BABY & ME,
The Shojo Beat Manga Edition

STORY & ART BY
MARIMO RAGAWA

English Adaptation/Lance Caselman
Translation/JN Productions
Touch-up Art & Lettering/Vanessa Satone
Design/Yuki Ameda
Editor/Shaenon K. Garrity

Editor in Chief, Books/Alvin Lu
Editor in Chief, Magazines/Marc Weidenbaum
VP, Publishing Licensing/Rika Inouye
VP, Sales and Product Marketing/Gonzalo Ferreyra
VP, Creative/Linda Espinosa
Publisher/Hyoe Narita

Akachan to Boku by Marimo Ragawa © Marimo Ragawa 1994. All rights reserved. First published in Japan in 1995 by HAKUSENSHA, Inc., Tokyo. English language translation rights arranged with HAKUSENSHA, Inc., Tokyo. The stories, characters and incidents mentioned in this publication are entirely fictional.

Printed in Canada

Published by VIZ Media, LLC
P.O. Box 77010
San Francisco, CA 94107

Shojo Beat Manga Edition
10 9 8 7 6 5 4 3 2 1
First printing, December 2008

VIZ
MEDIA

store.viz.com

Creator: Marimo Ragawa

SBM Title: *Baby & Me*

Date of Birth: September 21

Blood Type: B

Major Works: *Time Limit, Baby & Me, N.Y. N.Y.,* and *Shanimuni-Go* (Desperately—Go)

• •

Marimo Ragawa first started submitting manga to a comic maga-zine when she was 12 years old. She kept up her submissions for four years, but to no avail. She decided to submit her work to the magazine *Hana to Yume,* where she received Top Prize in the Monthly Manga Contest as well as an honorable mention (Kasaku) in the magazine's Big Challenge contest. Her first manga was titled *Time Limit. Baby & Me* was honored with a Shogakukan Manga Award in 1995 and was spun off into an anime.

Ragawa's work showcases some very cute and expressive line work along with an incredible ability to depict complex emotions and relationships. Some of her other works include *N.Y. N.Y.* and the tennis manga *Shanimuni-Go.*

Ragawa has two brothers and two sisters.

Shojo Beat

BABY & Me

Vol. 11

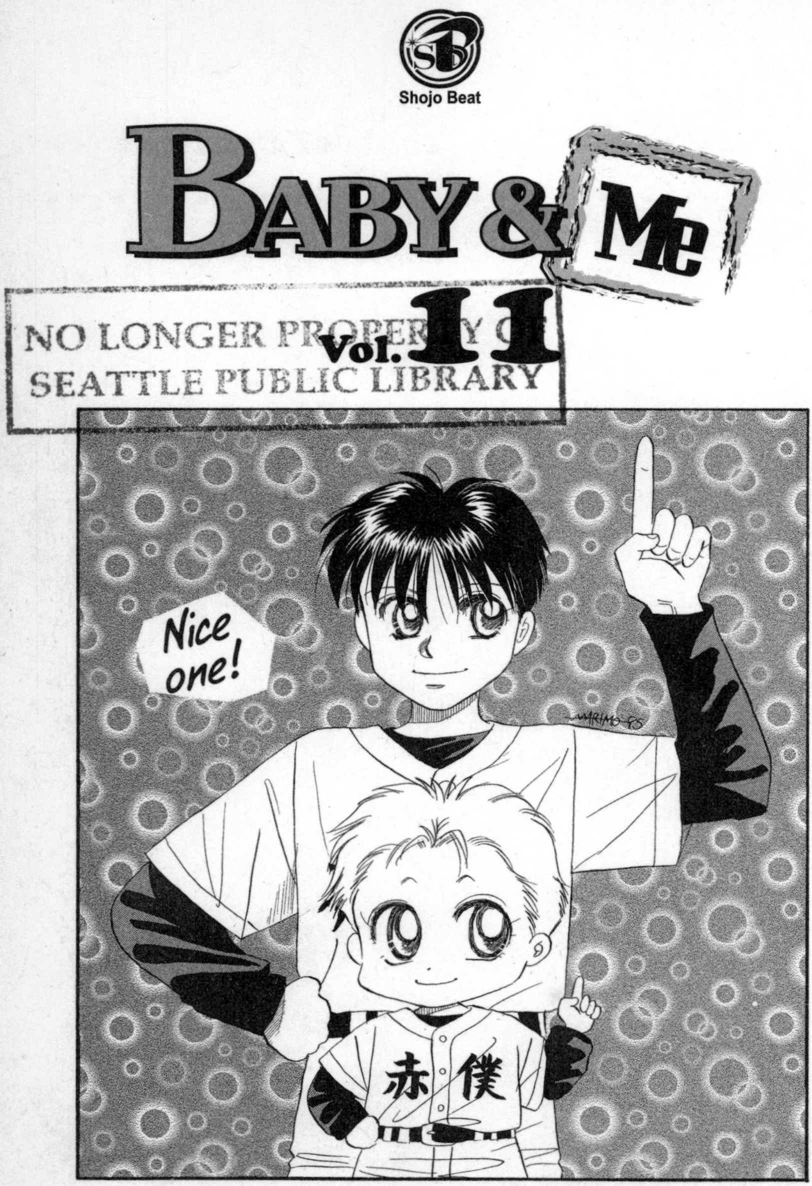
Nice one!
赤 僕

Story & Art by Marimo Ragawa

BABY & Me

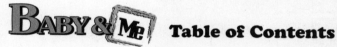

Table of Contents

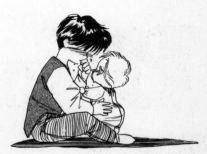

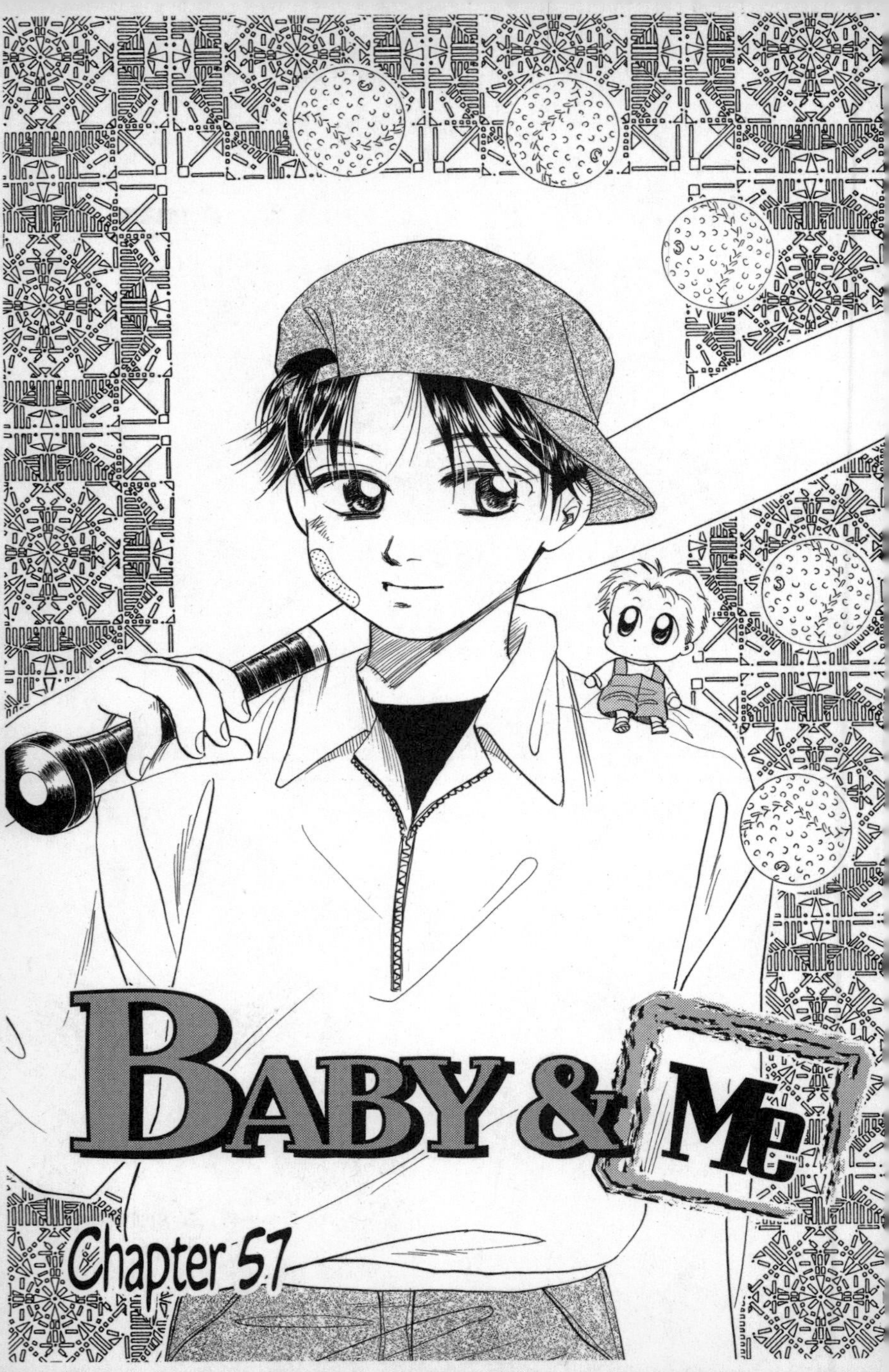
BABY & ME
Chapter 57

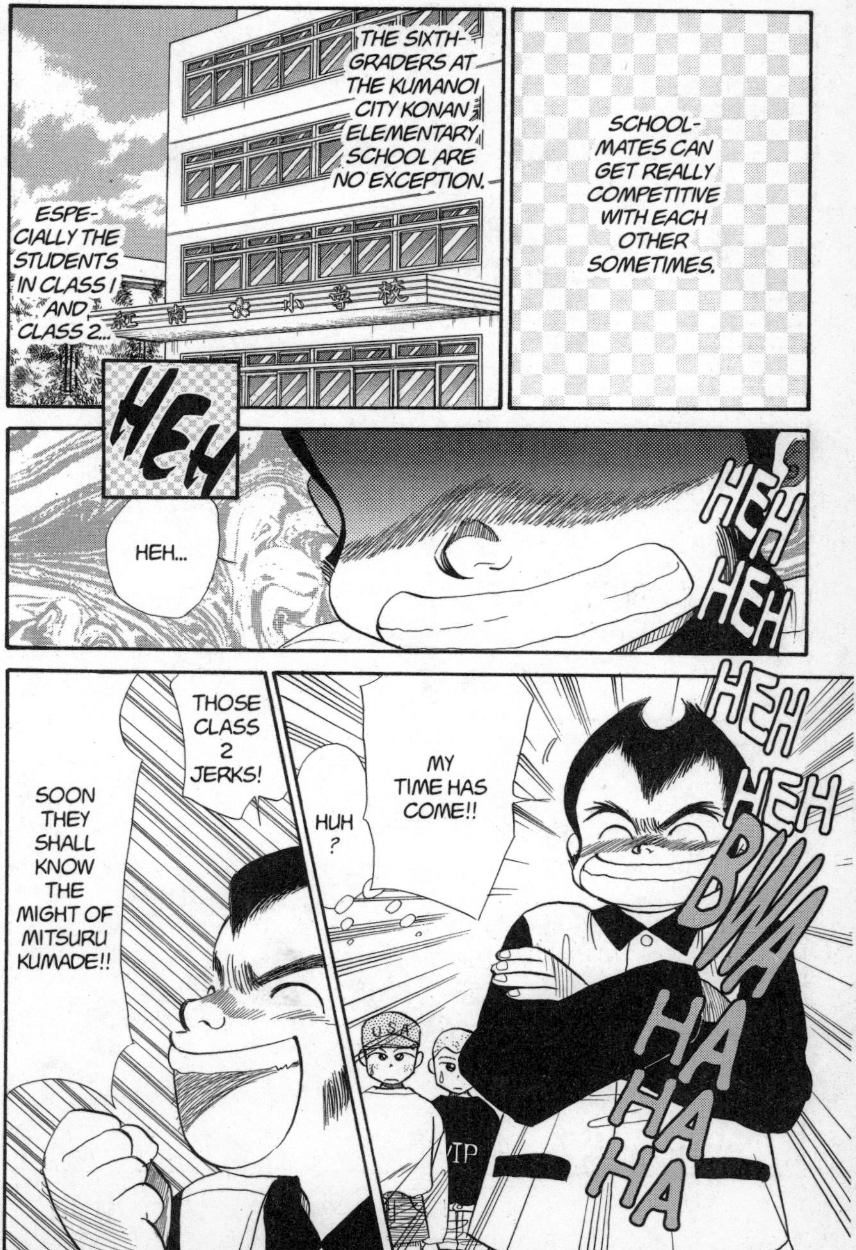
SCHOOL-MATES CAN GET REALLY COMPETITIVE WITH EACH OTHER SOMETIMES.
THE SIXTH-GRADERS AT THE KUMANOI CITY KONAN ELEMENTARY SCHOOL ARE NO EXCEPTION.
紅南小学校
ESPE-CIALLY THE STUDENTS IN CLASS 1 AND CLASS 2...
HEH
HEH HEH
HEH...
HEH HEH
BWAHAHAHAHA
MY TIME HAS COME!!
USA
VIP
HUH?
THOSE CLASS 2 JERKS!
SOON THEY SHALL KNOW THE MIGHT OF MITSURU KUMADE!!

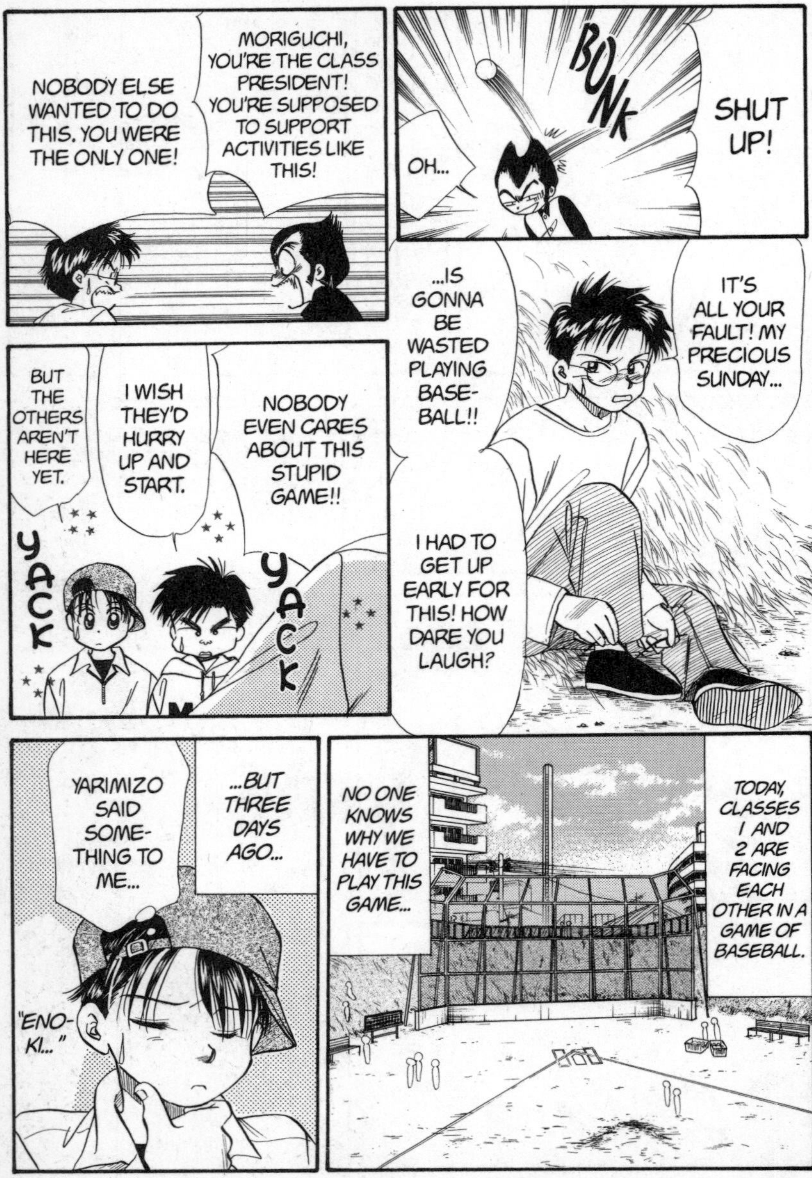
SHUT UP!
BONK
OH...
MORIGUCHI, YOU'RE THE CLASS PRESIDENT! YOU'RE SUPPOSED TO SUPPORT ACTIVITIES LIKE THIS!
NOBODY ELSE WANTED TO DO THIS. YOU WERE THE ONLY ONE!
IT'S ALL YOUR FAULT! MY PRECIOUS SUNDAY...
...IS GONNA BE WASTED PLAYING BASE-BALL!!
I HAD TO GET UP EARLY FOR THIS! HOW DARE YOU LAUGH?
NOBODY EVEN CARES ABOUT THIS STUPID GAME!!
YACK
I WISH THEY'D HURRY UP AND START.
BUT THE OTHERS AREN'T HERE YET.
YACK
TODAY, CLASSES 1 AND 2 ARE FACING EACH OTHER IN A GAME OF BASEBALL.
NO ONE KNOWS WHY WE HAVE TO PLAY THIS GAME...
...BUT THREE DAYS AGO...
YARIMIZO SAID SOME-THING TO ME...
"ENO-KI..."

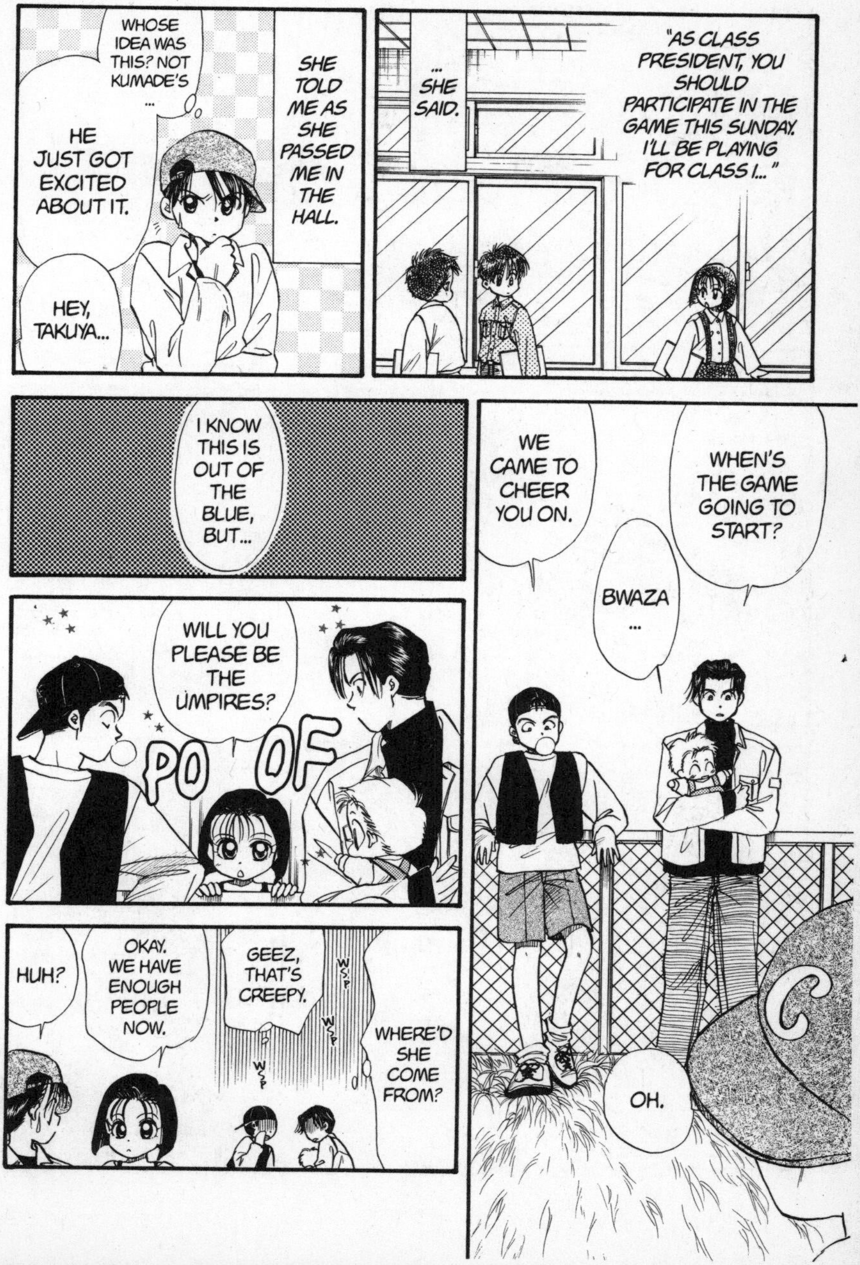
"AS CLASS PRESIDENT, YOU SHOULD PARTICIPATE IN THE GAME THIS SUNDAY. I'LL BE PLAYING FOR CLASS I..."
...SHE SAID.
SHE TOLD ME AS SHE PASSED ME IN THE HALL.
WHOSE IDEA WAS THIS? NOT KUMADE'S ...
HE JUST GOT EXCITED ABOUT IT.
HEY, TAKUYA...
WHEN'S THE GAME GOING TO START?
WE CAME TO CHEER YOU ON.
BWAZA ...
OH.
I KNOW THIS IS OUT OF THE BLUE, BUT...
WILL YOU PLEASE BE THE UMPIRES?
PO OF
WHERE'D SHE COME FROM?
WSP
WSP
GEEZ, THAT'S CREEPY.
WSP
OKAY. WE HAVE ENOUGH PEOPLE NOW.
HUH?

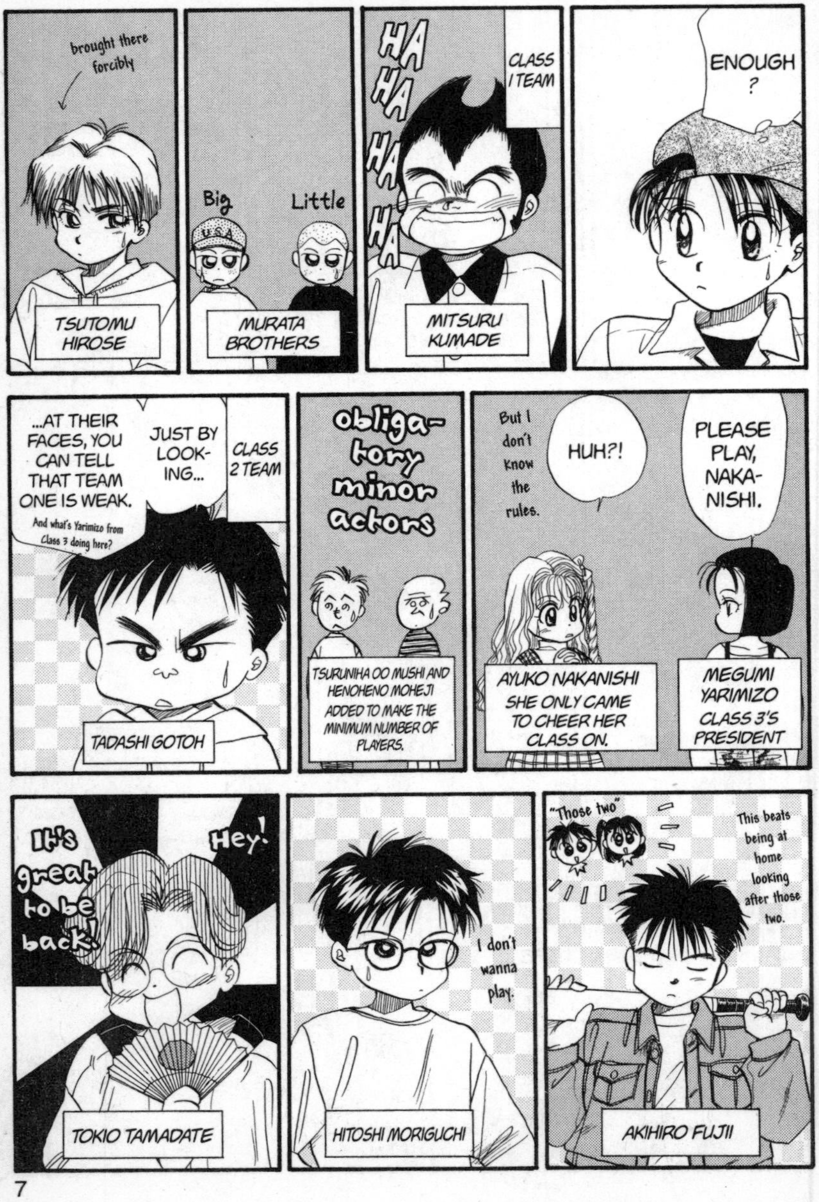
ENOUGH ?
CLASS 1 TEAM
HA HA HA HA HA
MITSURU KUMADE
Big
Little
MURATA BROTHERS
brought there forcibly
TSUTOMU HIROSE
PLEASE PLAY, NAKA-NISHI.
HUH?!
But I don't know the rules.
MEGUMI YARIMIZO CLASS 3'S PRESIDENT
AYUKO NAKANISHI SHE ONLY CAME TO CHEER HER CLASS ON.
obliga-tory minor actors
TSURUNIHA OO MUSHI AND HENOHENO MOHEJI ADDED TO MAKE THE MINIMUM NUMBER OF PLAYERS.
CLASS 2 TEAM
JUST BY LOOK-ING...
...AT THEIR FACES, YOU CAN TELL THAT TEAM ONE IS WEAK.
And what's Yarimizo from Class 3 doing here?
TADASHI GOTOH
This beats being at home looking after those two.
"Those two"
AKIHIRO FUJII
I don't wanna play.
HITOSHI MORIGUCHI
Hey!
It's great to be back!
TOKIO TAMADATE

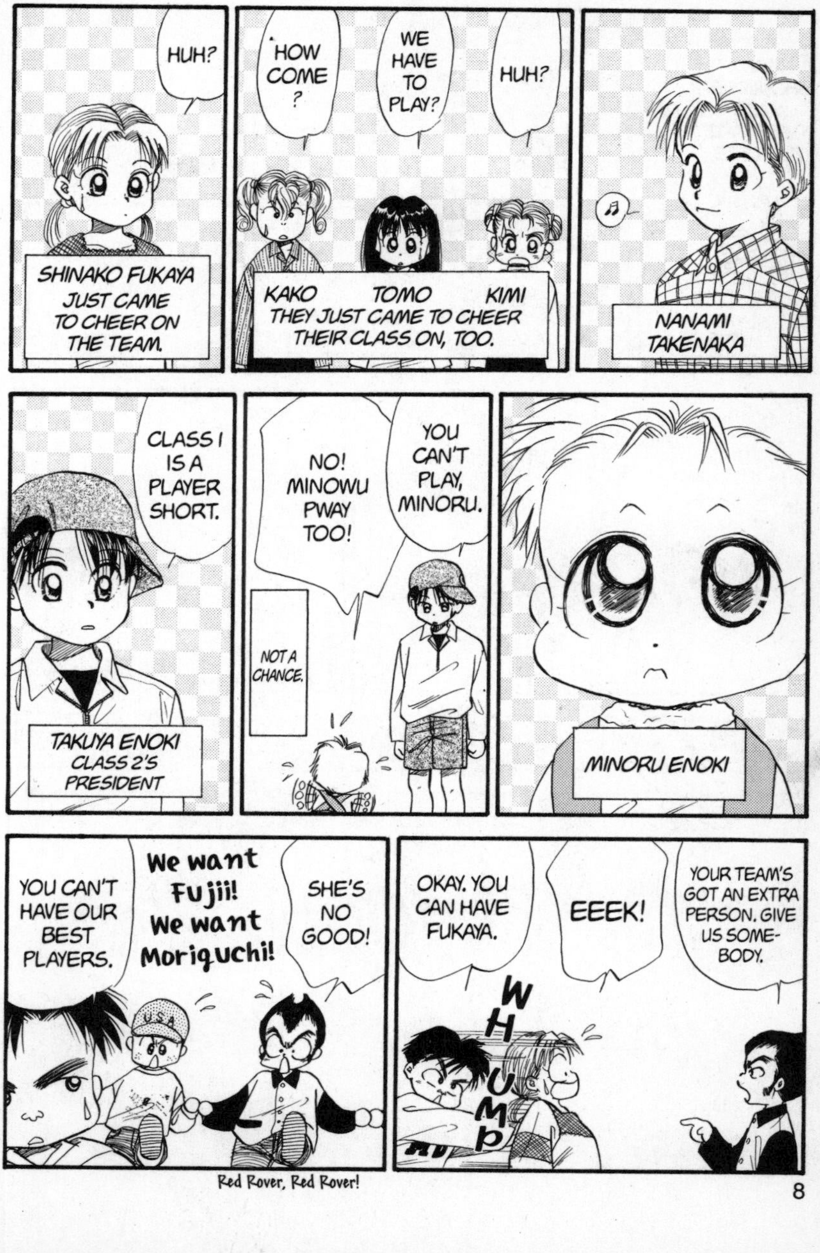
NANAMI TAKENAKA
HUH?
WE HAVE TO PLAY?
HOW COME?
KAKO TOMO KIMI THEY JUST CAME TO CHEER THEIR CLASS ON, TOO.
HUH?
SHINAKO FUKAYA JUST CAME TO CHEER ON THE TEAM.
MINORU ENOKI
YOU CAN'T PLAY, MINORU.
NO! MINOWU PWAY TOO!
NOT A CHANCE.
CLASS I IS A PLAYER SHORT.
TAKUYA ENOKI CLASS 2'S PRESIDENT
YOUR TEAM'S GOT AN EXTRA PERSON. GIVE US SOMEBODY.
EEEK!
OKAY. YOU CAN HAVE FUKAYA.
WHUMP
SHE'S NO GOOD!
We want Fujii! We want Moriguchi!
YOU CAN'T HAVE OUR BEST PLAYERS.

Red Rover, Red Rover!

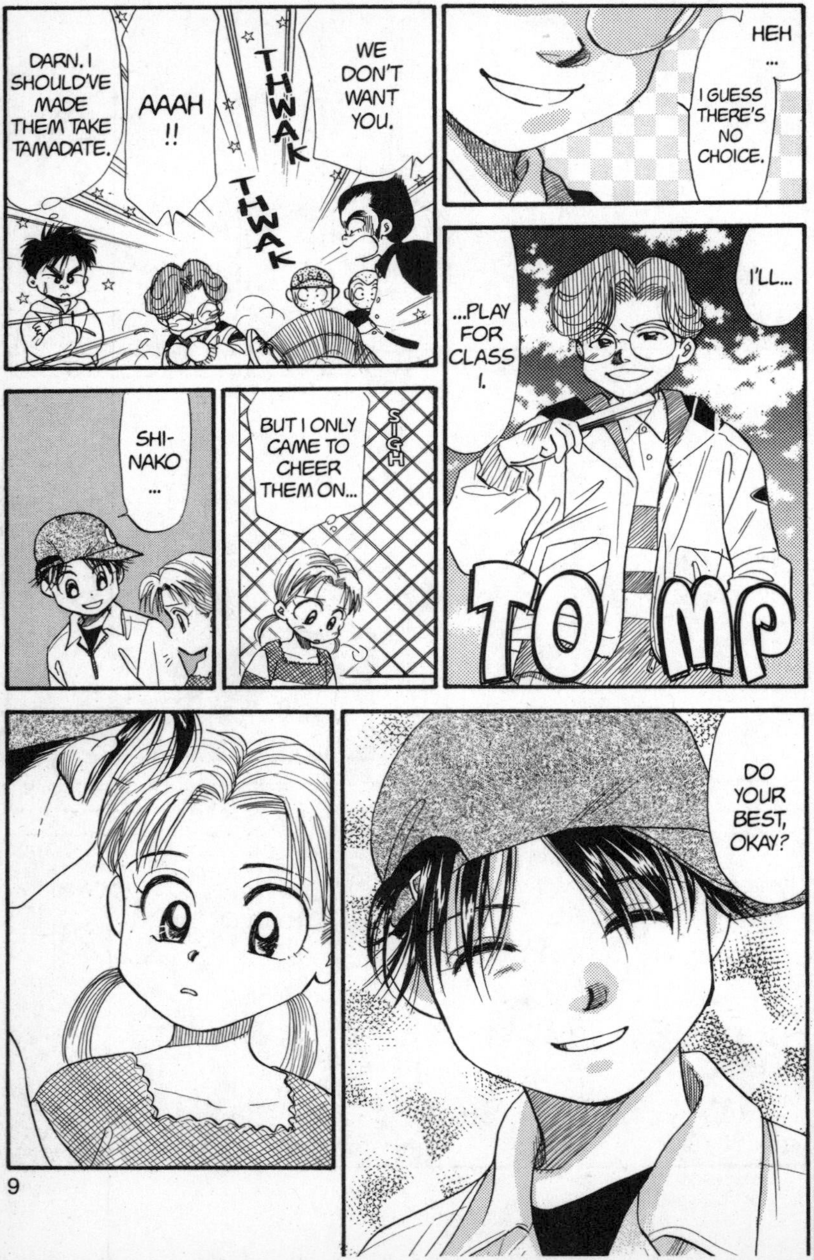
HEH ...
I GUESS THERE'S NO CHOICE.
WE DON'T WANT YOU.
THWAK
THWAK
AAAH !!
DARN. I SHOULD'VE MADE THEM TAKE TAMADATE.
I'LL...
...PLAY FOR CLASS I.
TOMP
SIGH
BUT I ONLY CAME TO CHEER THEM ON...
SHI-NAKO ...
DO YOUR BEST, OKAY?

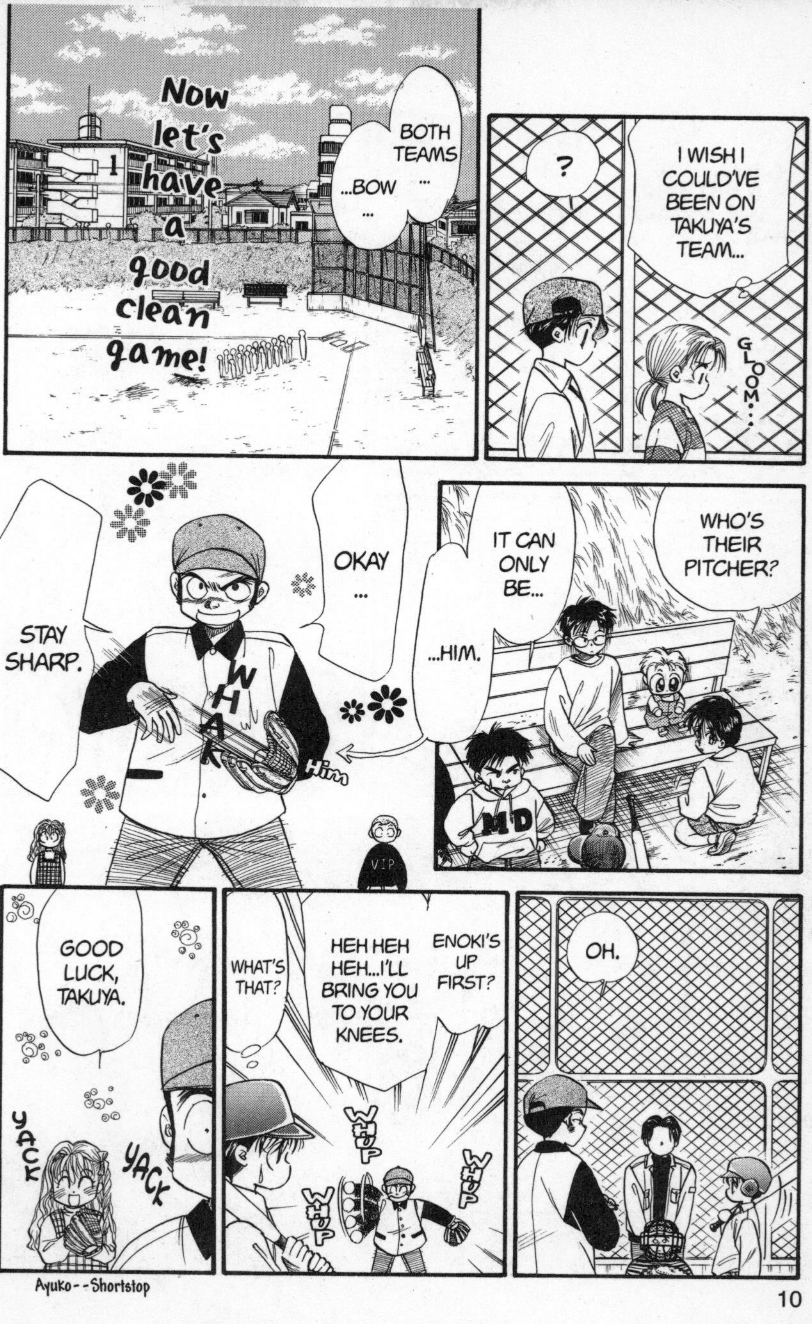
I WISH I COULD'VE BEEN ON TAKUYA'S TEAM...
?
GLOOM...
BOTH TEAMS ... ...BOW ...
Now let's have a good clean game!
WHO'S THEIR PITCHER?
IT CAN ONLY BE...
...HIM.
OKAY ...
STAY SHARP.
WHAK
Him
VIP
MD
OH.
ENOKI'S UP FIRST?
HEH HEH HEH...I'LL BRING YOU TO YOUR KNEES.
WHAT'S THAT?
WHUP
WHUP
WHUP
GOOD LUCK, TAKUYA.
YACK
YACK

Ayuko--Shortstop

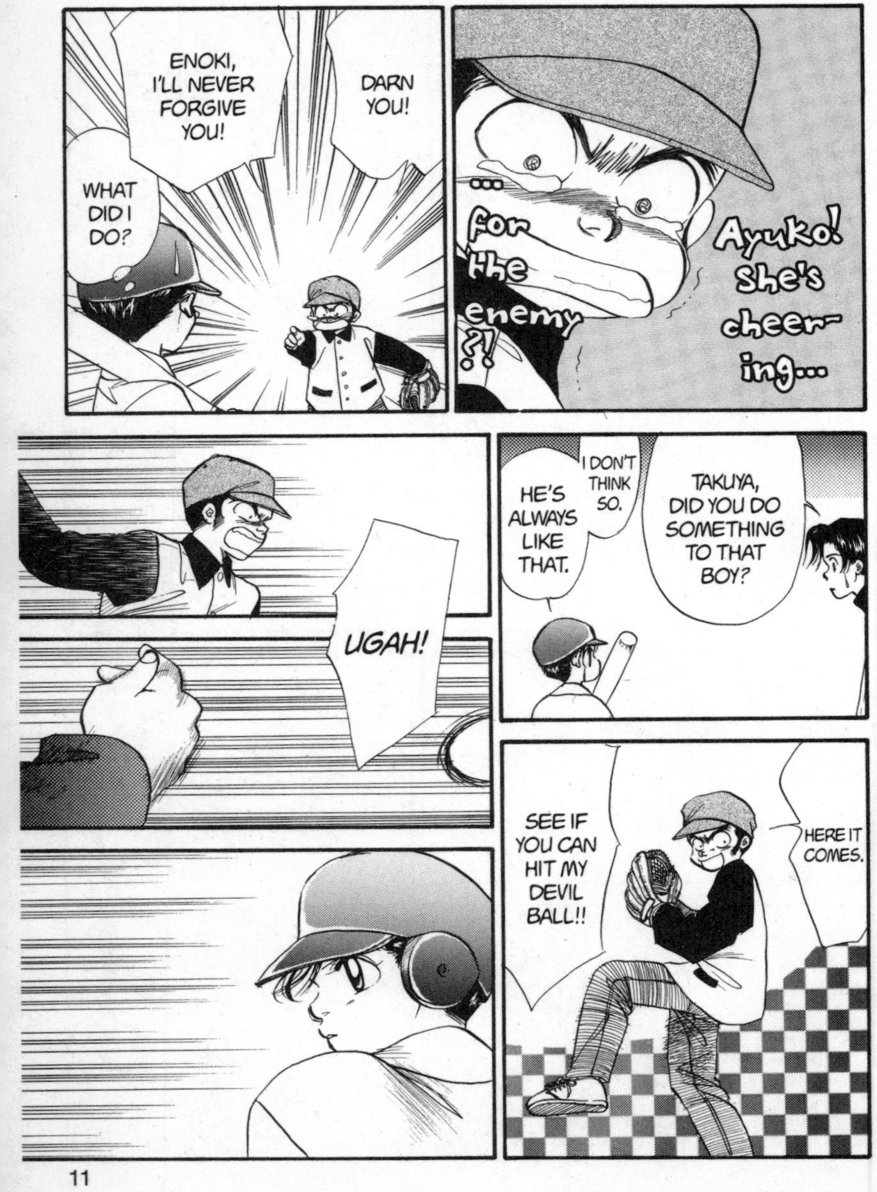
Ayuko! She's cheer-ing...
...for the enemy?!
DARN YOU!
ENOKI, I'LL NEVER FORGIVE YOU!
WHAT DID I DO?
TAKUYA, DID YOU DO SOMETHING TO THAT BOY?
I DON'T THINK SO.
HE'S ALWAYS LIKE THAT.
UGAH!
HERE IT COMES.
SEE IF YOU CAN HIT MY DEVIL BALL!!

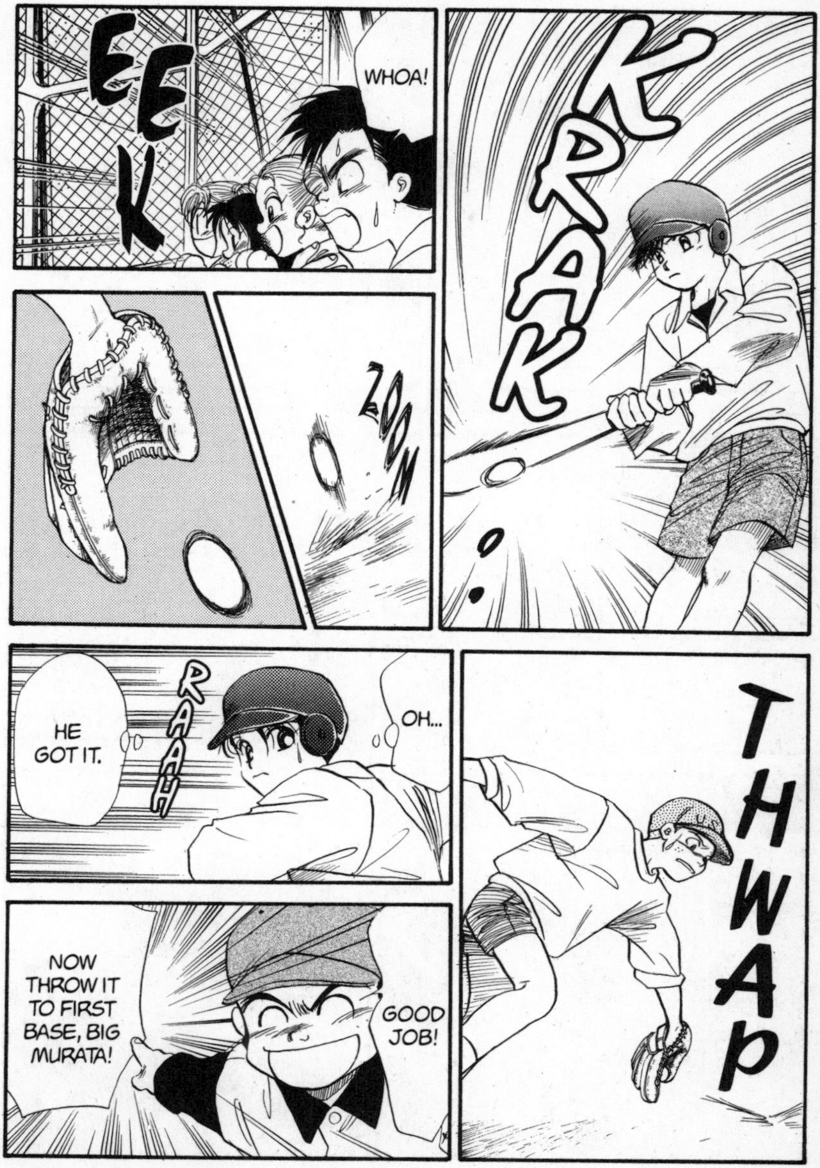
KRAK
WHOA!
EEEK
ZOOM
THWAP
OH...
RAAH
HE GOT IT.
GOOD JOB!
NOW THROW IT TO FIRST BASE, BIG MURATA!

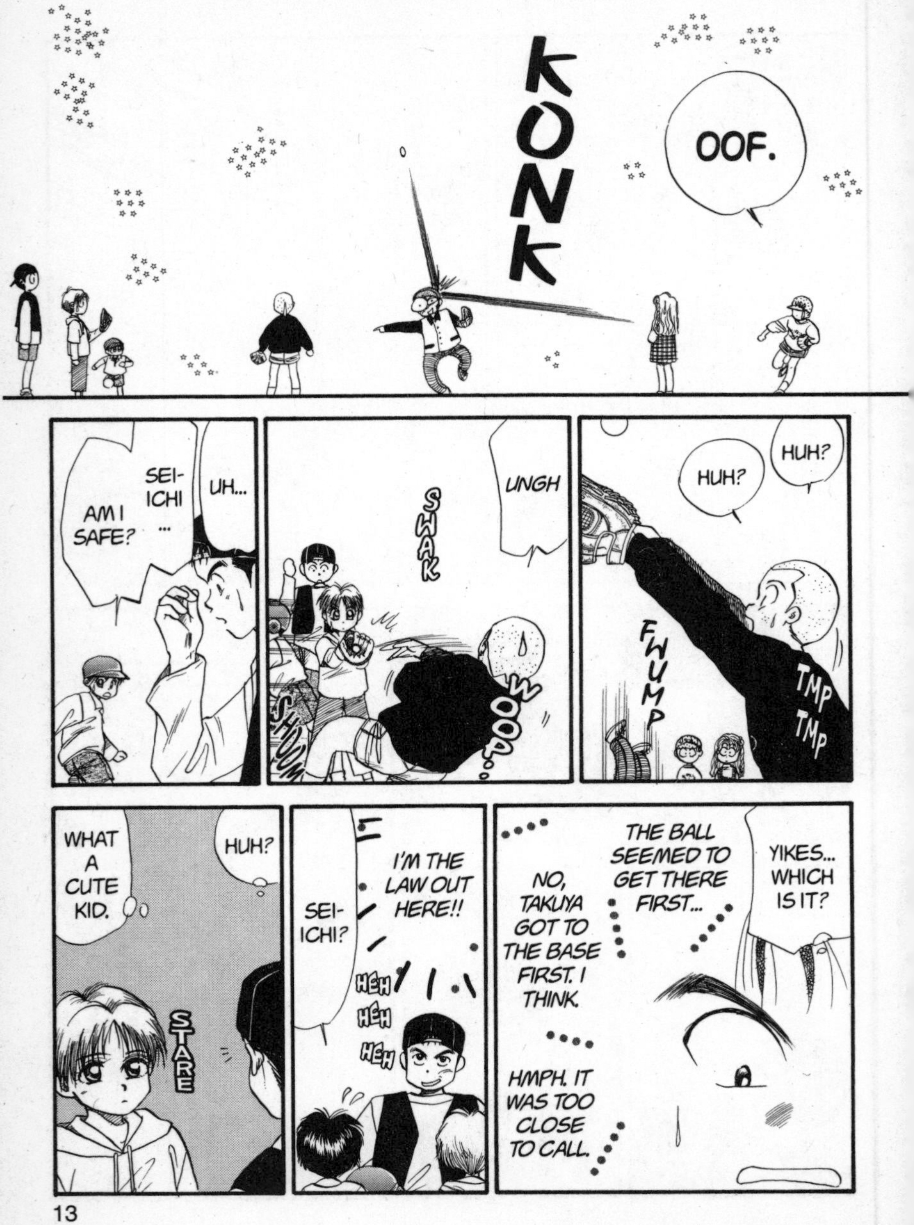
OOF.
KONK
HUH?
HUH?
FWUMP
TMP TMP
UNGH
SWAK
WOOP...
UH...
SEI-ICHI...
AM I SAFE?
YIKES... WHICH IS IT?
THE BALL SEEMED TO GET THERE FIRST...
NO, TAKUYA GOT TO THE BASE FIRST. I THINK.
....
HMPH. IT WAS TOO CLOSE TO CALL.
I'M THE LAW OUT HERE!!
SEI-ICHI?
HEH HEH HEH
HUH?
WHAT A CUTE KID.
STARE

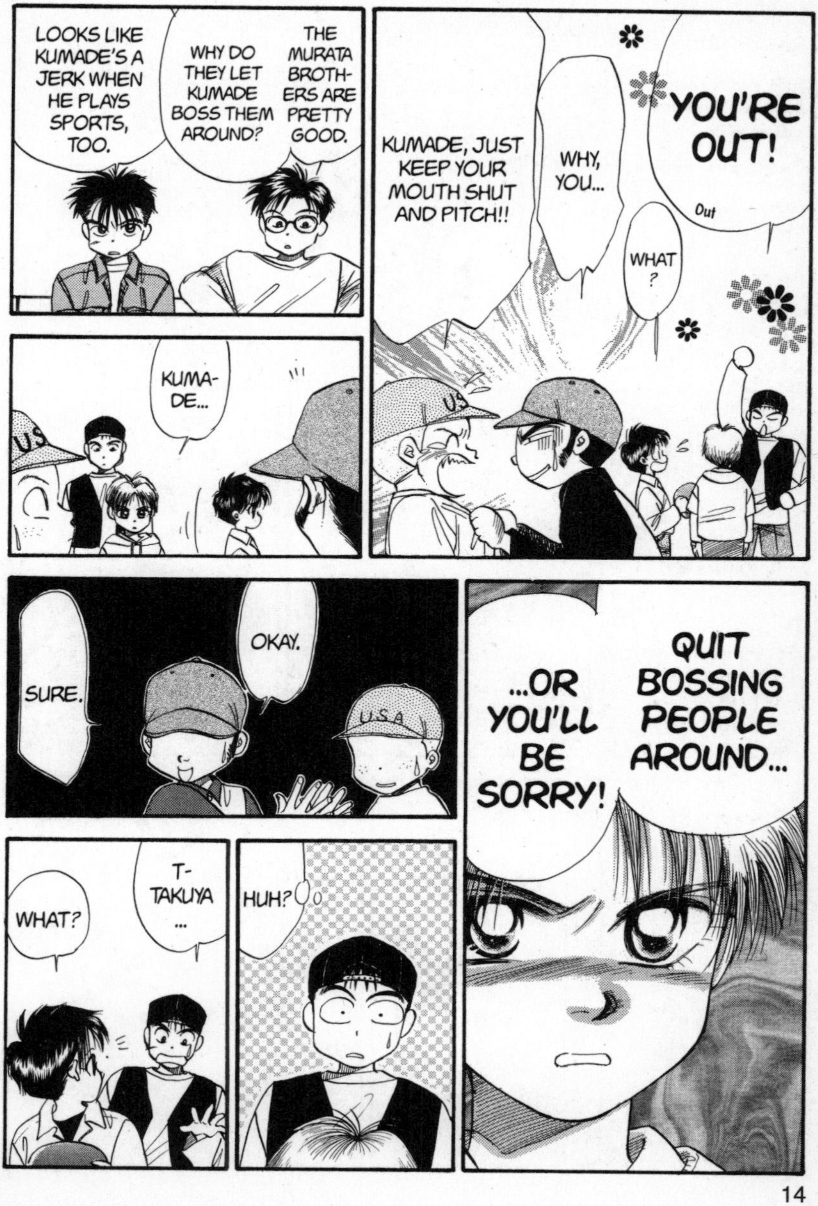
YOU'RE OUT!
Out
WHAT?
WHY, YOU...
KUMADE, JUST KEEP YOUR MOUTH SHUT AND PITCH!!
THE MURATA BROTHERS ARE PRETTY GOOD.
WHY DO THEY LET KUMADE BOSS THEM AROUND?
LOOKS LIKE KUMADE'S A JERK WHEN HE PLAYS SPORTS, TOO.
KUMADE...
QUIT BOSSING PEOPLE AROUND...
...OR YOU'LL BE SORRY!
OKAY.
SURE.
HUH?
T-TAKUYA...
WHAT?

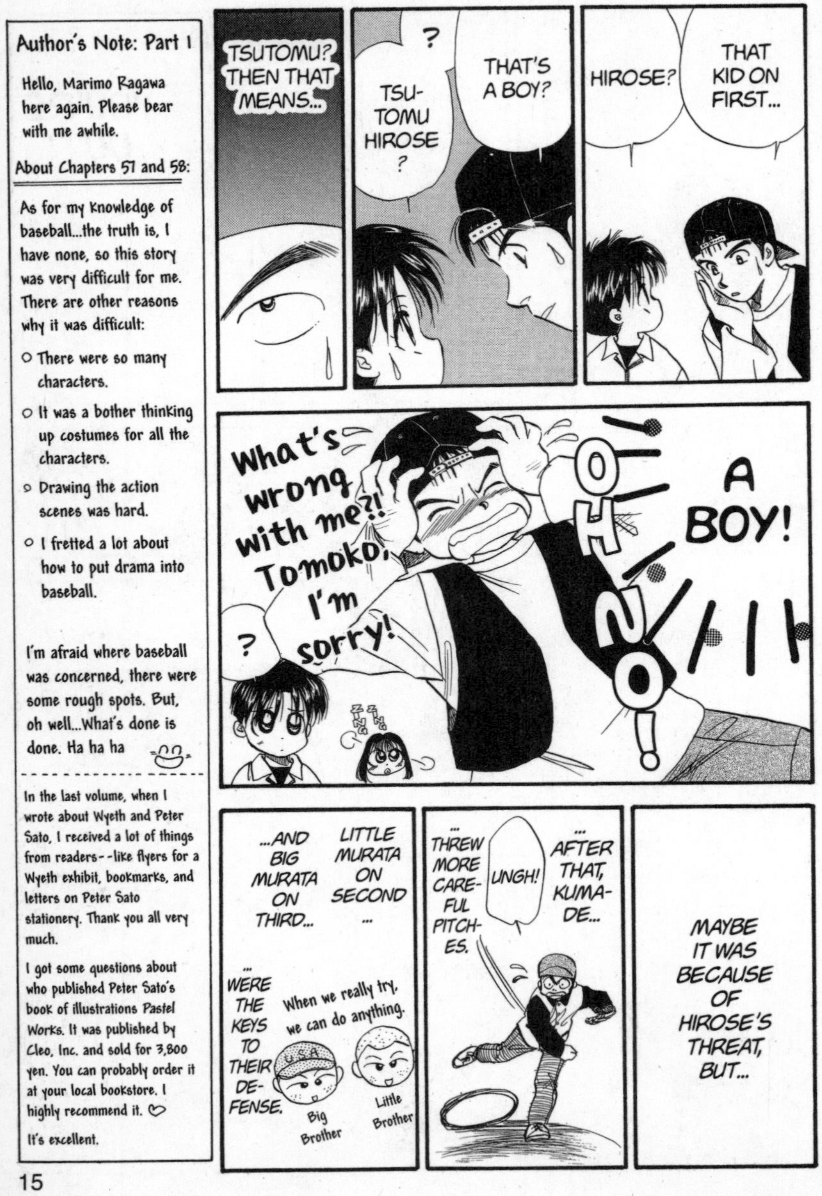
THAT KID ON FIRST...
HIROSE?
THAT'S A BOY?
?
TSU-TOMU HIROSE ?
TSUTOMU? THEN THAT MEANS...
A BOY!
OH NO!!
What's wrong with me?! Tomoko, I'm sorry!
?
MAYBE IT WAS BECAUSE OF HIROSE'S THREAT, BUT...
...AFTER THAT, KUMA-DE...
UNGH!
...THREW MORE CARE-FUL PITCH-ES.
LITTLE MURATA ON SECOND...
...AND BIG MURATA ON THIRD...
...WERE THE KEYS TO THEIR DE-FENSE.
When we really try, we can do anything.
Little Brother
Big Brother

Author's Note: Part 1

Hello, Marimo Ragawa here again. Please bear with me awhile.

About Chapters 57 and 58:

As for my knowledge of baseball...the truth is, I have none, so this story was very difficult for me. There are other reasons why it was difficult:

- There were so many characters.
- It was a bother thinking up costumes for all the characters.
- Drawing the action scenes was hard.
- I fretted a lot about how to put drama into baseball.

I'm afraid where baseball was concerned, there were some rough spots. But, oh well...What's done is done. Ha ha ha

---

In the last volume, when I wrote about Wyeth and Peter Sato, I received a lot of things from readers--like flyers for a Wyeth exhibit, bookmarks, and letters on Peter Sato stationery. Thank you all very much.

I got some questions about who published Peter Sato's book of illustrations Pastel Works. It was published by Cleo, Inc. and sold for 3,800 yen. You can probably order it at your local bookstore. I highly recommend it. ♡ It's excellent.

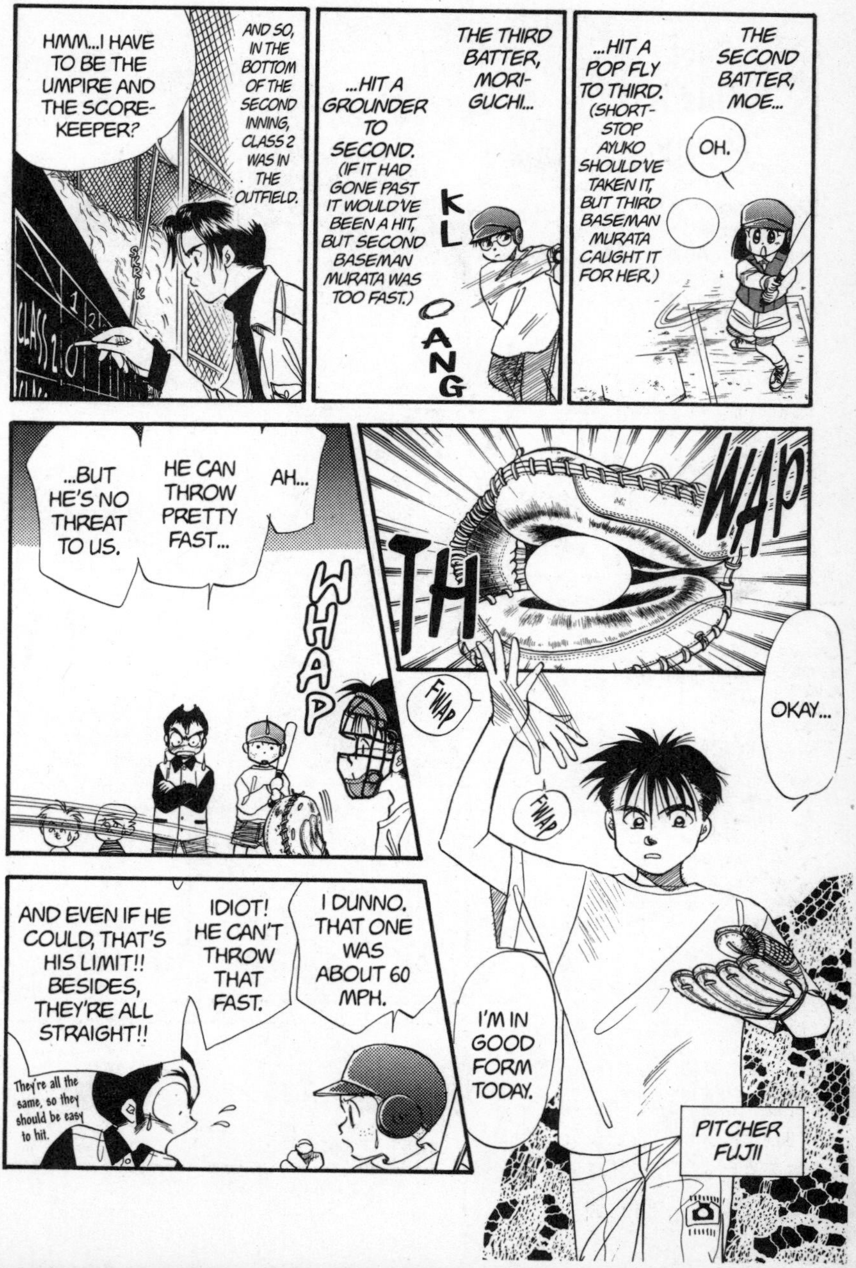
THE SECOND BATTER, MOE...
OH.
...HIT A POP FLY TO THIRD. (SHORTSTOP AYUKO SHOULD'VE TAKEN IT, BUT THIRD BASEMAN MURATA CAUGHT IT FOR HER.)
THE THIRD BATTER, MORIGUCHI...
KL
OANG
...HIT A GROUNDER TO SECOND. (IF IT HAD GONE PAST IT WOULD'VE BEEN A HIT, BUT SECOND BASEMAN MURATA WAS TOO FAST.)
AND SO, IN THE BOTTOM OF THE SECOND INNING, CLASS 2 WAS IN THE OUTFIELD.
HMM...I HAVE TO BE THE UMPIRE AND THE SCOREKEEPER?
SKRIK
WAP
TH
FWAP
FWAP
OKAY...
I'M IN GOOD FORM TODAY.
PITCHER FUJII
AH...
HE CAN THROW PRETTY FAST...
...BUT HE'S NO THREAT TO US.
WHHAP
I DUNNO. THAT ONE WAS ABOUT 60 MPH.
IDIOT! HE CAN'T THROW THAT FAST.
AND EVEN IF HE COULD, THAT'S HIS LIMIT!! BESIDES, THEY'RE ALL STRAIGHT!!
They're all the same, so they should be easy to hit.

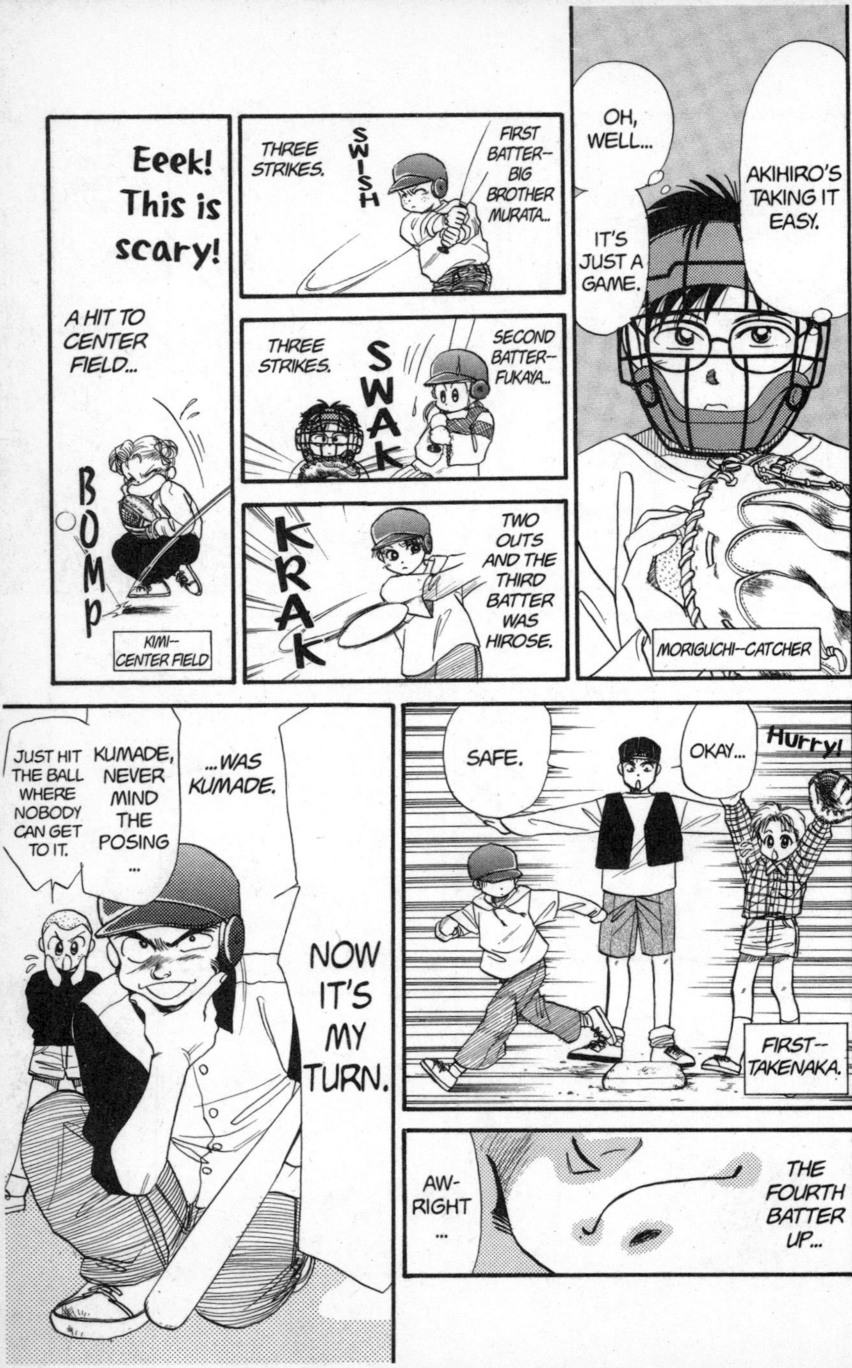
AKIHIRO'S TAKING IT EASY.
OH, WELL...
IT'S JUST A GAME.
MORIGUCHI--CATCHER
FIRST BATTER--BIG BROTHER MURATA...
SWISH
THREE STRIKES.
SECOND BATTER--FUKAYA...
SWAK
THREE STRIKES.
TWO OUTS AND THE THIRD BATTER WAS HIROSE.
KRAK
Eeek! This is scary!
A HIT TO CENTER FIELD...
BOMP
KIMI--CENTER FIELD
Hurry!
OKAY...
SAFE.
FIRST--TAKENAKA.
THE FOURTH BATTER UP...
AW-RIGHT ...
...WAS KUMADE.
KUMADE, NEVER MIND THE POSING ...
JUST HIT THE BALL WHERE NOBODY CAN GET TO IT.
NOW IT'S MY TURN.

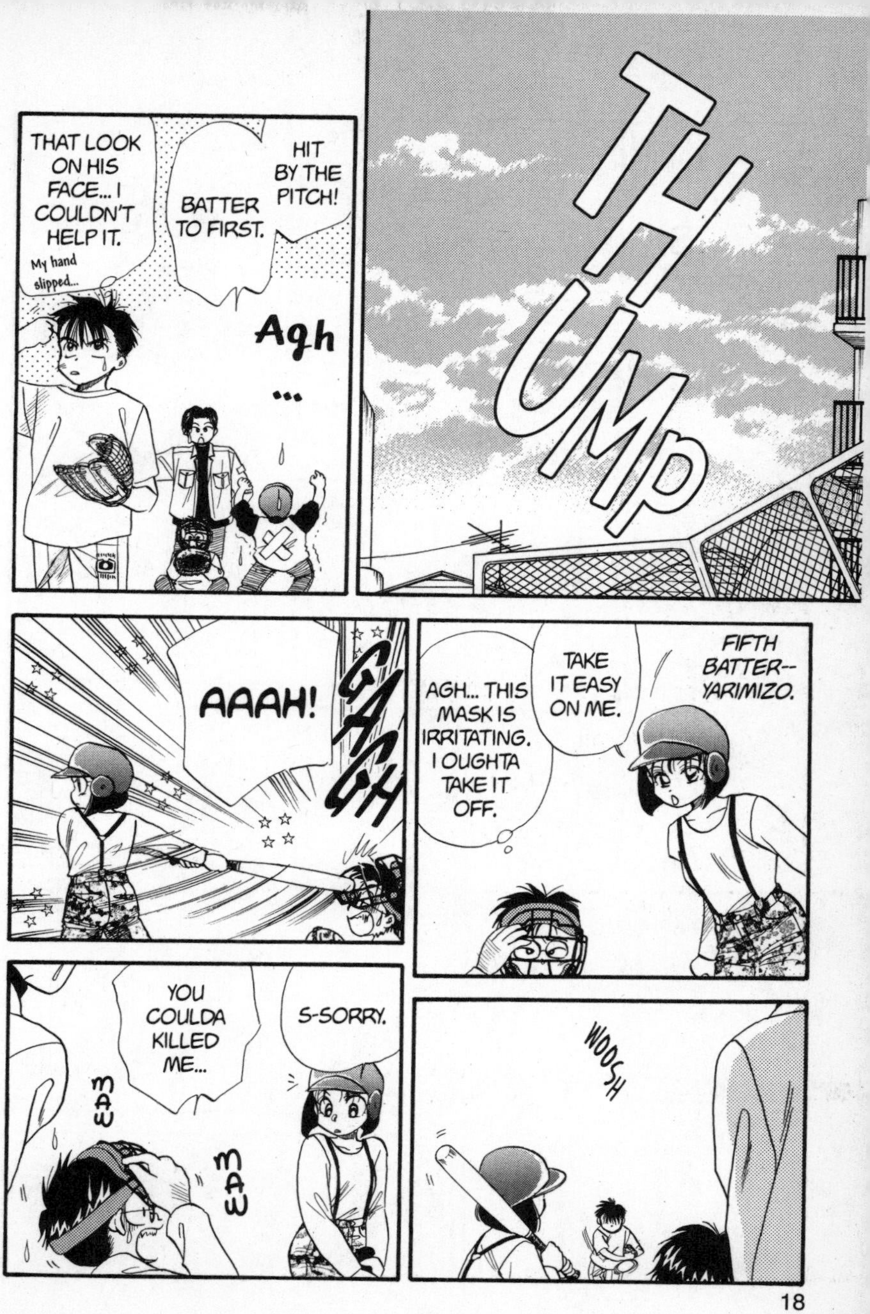
THUMP
HIT BY THE PITCH!
BATTER TO FIRST.
THAT LOOK ON HIS FACE... I COULDN'T HELP IT.
My hand slipped...
Agh ...
FIFTH BATTER-- YARIMIZO.
TAKE IT EASY ON ME.
AGH... THIS MASK IS IRRITATING. I OUGHTA TAKE IT OFF.
GASH
AAAH!
WOOSH
S-SORRY.
YOU COULDA KILLED ME...
MAW
MAW

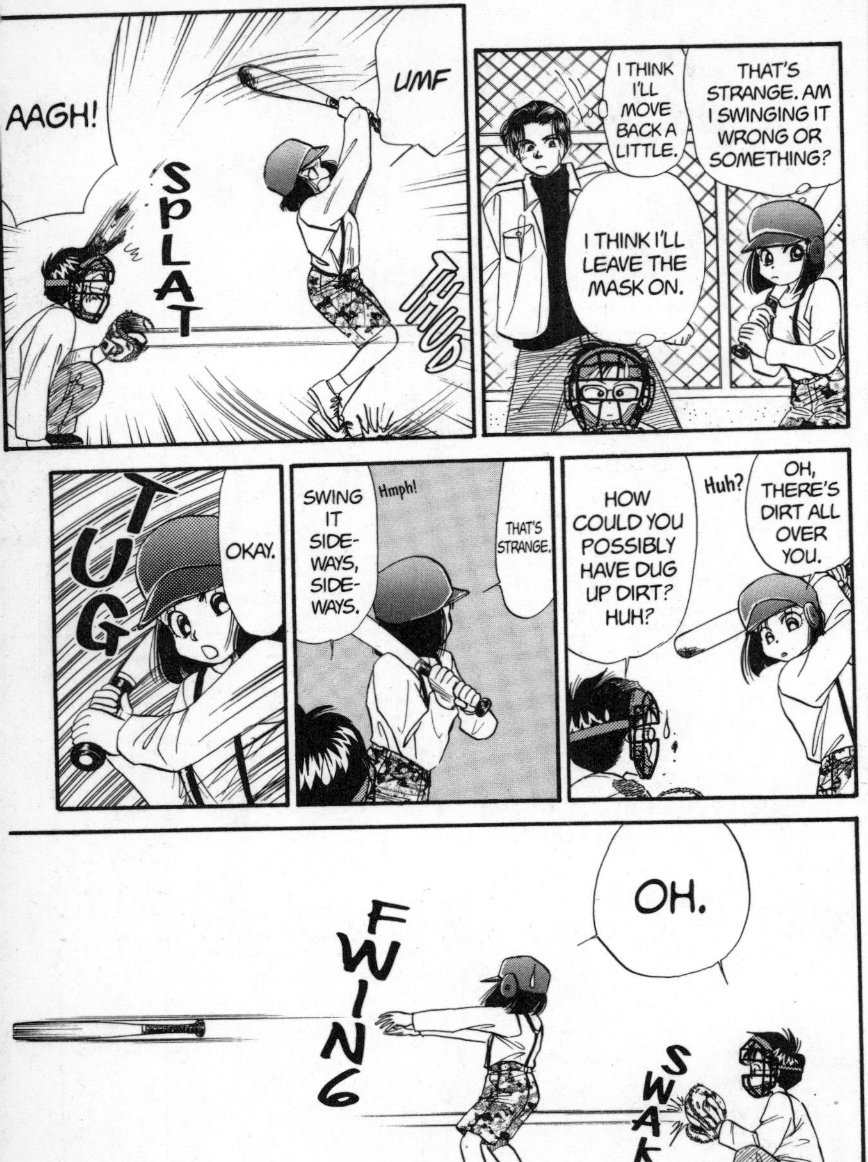
THAT'S STRANGE. AM I SWINGING IT WRONG OR SOMETHING?
I THINK I'LL MOVE BACK A LITTLE.
I THINK I'LL LEAVE THE MASK ON.
UMF
THUD
SPLAT
AAGH!
OH, THERE'S DIRT ALL OVER YOU.
Huh?
HOW COULD YOU POSSIBLY HAVE DUG UP DIRT? HUH?
THAT'S STRANGE.
Hmph!
SWING IT SIDEWAYS, SIDEWAYS.
OKAY.
TUG
OH.
FWING
SWAK

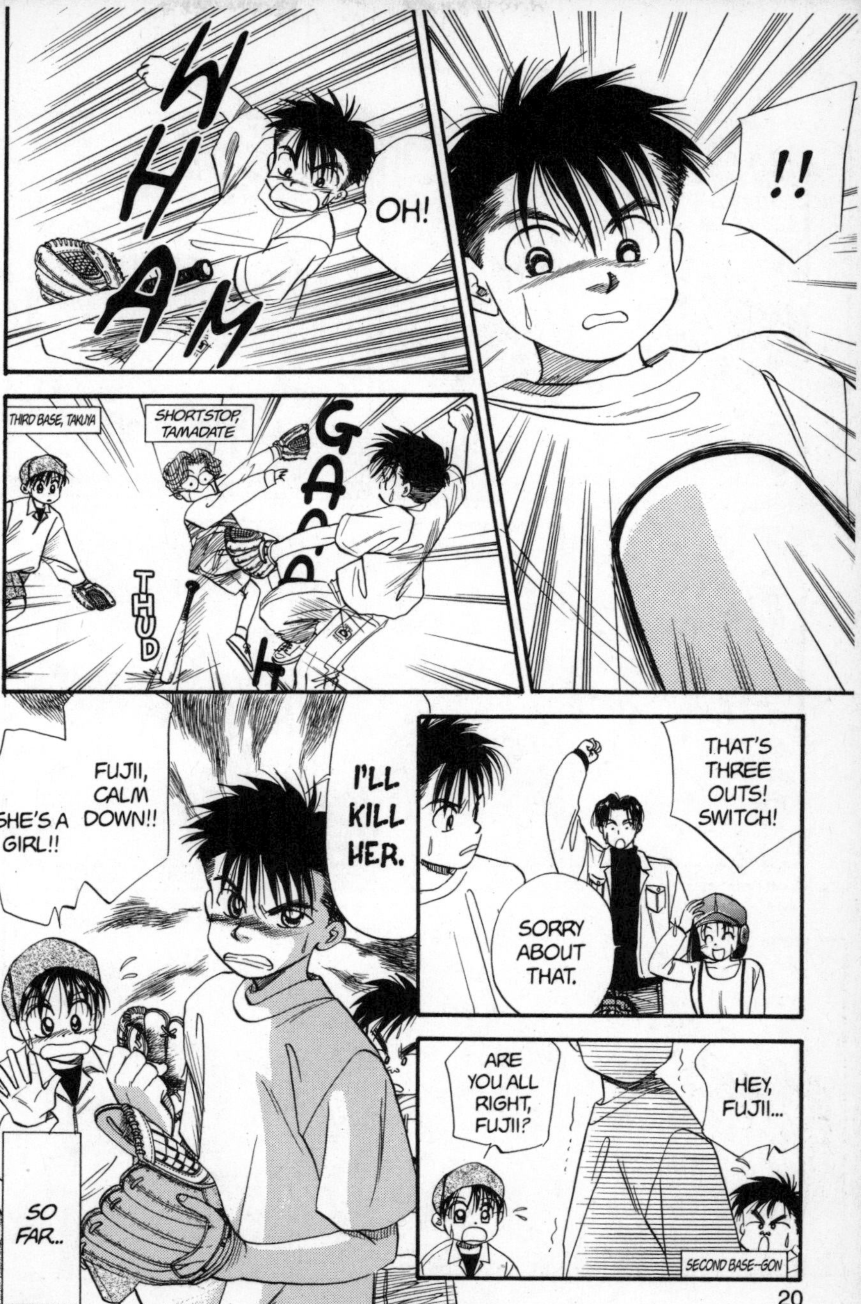
!!
SHAM
OH!
SHORTSTOP, TAMADATE
THIRD BASE, TAKUYA
THUD
THAT'S THREE OUTS! SWITCH!
SORRY ABOUT THAT.
HEY, FUJII...
ARE YOU ALL RIGHT, FUJII?
SECOND BASE—GON
I'LL KILL HER.
FUJII, CALM DOWN!!
SHE'S A GIRL!!
SO FAR...

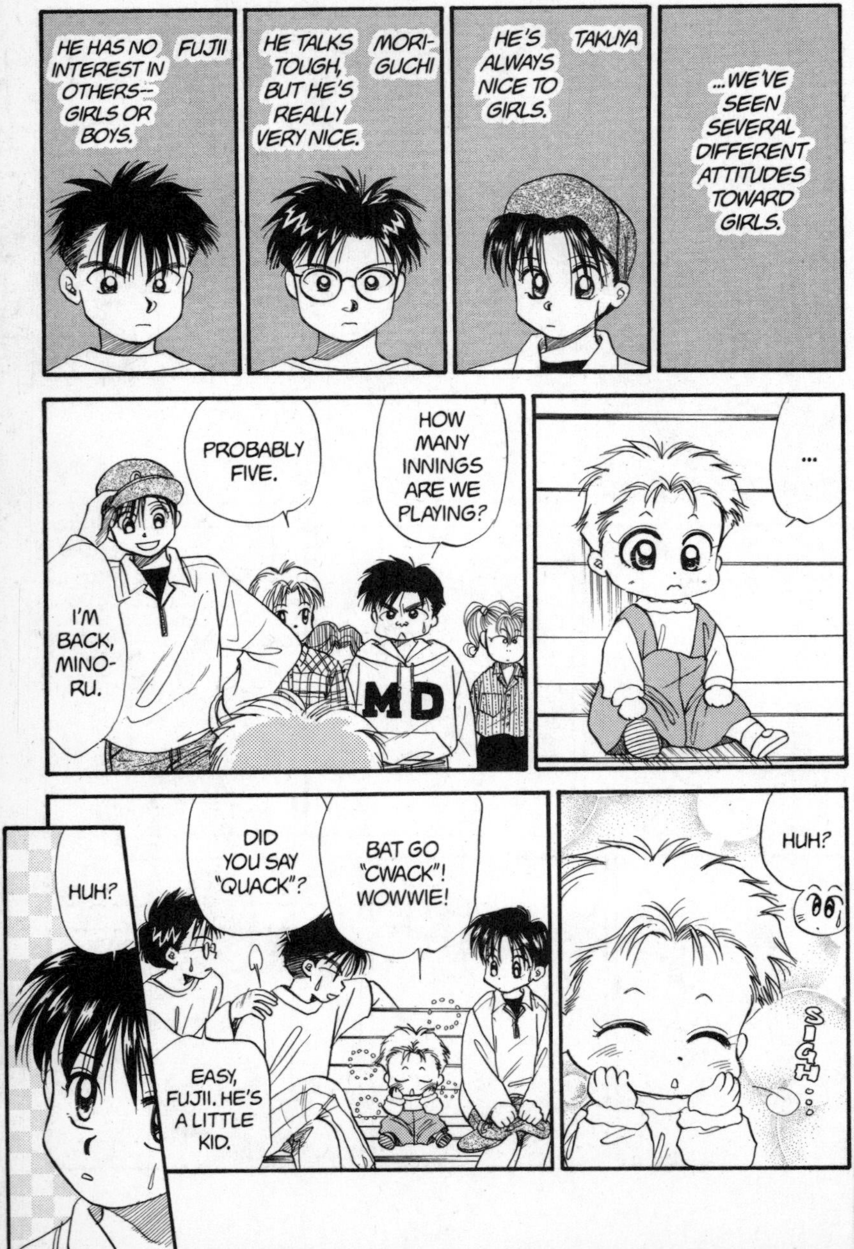
...WE'VE SEEN SEVERAL DIFFERENT ATTITUDES TOWARD GIRLS.
TAKUYA
HE'S ALWAYS NICE TO GIRLS.
MORI-GUCHI
HE TALKS TOUGH, BUT HE'S REALLY VERY NICE.
FUJII
HE HAS NO INTEREST IN OTHERS-- GIRLS OR BOYS.
...
HOW MANY INNINGS ARE WE PLAYING?
PROBABLY FIVE.
I'M BACK, MINO-RU.
HUH?
SIGH...
BAT GO "CWACK"! WOWWIE!
DID YOU SAY "QUACK"?
HUH?
EASY, FUJII. HE'S A LITTLE KID.

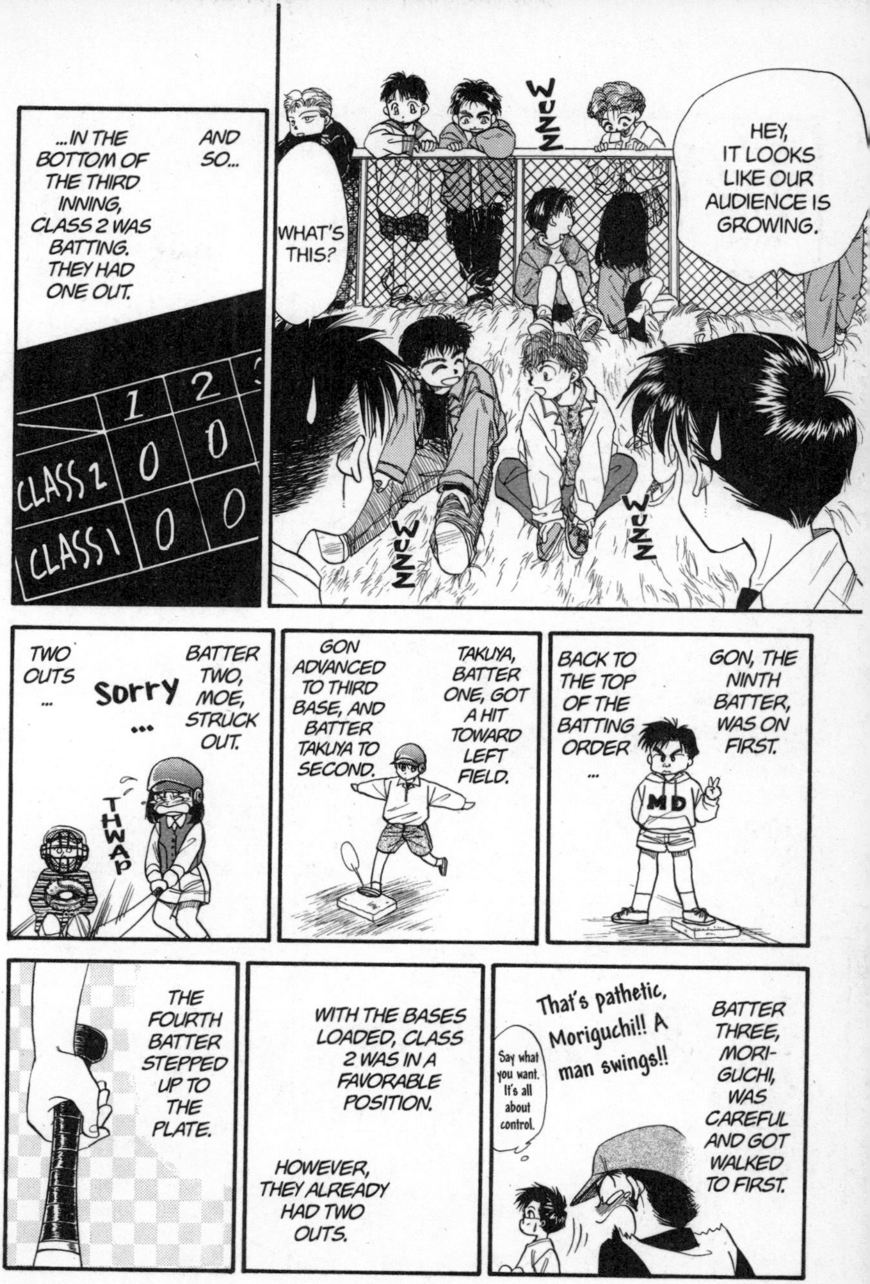
HEY, IT LOOKS LIKE OUR AUDIENCE IS GROWING.
WUZZ
WHAT'S THIS?
WUZZ
WUZZ
AND SO...
...IN THE BOTTOM OF THE THIRD INNING, CLASS 2 WAS BATTING. THEY HAD ONE OUT.
1 2
CLASS 2 0 0
CLASS 1 0 0
GON, THE NINTH BATTER, WAS ON FIRST.
BACK TO THE TOP OF THE BATTING ORDER ...
MD
TAKUYA, BATTER ONE, GOT A HIT TOWARD LEFT FIELD.
GON ADVANCED TO THIRD BASE, AND BATTER TAKUYA TO SECOND.
BATTER TWO, MOE, STRUCK OUT.
Sorry ...
THWAP
TWO OUTS ...
BATTER THREE, MORI-GUCHI, WAS CAREFUL AND GOT WALKED TO FIRST.
That's pathetic, Moriguchi!! A man swings!!
Say what you want. It's all about control.
WITH THE BASES LOADED, CLASS 2 WAS IN A FAVORABLE POSITION.
HOWEVER, THEY ALREADY HAD TWO OUTS.
THE FOURTH BATTER STEPPED UP TO THE PLATE.

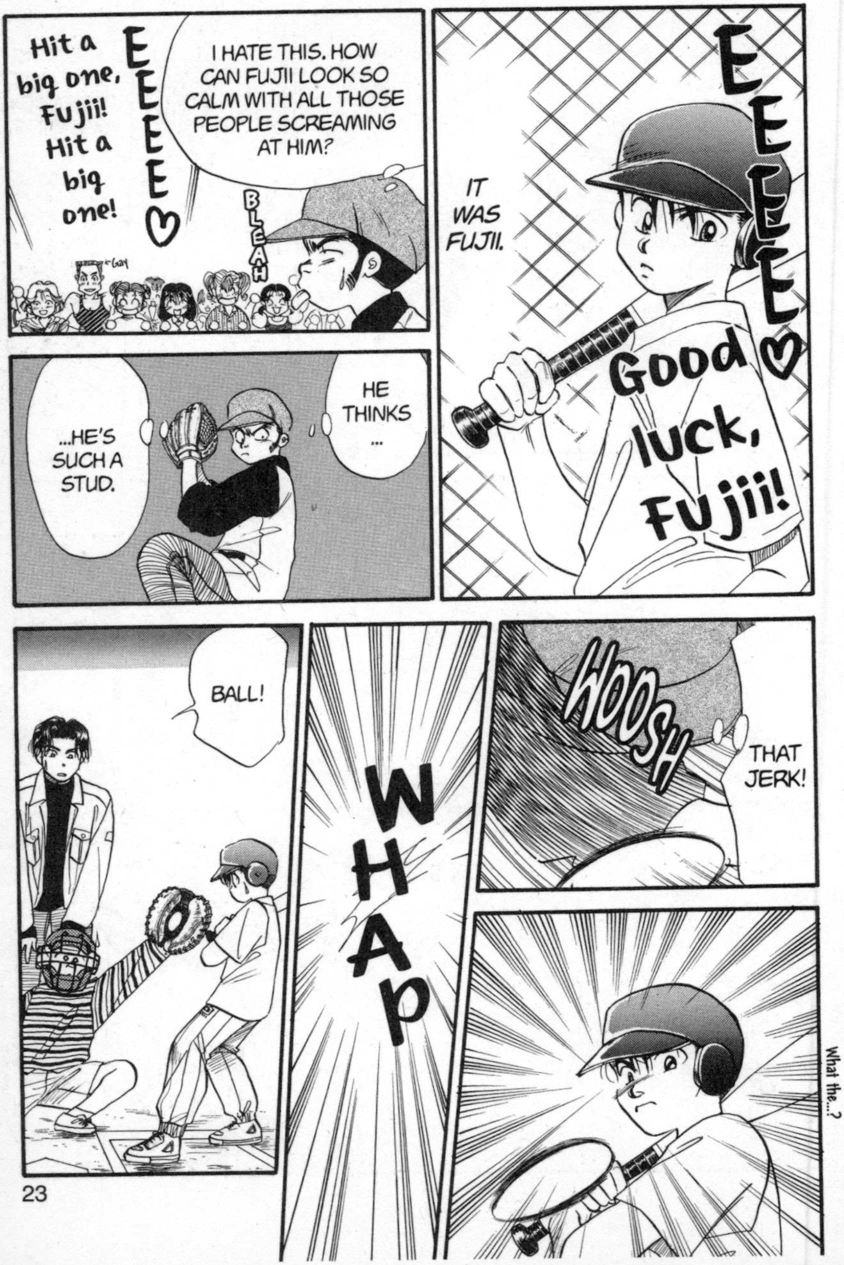

EEEEE♥
IT WAS FUJII.
Good luck, Fujii!
Hit a big one, Fujii! Hit a big one!
EEEEE♥
I HATE THIS. HOW CAN FUJII LOOK SO CALM WITH ALL THOSE PEOPLE SCREAMING AT HIM?
BLEAH
←Gay
HE THINKS ...
...HE'S SUCH A STUD.
WOOSH
THAT JERK!
What the...?
WHAp
BALL!

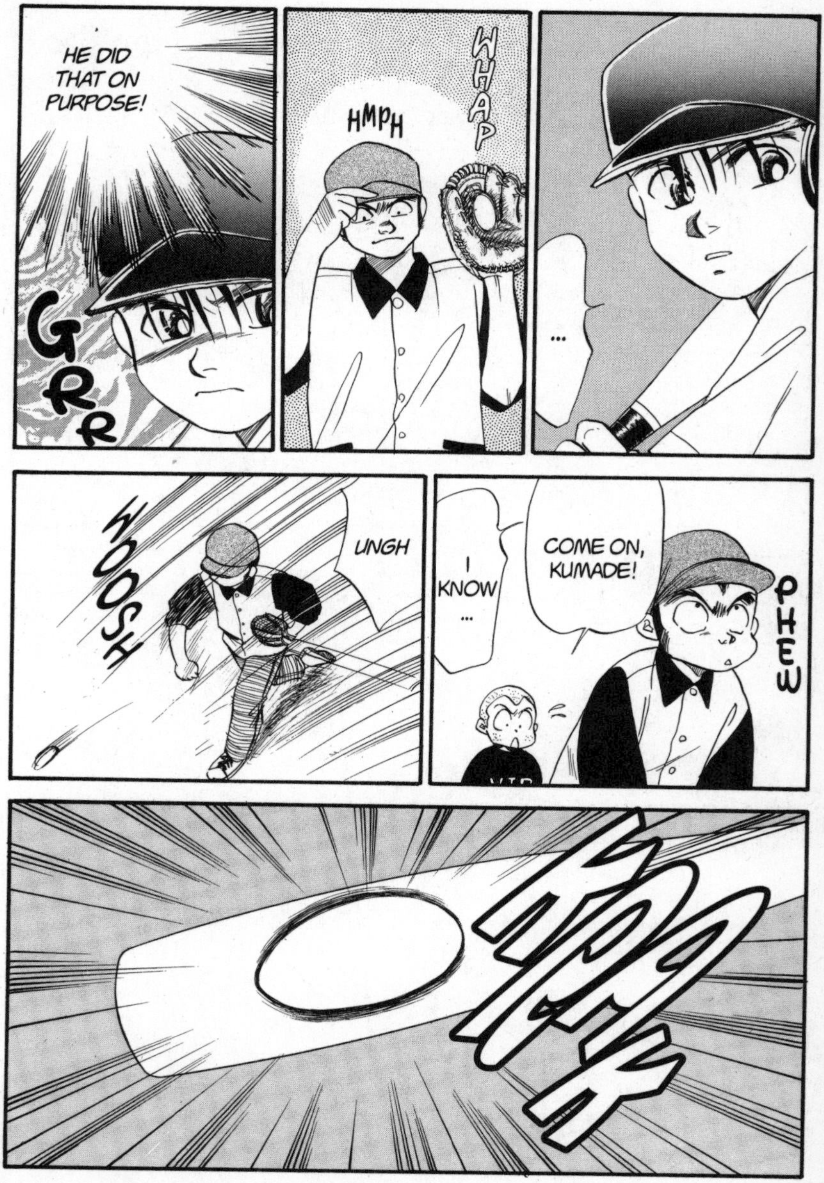
...
WHAP
HMPH
HE DID THAT ON PURPOSE!
GRR
COME ON, KUMADE!
I KNOW ...
PHEW
UNGH
WOOOSH

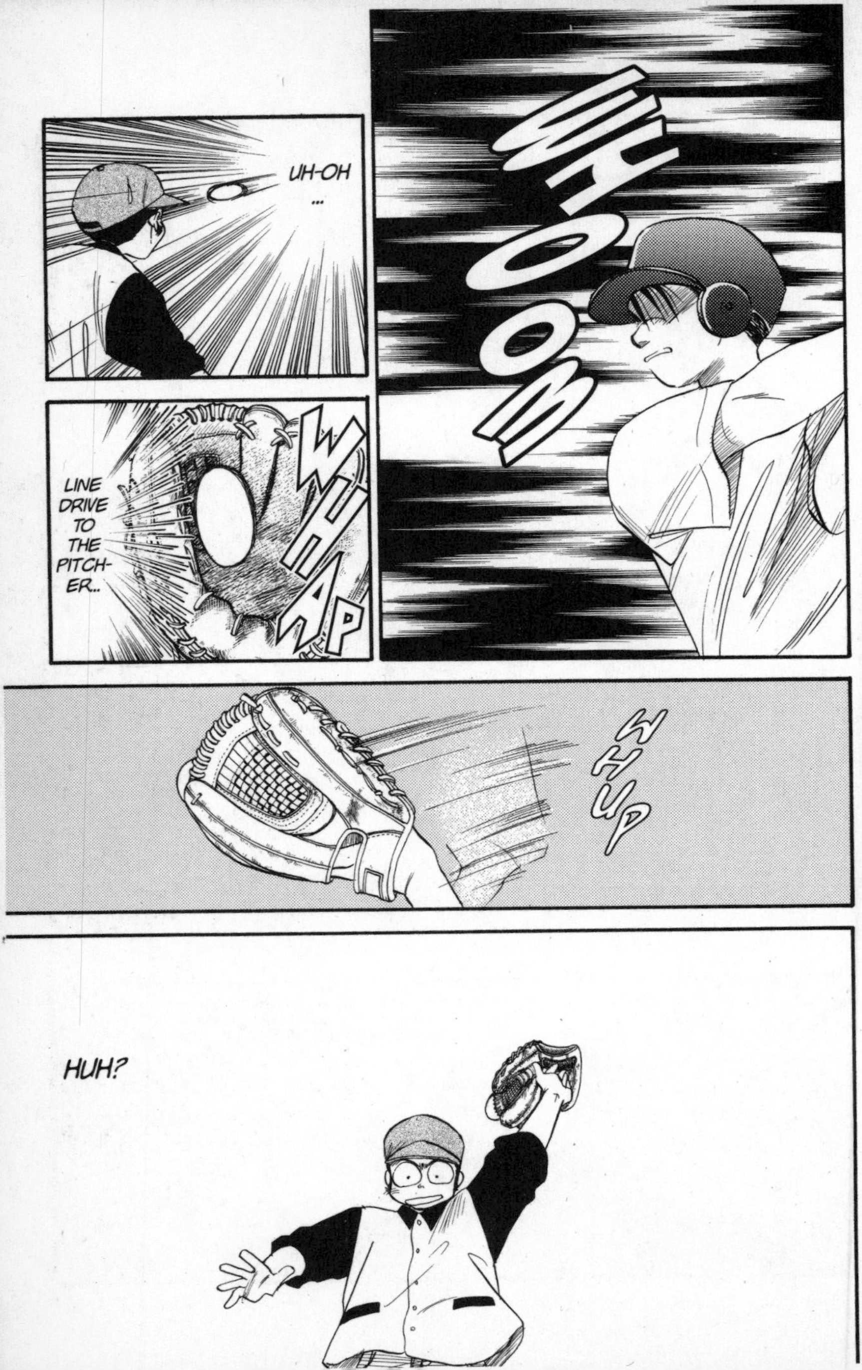
WHOOOOM
UH-OH ...
LINE DRIVE TO THE PITCHER...
WHAP
WHUP
HUH?

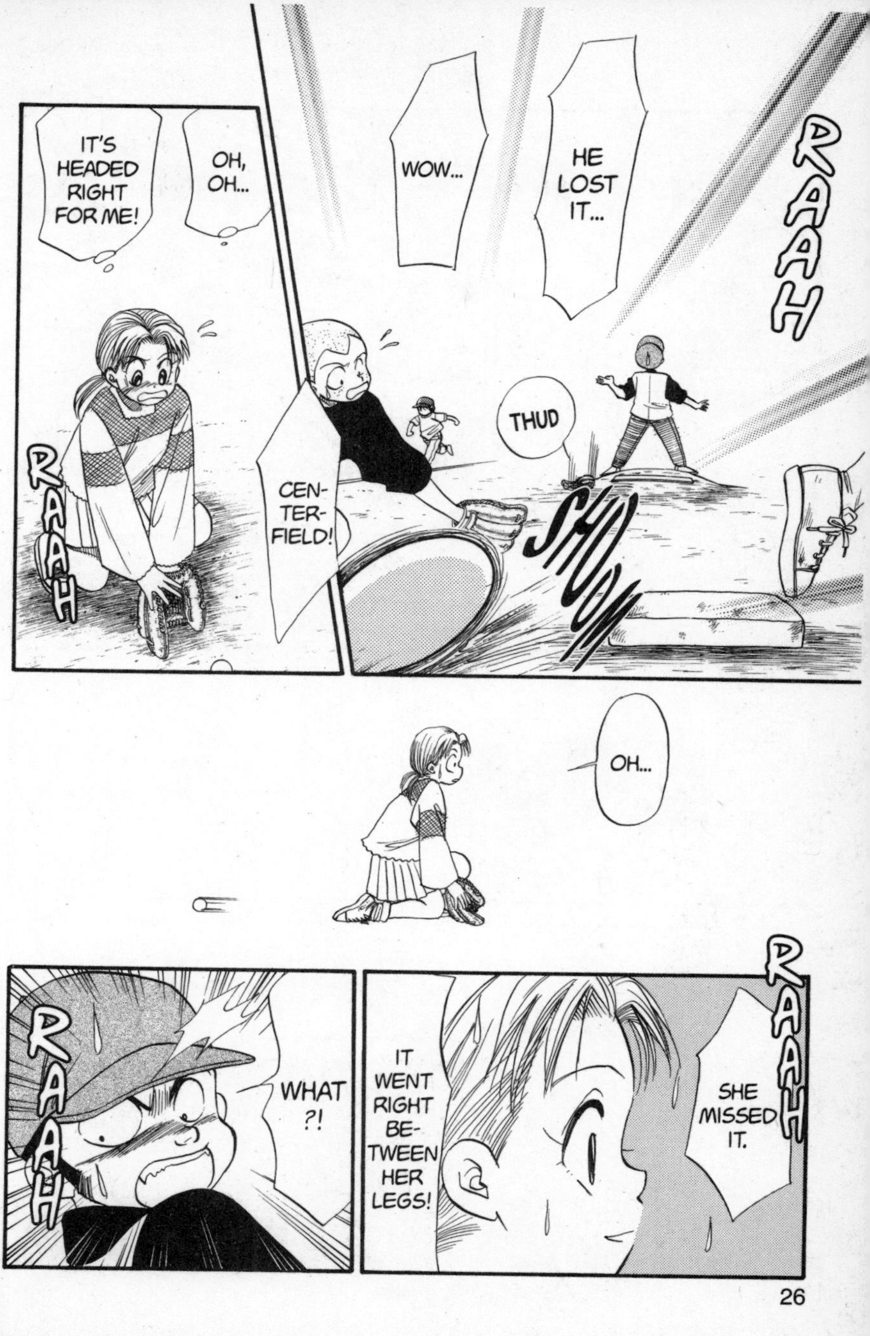
RAAAH
HE LOST IT...
WOW...
THUD
SHWOW
CENTER-FIELD!
OH, OH...
IT'S HEADED RIGHT FOR ME!
RAAAH
OH...
RAAAH
SHE MISSED IT.
IT WENT RIGHT BE-TWEEN HER LEGS!
WHAT?!
RAAAH

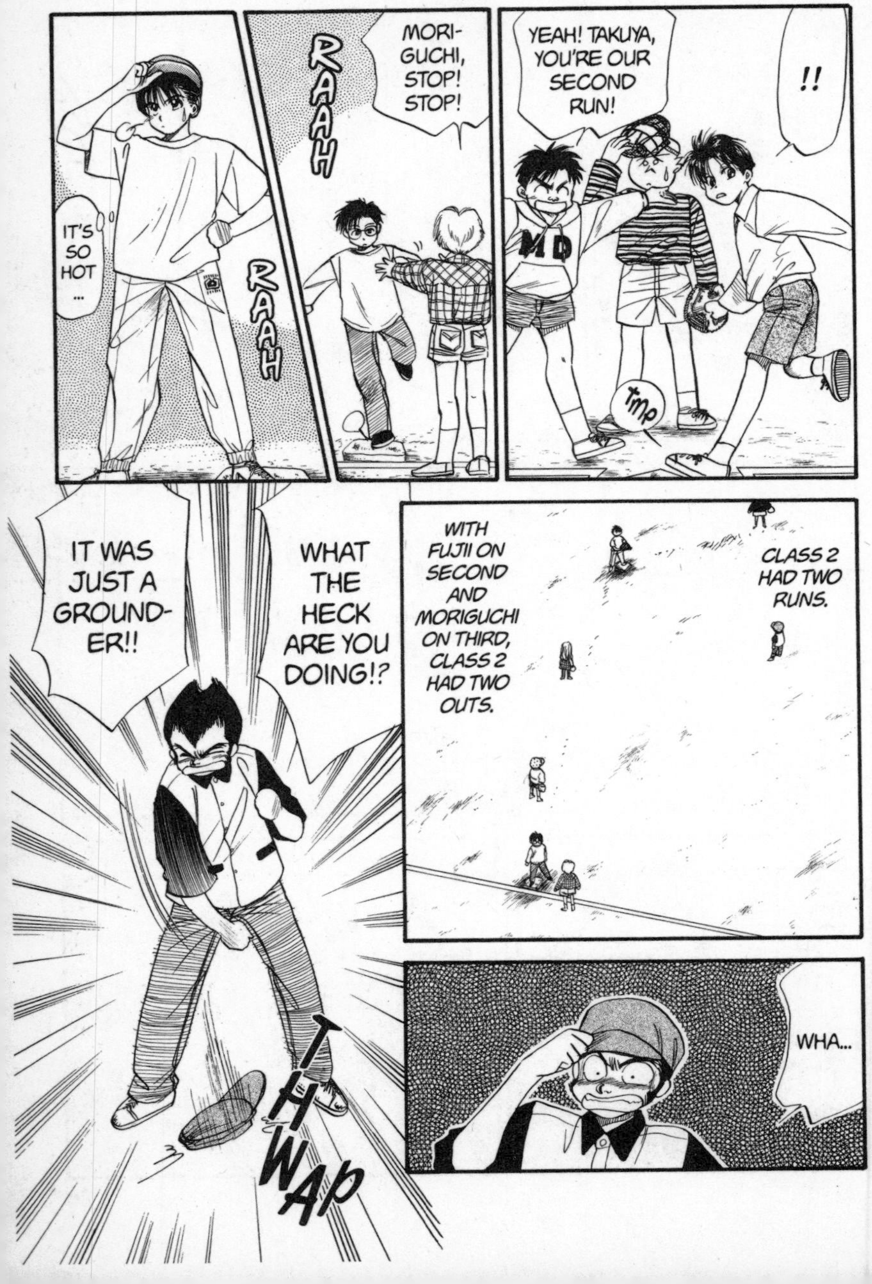
!!
YEAH! TAKUYA, YOU'RE OUR SECOND RUN!
tmp
MORI-GUCHI, STOP! STOP!
RAAAH
RAAAH
IT'S SO HOT ...
CLASS 2 HAD TWO RUNS.
WITH FUJII ON SECOND AND MORIGUCHI ON THIRD, CLASS 2 HAD TWO OUTS.
WHA...
WHAT THE HECK ARE YOU DOING!?
IT WAS JUST A GROUNDER!!
THWAP

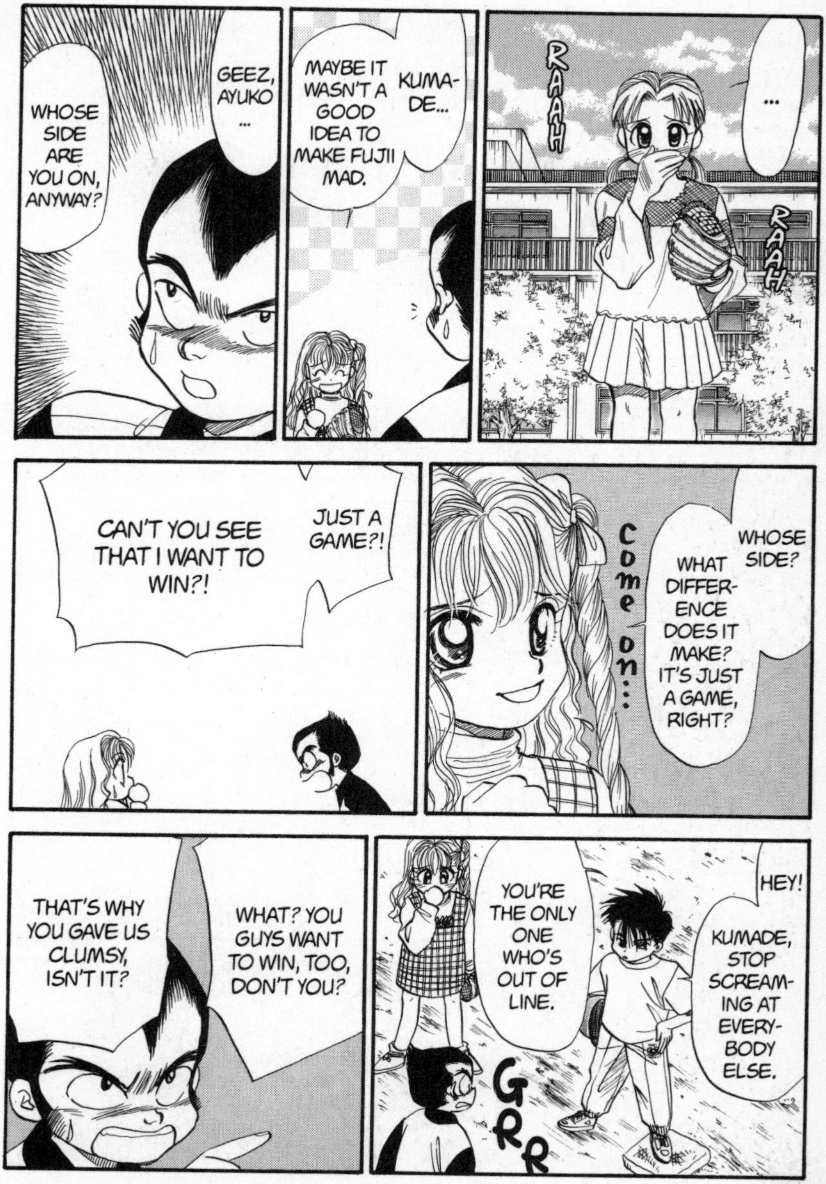
RAAAH
...
RAAAH
KUMA-DE...
MAYBE IT WASN'T A GOOD IDEA TO MAKE FUJII MAD.
GEEZ, AYUKO ...
WHOSE SIDE ARE YOU ON, ANYWAY?
WHOSE SIDE?
WHAT DIFFER-ENCE DOES IT MAKE? IT'S JUST A GAME, RIGHT?
Come on...
JUST A GAME?!
CAN'T YOU SEE THAT I WANT TO WIN?!
HEY!
KUMADE, STOP SCREAM-ING AT EVERY-BODY ELSE.
YOU'RE THE ONLY ONE WHO'S OUT OF LINE.
GRR
WHAT? YOU GUYS WANT TO WIN, TOO, DON'T YOU?
THAT'S WHY YOU GAVE US CLUMSY, ISN'T IT?

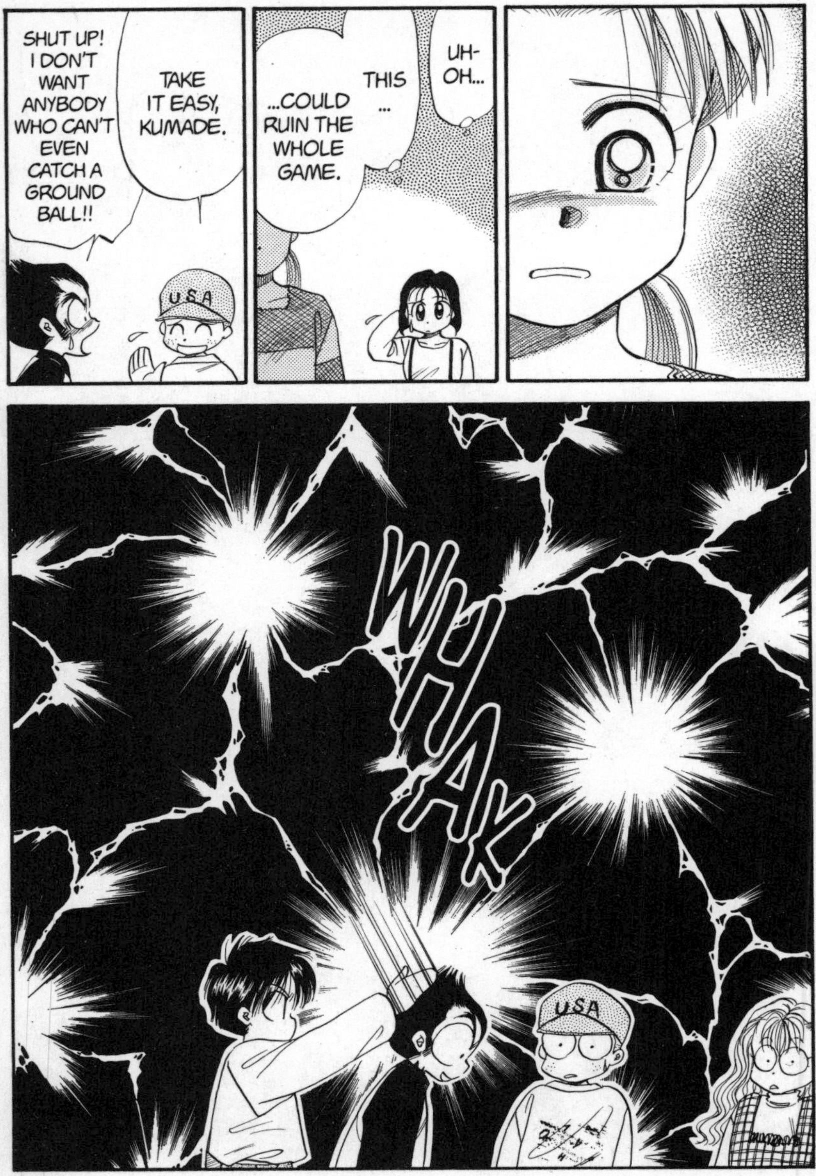
UH-OH...
THIS ...
...COULD RUIN THE WHOLE GAME.
TAKE IT EASY, KUMADE.
SHUT UP! I DON'T WANT ANYBODY WHO CAN'T EVEN CATCH A GROUND BALL!!
USA
WHHAK
USA

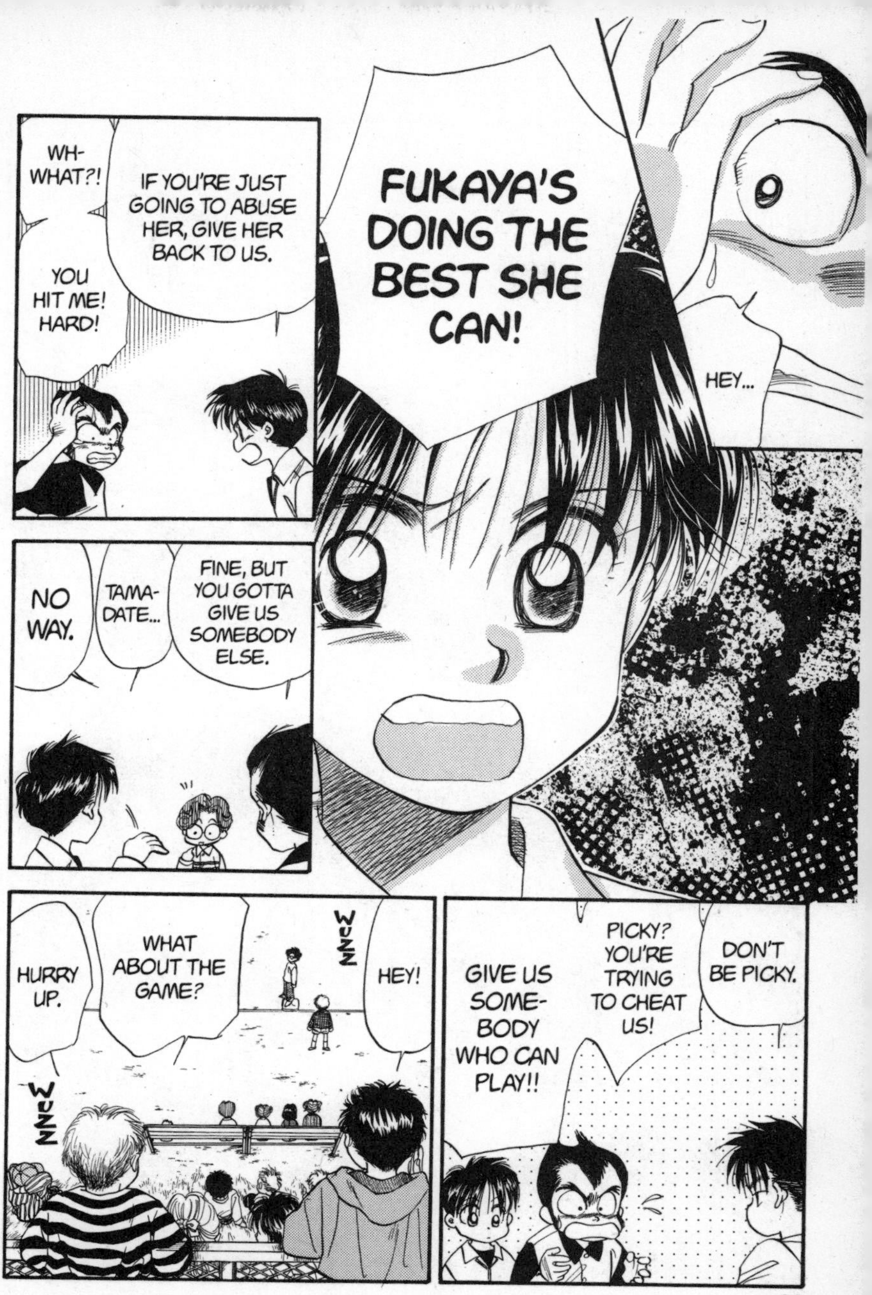
HEY...
FUKAYA'S DOING THE BEST SHE CAN!
IF YOU'RE JUST GOING TO ABUSE HER, GIVE HER BACK TO US.
WH- WHAT?!
YOU HIT ME! HARD!
FINE, BUT YOU GOTTA GIVE US SOMEBODY ELSE.
TAMA- DATE...
NO WAY.
DON'T BE PICKY.
PICKY? YOU'RE TRYING TO CHEAT US!
GIVE US SOME- BODY WHO CAN PLAY!!
HEY!
WUZZ
WHAT ABOUT THE GAME?
HURRY UP.
WUZZ

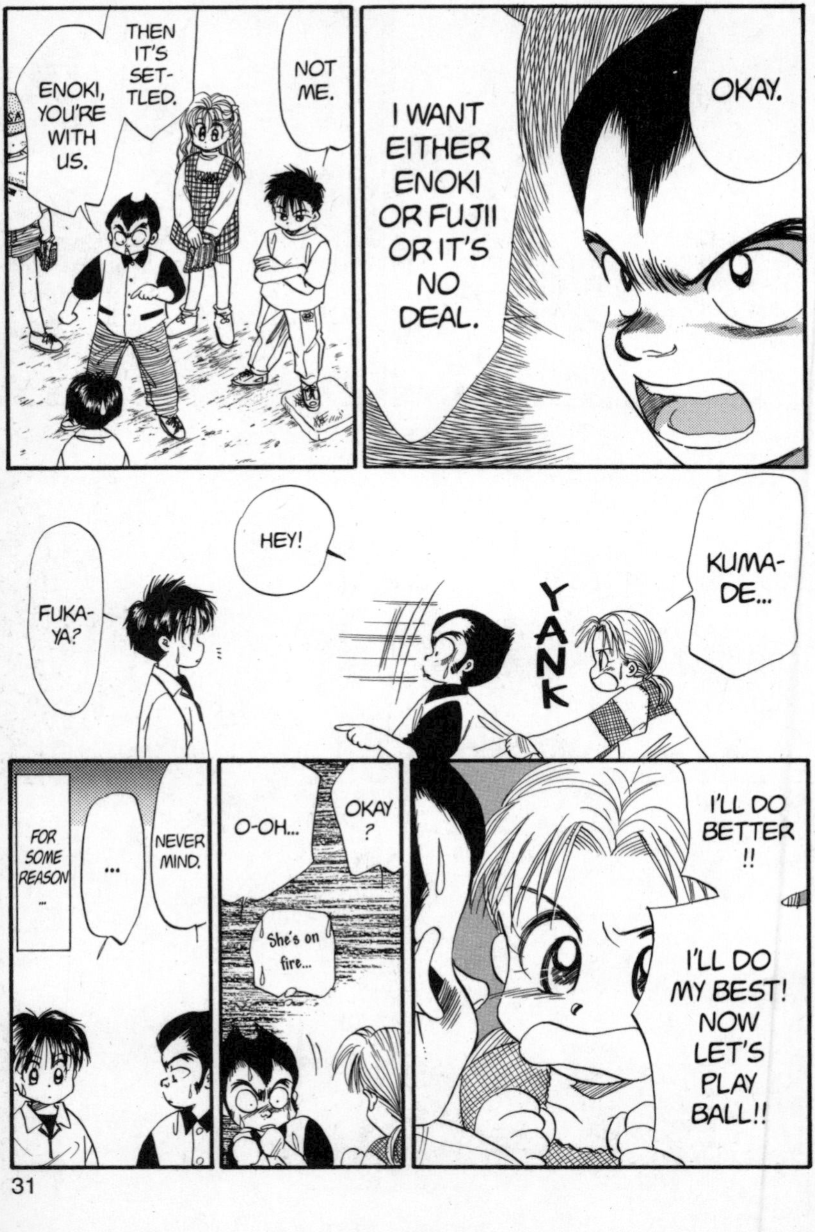
OKAY.
I WANT EITHER ENOKI OR FUJII OR IT'S NO DEAL.
NOT ME.
THEN IT'S SET-TLED.
ENOKI, YOU'RE WITH US.
KUMA-DE...
YANK
HEY!
FUKA-YA?
I'LL DO BETTER !!
I'LL DO MY BEST! NOW LET'S PLAY BALL!!
OKAY ?
O-OH...
She's on fire...
NEVER MIND.
...
FOR SOME REASON ...

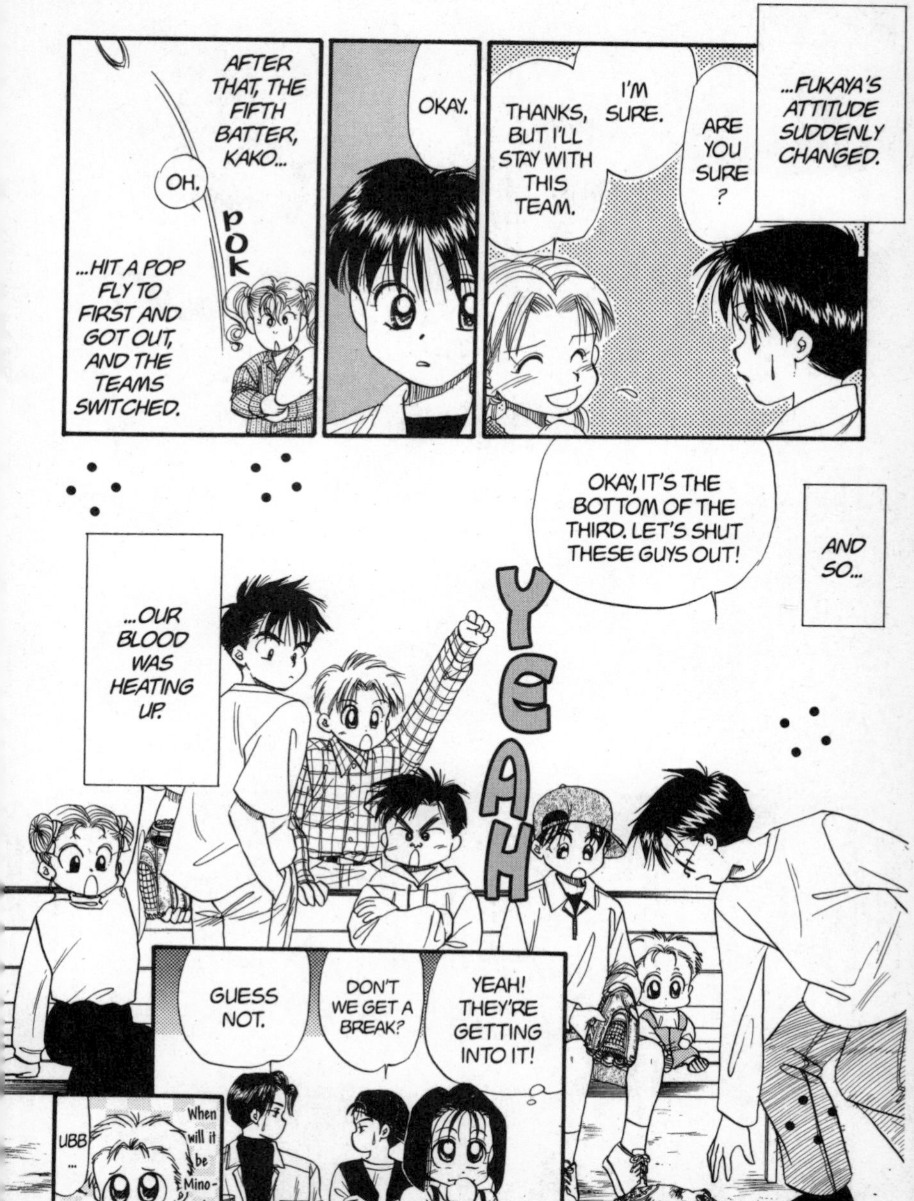
...FUKAYA'S ATTITUDE SUDDENLY CHANGED.
ARE YOU SURE?
I'M SURE.
THANKS, BUT I'LL STAY WITH THIS TEAM.
OKAY.
AFTER THAT, THE FIFTH BATTER, KAKO...
OH.
POK
...HIT A POP FLY TO FIRST AND GOT OUT, AND THE TEAMS SWITCHED.
AND SO...
OKAY, IT'S THE BOTTOM OF THE THIRD. LET'S SHUT THESE GUYS OUT!
YEAH
...OUR BLOOD WAS HEATING UP.
YEAH! THEY'RE GETTING INTO IT!
DON'T WE GET A BREAK?
GUESS NOT.
When will it be Mino-ru's turn?
UBB...

Chapter 57 / The End

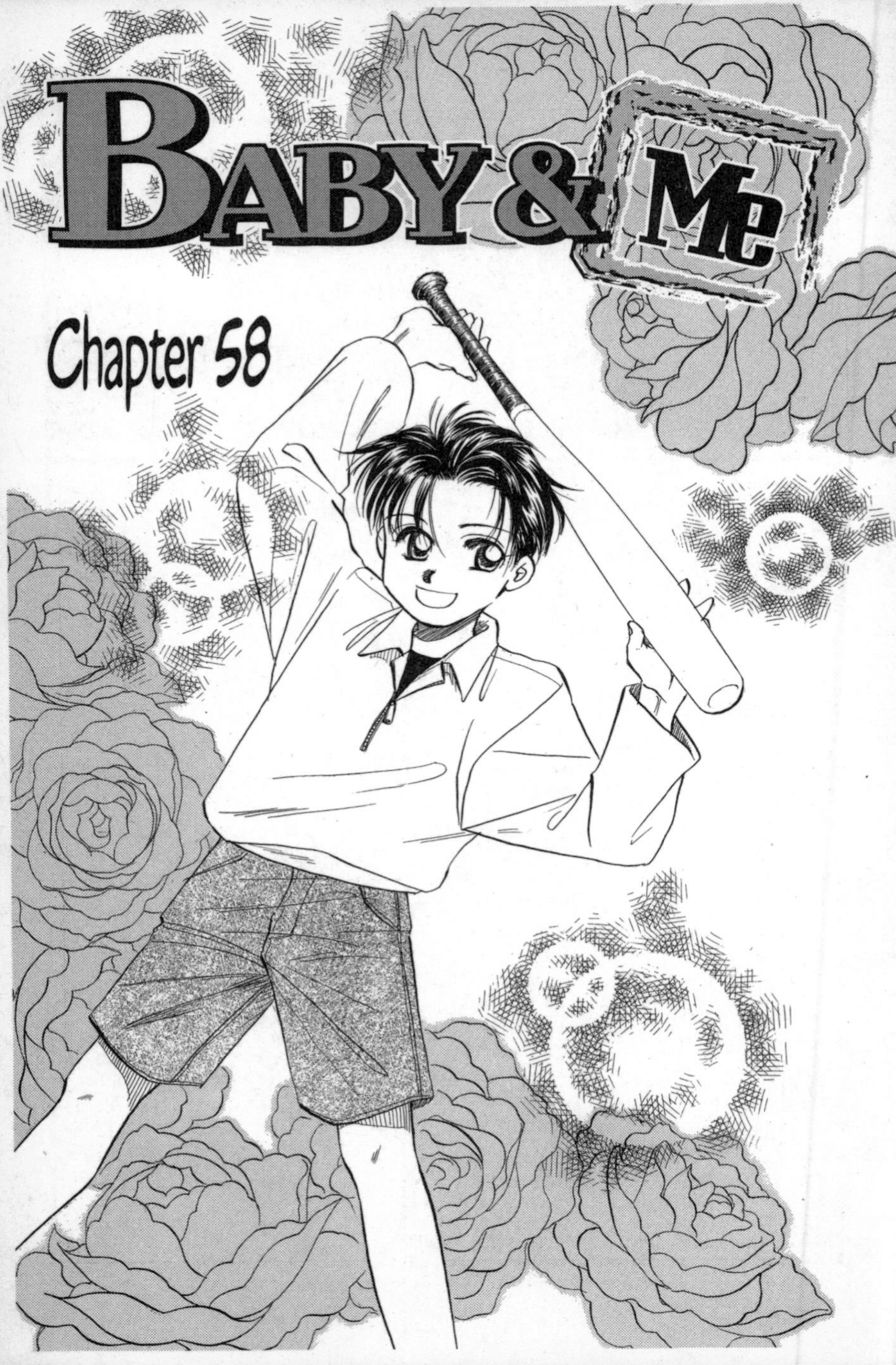
BABY & Me
Chapter 58

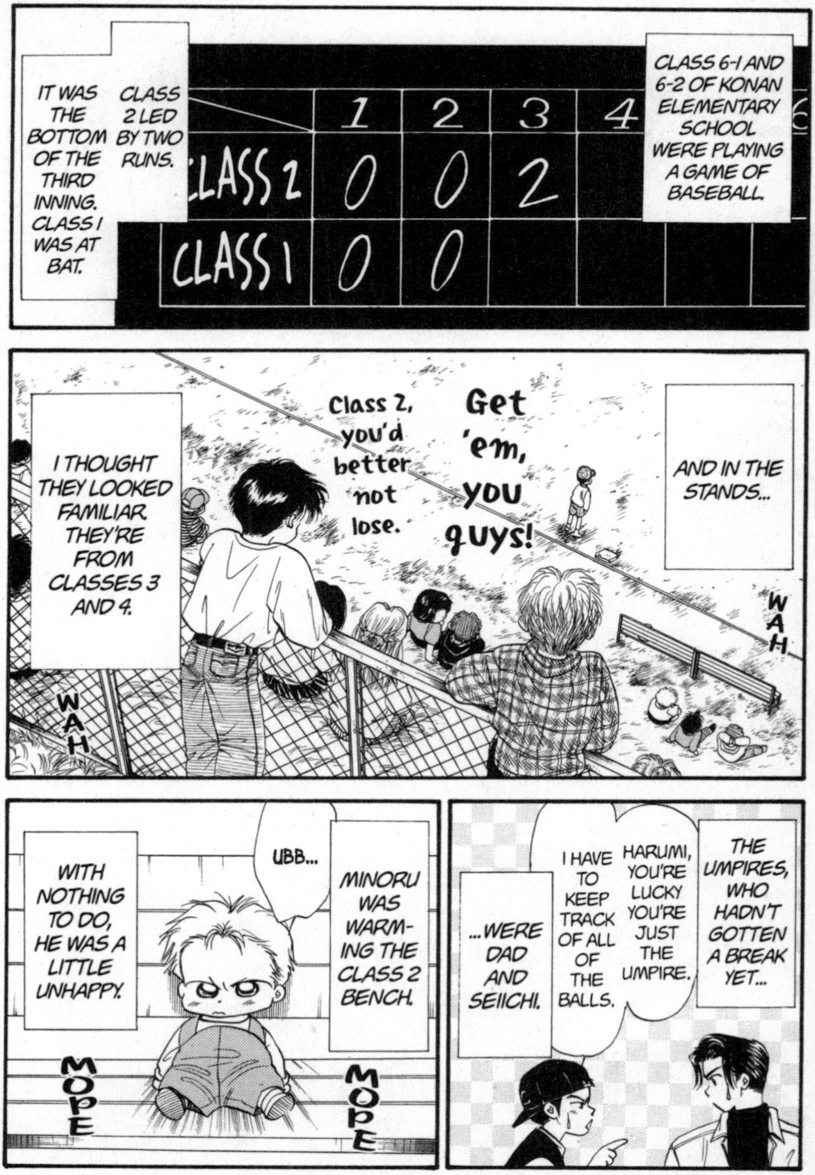
CLASS 6-1 AND 6-2 OF KONAN ELEMENTARY SCHOOL WERE PLAYING A GAME OF BASEBALL.
1 2 3 4
CLASS 2 0 0 2
CLASS 1 0 0
CLASS 2 LED BY TWO RUNS.
IT WAS THE BOTTOM OF THE THIRD INNING. CLASS 1 WAS AT BAT.
AND IN THE STANDS...
WAH
Get 'em, you guys!
Class 2, you'd better not lose.
I THOUGHT THEY LOOKED FAMILIAR. THEY'RE FROM CLASSES 3 AND 4.
WAH
THE UMPIRES, WHO HADN'T GOTTEN A BREAK YET...
HARUMI, YOU'RE LUCKY YOU'RE JUST THE UMPIRE.
I HAVE TO KEEP TRACK OF ALL OF THE BALLS.
...WERE DAD AND SEIICHI.
MINORU WAS WARMING THE CLASS 2 BENCH.
UBB...
MOPE
MOPE
WITH NOTHING TO DO, HE WAS A LITTLE UNHAPPY.

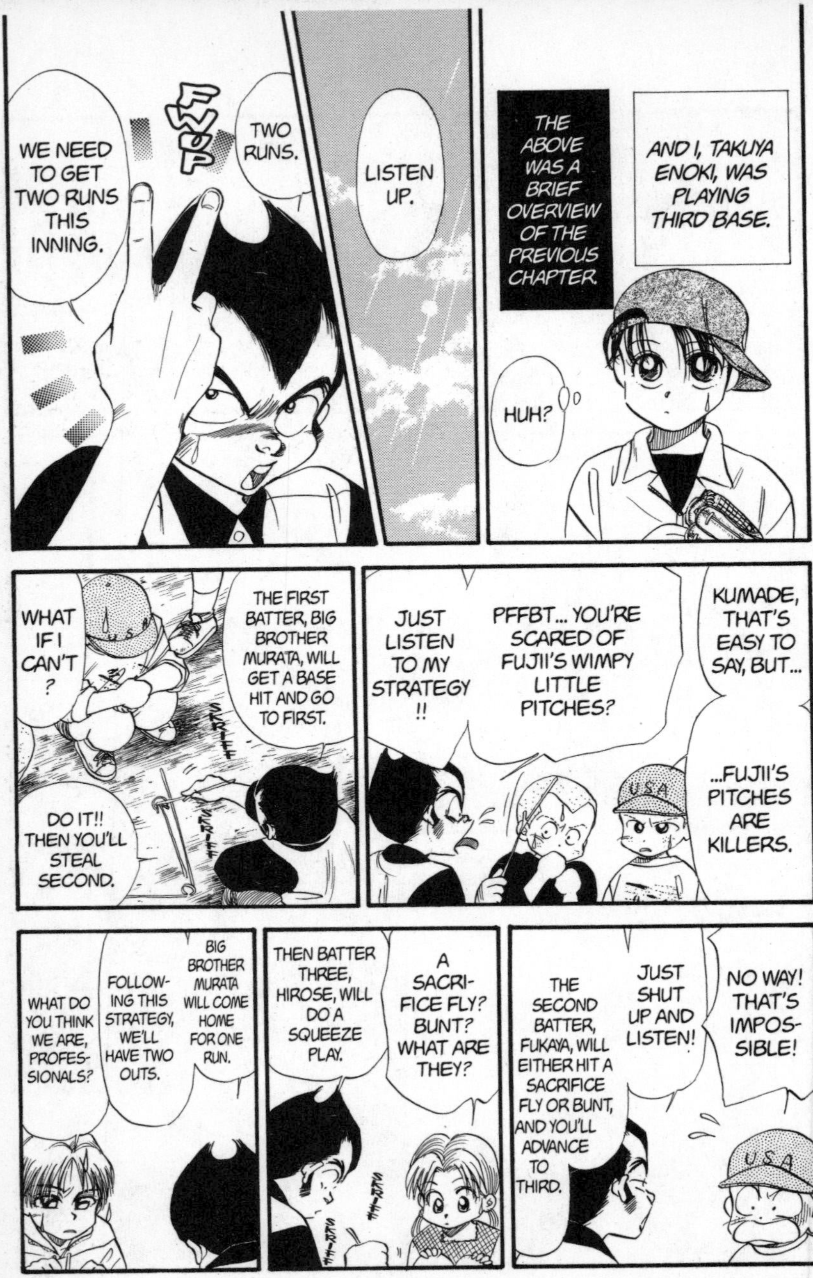
AND I, TAKUYA ENOKI, WAS PLAYING THIRD BASE.
THE ABOVE WAS A BRIEF OVERVIEW OF THE PREVIOUS CHAPTER.
HUH?
LISTEN UP.
TWO RUNS.
FWUP
WE NEED TO GET TWO RUNS THIS INNING.
KUMADE, THAT'S EASY TO SAY, BUT...
...FUJII'S PITCHES ARE KILLERS.
PFFBT... YOU'RE SCARED OF FUJII'S WIMPY LITTLE PITCHES?
JUST LISTEN TO MY STRATEGY !!
THE FIRST BATTER, BIG BROTHER MURATA, WILL GET A BASE HIT AND GO TO FIRST.
WHAT IF I CAN'T ?
SKRIFF
SKRIFF
DO IT!! THEN YOU'LL STEAL SECOND.
NO WAY! THAT'S IMPOSSIBLE!
JUST SHUT UP AND LISTEN!
THE SECOND BATTER, FUKAYA, WILL EITHER HIT A SACRIFICE FLY OR BUNT, AND YOU'LL ADVANCE TO THIRD.
A SACRIFICE FLY? BUNT? WHAT ARE THEY?
THEN BATTER THREE, HIROSE, WILL DO A SQUEEZE PLAY.
SKRIFF
SKRIFF
BIG BROTHER MURATA WILL COME HOME FOR ONE RUN.
FOLLOWING THIS STRATEGY, WE'LL HAVE TWO OUTS.
WHAT DO YOU THINK WE ARE, PROFESSIONALS?

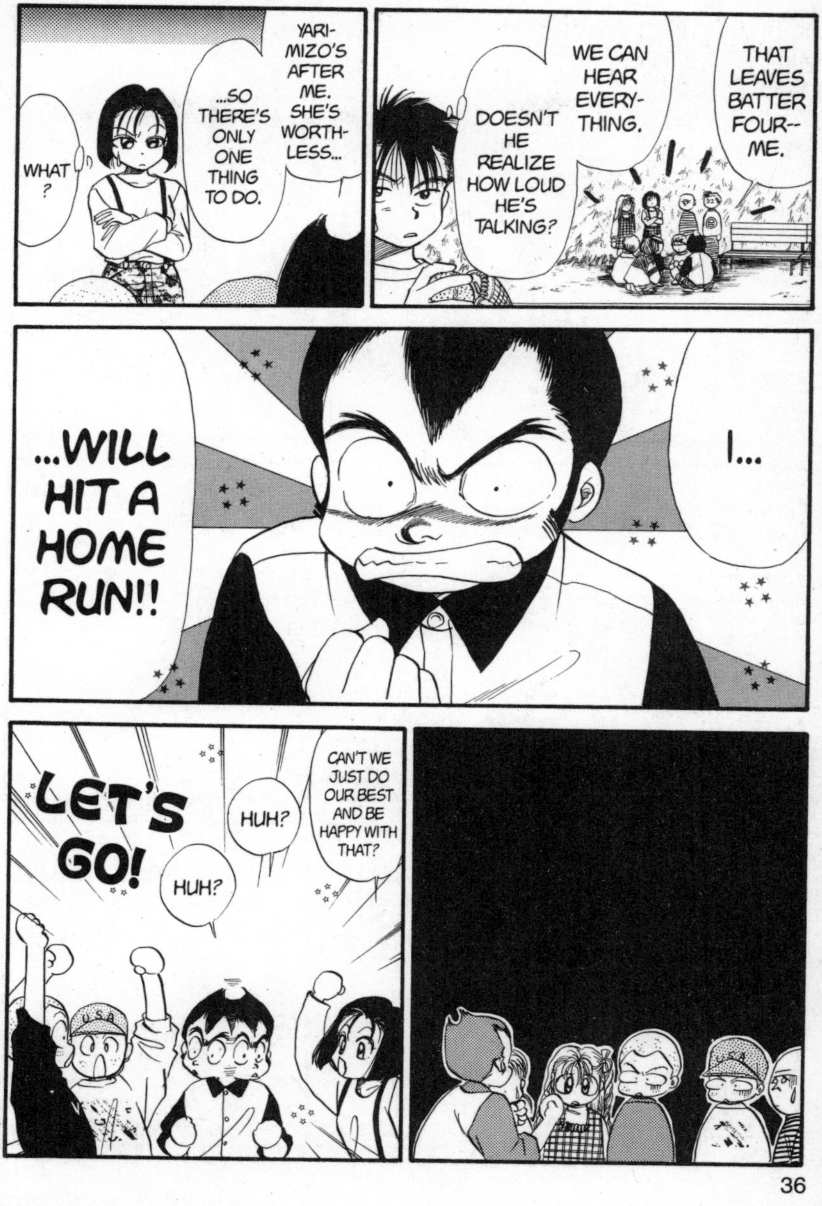
THAT LEAVES BATTER FOUR-- ME.
WE CAN HEAR EVERY-THING.
DOESN'T HE REALIZE HOW LOUD HE'S TALKING?
YARI-MIZO'S AFTER ME. SHE'S WORTH-LESS...
...SO THERE'S ONLY ONE THING TO DO.
WHAT?
I...
...WILL HIT A HOME RUN!!
CAN'T WE JUST DO OUR BEST AND BE HAPPY WITH THAT?
HUH?
HUH?
LET'S GO!

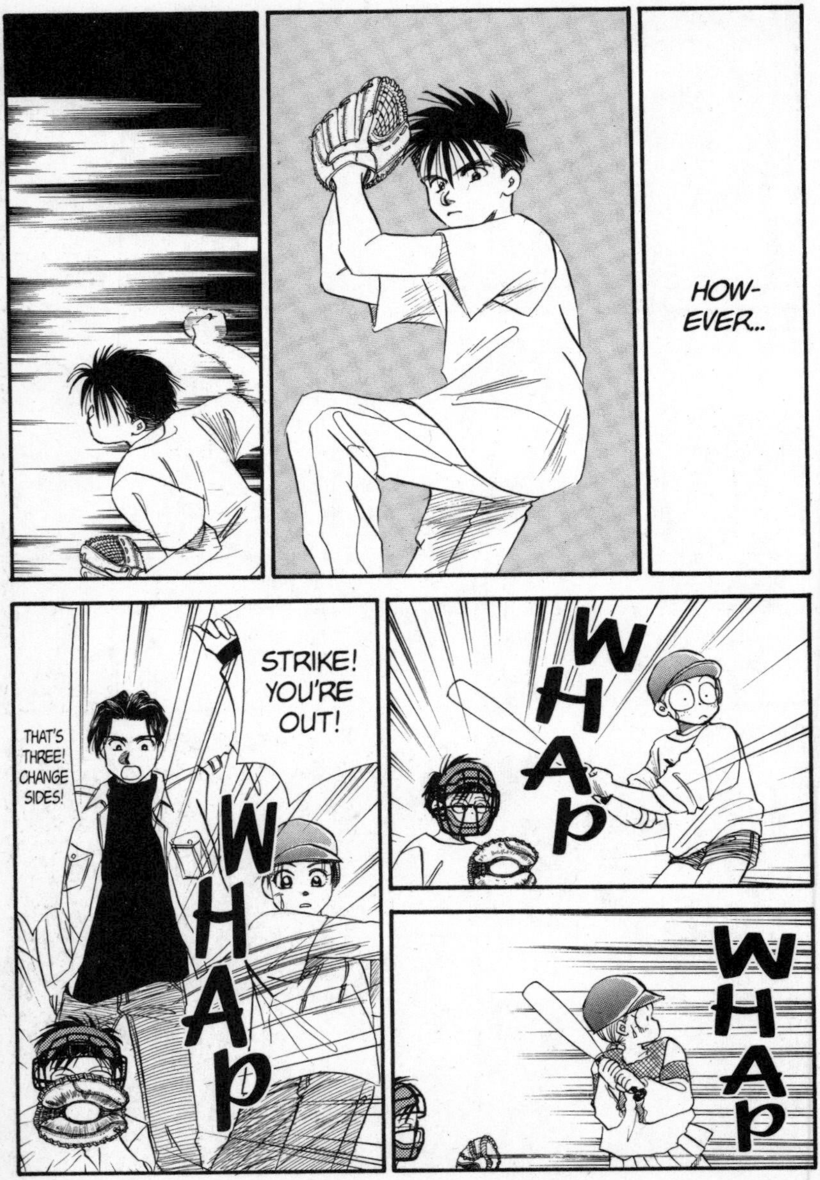
HOW-EVER...
WHAp
WHAp
STRIKE! YOU'RE OUT!
THAT'S THREE! CHANGE SIDES!
WHAp

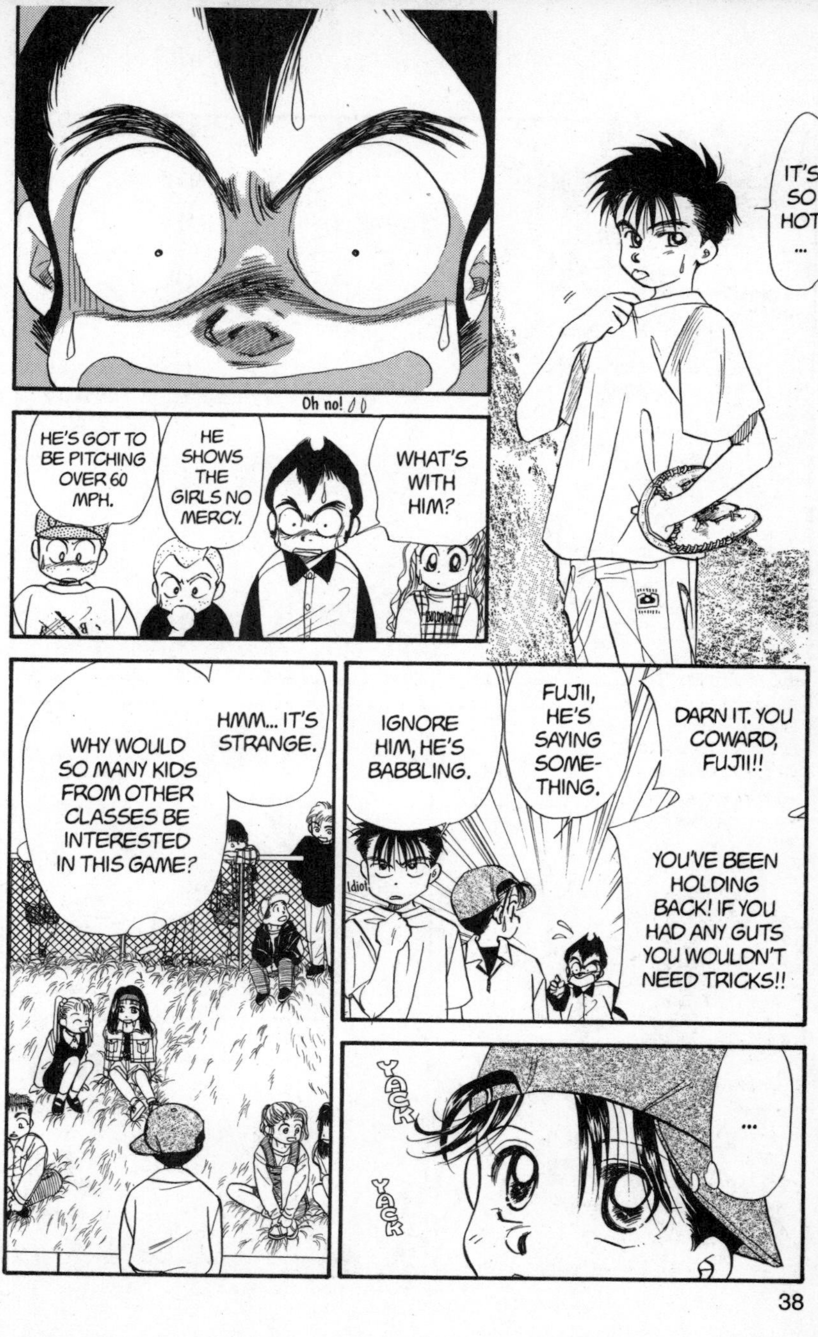
IT'S SO HOT ...
Oh no!
WHAT'S WITH HIM?
HE SHOWS THE GIRLS NO MERCY.
HE'S GOT TO BE PITCHING OVER 60 MPH.
DARN IT. YOU COWARD, FUJII!!
YOU'VE BEEN HOLDING BACK! IF YOU HAD ANY GUTS YOU WOULDN'T NEED TRICKS!!
FUJII, HE'S SAYING SOME-THING.
IGNORE HIM, HE'S BABBLING.
Idiot
...
YACK
YACK
HMM... IT'S STRANGE.
WHY WOULD SO MANY KIDS FROM OTHER CLASSES BE INTERESTED IN THIS GAME?

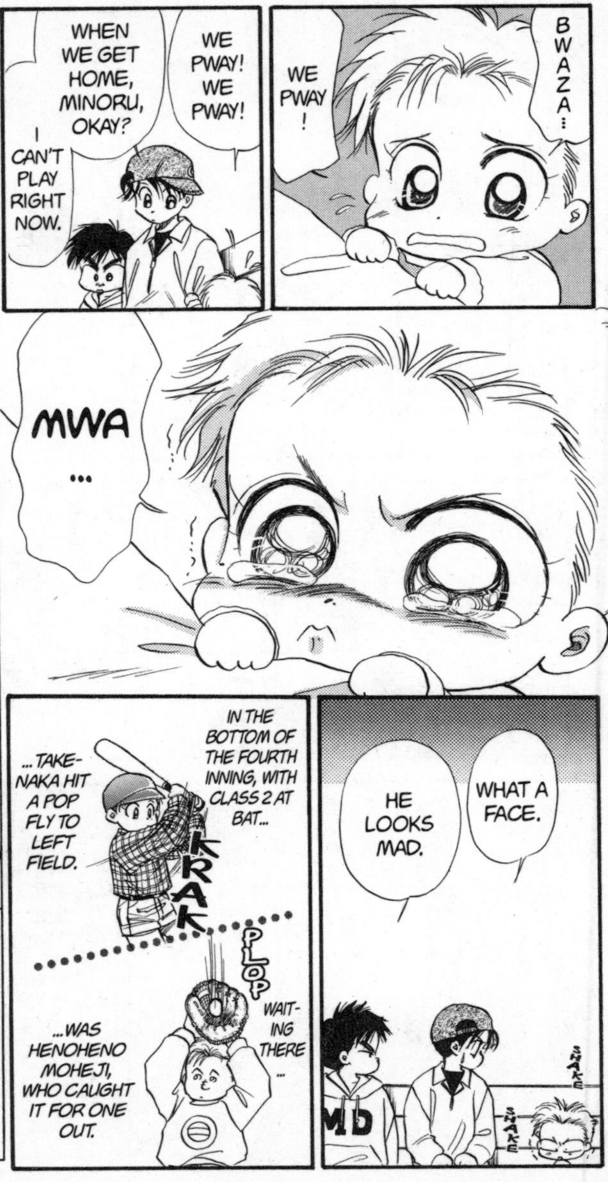
BWAZA...
WE PWAY!
WE PWAY! WE PWAY!
WHEN WE GET HOME, MINORU, OKAY?
I CAN'T PLAY RIGHT NOW.
MWA...
WHAT A FACE.
HE LOOKS MAD.
SHAKE
SHAKE
IN THE BOTTOM OF THE FOURTH INNING, WITH CLASS 2 AT BAT...
...TAKE-NAKA HIT A POP FLY TO LEFT FIELD.
KRAK
PLOP
WAIT-ING THERE...
...WAS HENOHENO MOHEJI, WHO CAUGHT IT FOR ONE OUT.
MD

Author's Note: Part 2

Celebrating the Acceptance of the Shogakukan Manga Award

On March 3, 1995, I attended the 40th Annual Shogakukan Manga Awards Presentations.

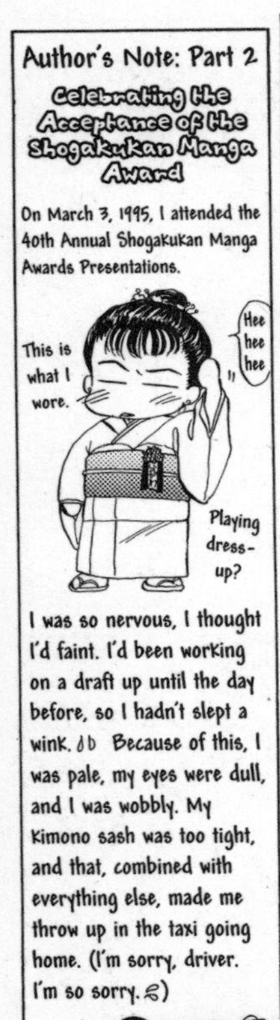
This is what I wore.
Hee hee hee
Playing dress-up?

I was so nervous, I thought I'd faint. I'd been working on a draft up until the day before, so I hadn't slept a wink. Because of this, I was pale, my eyes were dull, and I was wobbly. My kimono sash was too tight, and that, combined with everything else, made me throw up in the taxi going home. (I'm sorry, driver. I'm so sorry.)

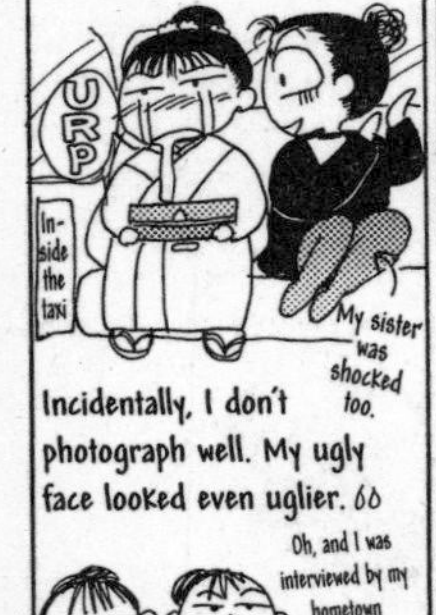
URP
Inside the taxi
My sister was shocked too.

Incidentally, I don't photograph well. My ugly face looked even uglier.

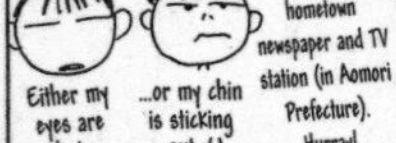
Either my eyes are shut...
...or my chin is sticking out.
Oh, and I was interviewed by my hometown newspaper and TV station (in Aomori Prefecture). Hurray!

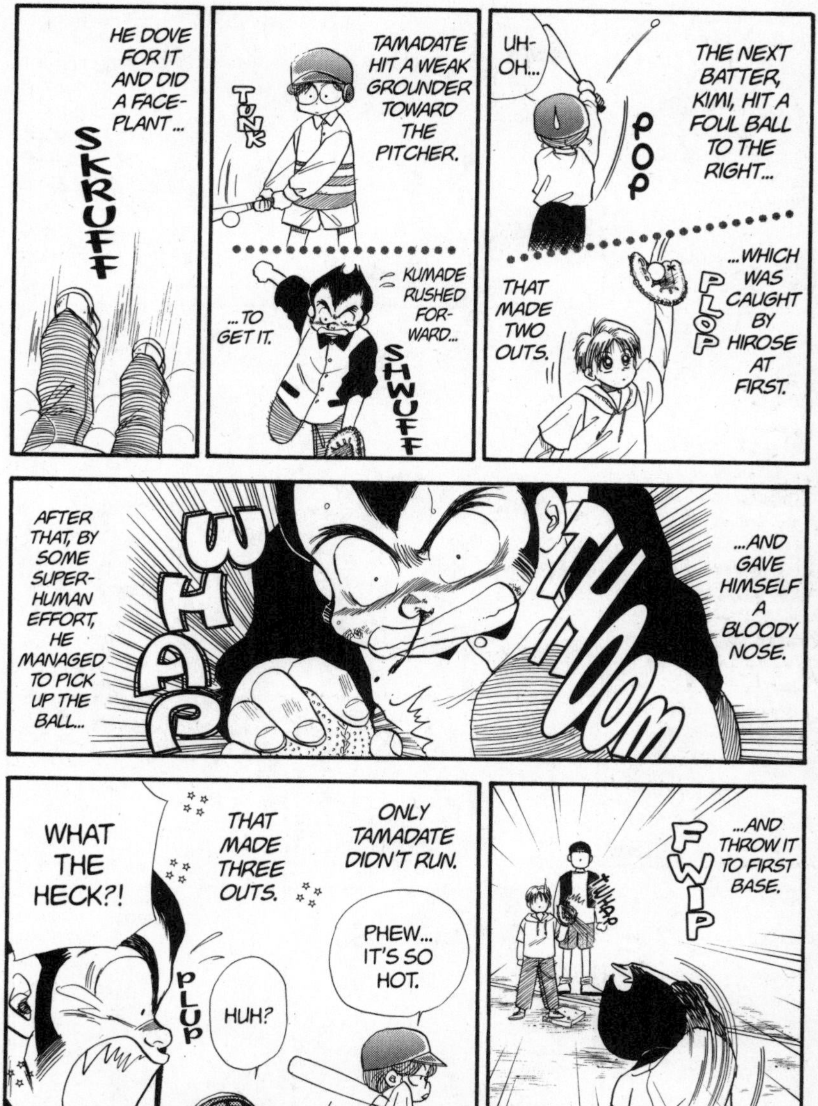

UH-OH...
THE NEXT BATTER, KIMI, HIT A FOUL BALL TO THE RIGHT...
POP
...WHICH WAS CAUGHT BY HIROSE AT FIRST.
PLOP
THAT MADE TWO OUTS.
TAMADATE HIT A WEAK GROUNDER TOWARD THE PITCHER.
TUNK
KUMADE RUSHED FORWARD...
...TO GET IT.
SHWUFF
HE DOVE FOR IT AND DID A FACE-PLANT...
SKRUFF
...AND GAVE HIMSELF A BLOODY NOSE.
THOOM
WHAP
AFTER THAT, BY SOME SUPER-HUMAN EFFORT, HE MANAGED TO PICK UP THE BALL...
FWIP
...AND THROW IT TO FIRST BASE.
THWAP
ONLY TAMADATE DIDN'T RUN.
PHEW... IT'S SO HOT.
THAT MADE THREE OUTS.
HUH?
WHAT THE HECK?!
PLUP
PLUP

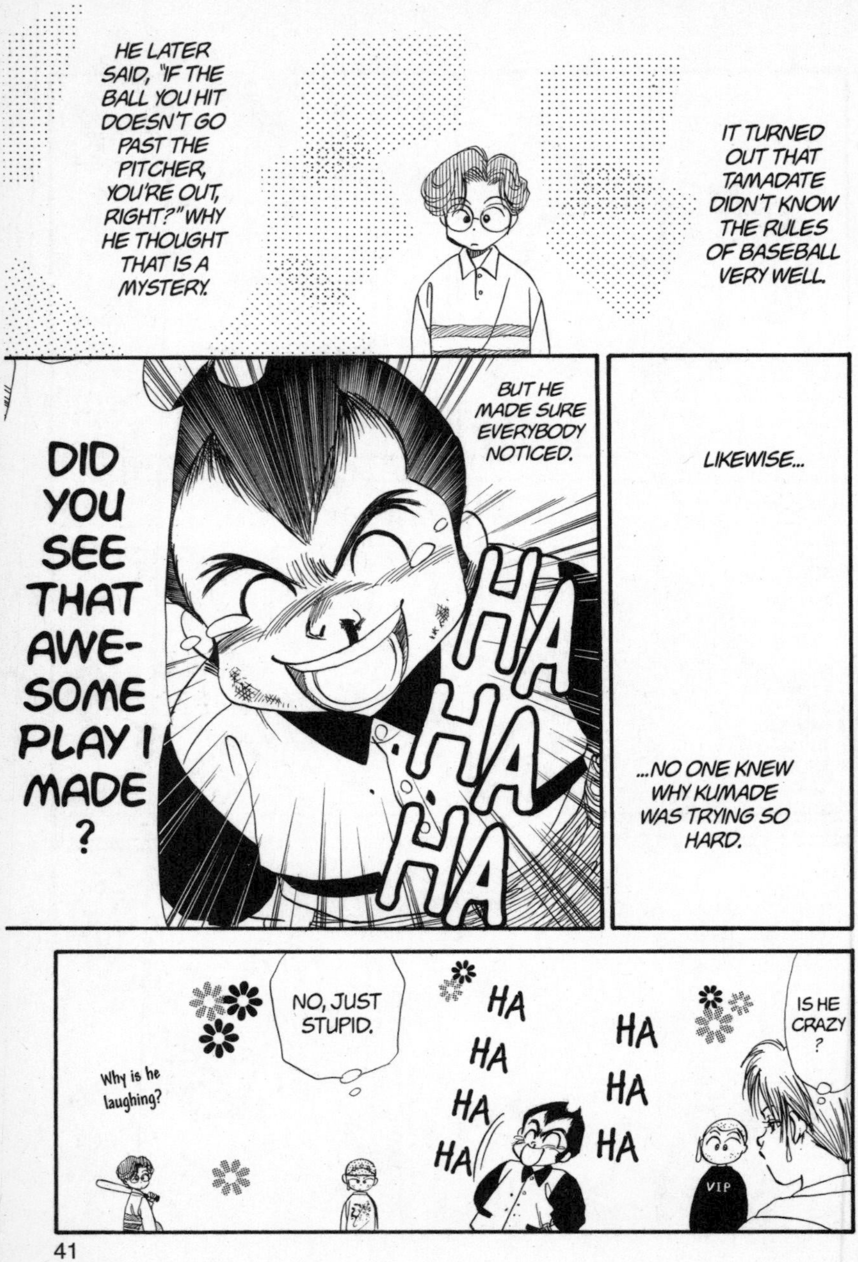
IT TURNED OUT THAT TAMADATE DIDN'T KNOW THE RULES OF BASEBALL VERY WELL.
HE LATER SAID, "IF THE BALL YOU HIT DOESN'T GO PAST THE PITCHER, YOU'RE OUT, RIGHT?" WHY HE THOUGHT THAT IS A MYSTERY.
LIKEWISE...
...NO ONE KNEW WHY KUMADE WAS TRYING SO HARD.
BUT HE MADE SURE EVERYBODY NOTICED.
HA HA HA HA
DID YOU SEE THAT AWE-SOME PLAY I MADE?
IS HE CRAZY?
HA HA HA
HA HA HA HA
NO, JUST STUPID.
Why is he laughing?

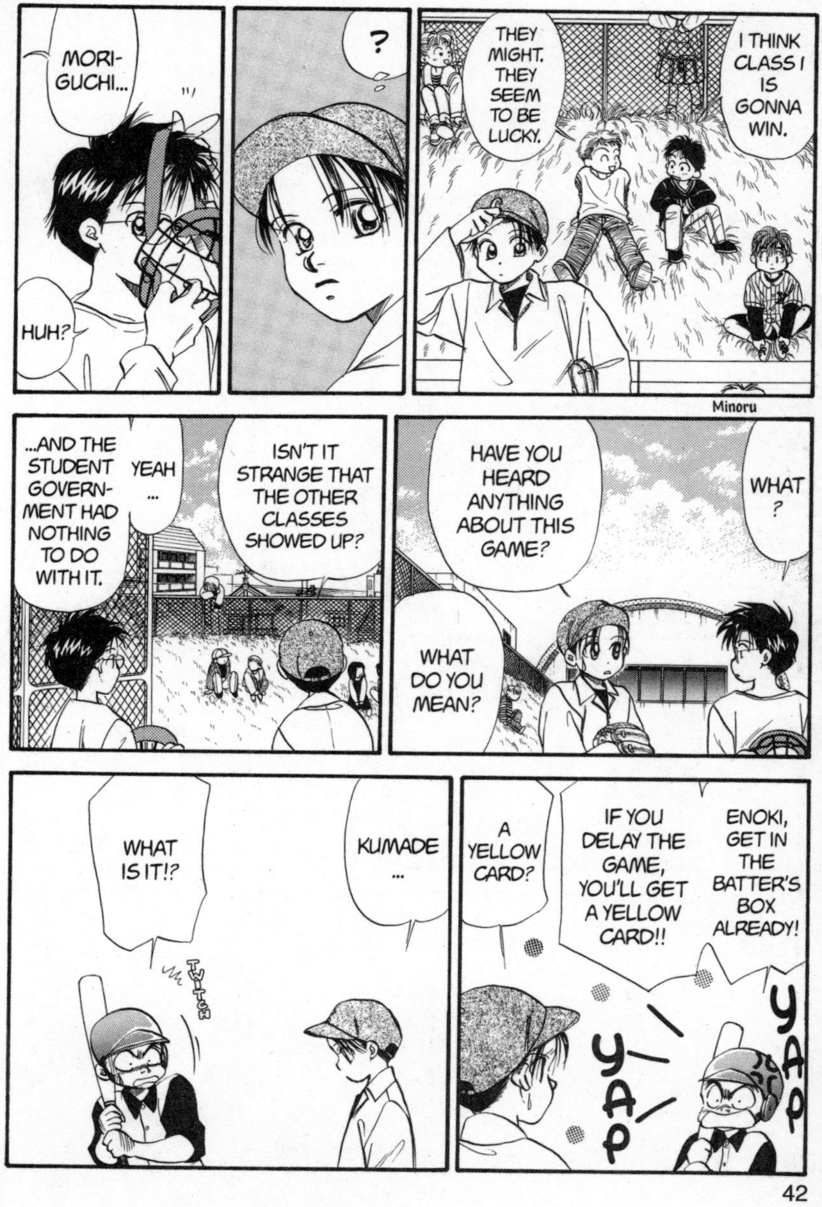
I THINK CLASS I IS GONNA WIN.
THEY MIGHT. THEY SEEM TO BE LUCKY.
Minoru
?
MORI-GUCHI...
HUH?
WHAT ?
HAVE YOU HEARD ANYTHING ABOUT THIS GAME?
WHAT DO YOU MEAN?
ISN'T IT STRANGE THAT THE OTHER CLASSES SHOWED UP?
YEAH ...
...AND THE STUDENT GOVERN-MENT HAD NOTHING TO DO WITH IT.
ENOKI, GET IN THE BATTER'S BOX ALREADY!
IF YOU DELAY THE GAME, YOU'LL GET A YELLOW CARD!!
A YELLOW CARD?
YAP
YAP
KUMADE ...
WHAT IS IT!?
TWITCH

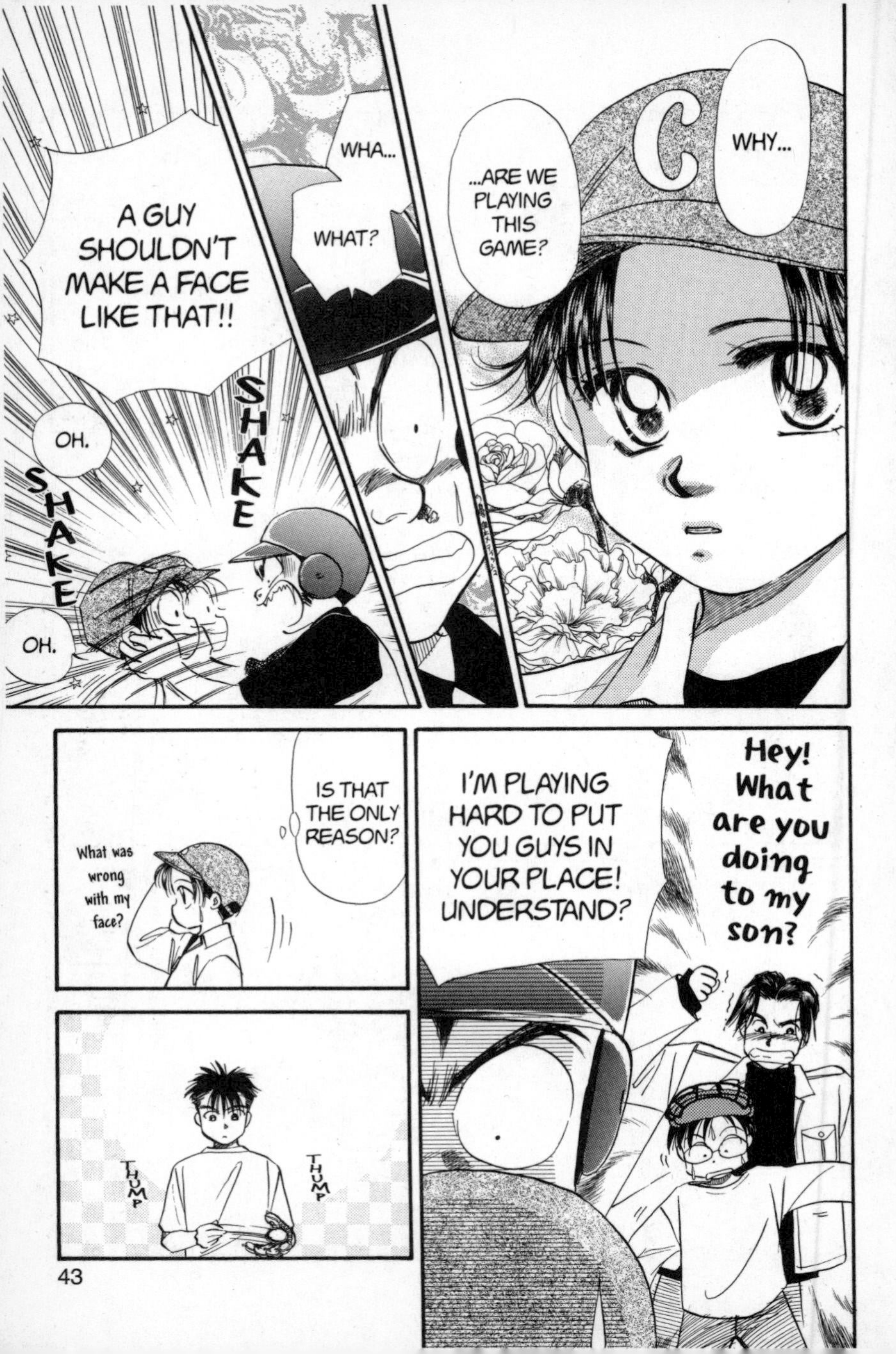
WHY...
...ARE WE PLAYING THIS GAME?
WHA...
WHAT?
A GUY SHOULDN'T MAKE A FACE LIKE THAT!!
SHAKE
SHAKE
OH.
OH.
Hey! What are you doing to my son?
I'M PLAYING HARD TO PUT YOU GUYS IN YOUR PLACE! UNDERSTAND?
IS THAT THE ONLY REASON?
What was wrong with my face?
THUMP
THUMP

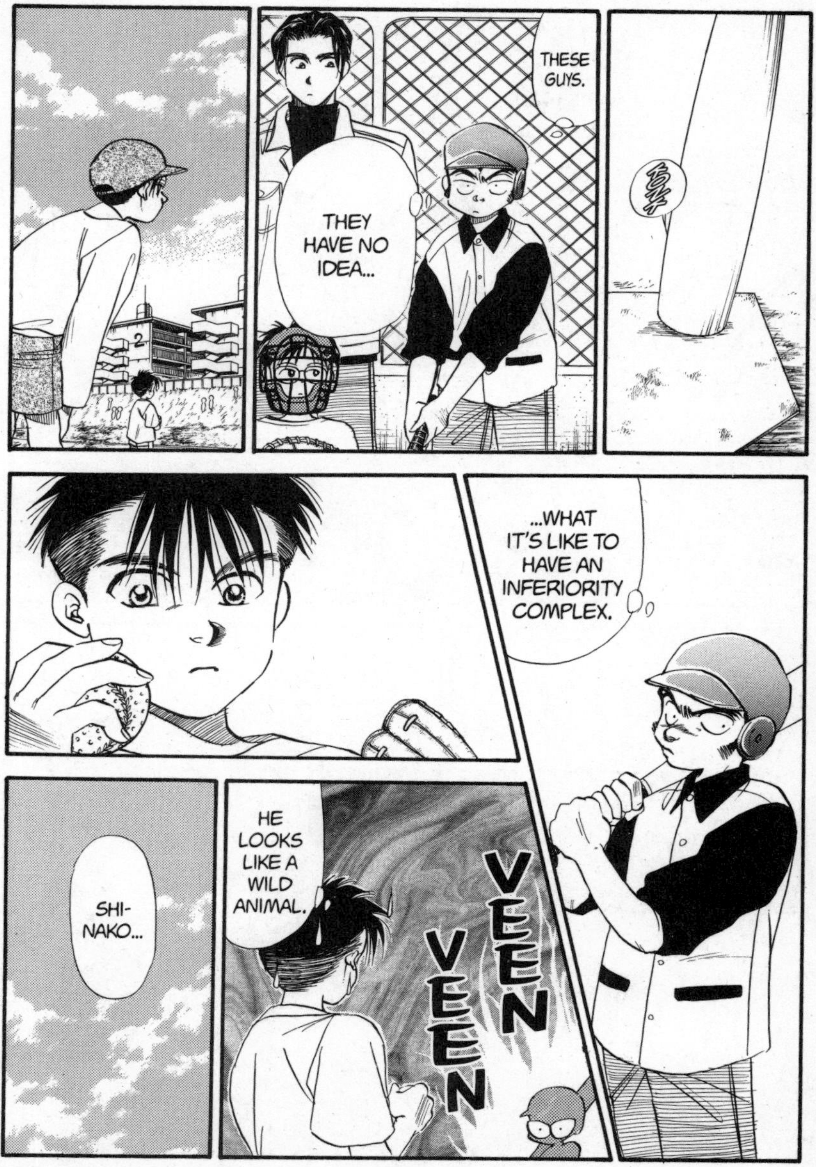
TONK
THESE GUYS.
THEY HAVE NO IDEA...
...WHAT IT'S LIKE TO HAVE AN INFERIORITY COMPLEX.
HE LOOKS LIKE A WILD ANIMAL.
VEEN VEEN
SHI-NAKO...

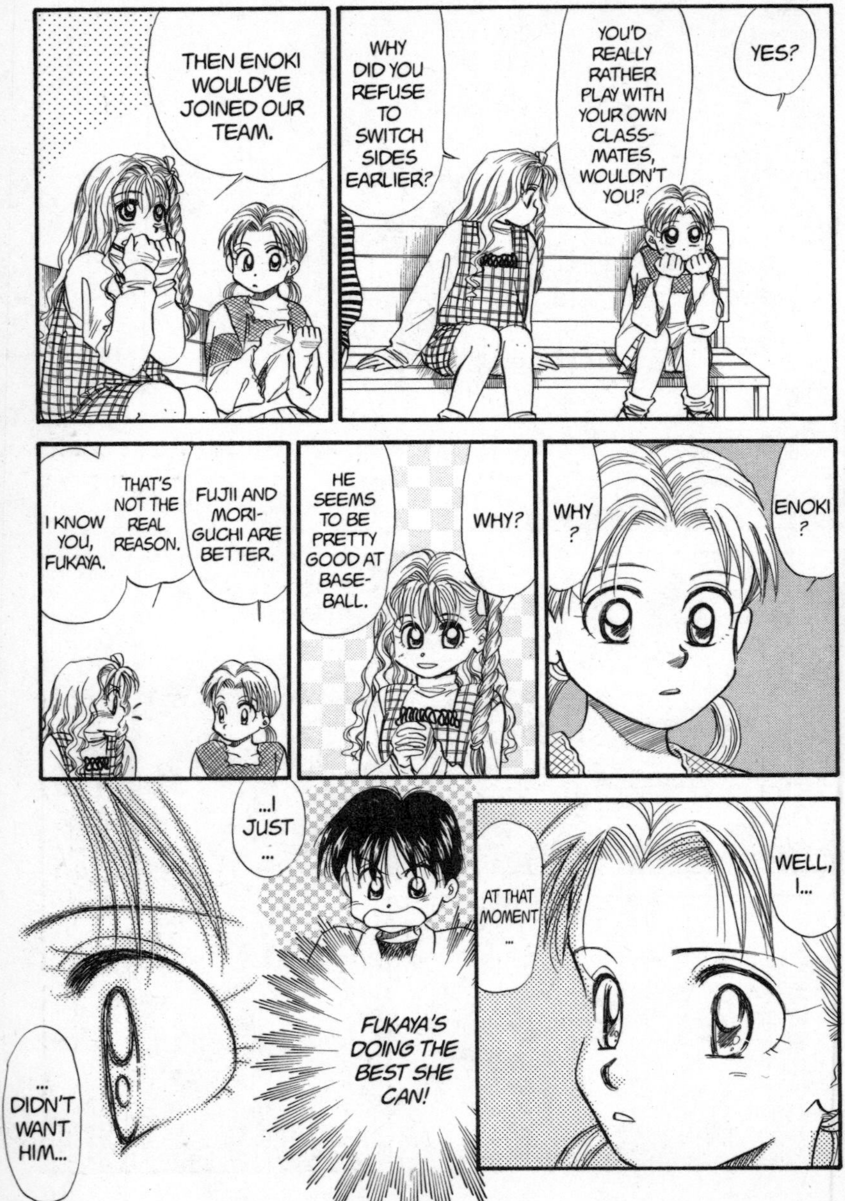
YES?
YOU'D REALLY RATHER PLAY WITH YOUR OWN CLASS-MATES, WOULDN'T YOU?
WHY DID YOU REFUSE TO SWITCH SIDES EARLIER?
THEN ENOKI WOULD'VE JOINED OUR TEAM.
ENOKI?
WHY?
WHY?
HE SEEMS TO BE PRETTY GOOD AT BASE-BALL.
FUJII AND MORI-GUCHI ARE BETTER.
THAT'S NOT THE REAL REASON.
I KNOW YOU, FUKAYA.
WELL, I...
AT THAT MOMENT ...
...I JUST ...
FUKAYA'S DOING THE BEST SHE CAN!
... DIDN'T WANT HIM...

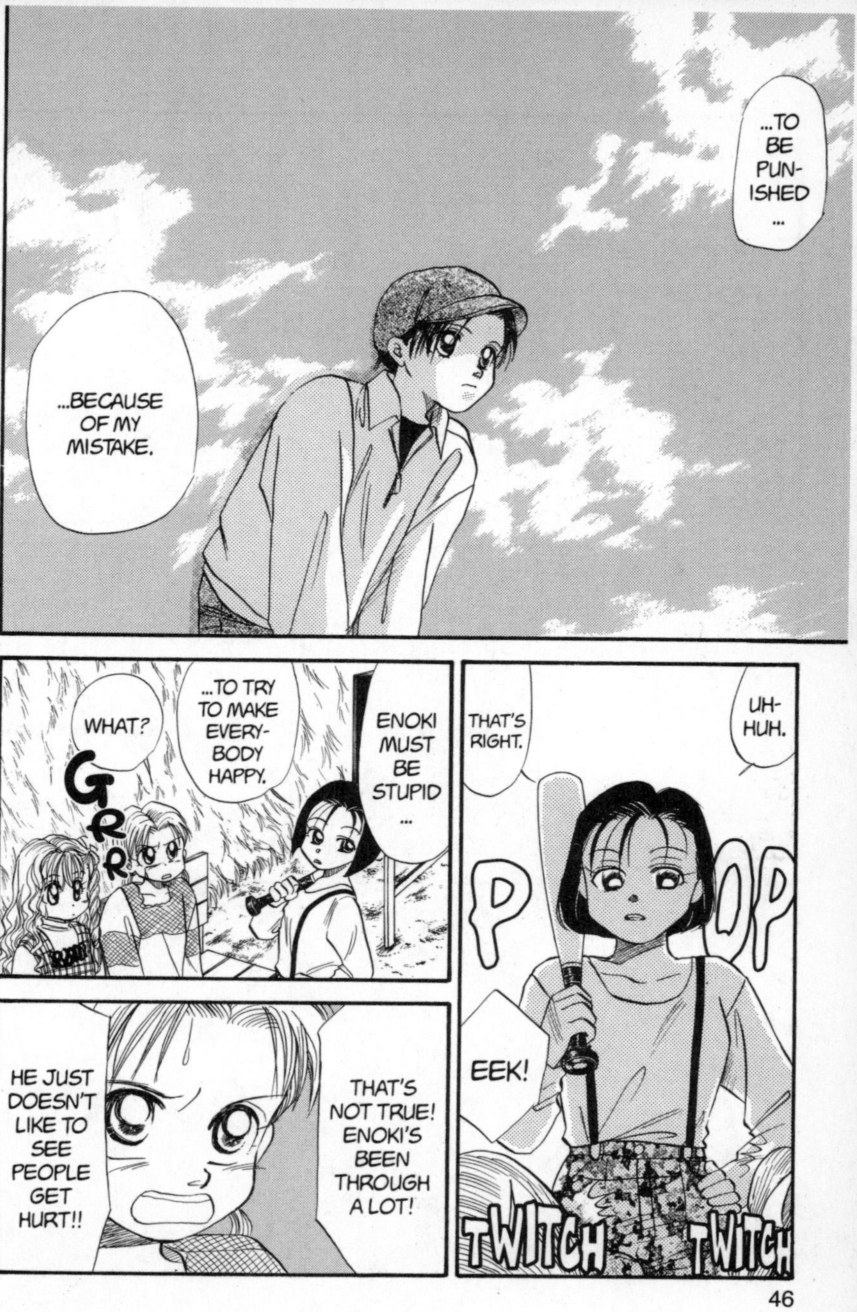
...TO BE PUN-ISHED ...
...BECAUSE OF MY MISTAKE.
UH-HUH.
THAT'S RIGHT.
POP
EEK!
TWITCH
TWITCH
ENOKI MUST BE STUPID ...
...TO TRY TO MAKE EVERY-BODY HAPPY.
WHAT?
GRR
THAT'S NOT TRUE! ENOKI'S BEEN THROUGH A LOT!
HE JUST DOESN'T LIKE TO SEE PEOPLE GET HURT!!

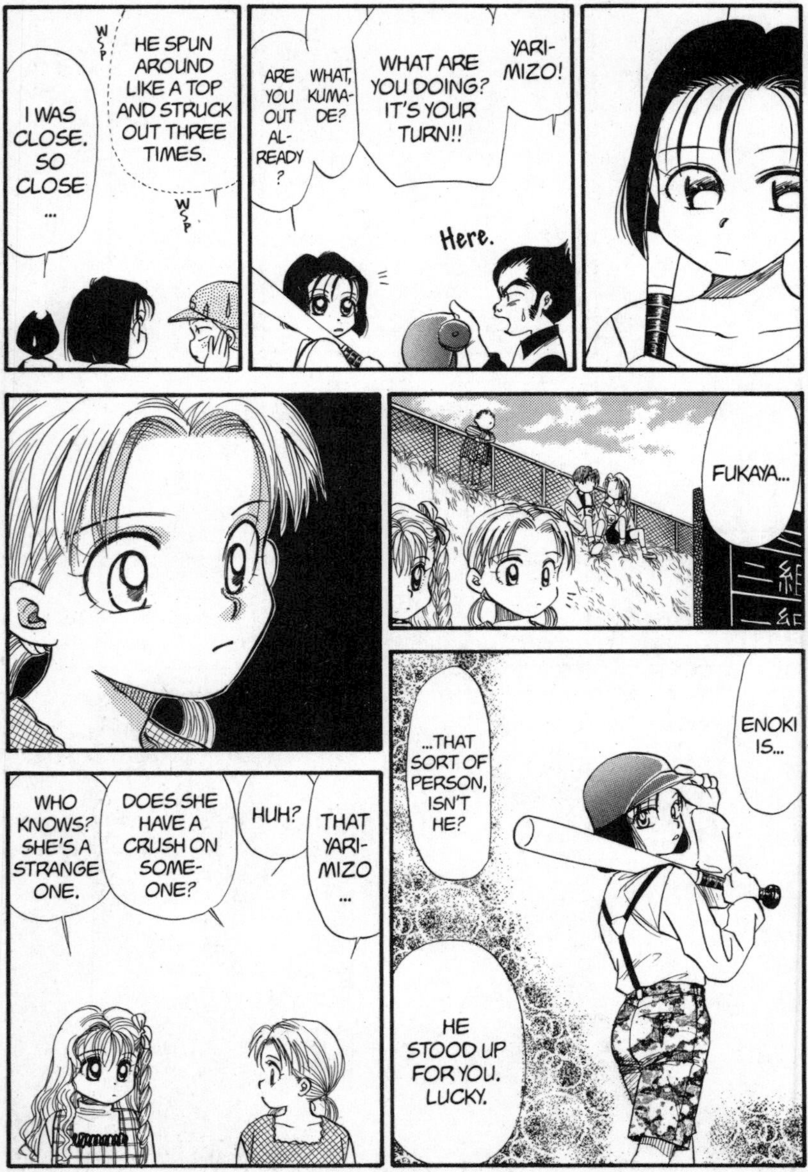
YARI-MIZO!
WHAT ARE YOU DOING? IT'S YOUR TURN!!
WHAT, KUMA-DE?
ARE YOU OUT AL-READY?
Here.
WSP
HE SPUN AROUND LIKE A TOP AND STRUCK OUT THREE TIMES.
WSP
I WAS CLOSE. SO CLOSE ...
FUKAYA...
ENOKI IS...
...THAT SORT OF PERSON, ISN'T HE?
HE STOOD UP FOR YOU. LUCKY.
THAT YARI-MIZO ...
HUH?
DOES SHE HAVE A CRUSH ON SOME-ONE?
WHO KNOWS? SHE'S A STRANGE ONE.

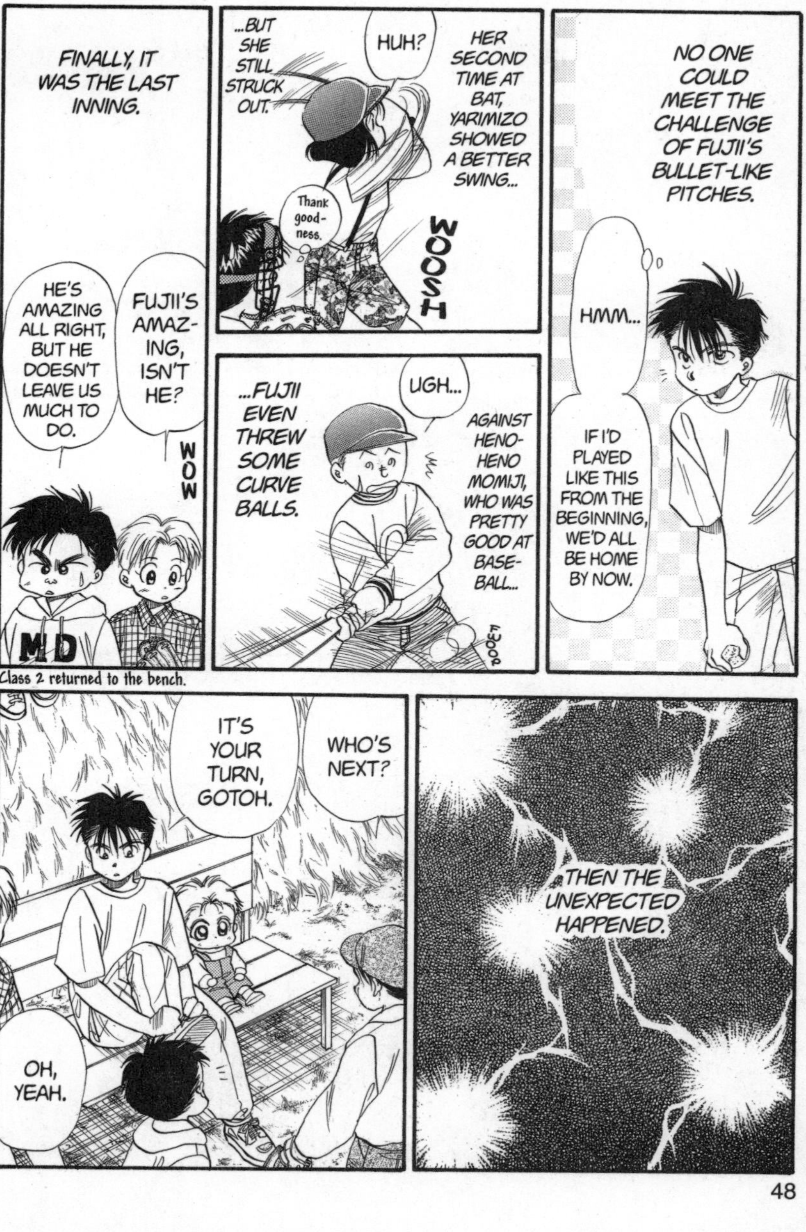
FINALLY, IT WAS THE LAST INNING.
FUJII'S AMAZING, ISN'T HE?
HE'S AMAZING ALL RIGHT, BUT HE DOESN'T LEAVE US MUCH TO DO.
WOW
HER SECOND TIME AT BAT, YARIMIZO SHOWED A BETTER SWING...
HUH?
...BUT SHE STILL STRUCK OUT.
Thank goodness.
WOOSH
AGAINST HENO-HENO MOMIJI, WHO WAS PRETTY GOOD AT BASE-BALL...
...FUJII EVEN THREW SOME CURVE BALLS.
UGH...
FWOOP
NO ONE COULD MEET THE CHALLENGE OF FUJII'S BULLET-LIKE PITCHES.
HMM...
IF I'D PLAYED LIKE THIS FROM THE BEGINNING, WE'D ALL BE HOME BY NOW.
Class 2 returned to the bench.
WHO'S NEXT?
IT'S YOUR TURN, GOTOH.
OH, YEAH.
THEN THE UNEXPECTED HAPPENED.

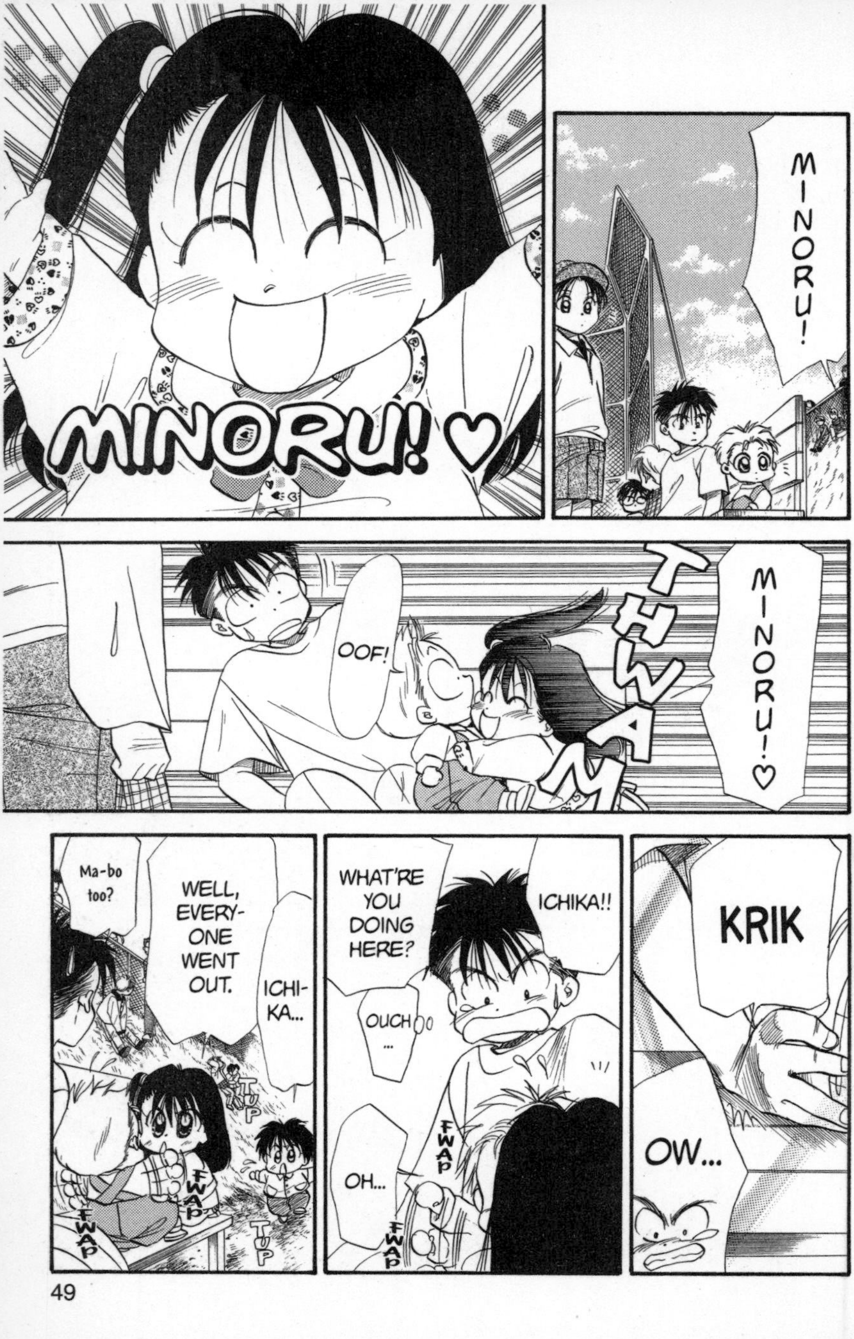
MINORU!
MINORU! ♥
MINORU! ♥
THWAM
OOF!
KRIK
OW...
ICHIKA!!
WHAT'RE YOU DOING HERE?
OUCH...
FWAP
OH...
FWAP
ICHI-KA...
WELL, EVERY-ONE WENT OUT.
Ma-bo too?
TUP
FWAP
TUP
FWAP

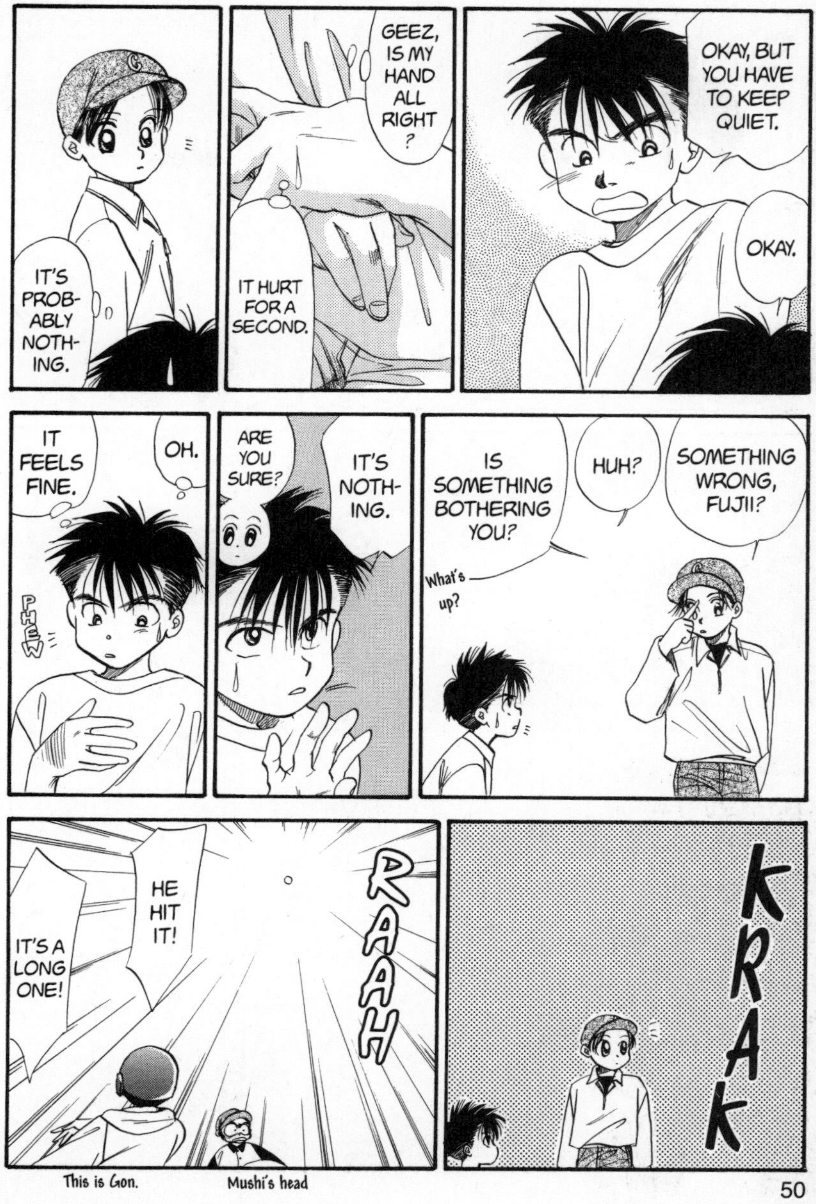
OKAY, BUT YOU HAVE TO KEEP QUIET.
OKAY.
GEEZ, IS MY HAND ALL RIGHT?
IT HURT FOR A SECOND.
IT'S PROB-ABLY NOTH-ING.
SOMETHING WRONG, FUJII?
HUH?
IS SOMETHING BOTHERING YOU?
What's up?
IT'S NOTH-ING.
ARE YOU SURE?
OH.
IT FEELS FINE.
PHEW
KRAK
RAAAH
HE HIT IT!
IT'S A LONG ONE!

This is Gon.

Mushi's head

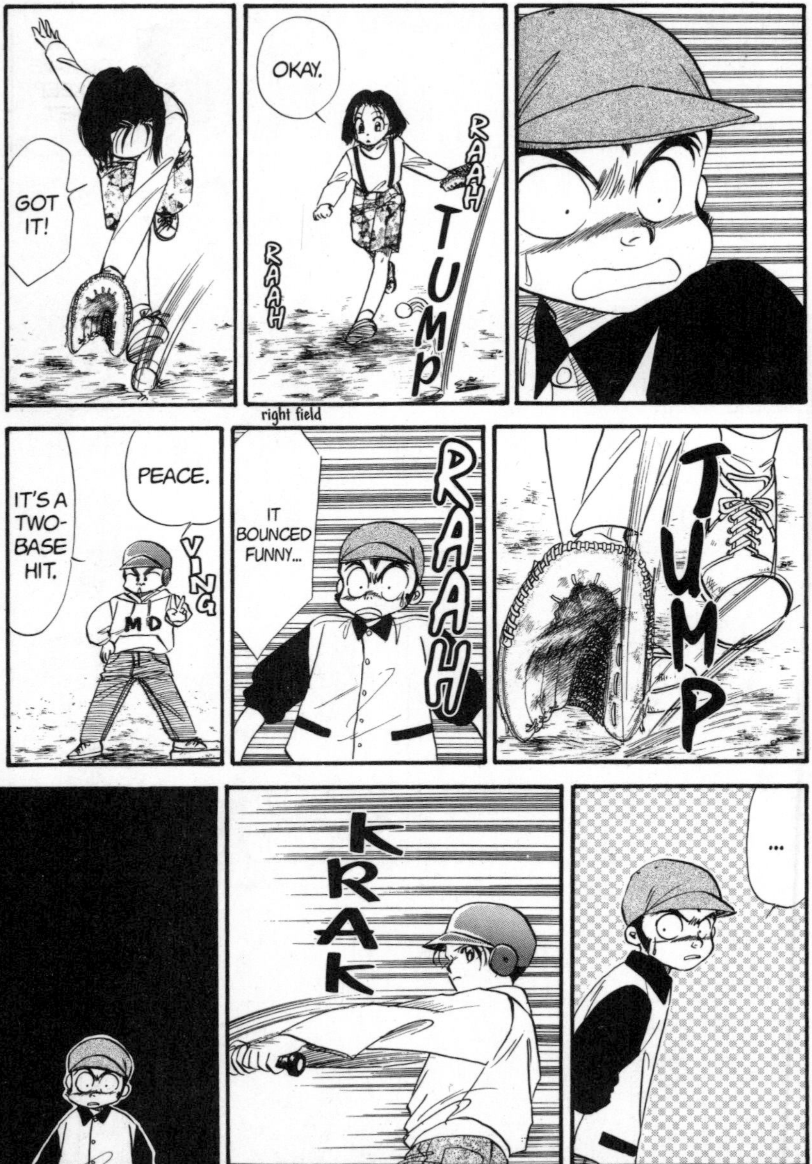
OKAY.
RAAAH
TUMP
RAAAH
right field
GOT IT!
TUMP
IT BOUNCED FUNNY...
RAAAH
PEACE.
VING
IT'S A TWO-BASE HIT.
...
KRAK

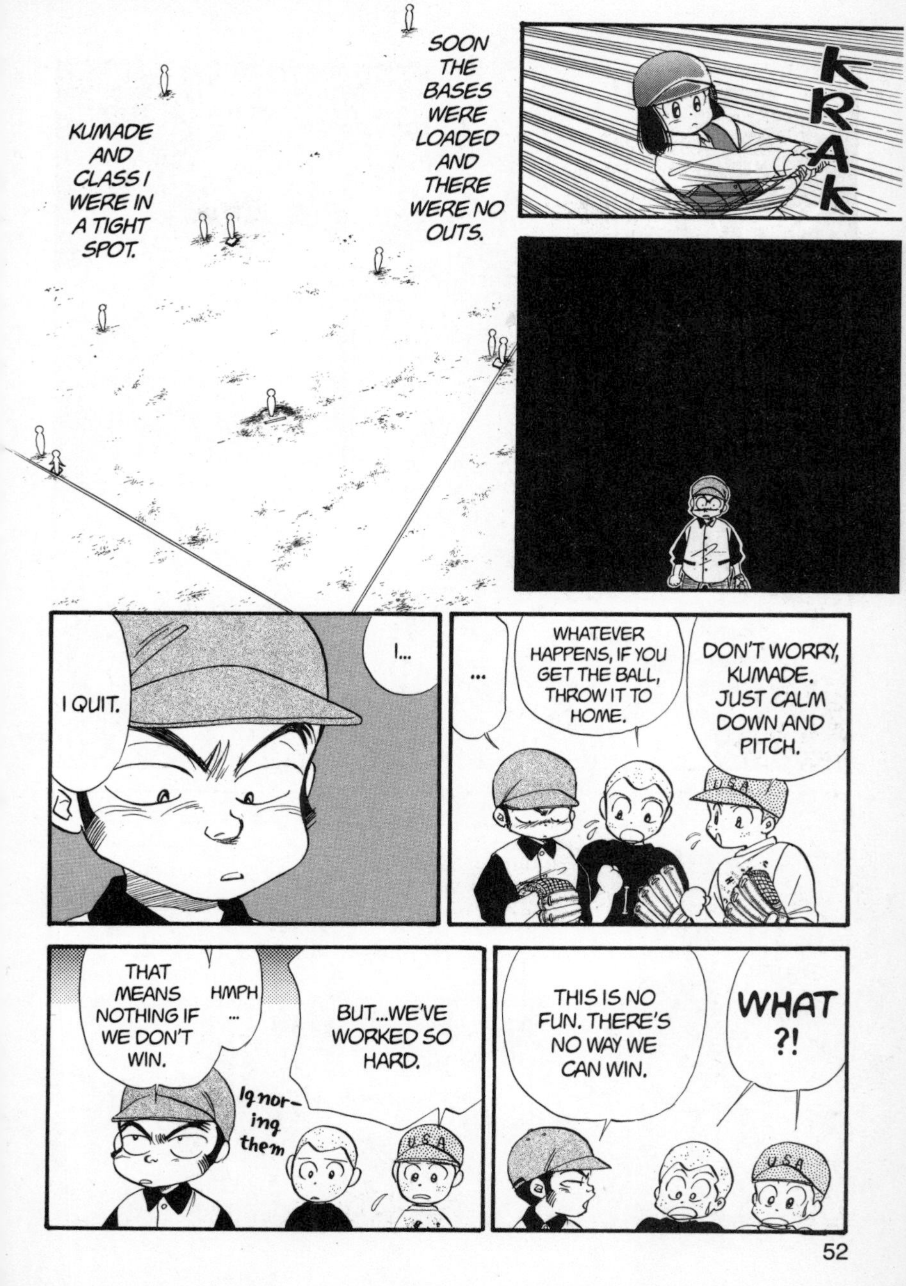
KRAK
SOON THE BASES WERE LOADED AND THERE WERE NO OUTS.
KUMADE AND CLASS I WERE IN A TIGHT SPOT.
DON'T WORRY, KUMADE. JUST CALM DOWN AND PITCH.
WHATEVER HAPPENS, IF YOU GET THE BALL, THROW IT TO HOME.
...
I...
I QUIT.
WHAT ?!
THIS IS NO FUN. THERE'S NO WAY WE CAN WIN.
BUT...WE'VE WORKED SO HARD.
HMPH ...
THAT MEANS NOTHING IF WE DON'T WIN.
Ignor-ing them

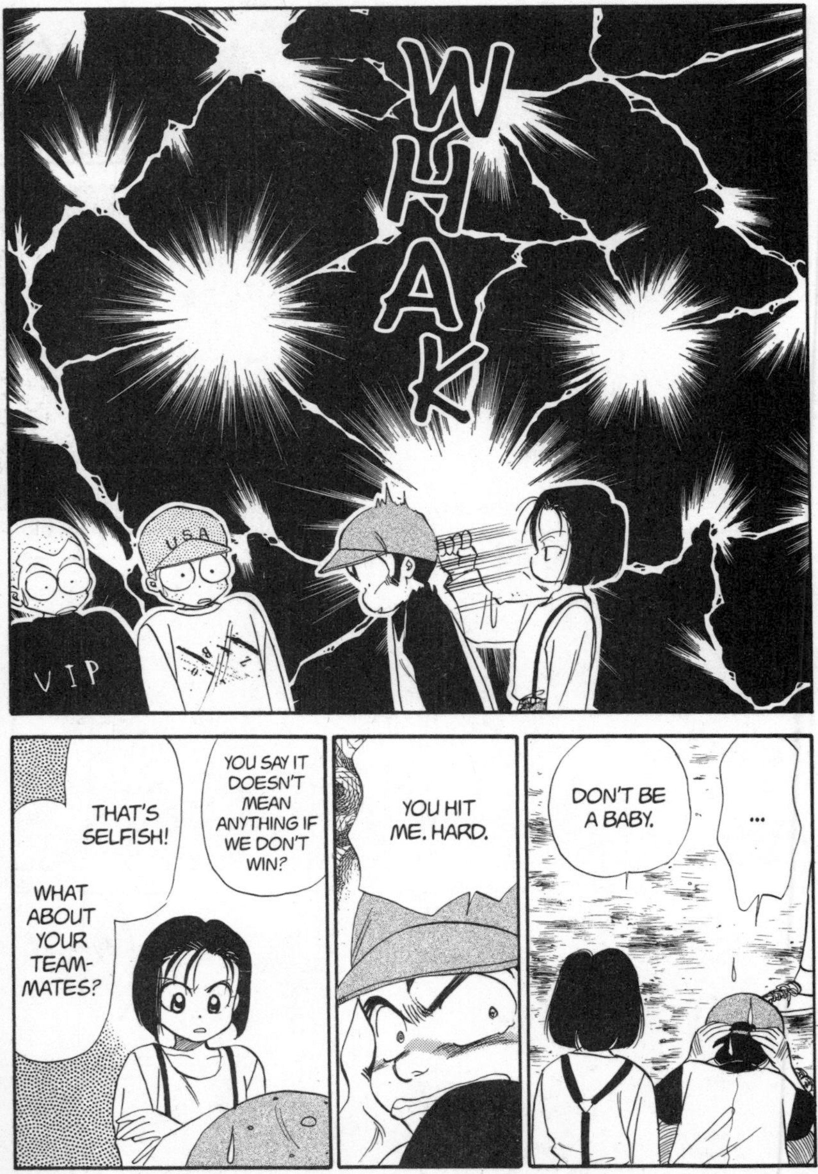
WHAK
VIP
...
DON'T BE A BABY.
YOU HIT ME. HARD.
YOU SAY IT DOESN'T MEAN ANYTHING IF WE DON'T WIN?
THAT'S SELFISH!
WHAT ABOUT YOUR TEAM-MATES?

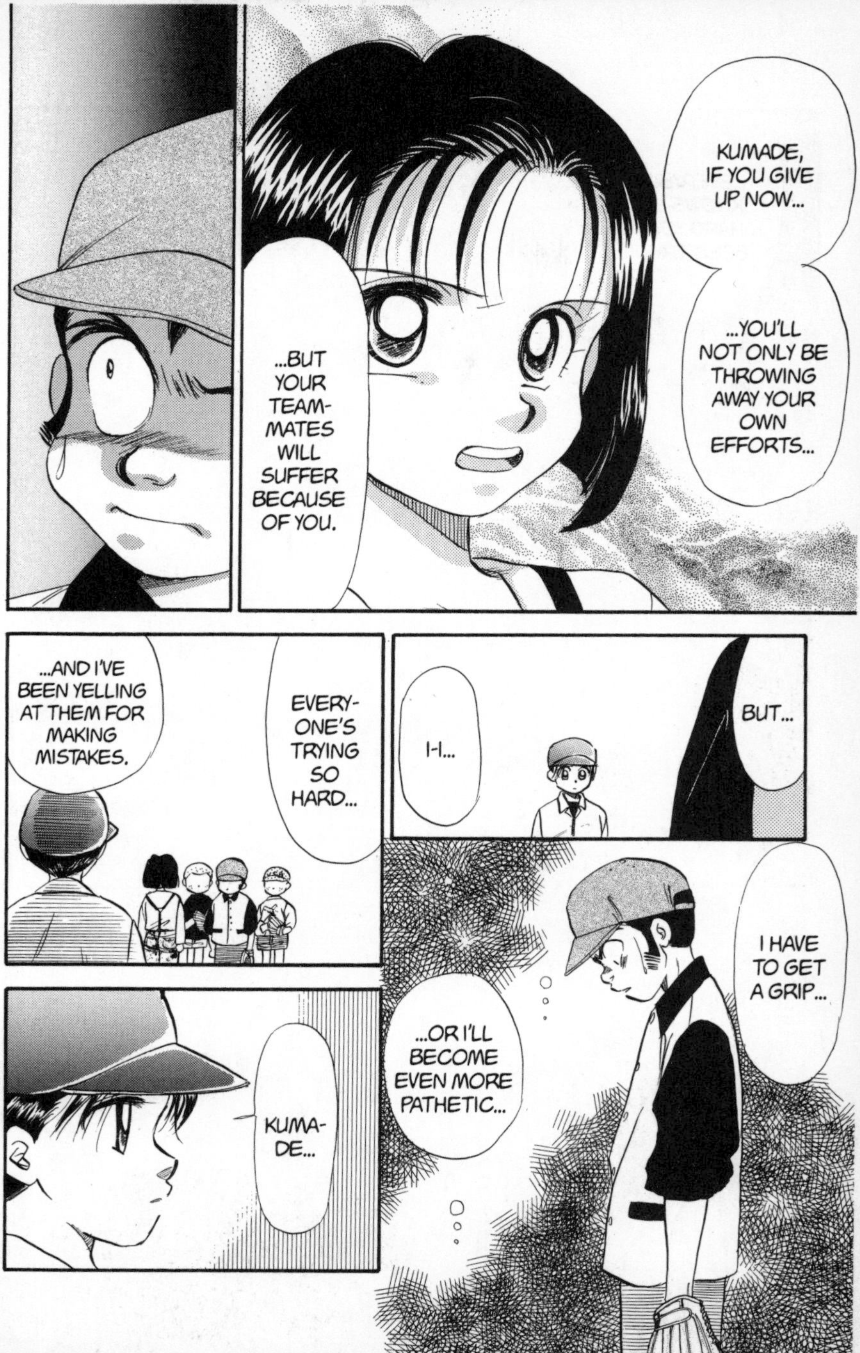
KUMADE, IF YOU GIVE UP NOW...
...YOU'LL NOT ONLY BE THROWING AWAY YOUR OWN EFFORTS...
...BUT YOUR TEAM-MATES WILL SUFFER BECAUSE OF YOU.
BUT...
I-I...
EVERY-ONE'S TRYING SO HARD...
...AND I'VE BEEN YELLING AT THEM FOR MAKING MISTAKES.
I HAVE TO GET A GRIP...
...OR I'LL BECOME EVEN MORE PATHETIC...
KUMA-DE...

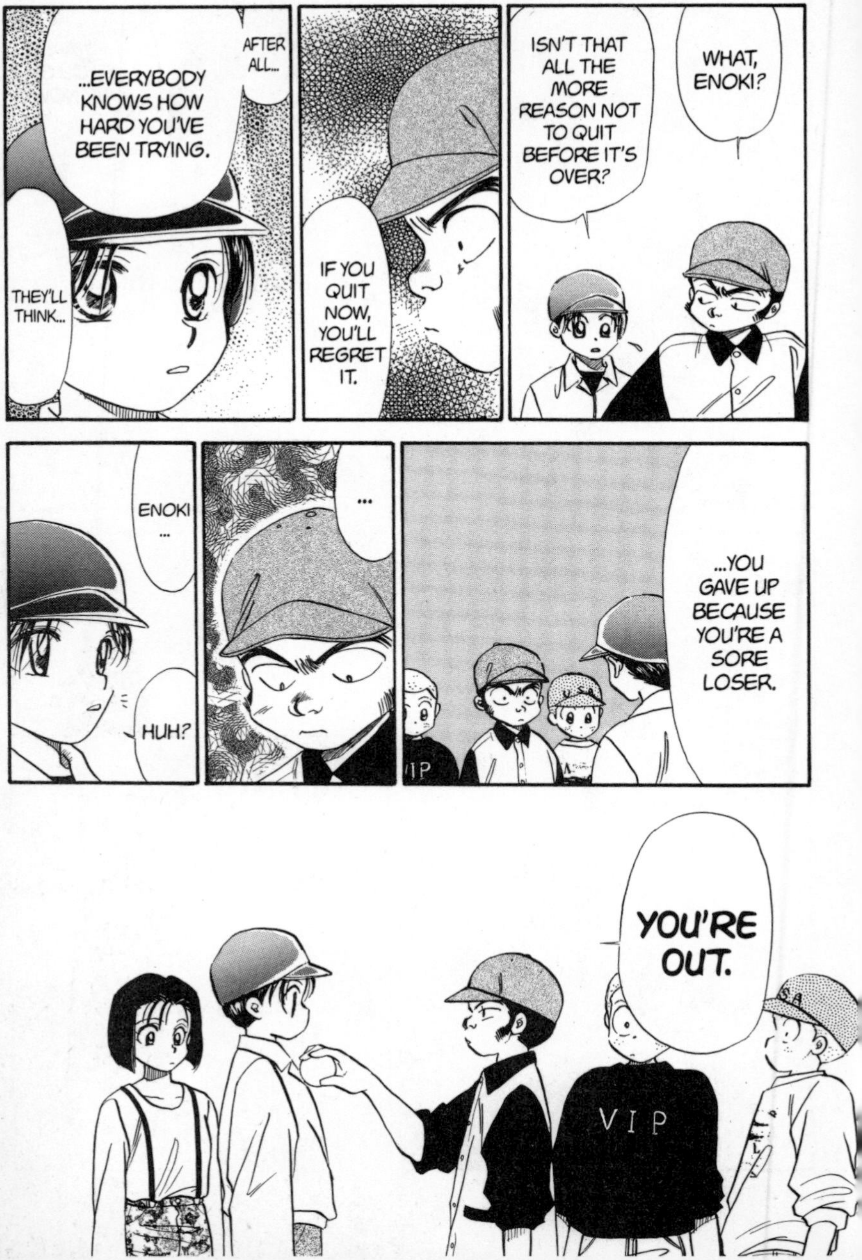
WHAT, ENOKI?
ISN'T THAT ALL THE MORE REASON NOT TO QUIT BEFORE IT'S OVER?
IF YOU QUIT NOW, YOU'LL REGRET IT.
AFTER ALL...
...EVERYBODY KNOWS HOW HARD YOU'VE BEEN TRYING.
THEY'LL THINK...
...YOU GAVE UP BECAUSE YOU'RE A SORE LOSER.
...
ENOKI ...
HUH?
YOU'RE OUT.
VIP

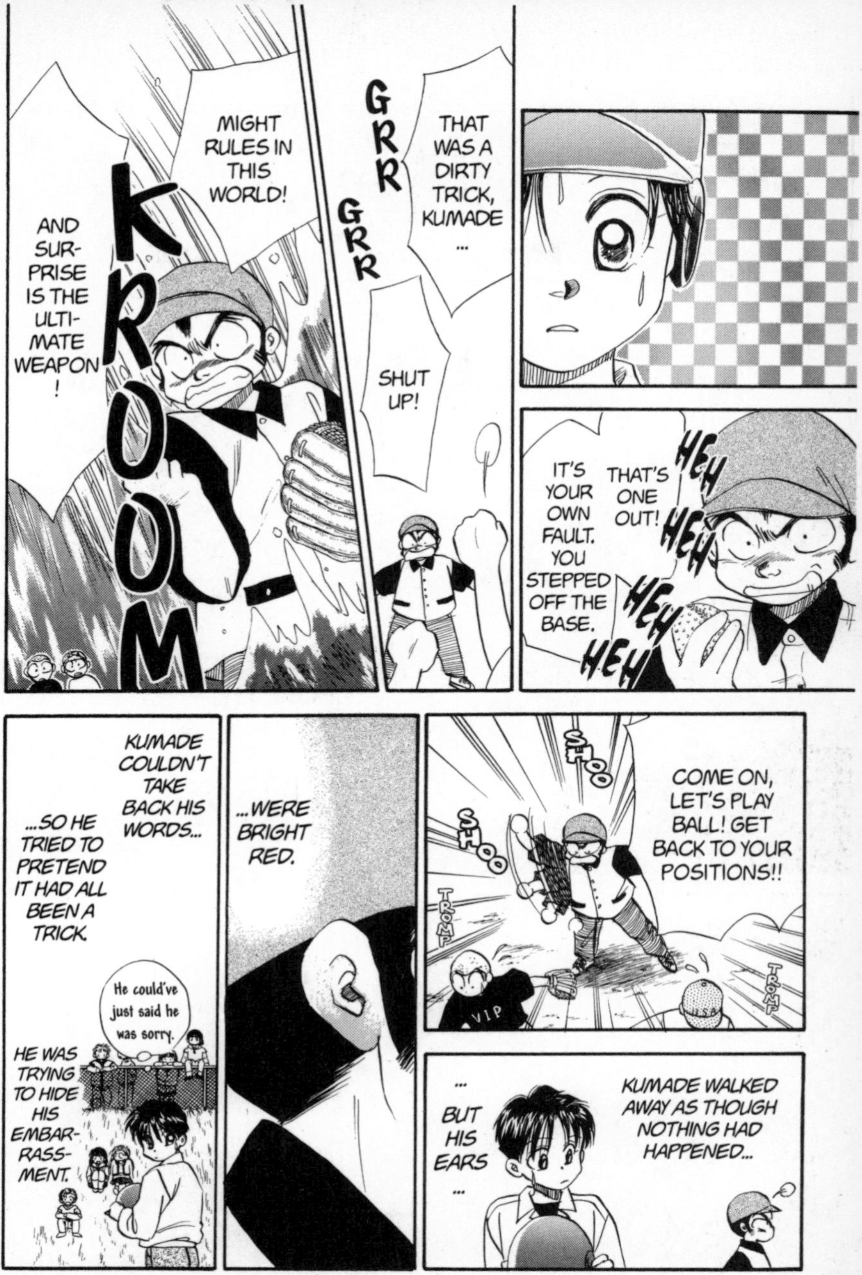
HEH HEH HEH HEH
THAT'S ONE OUT!
IT'S YOUR OWN FAULT. YOU STEPPED OFF THE BASE.
THAT WAS A DIRTY TRICK, KUMADE...
GRR GRR
SHUT UP!
MIGHT RULES IN THIS WORLD!
AND SURPRISE IS THE ULTIMATE WEAPON!
KROOM
COME ON, LET'S PLAY BALL! GET BACK TO YOUR POSITIONS!!
SHOO SHOO
TROMP TROMP
KUMADE WALKED AWAY AS THOUGH NOTHING HAD HAPPENED...
...BUT HIS EARS...
...WERE BRIGHT RED.
KUMADE COULDN'T TAKE BACK HIS WORDS...
...SO HE TRIED TO PRETEND IT HAD ALL BEEN A TRICK.
He could've just said he was sorry.
HE WAS TRYING TO HIDE HIS EMBARRASSMENT.

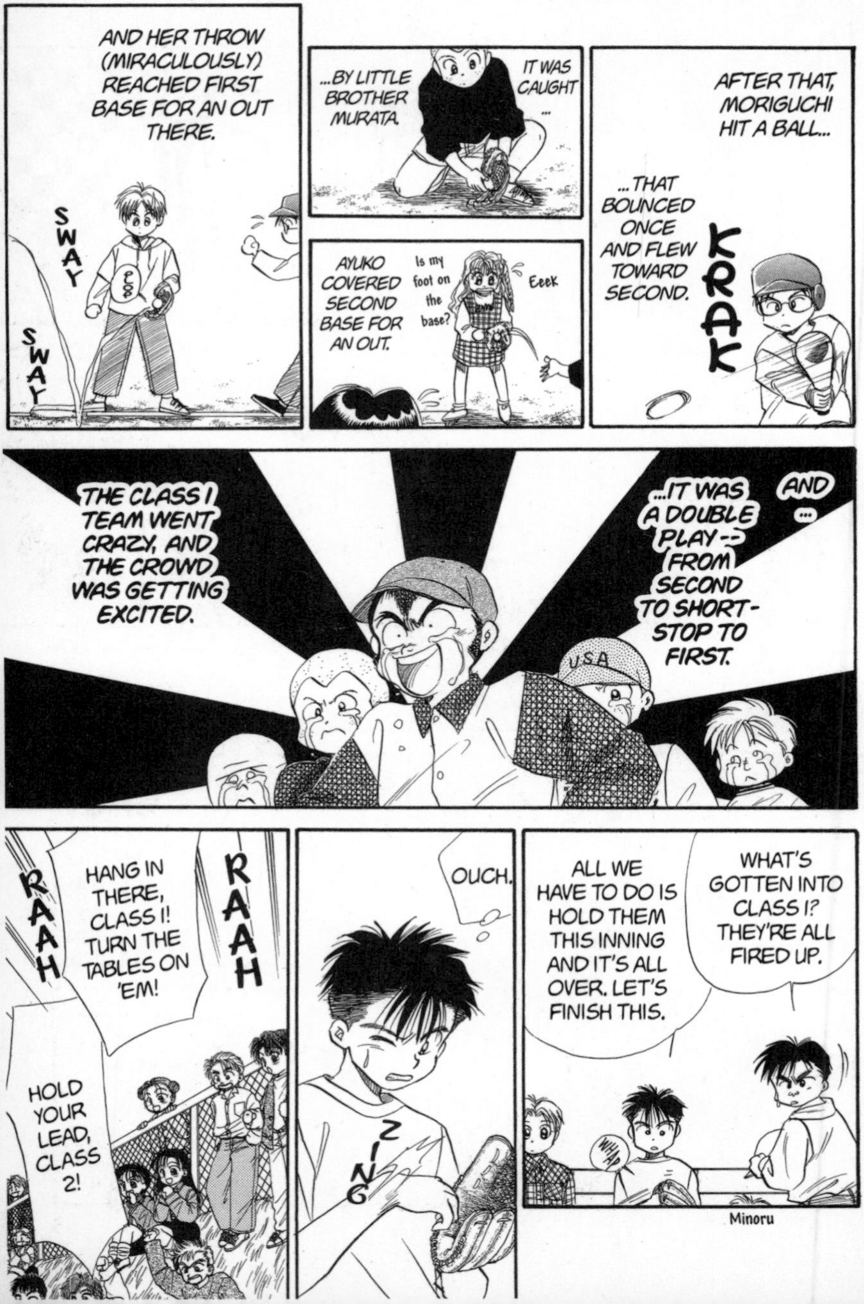
AFTER THAT, MORIGUCHI HIT A BALL...
...THAT BOUNCED ONCE AND FLEW TOWARD SECOND.
KRAK
IT WAS CAUGHT...
...BY LITTLE BROTHER MURATA.
Eeek
Is my foot on the base?
AYUKO COVERED SECOND BASE FOR AN OUT.
AND HER THROW (MIRACULOUSLY) REACHED FIRST BASE FOR AN OUT THERE.
SWAY
SWAY
AND...
...IT WAS A DOUBLE PLAY-- FROM SECOND TO SHORTSTOP TO FIRST.
USA
THE CLASS I TEAM WENT CRAZY, AND THE CROWD WAS GETTING EXCITED.
WHAT'S GOTTEN INTO CLASS I? THEY'RE ALL FIRED UP.
ALL WE HAVE TO DO IS HOLD THEM THIS INNING AND IT'S ALL OVER. LET'S FINISH THIS.
WHAP
Minoru
OUCH.
ZING
RAAH
HANG IN THERE, CLASS I! TURN THE TABLES ON 'EM!
RAAH
HOLD YOUR LEAD, CLASS 2!

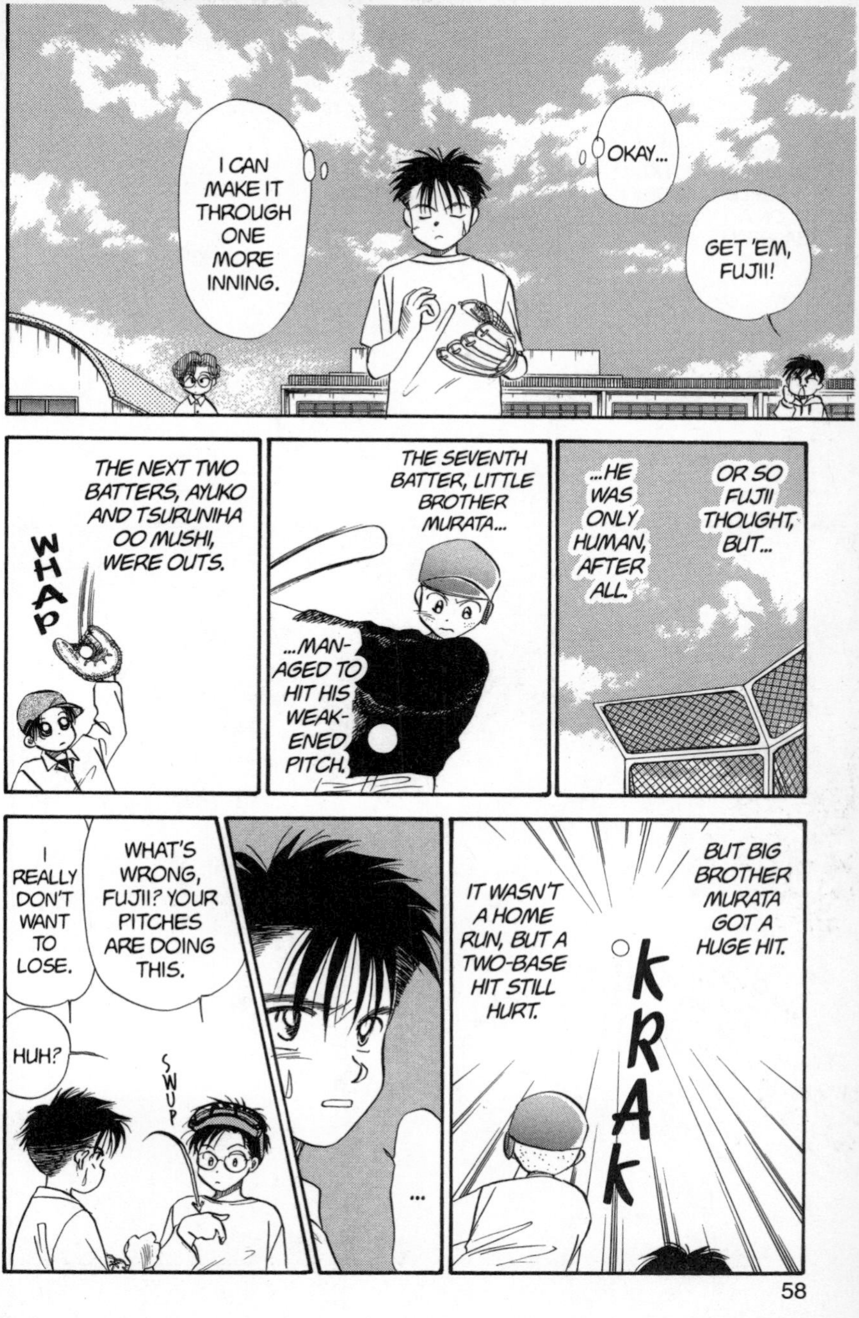

OKAY...
GET 'EM, FUJII!
I CAN MAKE IT THROUGH ONE MORE INNING.
OR SO FUJII THOUGHT, BUT...
...HE WAS ONLY HUMAN, AFTER ALL.
THE SEVENTH BATTER, LITTLE BROTHER MURATA...
...MANAGED TO HIT HIS WEAKENED PITCH.
THE NEXT TWO BATTERS, AYUKO AND TSURUNIHA OO MUSHI, WERE OUTS.
WHAP
BUT BIG BROTHER MURATA GOT A HUGE HIT.
KRAK
IT WASN'T A HOME RUN, BUT A TWO-BASE HIT STILL HURT.
...
WHAT'S WRONG, FUJII? YOUR PITCHES ARE DOING THIS.
I REALLY DON'T WANT TO LOSE.
HUH?
SWUP

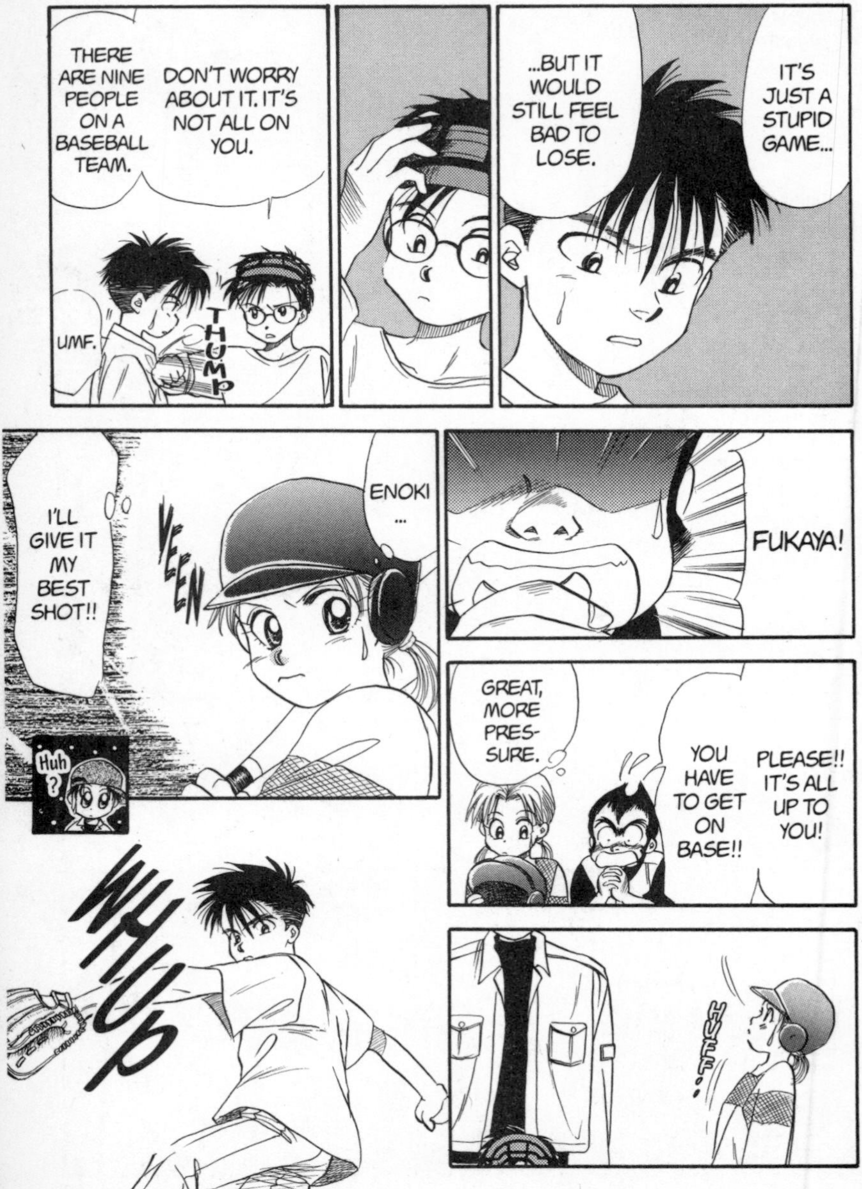
IT'S JUST A STUPID GAME...
...BUT IT WOULD STILL FEEL BAD TO LOSE.
DON'T WORRY ABOUT IT. IT'S NOT ALL ON YOU.
THERE ARE NINE PEOPLE ON A BASEBALL TEAM.
THUMP
UMF.
FUKAYA!
PLEASE!! IT'S ALL UP TO YOU!
YOU HAVE TO GET ON BASE!!
GREAT, MORE PRES-SURE.
ENOKI ...
VEEN
I'LL GIVE IT MY BEST SHOT!!
Huh ?
HUFF..
WHUP

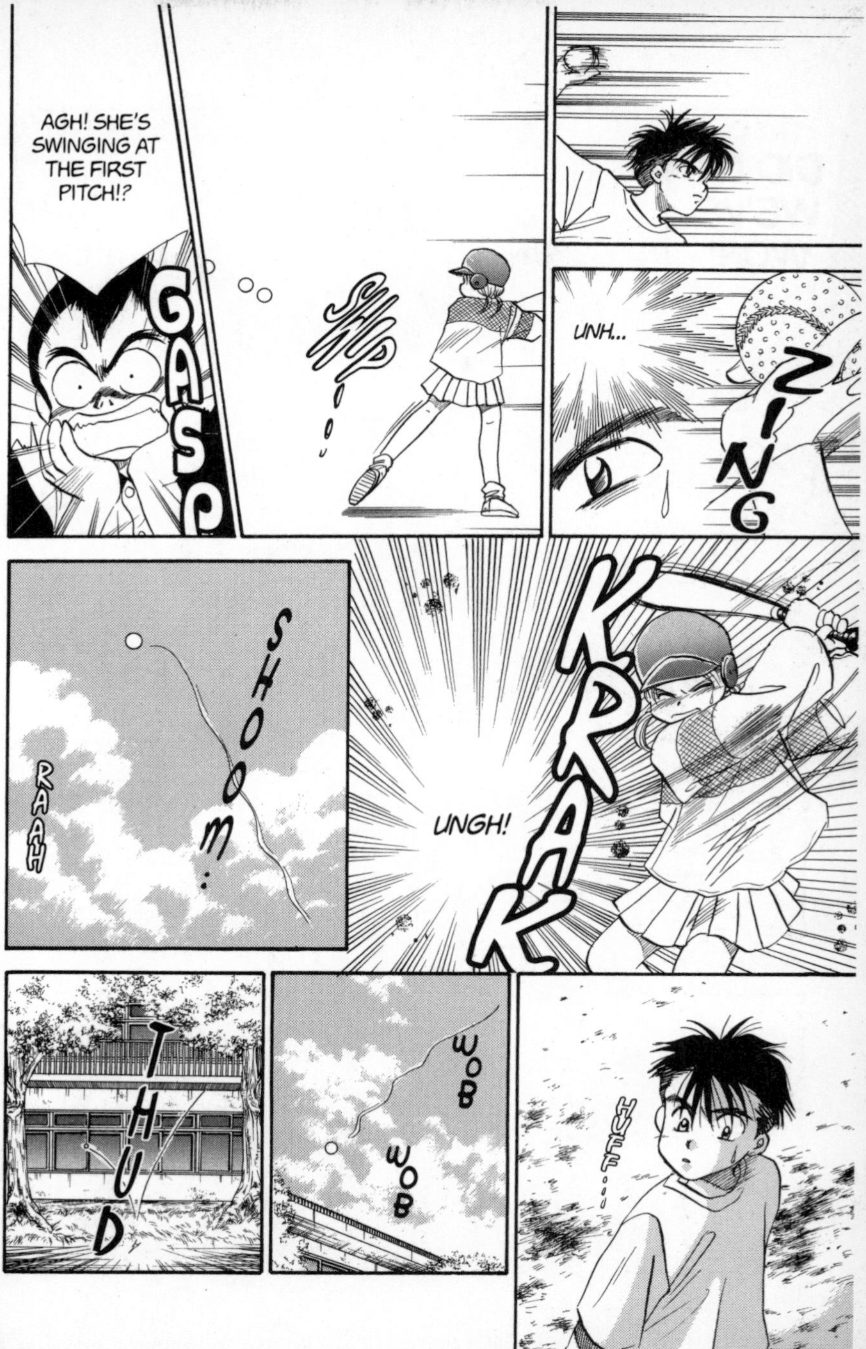
UNH...
ZING
SHIP...
AGH! SHE'S SWINGING AT THE FIRST PITCH!?
GASP
UNGH!
KRAAK
SHOOM...
RAAAH
HUFF...
WOB
WOB
THUD

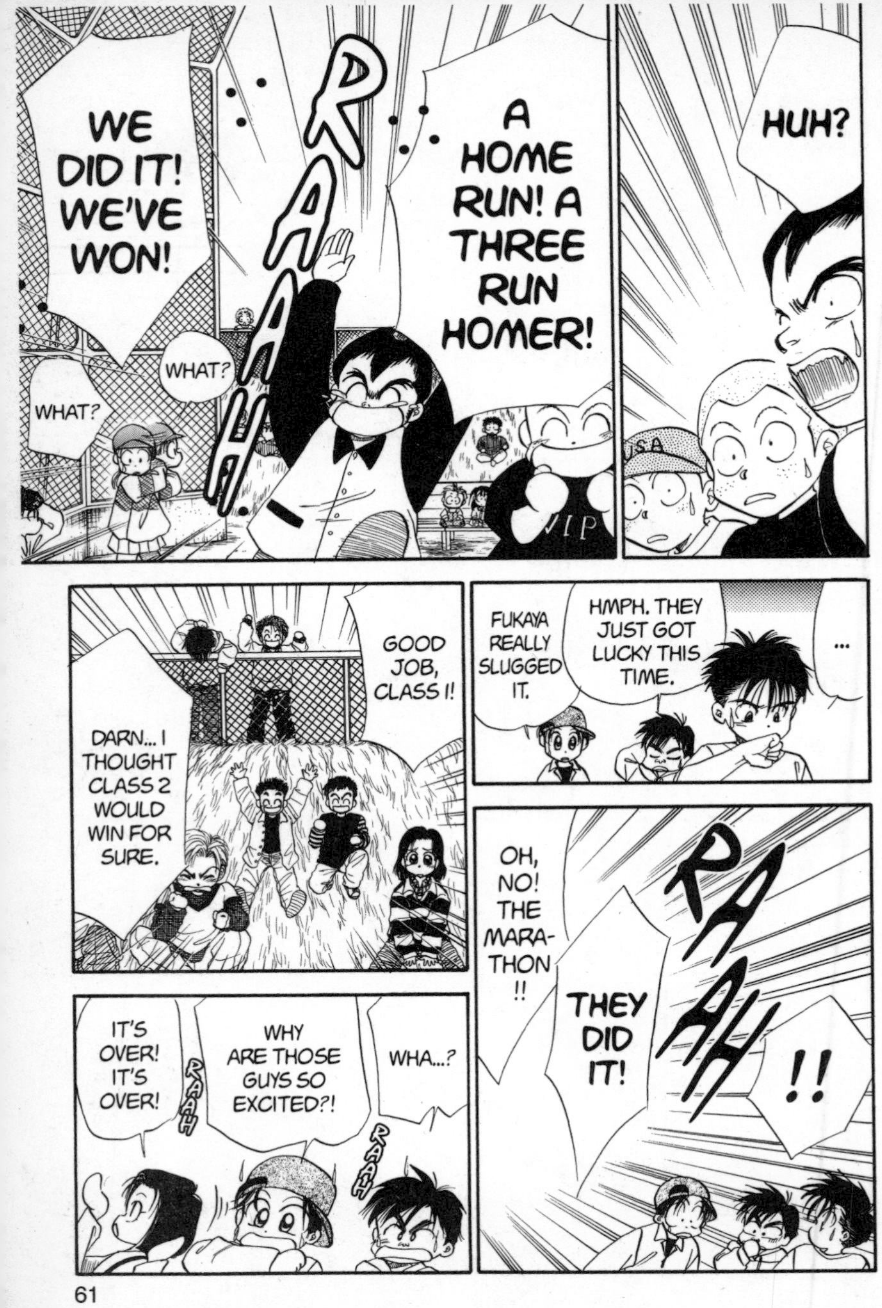
HUH?
A HOME RUN! A THREE RUN HOMER!
RAAAH
WE DID IT! WE'VE WON!
WHAT?
WHAT?
...
HMPH. THEY JUST GOT LUCKY THIS TIME.
FUKAYA REALLY SLUGGED IT.
RAAAH !!
THEY DID IT!
OH, NO! THE MARA-THON !!
GOOD JOB, CLASS 1!
DARN... I THOUGHT CLASS 2 WOULD WIN FOR SURE.
WHA...?
RAAAH
WHY ARE THOSE GUYS SO EXCITED?!
RAAAH
IT'S OVER! IT'S OVER!

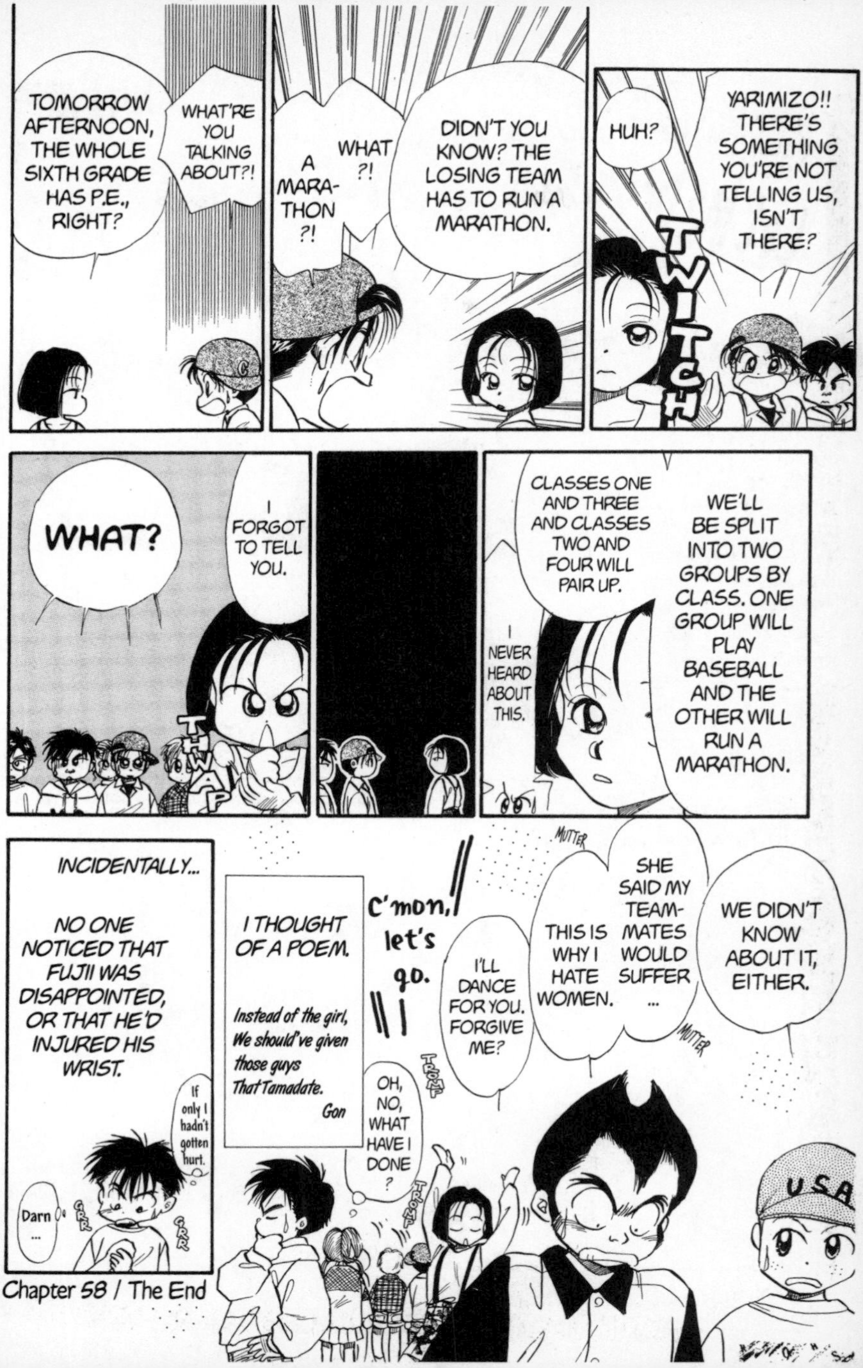
YARIMIZO!! THERE'S SOMETHING YOU'RE NOT TELLING US, ISN'T THERE?
HUH?
TWITCH
DIDN'T YOU KNOW? THE LOSING TEAM HAS TO RUN A MARATHON.
WHAT?!
A MARA-THON?!
WHAT'RE YOU TALKING ABOUT?!
TOMORROW AFTERNOON, THE WHOLE SIXTH GRADE HAS P.E., RIGHT?
WE'LL BE SPLIT INTO TWO GROUPS BY CLASS. ONE GROUP WILL PLAY BASEBALL AND THE OTHER WILL RUN A MARATHON.
CLASSES ONE AND THREE AND CLASSES TWO AND FOUR WILL PAIR UP.
I NEVER HEARD ABOUT THIS.
I FORGOT TO TELL YOU.
WHAT?
THWAP
WE DIDN'T KNOW ABOUT IT, EITHER.
MUTTER
SHE SAID MY TEAM-MATES WOULD SUFFER ...
MUTTER
THIS IS WHY I HATE WOMEN.
I'LL DANCE FOR YOU. FORGIVE ME?
TROMP
OH, NO, WHAT HAVE I DONE?
TROMP
C'mon, let's go.
I THOUGHT OF A POEM.
Instead of the girl, We should've given those guys That Tamadate. Gon
INCIDENTALLY...
NO ONE NOTICED THAT FUJII WAS DISAPPOINTED, OR THAT HE'D INJURED HIS WRIST.
If only I hadn't gotten hurt.
Darn ...
GRR
GRR

Chapter 58 / The End

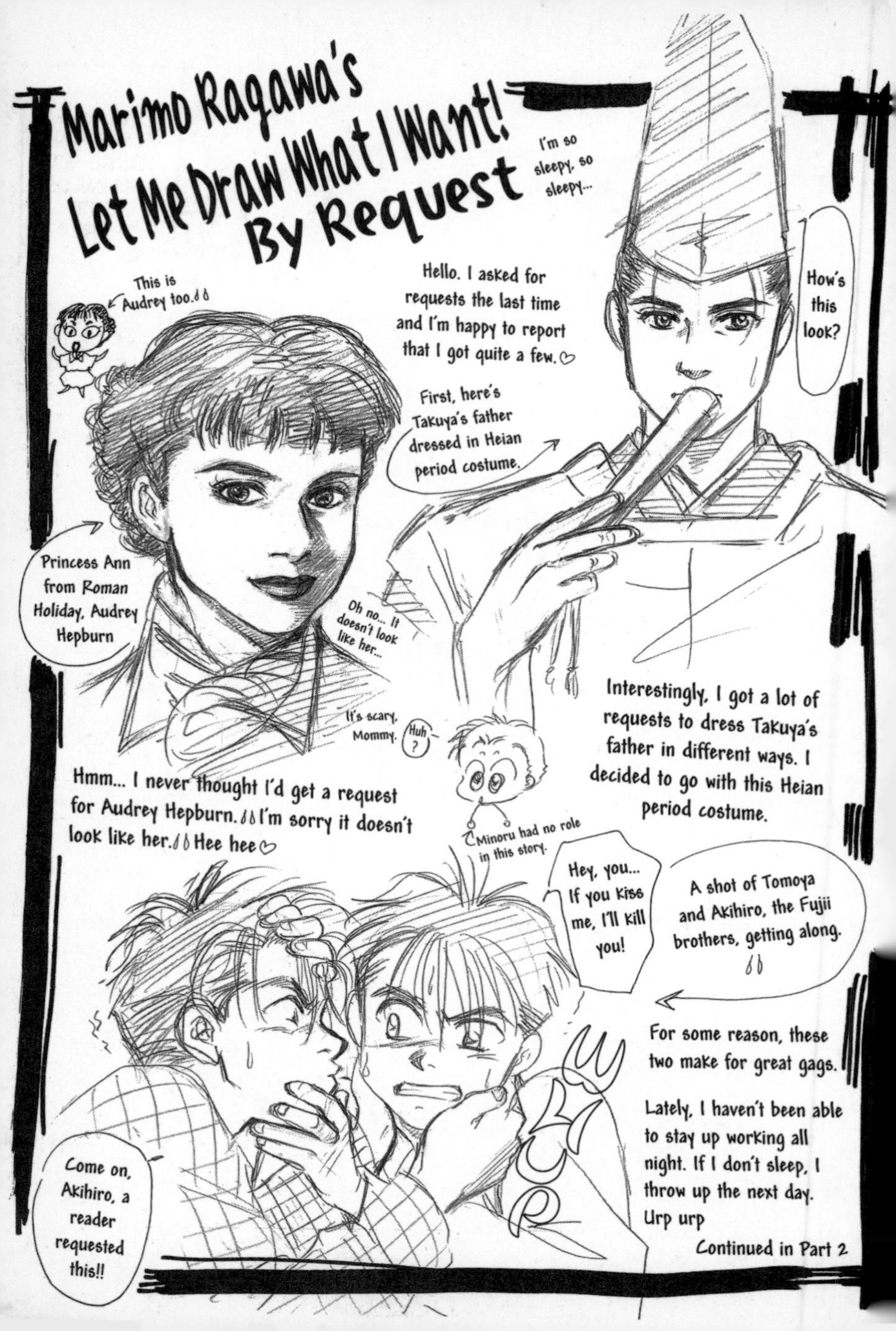

Marimo Ragawa's
Let Me Draw What I Want!
By Request
I'm so sleepy, so sleepy...
How's this look?
Hello. I asked for requests the last time and I'm happy to report that I got quite a few.♡
First, here's Takuya's father dressed in Heian period costume.
This is Audrey too.
Princess Ann from Roman Holiday, Audrey Hepburn
Oh no... It doesn't look like her...
It's scary, Mommy.
Huh?
Interestingly, I got a lot of requests to dress Takuya's father in different ways. I decided to go with this Heian period costume.
Hmm... I never thought I'd get a request for Audrey Hepburn. I'm sorry it doesn't look like her. Hee hee♡
Minoru had no role in this story.
A shot of Tomoya and Akihiro, the Fujii brothers, getting along.
Hey, you... If you kiss me, I'll kill you!
For some reason, these two make for great gags.
Come on, Akihiro, a reader requested this!!
Lately, I haven't been able to stay up working all night. If I don't sleep, I throw up the next day. Urp urp
Continued in Part 2

BABY & ME

Chapter 59

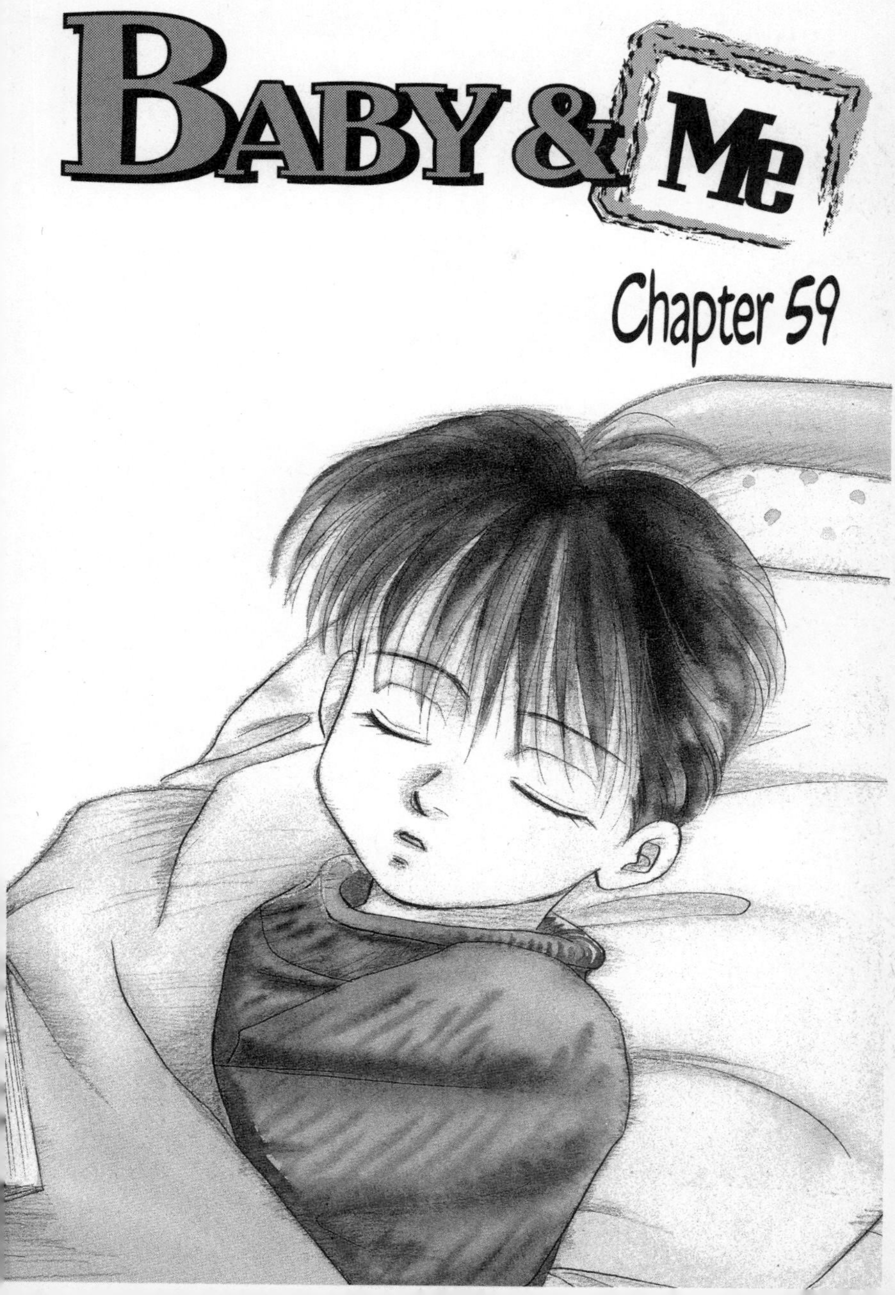

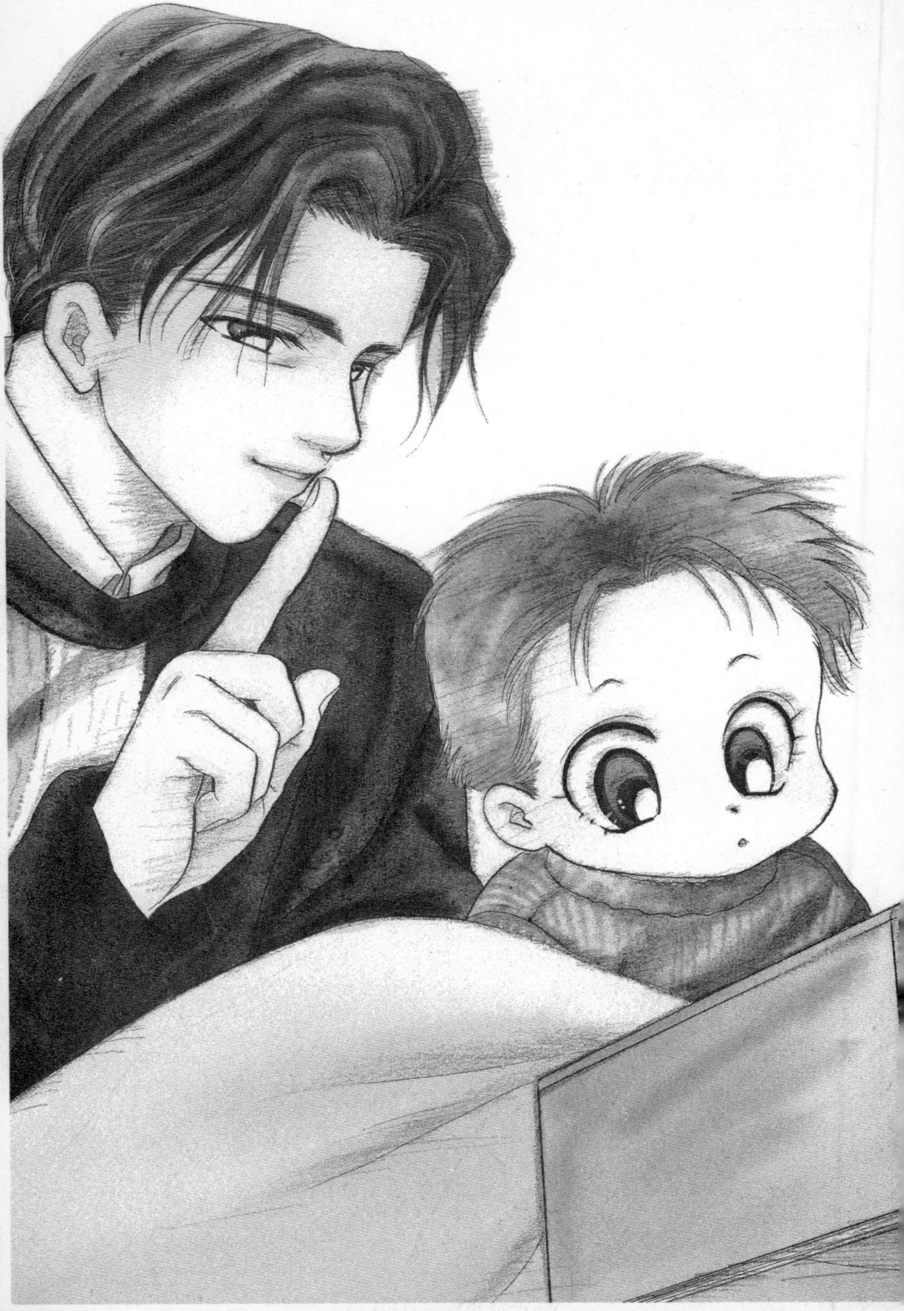

Marimo Ragawa's Let Me Draw What I Want! By Request

Part 2

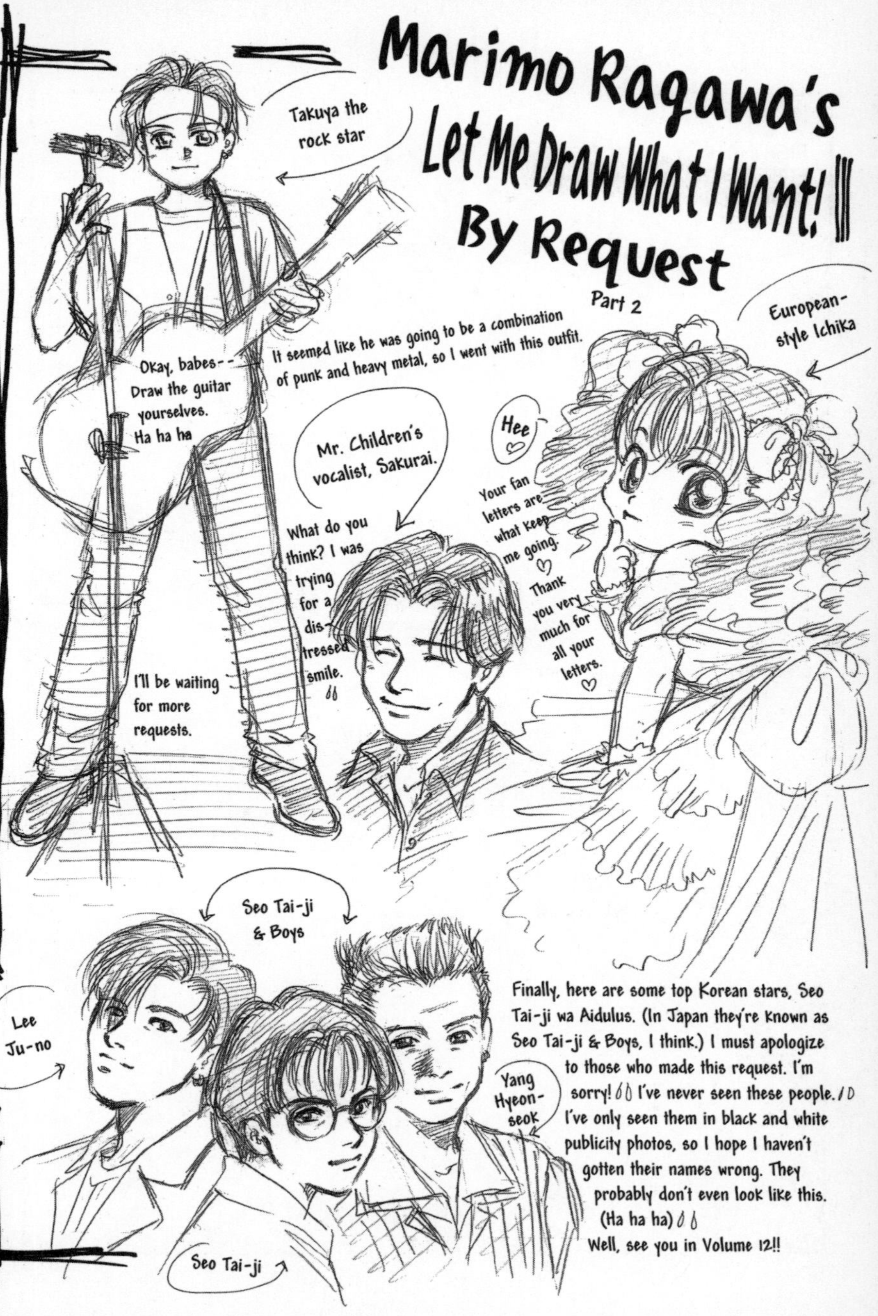
Takuya the rock star
It seemed like he was going to be a combination of punk and heavy metal, so I went with this outfit.
Okay, babes-- Draw the guitar yourselves. Ha ha ha
I'll be waiting for more requests.
Mr. Children's vocalist, Sakurai.
What do you think? I was trying for a distressed smile.
European-style Ichika
Hee ♡
Your fan letters are what keep me going. ♡ Thank you very much for all your letters. ♡
Seo Tai-ji & Boys
Lee Ju-no
Yang Hyeon-seok
Seo Tai-ji

Finally, here are some top Korean stars, Seo Tai-ji wa Aidulus. (In Japan they're known as Seo Tai-ji & Boys, I think.) I must apologize to those who made this request. I'm sorry! I've never seen these people. I've only seen them in black and white publicity photos, so I hope I haven't gotten their names wrong. They probably don't even look like this. (Ha ha ha)

Well, see you in Volume 12!!

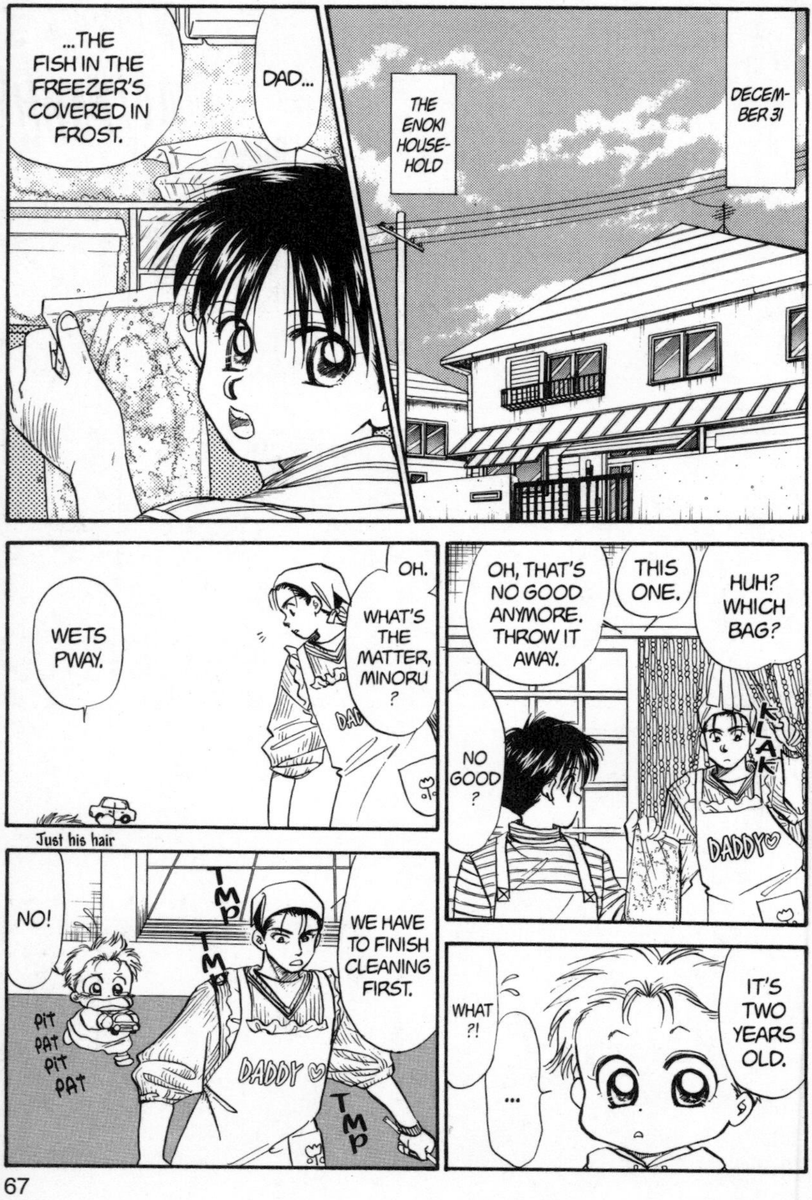
DECEMBER 31
THE ENOKI HOUSEHOLD
DAD...
...THE FISH IN THE FREEZER'S COVERED IN FROST.
HUH? WHICH BAG?
THIS ONE.
OH, THAT'S NO GOOD ANYMORE. THROW IT AWAY.
KLAK
NO GOOD?
IT'S TWO YEARS OLD.
WHAT?!
...
OH. WHAT'S THE MATTER, MINORU?
WETS PWAY.
Just his hair
WE HAVE TO FINISH CLEANING FIRST.
TMP
TMP
NO!
PIT PAT PIT PAT
TMP

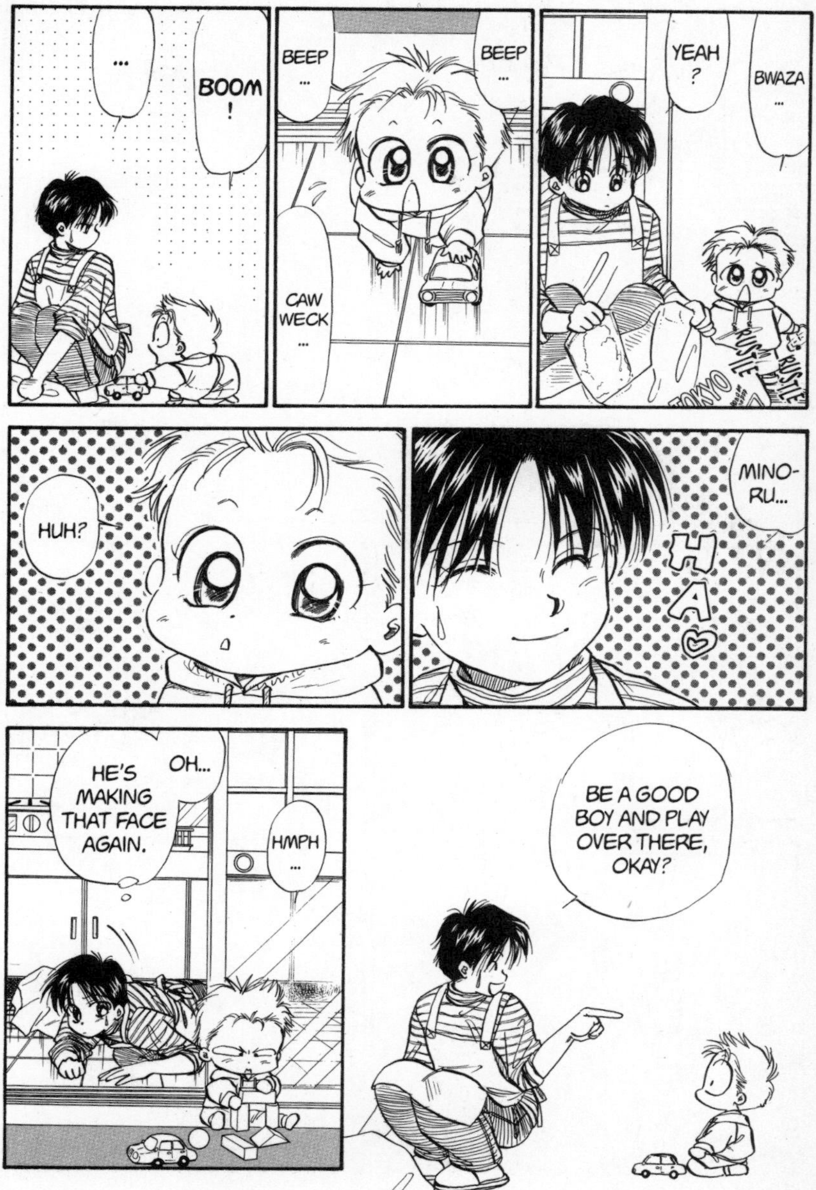
BWAZA ...
YEAH ?
BEEP ...
BEEP ...
CAW WECK ...
BOOM !
...
MINO-RU...
HA
HUH?
BE A GOOD BOY AND PLAY OVER THERE, OKAY?
OH...
HE'S MAKING THAT FACE AGAIN.
HMPH ...

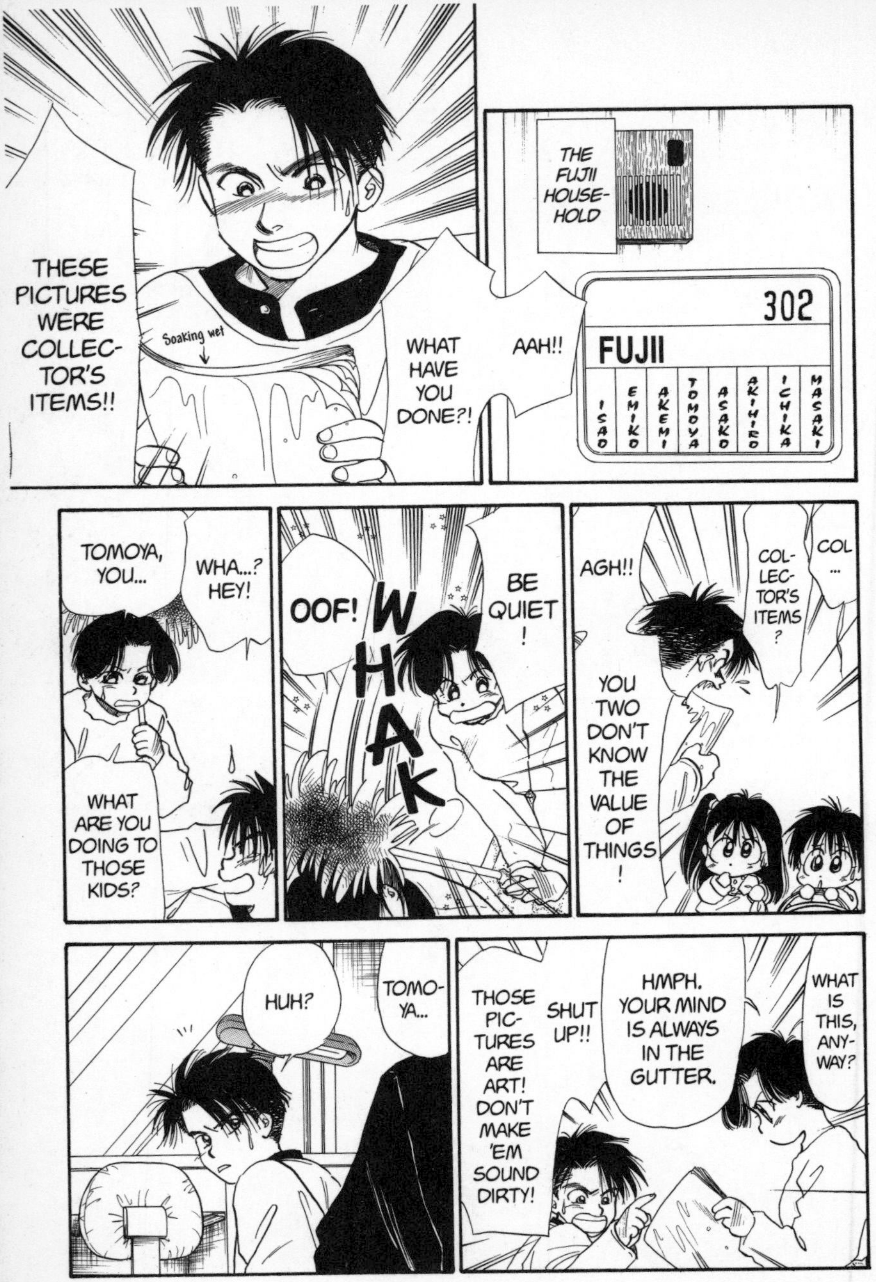
THE FUJII HOUSEHOLD
302
FUJII
ISAO EMIKO AKEMI TOMOYA ASAKO AKIHIRO ICHIKA MASAKI
AAH!!
WHAT HAVE YOU DONE?!
THESE PICTURES WERE COLLECTOR'S ITEMS!!
Soaking wet
COL...
COLLECTOR'S ITEMS?
AGH!!
YOU TWO DON'T KNOW THE VALUE OF THINGS!
BE QUIET!
WHAK
OOF!
WHA...? HEY!
TOMOYA, YOU...
WHAT ARE YOU DOING TO THOSE KIDS?
WHAT IS THIS, ANYWAY?
HMPH. YOUR MIND IS ALWAYS IN THE GUTTER.
SHUT UP!!
THOSE PICTURES ARE ART! DON'T MAKE 'EM SOUND DIRTY!
TOMOYA...
HUH?

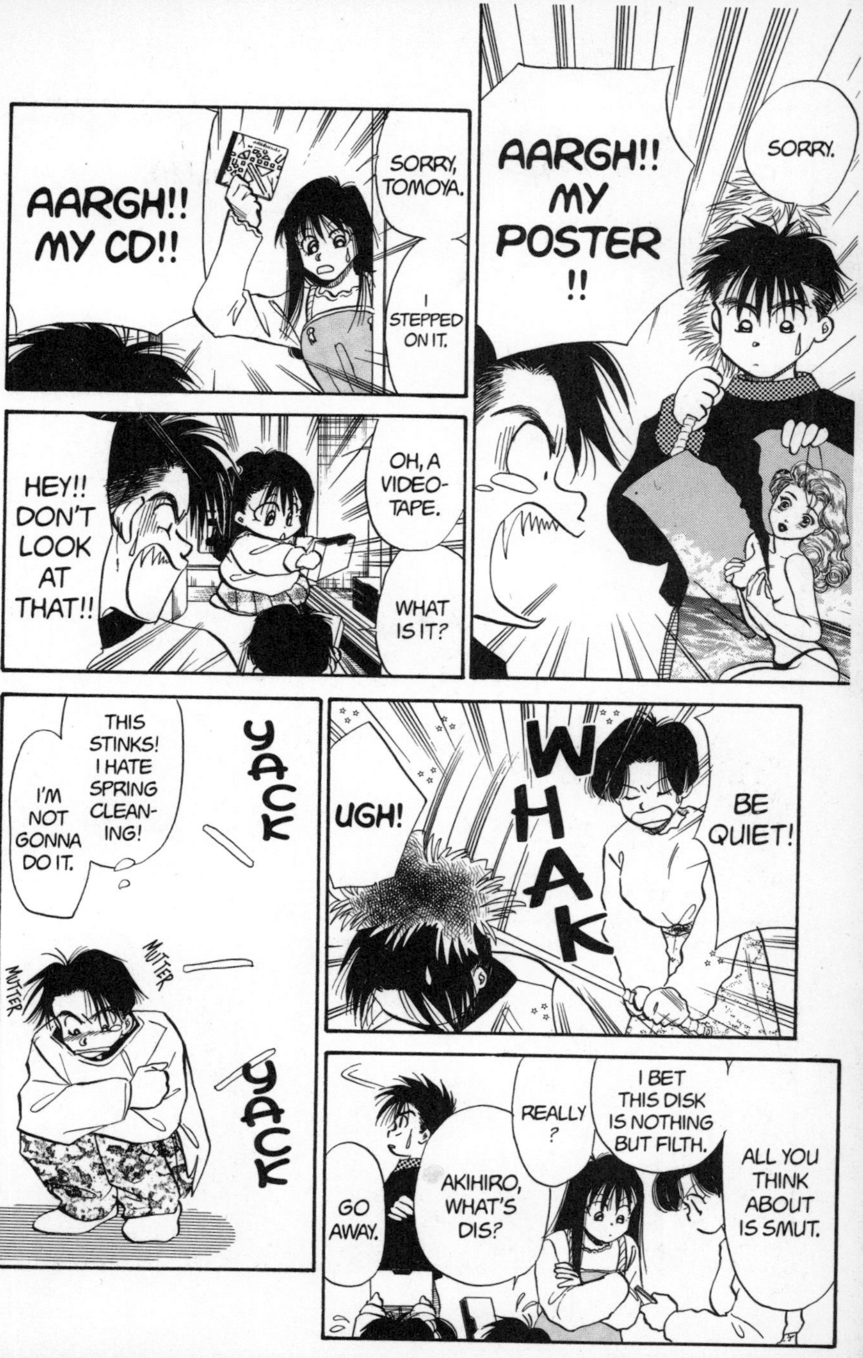
SORRY.
AARGH!! MY POSTER!!
SORRY, TOMOYA.
I STEPPED ON IT.
AARGH!! MY CD!!
OH, A VIDEO-TAPE.
WHAT IS IT?
HEY!! DON'T LOOK AT THAT!!
BE QUIET!
WHAK
UGH!
ALL YOU THINK ABOUT IS SMUT.
I BET THIS DISK IS NOTHING BUT FILTH.
REALLY?
AKIHIRO, WHAT'S DIS?
GO AWAY.
YACK
THIS STINKS! I HATE SPRING CLEAN-ING!
I'M NOT GONNA DO IT.
MUTTER
MUTTER
YACK

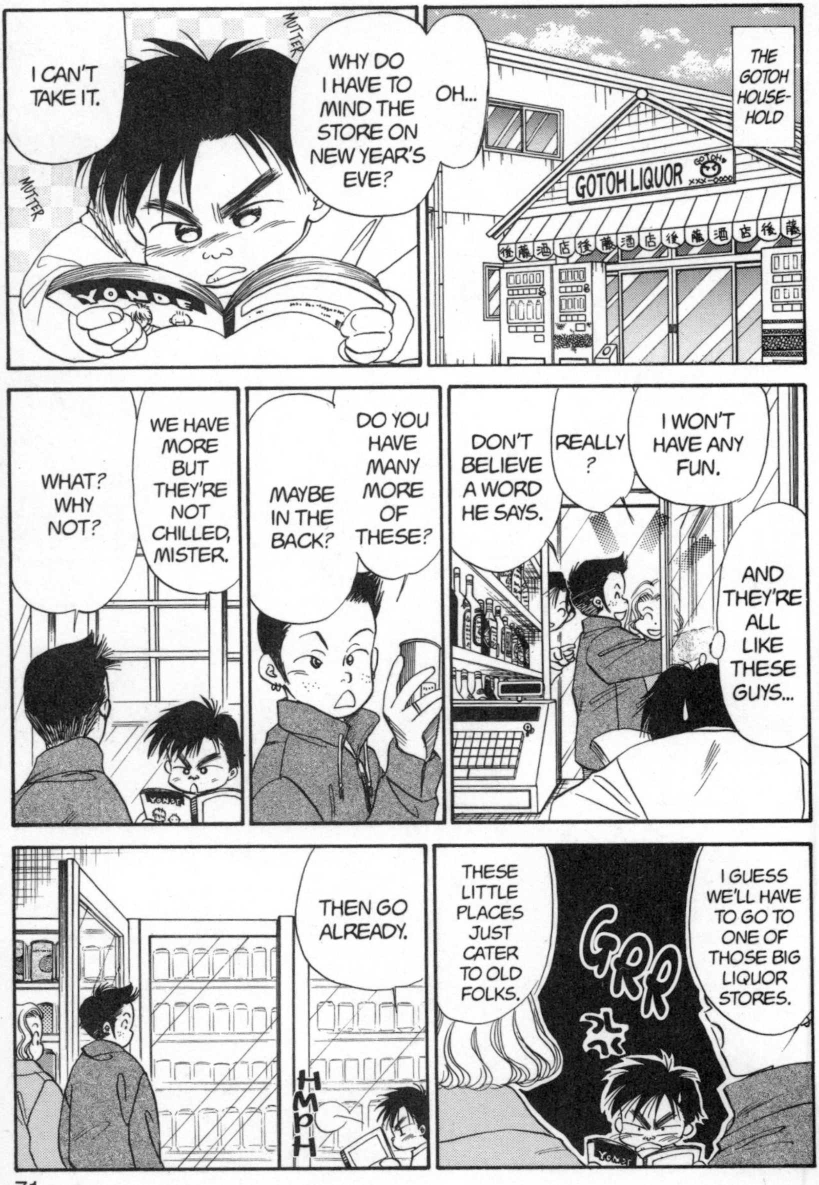
THE GOTOH HOUSEHOLD
OH...
GOTOH LIQUOR
WHY DO I HAVE TO MIND THE STORE ON NEW YEAR'S EVE?
MUTTER
I CAN'T TAKE IT.
MUTTER
I WON'T HAVE ANY FUN.
REALLY?
DON'T BELIEVE A WORD HE SAYS.
AND THEY'RE ALL LIKE THESE GUYS...
DO YOU HAVE MANY MORE OF THESE?
MAYBE IN THE BACK?
WE HAVE MORE BUT THEY'RE NOT CHILLED, MISTER.
WHAT? WHY NOT?
I GUESS WE'LL HAVE TO GO TO ONE OF THOSE BIG LIQUOR STORES.
GRR
THESE LITTLE PLACES JUST CATER TO OLD FOLKS.
THEN GO ALREADY.
HMPH

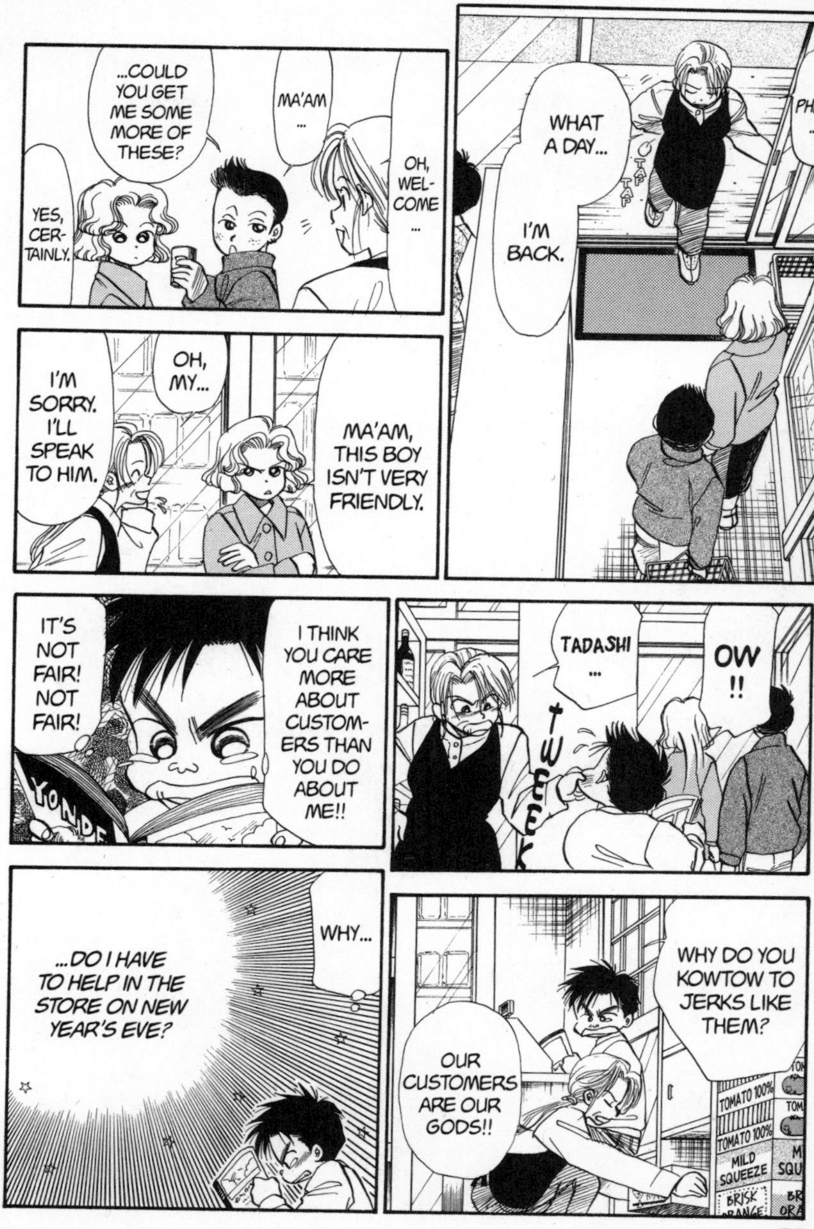
PHEW...
WHAT A DAY...
TAP TAP
I'M BACK.
OH, WELCOME...
MA'AM...
...COULD YOU GET ME SOME MORE OF THESE?
YES, CERTAINLY.
MA'AM, THIS BOY ISN'T VERY FRIENDLY.
OH, MY...
I'M SORRY. I'LL SPEAK TO HIM.
OW!!
TADASHI...
TWEEEK
I THINK YOU CARE MORE ABOUT CUSTOMERS THAN YOU DO ABOUT ME!!
IT'S NOT FAIR! NOT FAIR!
YONDE
WHY DO YOU KOWTOW TO JERKS LIKE THEM?
OUR CUSTOMERS ARE OUR GODS!!
TOMATO 100%
TOMATO 100%
MILD SQUEEZE
BRISK ORANGE
WHY...
...DO I HAVE TO HELP IN THE STORE ON NEW YEAR'S EVE?

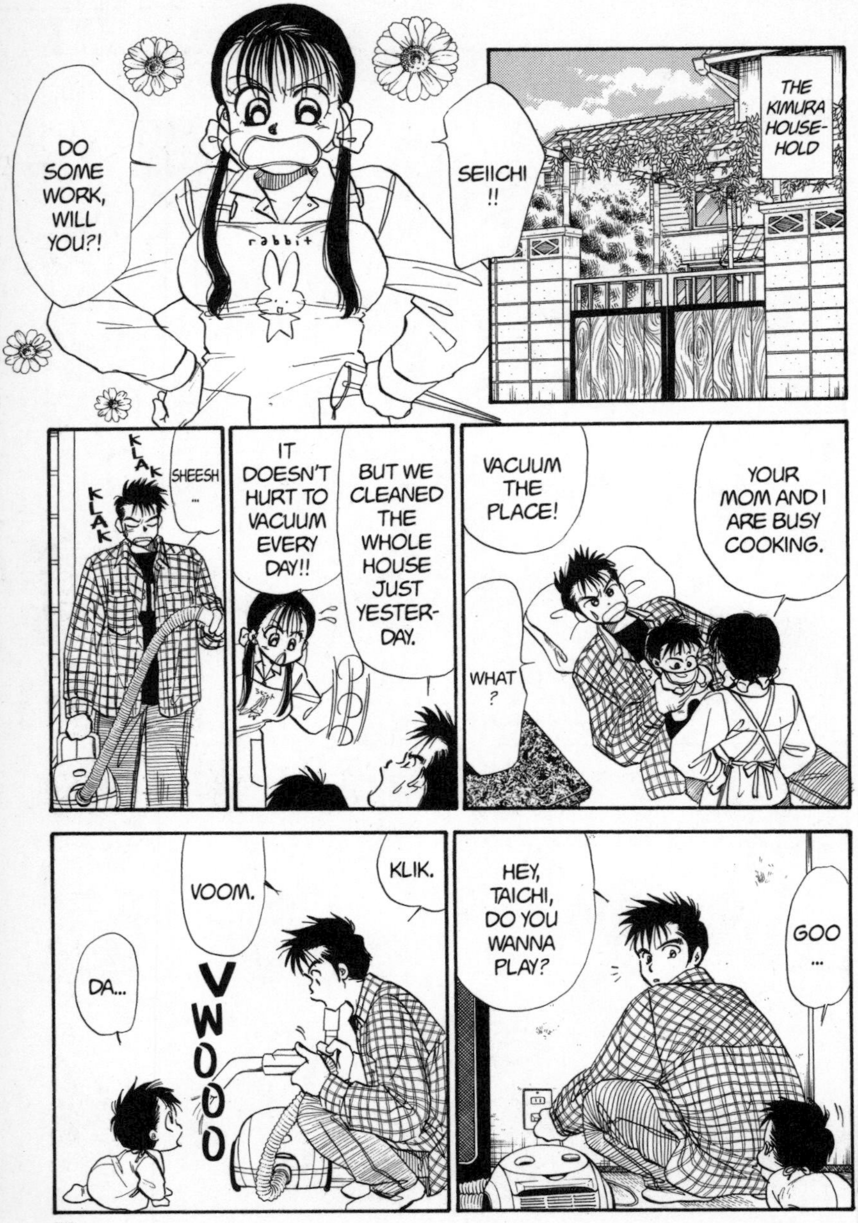

THE KIMURA HOUSE-HOLD
SEIICHI !!
DO SOME WORK, WILL YOU?!
YOUR MOM AND I ARE BUSY COOKING.
VACUUM THE PLACE!
WHAT ?
BUT WE CLEANED THE WHOLE HOUSE JUST YESTER-DAY.
IT DOESN'T HURT TO VACUUM EVERY DAY!!
SHEESH ...
KLAK
KLAK
GOO ...
HEY, TAICHI, DO YOU WANNA PLAY?
KLIK.
VOOM.
VWOOO
DA...

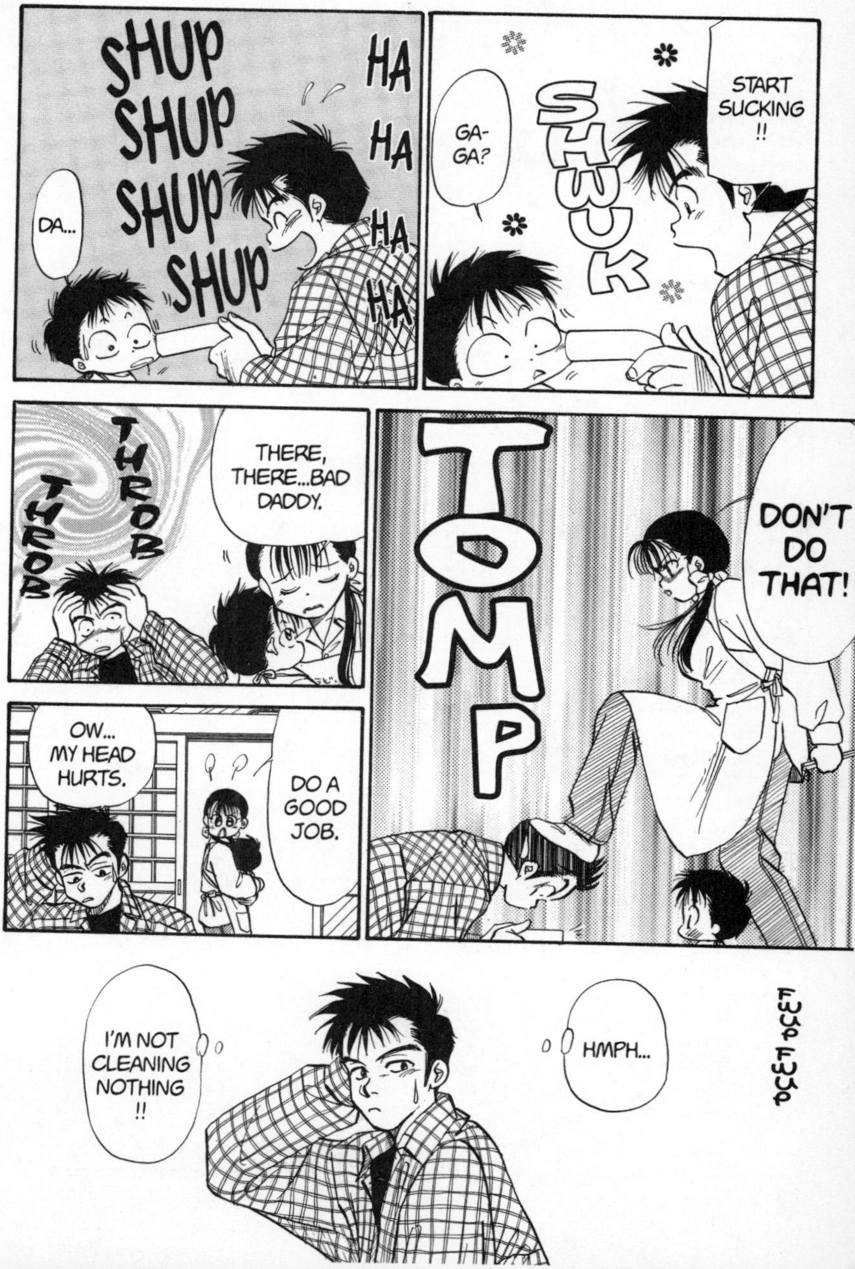
START SUCKING !!
SHWUK
GA-GA?
HA HA HA HA
SHUP SHUP SHUP SHUP
DA...
DON'T DO THAT!
TOMP
THERE, THERE...BAD DADDY.
THROB THROB
DO A GOOD JOB.
OW... MY HEAD HURTS.
FWUP FWUP
HMPH...
I'M NOT CLEANING NOTHING !!

Author's Note: Part 3

A reader inquired what kinds of liquor I like. Well, I mostly drink beer. I don't really care for sake, but I do like "Hi Sour" drinks (shôchu and citrus-flavored soda water.) I'm a cheap drunk. I still drink the same stuff I drank when I was a student.

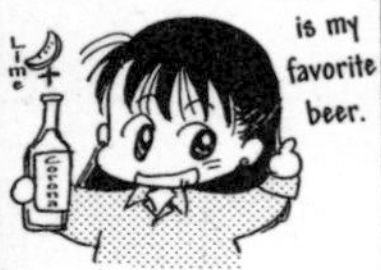

Lime
Corona

Corona is my favorite beer.

Corona beer comes in bottles. You just drop a wedge of lime into it and drink. I like Budweiser, too. I also like Lime and Lemon Sours. I can drink up to five glasses.

I like sweeter wines, so I prefer reds to whites. Madonna is delicious.

I don't like dry sake--I prefer smoother tasting ones. I like to sip it slowly when it's hot.

I mustn't forget cocktails. I love cocktails. I bought all the equipment to make them, but I have yet to make anything. I even have a cocktail recipe book. But cocktails are high in alcohol, so you can't slam them.

Continued in Part 4...

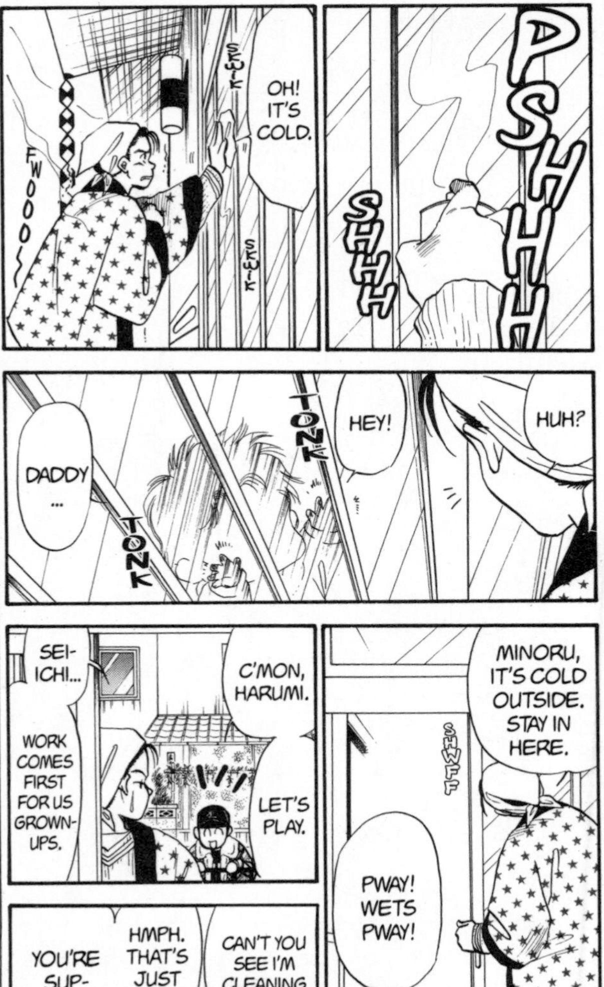

PSHHH
SHHH
OH! IT'S COLD.
SKWIK
SKWIK
FWOOO~
HUH?
HEY!
TONK
DADDY ...
TONK
MINORU, IT'S COLD OUTSIDE. STAY IN HERE.
SHWFF
PWAY! WETS PWAY!
C'MON, HARUMI.
SEI-ICHI...
LET'S PLAY.
WORK COMES FIRST FOR US GROWN-UPS.
CAN'T YOU SEE I'M CLEANING THE HOUSE?
HMPH. THAT'S JUST SAD.
YOU'RE SUP-POSED TO TAKE IT EASY ON NEW YEAR'S EVE.

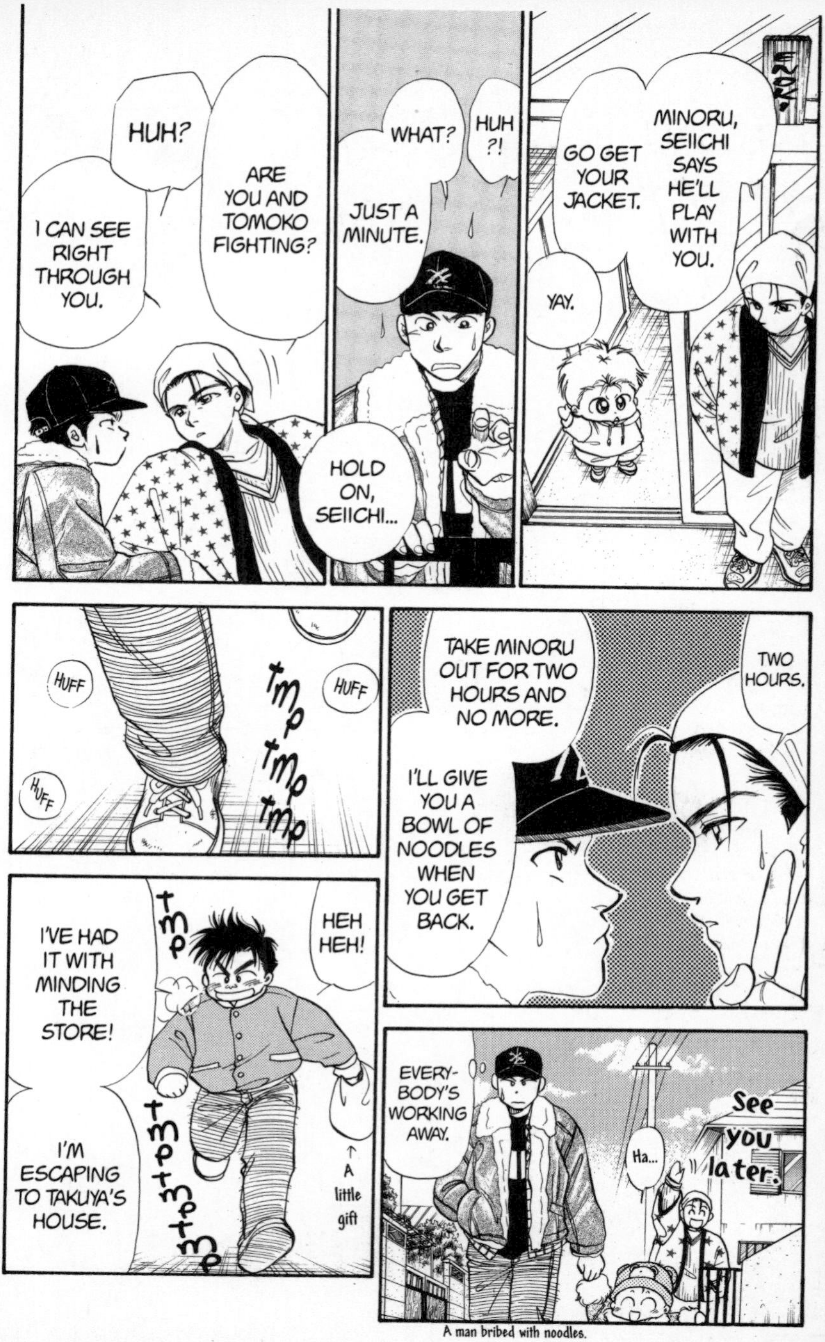
MINORU, SEIICHI SAYS HE'LL PLAY WITH YOU.
GO GET YOUR JACKET.
YAY.
HUH ?!
WHAT?
JUST A MINUTE.
HOLD ON, SEIICHI...
ARE YOU AND TOMOKO FIGHTING?
HUH?
I CAN SEE RIGHT THROUGH YOU.
TWO HOURS.
TAKE MINORU OUT FOR TWO HOURS AND NO MORE.
I'LL GIVE YOU A BOWL OF NOODLES WHEN YOU GET BACK.
HUFF
tmp tmp tmp
HUFF
HUFF
See you later.
Ha...
EVERY-BODY'S WORKING AWAY.
tmp
HEH HEH!
I'VE HAD IT WITH MINDING THE STORE!
I'M ESCAPING TO TAKUYA'S HOUSE.
tmp tmp tmp
↑ A little gift

A man bribed with noodles.

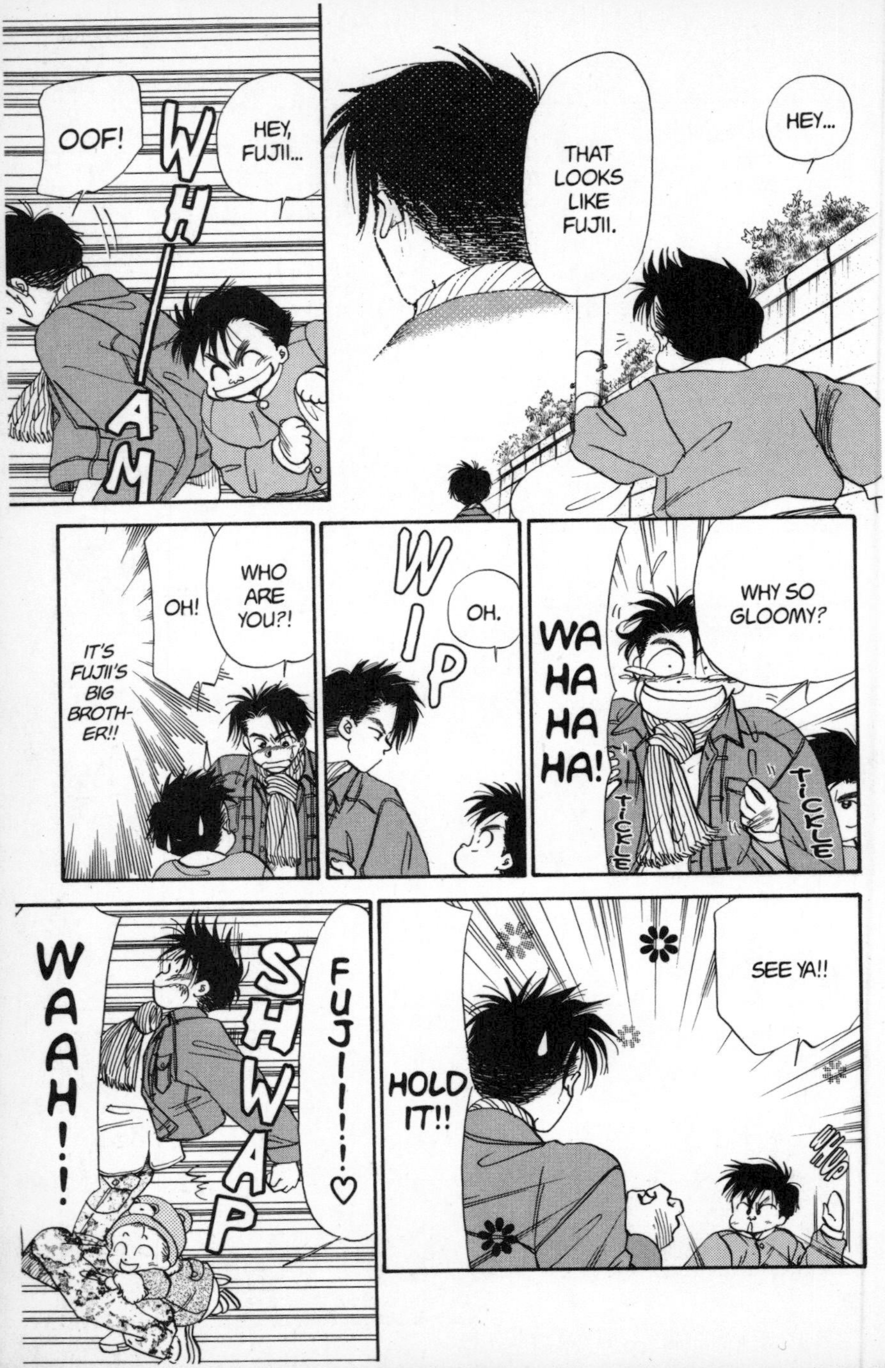
HEY...
THAT LOOKS LIKE FUJII.
HEY, FUJII...
WHAM
OOF!
WHY SO GLOOMY?
WA HA HA HA!
TICKLE
TICKLE
OH.
WIP
WHO ARE YOU?!
OH!
IT'S FUJII'S BIG BROTHER!!
SEE YA!!
HOLD IT!!
FUJII!!!♡
SHWAP
WAAH!!!

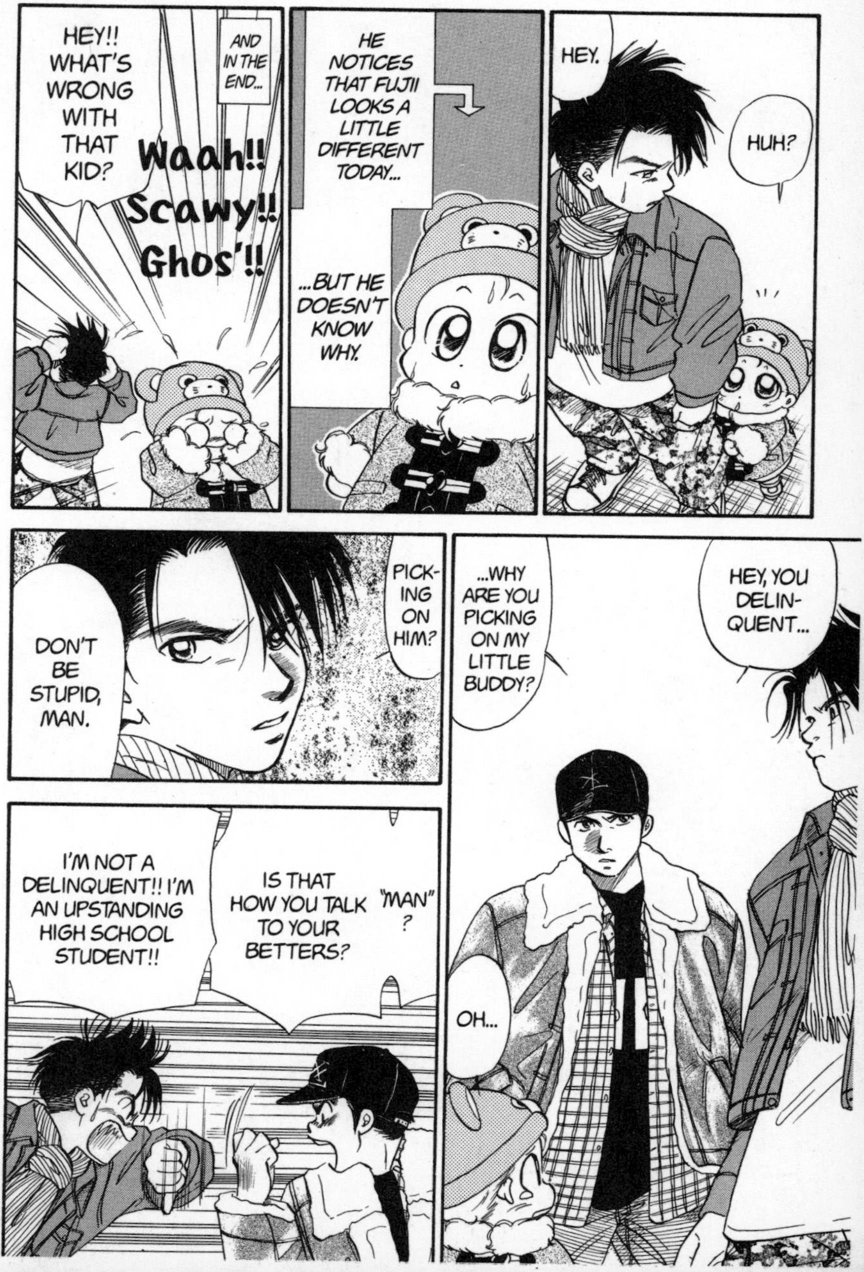
HEY.
HUH?
HE NOTICES THAT FUJII LOOKS A LITTLE DIFFERENT TODAY...
...BUT HE DOESN'T KNOW WHY.
AND IN THE END...
HEY!! WHAT'S WRONG WITH THAT KID?
Waah!! Scawy!! Ghos'!!
HEY, YOU DELIN-QUENT...
...WHY ARE YOU PICKING ON MY LITTLE BUDDY?
OH...
PICK-ING ON HIM?
DON'T BE STUPID, MAN.
"MAN"?
IS THAT HOW YOU TALK TO YOUR BETTERS?
I'M NOT A DELINQUENT!! I'M AN UPSTANDING HIGH SCHOOL STUDENT!!

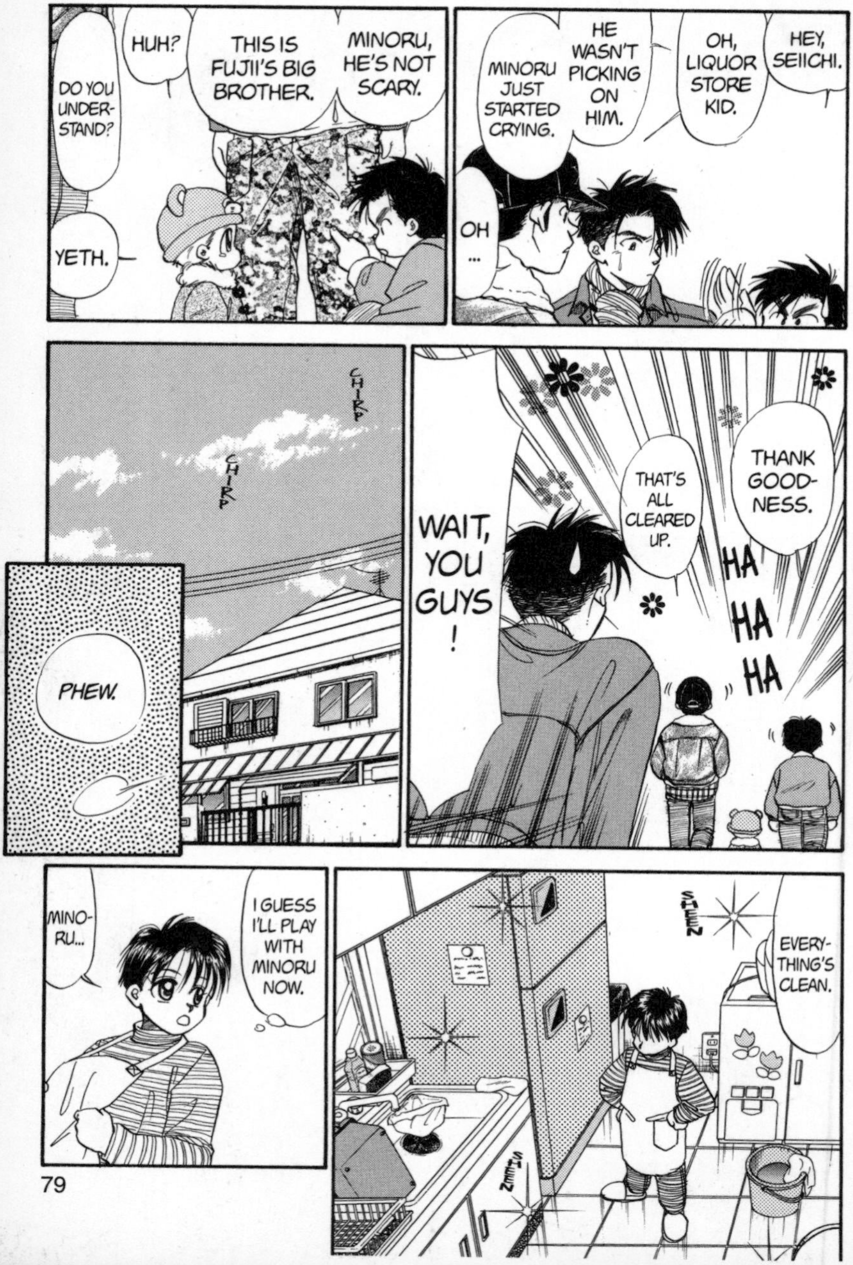
HEY, SEIICHI.
OH, LIQUOR STORE KID.
HE WASN'T PICKING ON HIM.
MINORU JUST STARTED CRYING.
OH ...
MINORU, HE'S NOT SCARY.
THIS IS FUJII'S BIG BROTHER.
HUH?
DO YOU UNDERSTAND?
YETH.
THANK GOODNESS.
THAT'S ALL CLEARED UP.
HA HA HA
WAIT, YOU GUYS!
CHIRP
CHIRP
PHEW.
SHEEN
EVERYTHING'S CLEAN.
SHEEN
I GUESS I'LL PLAY WITH MINORU NOW.
MINORU...

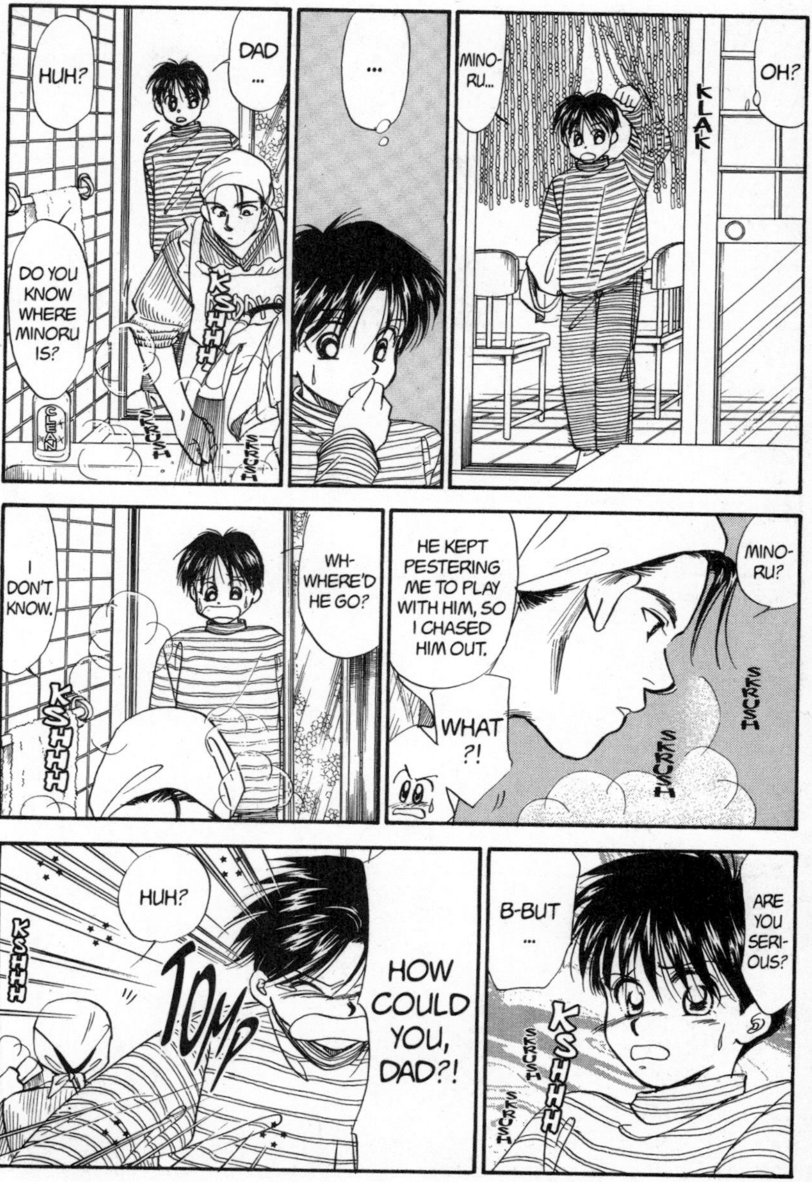
OH?
KLAK
MINO-RU...
...
DAD
...
HUH?
DO YOU KNOW WHERE MINORU IS?
KSHHHH
SKRUSH
SKRUSH
CLEAN
MINO-RU?
HE KEPT PESTERING ME TO PLAY WITH HIM, SO I CHASED HIM OUT.
SKRUSH
SKRUSH
WHAT ?!
WH-WHERE'D HE GO?
I DON'T KNOW.
KSHHHH
ARE YOU SERI-OUS?
B-BUT ...
KSHHHH
SKRUSH
SKRUSH
HUH?
HOW COULD YOU, DAD?!
TOMP
KSHHHH

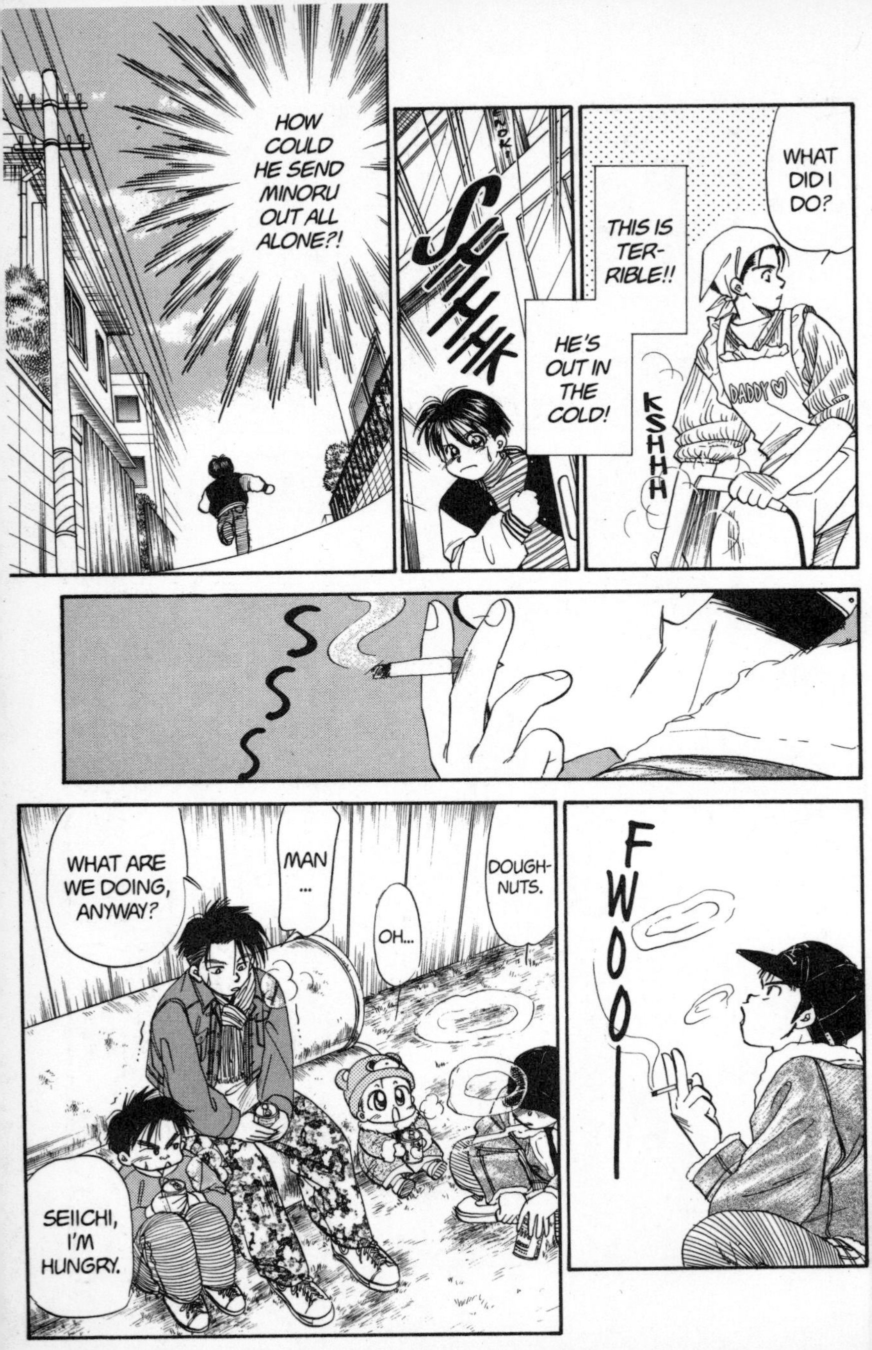
WHAT DID I DO?
THIS IS TERRIBLE!!
HE'S OUT IN THE COLD!
KSHHH
DADDY
SHHHHK
HOW COULD HE SEND MINORU OUT ALL ALONE?!
SSS
FWOO
DOUGH-NUTS.
OH...
MAN ...
WHAT ARE WE DOING, ANYWAY?
SEIICHI, I'M HUNGRY.

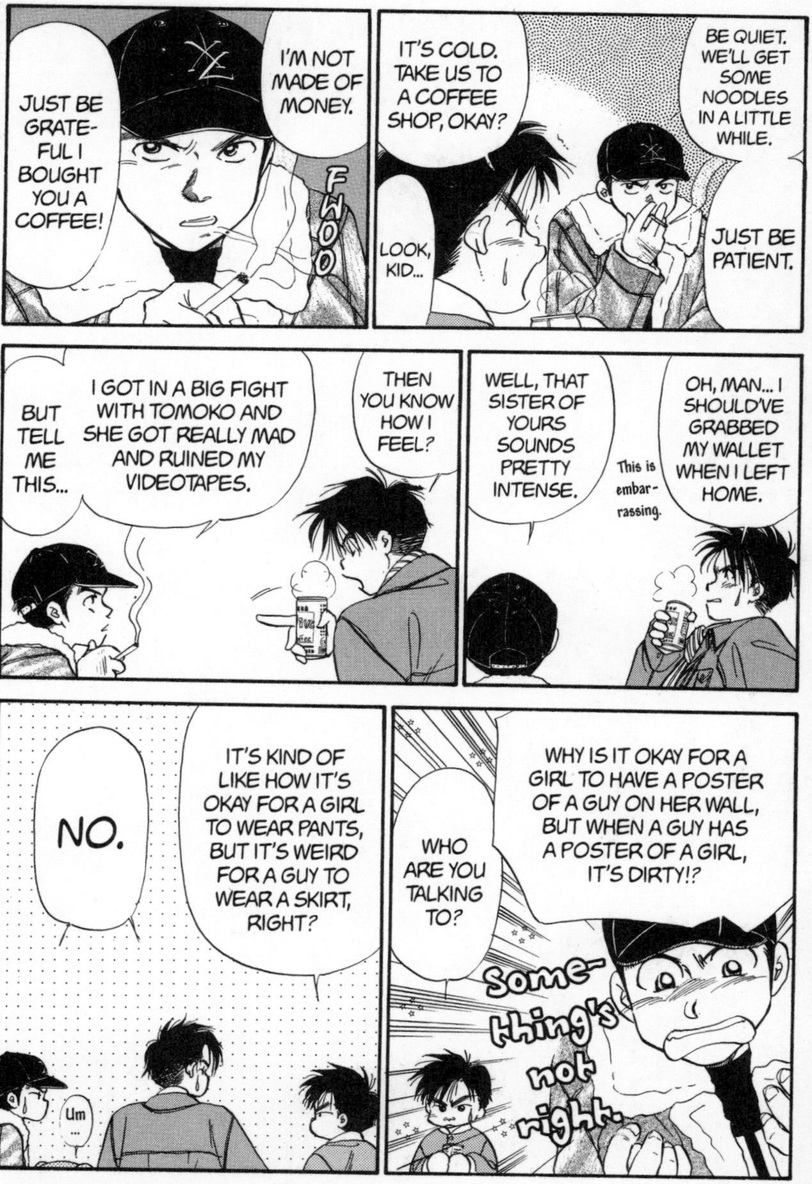
BE QUIET. WE'LL GET SOME NOODLES IN A LITTLE WHILE.
IT'S COLD. TAKE US TO A COFFEE SHOP, OKAY?
JUST BE PATIENT.
LOOK, KID...
I'M NOT MADE OF MONEY.
FWOO
JUST BE GRATEFUL I BOUGHT YOU A COFFEE!
OH, MAN... I SHOULD'VE GRABBED MY WALLET WHEN I LEFT HOME.
WELL, THAT SISTER OF YOURS SOUNDS PRETTY INTENSE.
This is embarrassing.
THEN YOU KNOW HOW I FEEL?
I GOT IN A BIG FIGHT WITH TOMOKO AND SHE GOT REALLY MAD AND RUINED MY VIDEOTAPES.
BUT TELL ME THIS...
WHY IS IT OKAY FOR A GIRL TO HAVE A POSTER OF A GUY ON HER WALL, BUT WHEN A GUY HAS A POSTER OF A GIRL, IT'S DIRTY!?
WHO ARE YOU TALKING TO?
Something's not right.
IT'S KIND OF LIKE HOW IT'S OKAY FOR A GIRL TO WEAR PANTS, BUT IT'S WEIRD FOR A GUY TO WEAR A SKIRT, RIGHT?
NO.
Um...

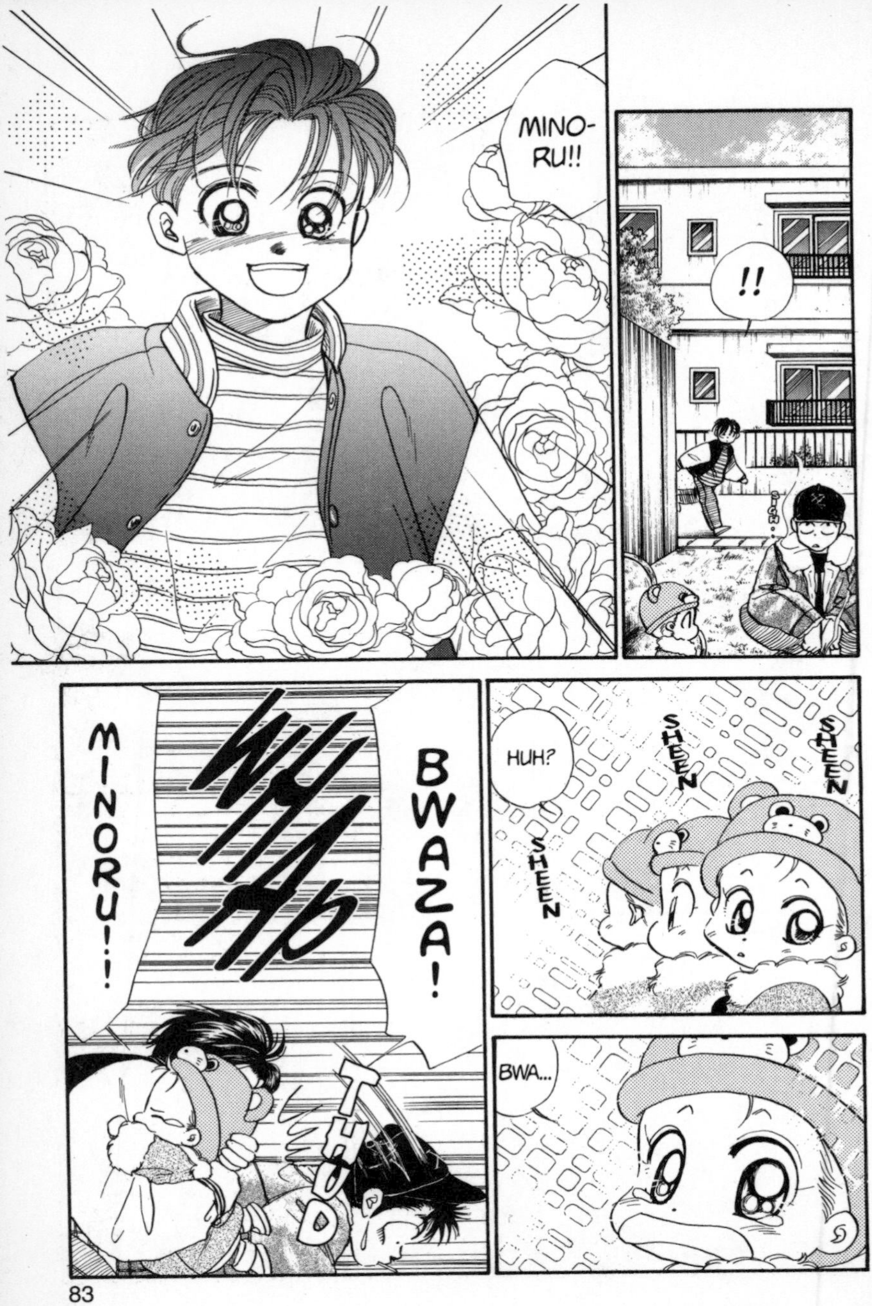
!!
SIGH...
MINO-RU!!
HUH?
SHEEN
SHEEN
SHEEN
BWA...
BWAZA!
WHAP
MINORU!!
THUD

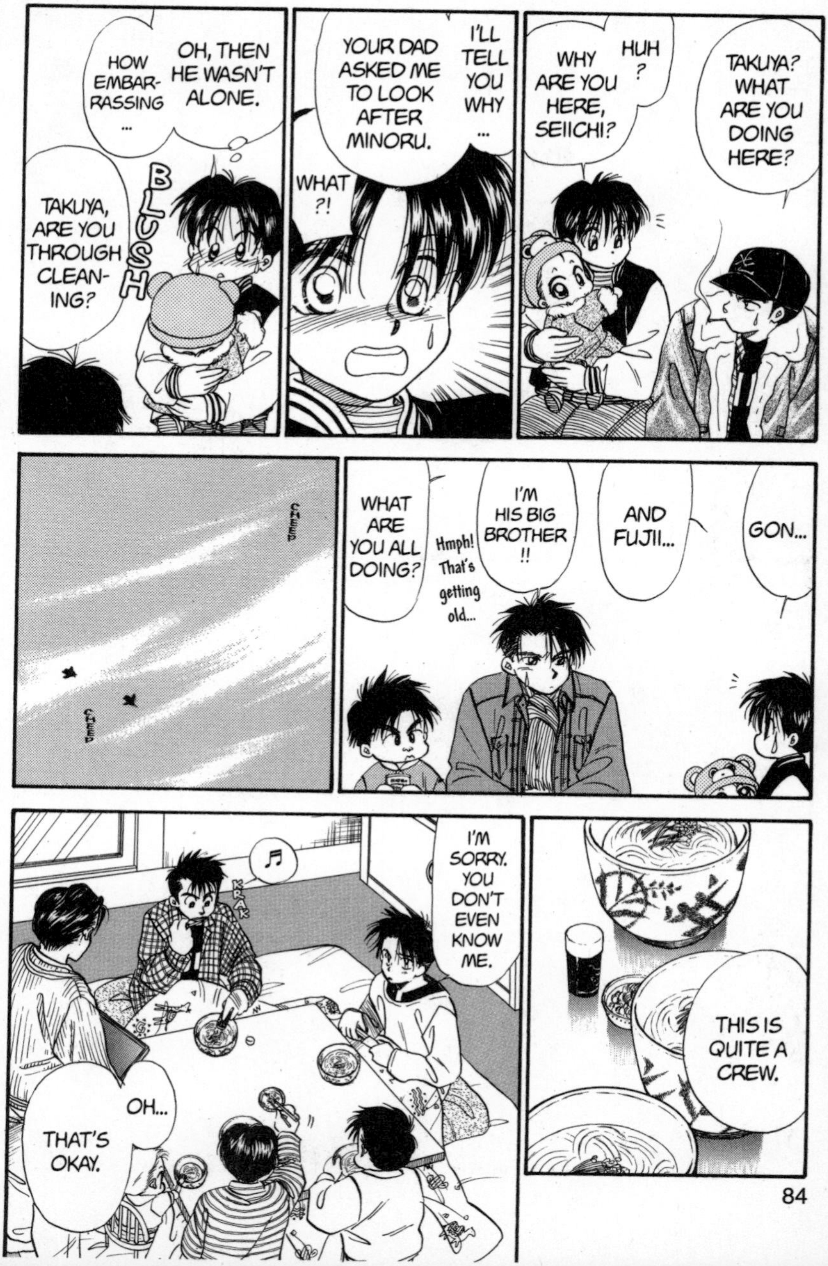
TAKUYA? WHAT ARE YOU DOING HERE?
HUH?
WHY ARE YOU HERE, SEIICHI?
I'LL TELL YOU WHY...
YOUR DAD ASKED ME TO LOOK AFTER MINORU.
WHAT?!
OH, THEN HE WASN'T ALONE.
HOW EMBARRASSING...
BLUSH
TAKUYA, ARE YOU THROUGH CLEANING?
GON...
AND FUJII...
I'M HIS BIG BROTHER!!
Hmph! That's getting old...
WHAT ARE YOU ALL DOING?
CHEEP
CHEEP
THIS IS QUITE A CREW.
I'M SORRY. YOU DON'T EVEN KNOW ME.
KRAK
OH... THAT'S OKAY.

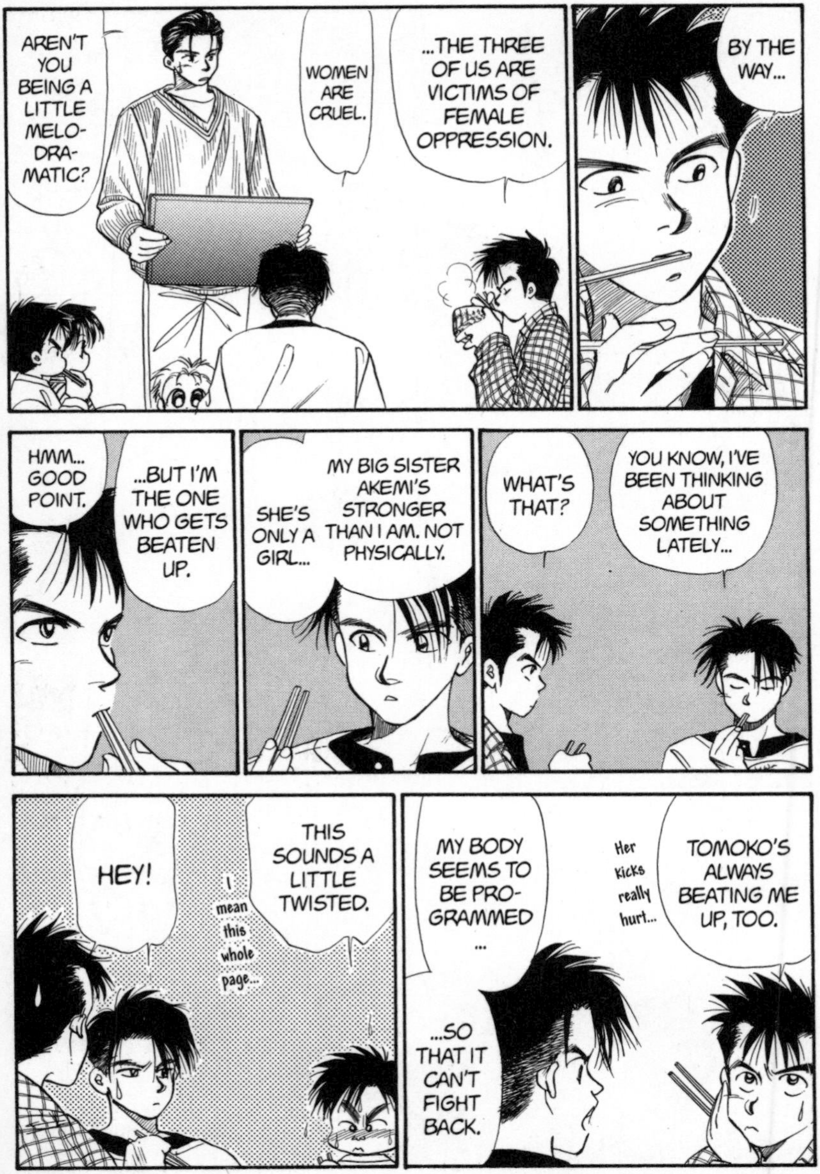
BY THE WAY...
...THE THREE OF US ARE VICTIMS OF FEMALE OPPRESSION.
WOMEN ARE CRUEL.
AREN'T YOU BEING A LITTLE MELO-DRA-MATIC?
YOU KNOW, I'VE BEEN THINKING ABOUT SOMETHING LATELY...
WHAT'S THAT?
MY BIG SISTER AKEMI'S STRONGER THAN I AM. NOT PHYSICALLY.
SHE'S ONLY A GIRL...
...BUT I'M THE ONE WHO GETS BEATEN UP.
HMM... GOOD POINT.
TOMOKO'S ALWAYS BEATING ME UP, TOO.
Her kicks really hurt...
MY BODY SEEMS TO BE PRO-GRAMMED...
...SO THAT IT CAN'T FIGHT BACK.
THIS SOUNDS A LITTLE TWISTED.
I mean this whole page...
HEY!

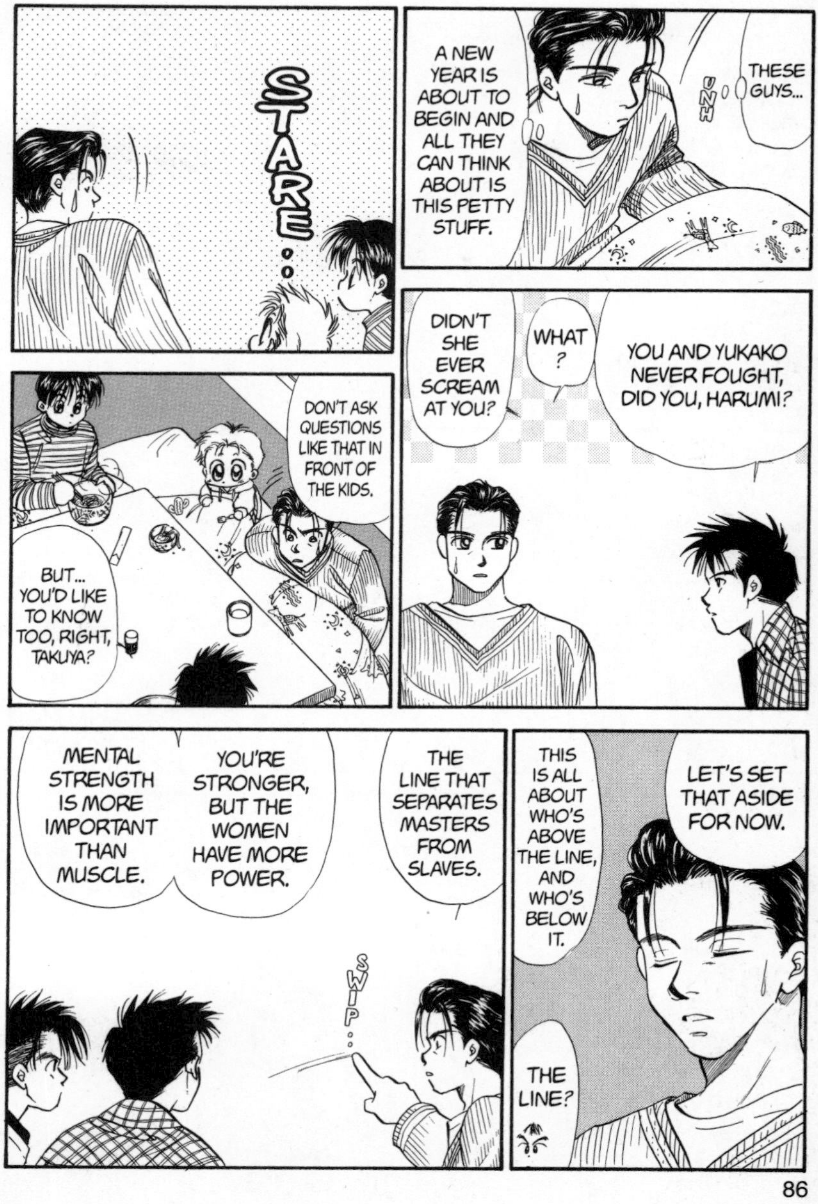
THESE GUYS...
UNH
A NEW YEAR IS ABOUT TO BEGIN AND ALL THEY CAN THINK ABOUT IS THIS PETTY STUFF.
STARE...
YOU AND YUKAKO NEVER FOUGHT, DID YOU, HARUMI?
WHAT?
DIDN'T SHE EVER SCREAM AT YOU?
DON'T ASK QUESTIONS LIKE THAT IN FRONT OF THE KIDS.
BUT... YOU'D LIKE TO KNOW TOO, RIGHT, TAKUYA?
LET'S SET THAT ASIDE FOR NOW.
THIS IS ALL ABOUT WHO'S ABOVE THE LINE, AND WHO'S BELOW IT.
THE LINE?
THE LINE THAT SEPARATES MASTERS FROM SLAVES.
YOU'RE STRONGER, BUT THE WOMEN HAVE MORE POWER.
MENTAL STRENGTH IS MORE IMPORTANT THAN MUSCLE.
SWIP..

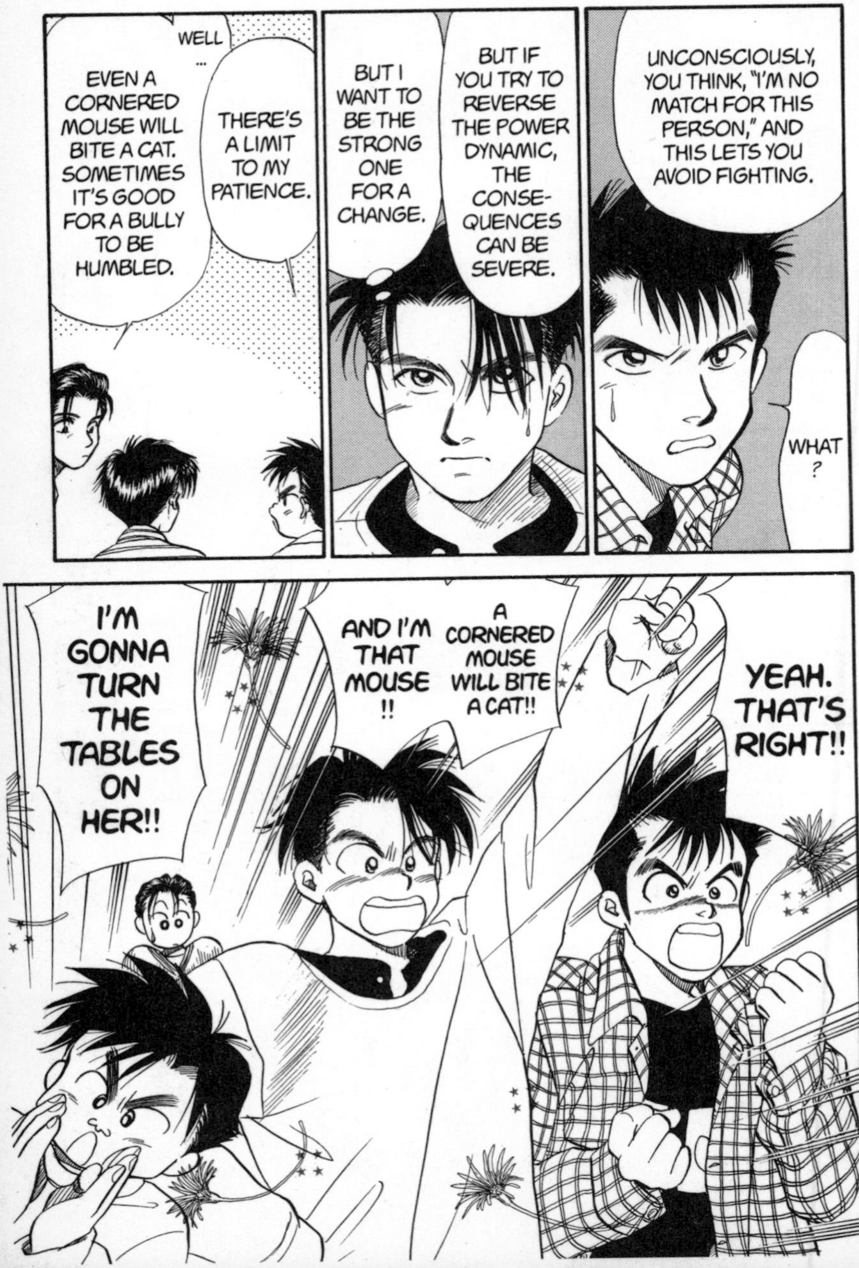
UNCONSCIOUSLY, YOU THINK, "I'M NO MATCH FOR THIS PERSON," AND THIS LETS YOU AVOID FIGHTING.
WHAT?
BUT IF YOU TRY TO REVERSE THE POWER DYNAMIC, THE CONSE-QUENCES CAN BE SEVERE.
BUT I WANT TO BE THE STRONG ONE FOR A CHANGE.
WELL ...
THERE'S A LIMIT TO MY PATIENCE.
EVEN A CORNERED MOUSE WILL BITE A CAT. SOMETIMES IT'S GOOD FOR A BULLY TO BE HUMBLED.
YEAH. THAT'S RIGHT!!
A CORNERED MOUSE WILL BITE A CAT!!
AND I'M THAT MOUSE!!
I'M GONNA TURN THE TABLES ON HER!!

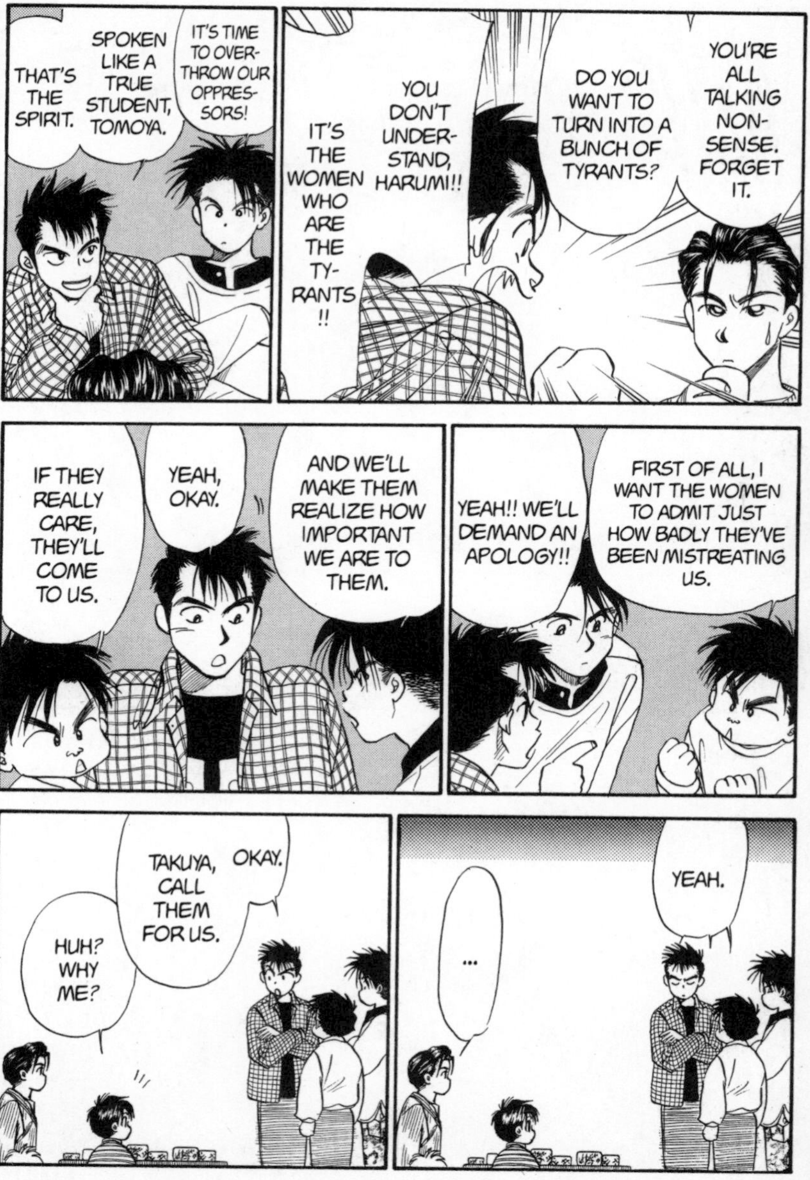
YOU'RE ALL TALKING NON-SENSE. FORGET IT.
DO YOU WANT TO TURN INTO A BUNCH OF TYRANTS?
YOU DON'T UNDER-STAND, HARUMI!!
IT'S THE WOMEN WHO ARE THE TY-RANTS !!
IT'S TIME TO OVER-THROW OUR OPPRES-SORS!
SPOKEN LIKE A TRUE STUDENT, TOMOYA.
THAT'S THE SPIRIT.
FIRST OF ALL, I WANT THE WOMEN TO ADMIT JUST HOW BADLY THEY'VE BEEN MISTREATING US.
YEAH!! WE'LL DEMAND AN APOLOGY!!
AND WE'LL MAKE THEM REALIZE HOW IMPORTANT WE ARE TO THEM.
YEAH, OKAY.
IF THEY REALLY CARE, THEY'LL COME TO US.
YEAH.
...
OKAY.
TAKUYA, CALL THEM FOR US.
HUH? WHY ME?

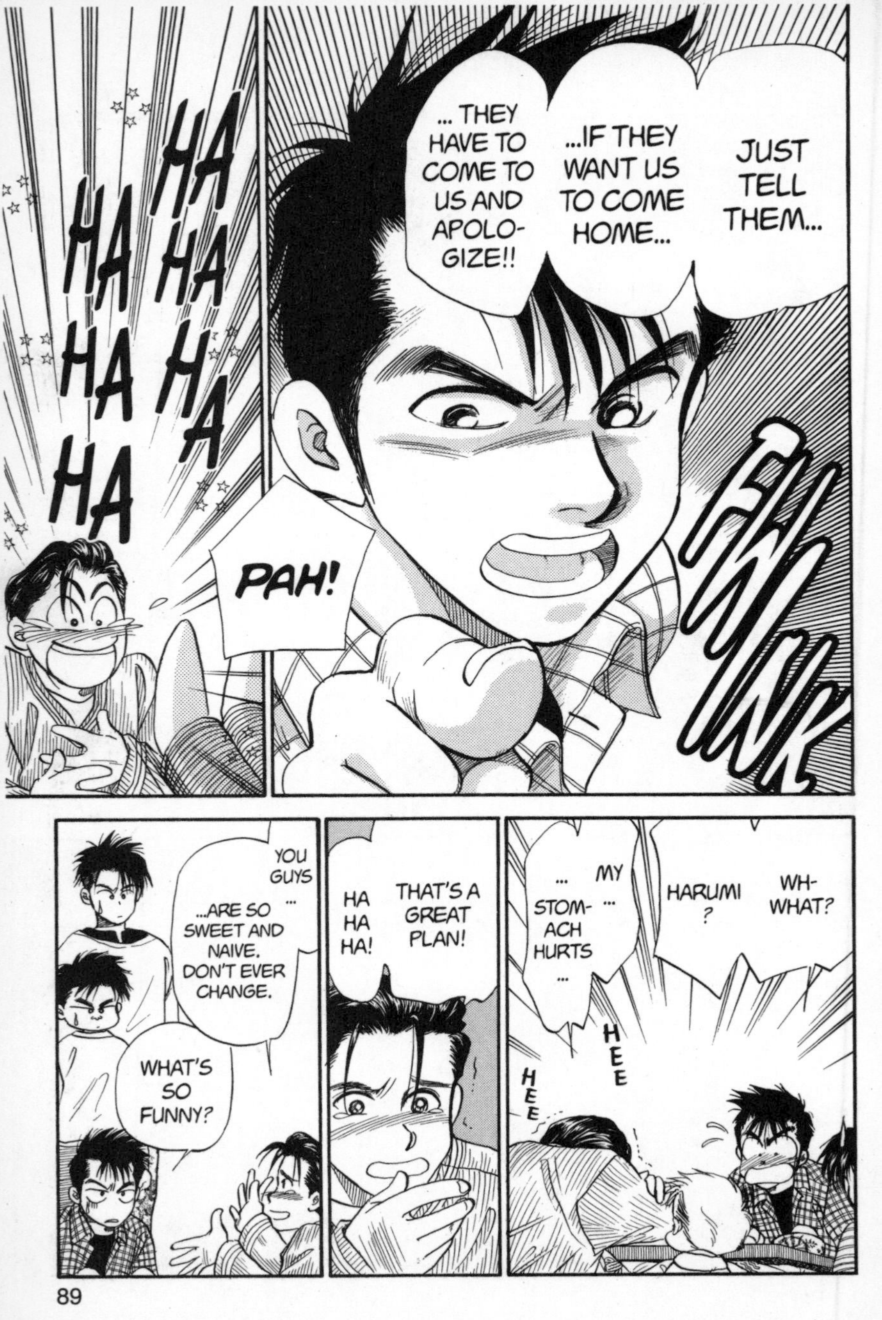
JUST TELL THEM...
...IF THEY WANT US TO COME HOME...
... THEY HAVE TO COME TO US AND APOLOGIZE!!
PAH!
HA HA HA HA HA
HA HA HA HA
WH-WHAT?
HARUMI?
MY...
... STOMACH HURTS...
HEE HEE
HEE
THAT'S A GREAT PLAN!
HA HA HA!
YOU GUYS...
...ARE SO SWEET AND NAIVE. DON'T EVER CHANGE.
WHAT'S SO FUNNY?

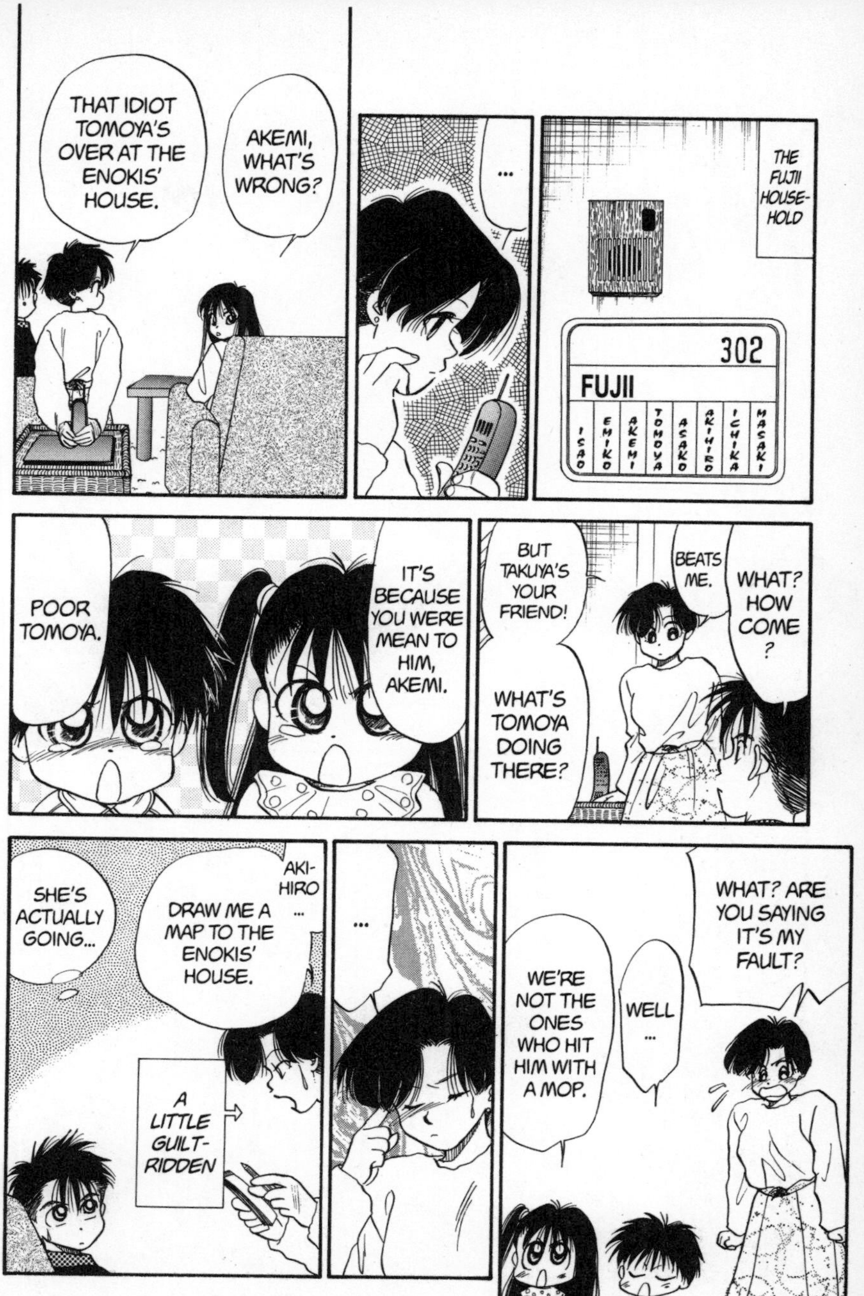
THE FUJII HOUSEHOLD
302
FUJII
ISAO EMIKO AKEMI TOMOYA ASAKO AKIHIRO ICHIKA MASAKI
...
AKEMI, WHAT'S WRONG?
THAT IDIOT TOMOYA'S OVER AT THE ENOKIS' HOUSE.
WHAT? HOW COME?
BEATS ME.
BUT TAKUYA'S YOUR FRIEND!
WHAT'S TOMOYA DOING THERE?
IT'S BECAUSE YOU WERE MEAN TO HIM, AKEMI.
POOR TOMOYA.
WHAT? ARE YOU SAYING IT'S MY FAULT?
WELL ...
WE'RE NOT THE ONES WHO HIT HIM WITH A MOP.
...
AKI-HIRO ...
DRAW ME A MAP TO THE ENOKIS' HOUSE.
SHE'S ACTUALLY GOING...
A LITTLE GUILT-RIDDEN

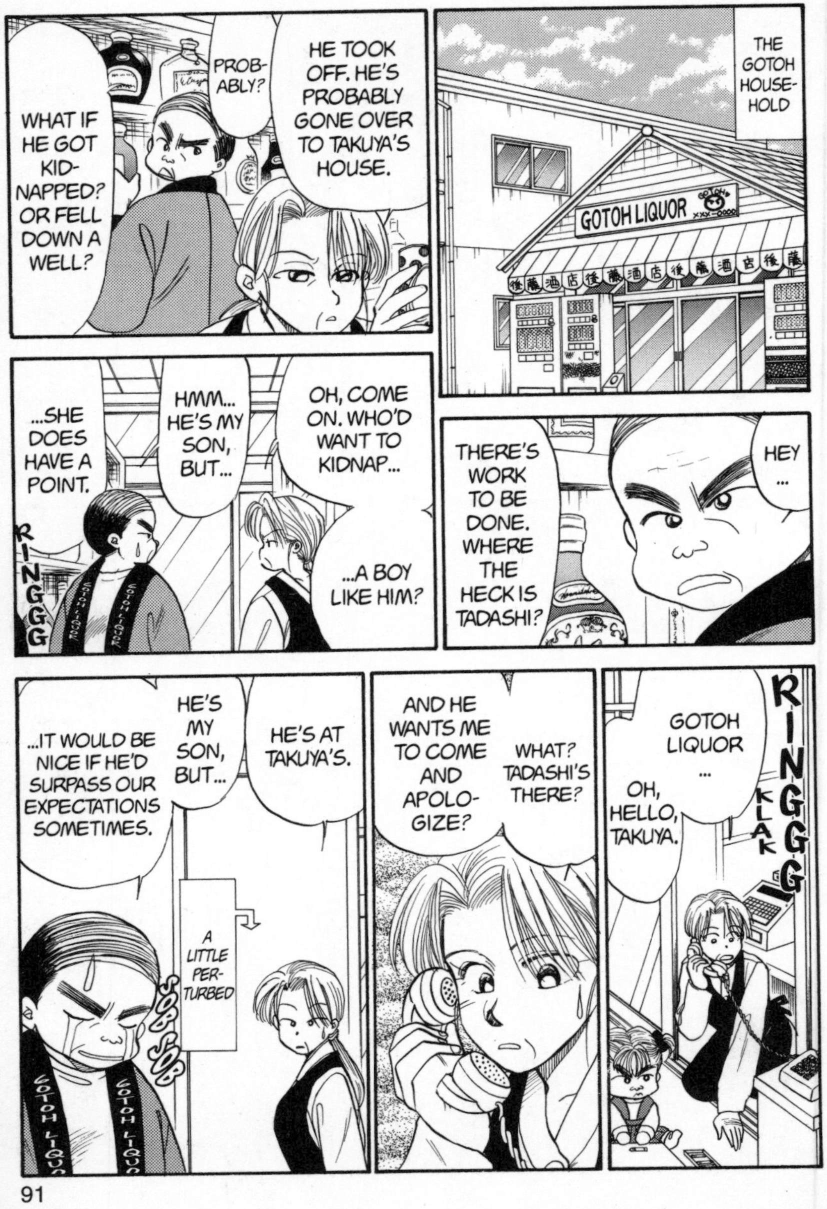
THE GOTOH HOUSEHOLD
GOTOH LIQUOR
GOTOH
XXX-0000
後藤酒店後藤酒店後藤酒店後藤
HE TOOK OFF. HE'S PROBABLY GONE OVER TO TAKUYA'S HOUSE.
PROBABLY?
WHAT IF HE GOT KIDNAPPED? OR FELL DOWN A WELL?
HEY...
THERE'S WORK TO BE DONE. WHERE THE HECK IS TADASHI?
OH, COME ON. WHO'D WANT TO KIDNAP...
...A BOY LIKE HIM?
HMM... HE'S MY SON, BUT...
...SHE DOES HAVE A POINT.
RINGGG
GOTOH LIQUOR
RINGGG
KLAK
GOTOH LIQUOR...
OH, HELLO, TAKUYA.
WHAT? TADASHI'S THERE?
AND HE WANTS ME TO COME AND APOLOGIZE?
HE'S AT TAKUYA'S.
HE'S MY SON, BUT...
...IT WOULD BE NICE IF HE'D SURPASS OUR EXPECTATIONS SOMETIMES.
A LITTLE PERTURBED
SOB SOB
GOTOH LIQUOR

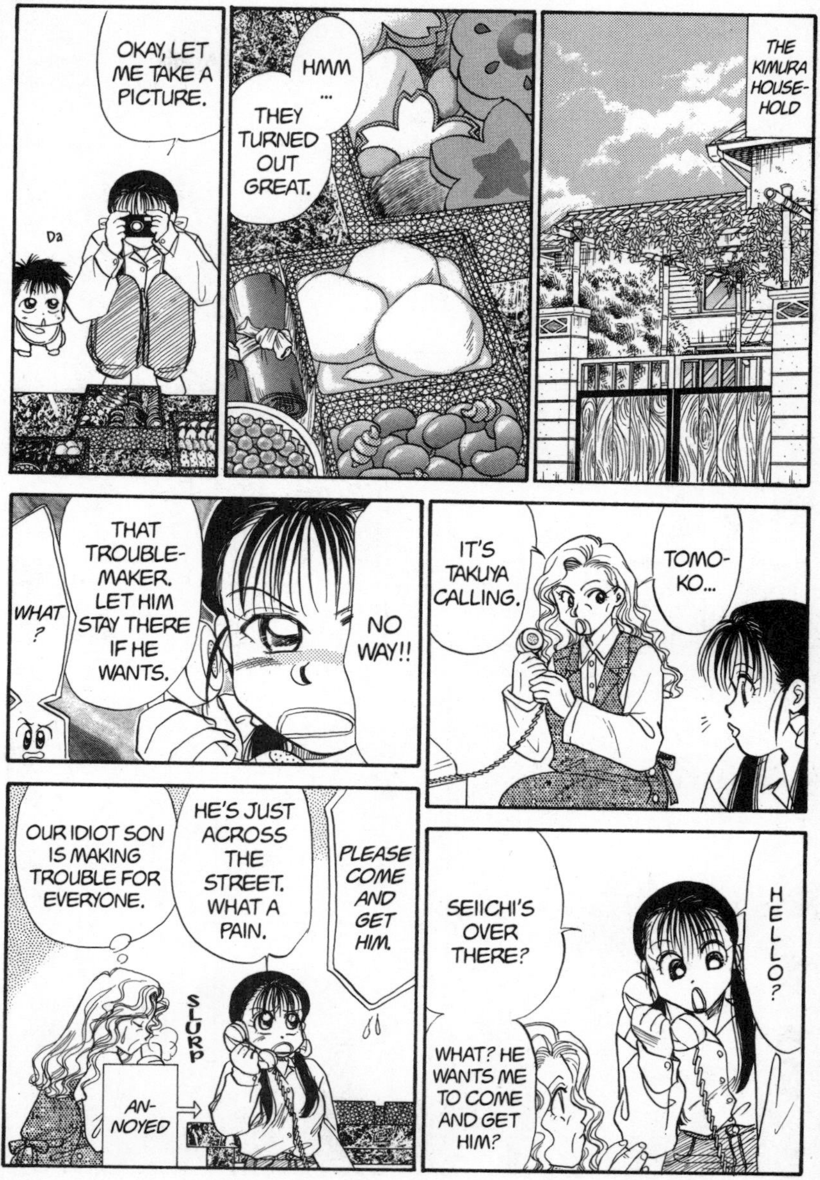
THE KIMURA HOUSEHOLD
HMM ...
THEY TURNED OUT GREAT.
OKAY, LET ME TAKE A PICTURE.
Da
TOMO-KO...
IT'S TAKUYA CALLING.
NO WAY!!
THAT TROUBLE-MAKER. LET HIM STAY THERE IF HE WANTS.
WHAT ?
HELLO?
SEIICHI'S OVER THERE?
WHAT? HE WANTS ME TO COME AND GET HIM?
PLEASE COME AND GET HIM.
HE'S JUST ACROSS THE STREET. WHAT A PAIN.
OUR IDIOT SON IS MAKING TROUBLE FOR EVERYONE.
SLURP
AN-NOYED

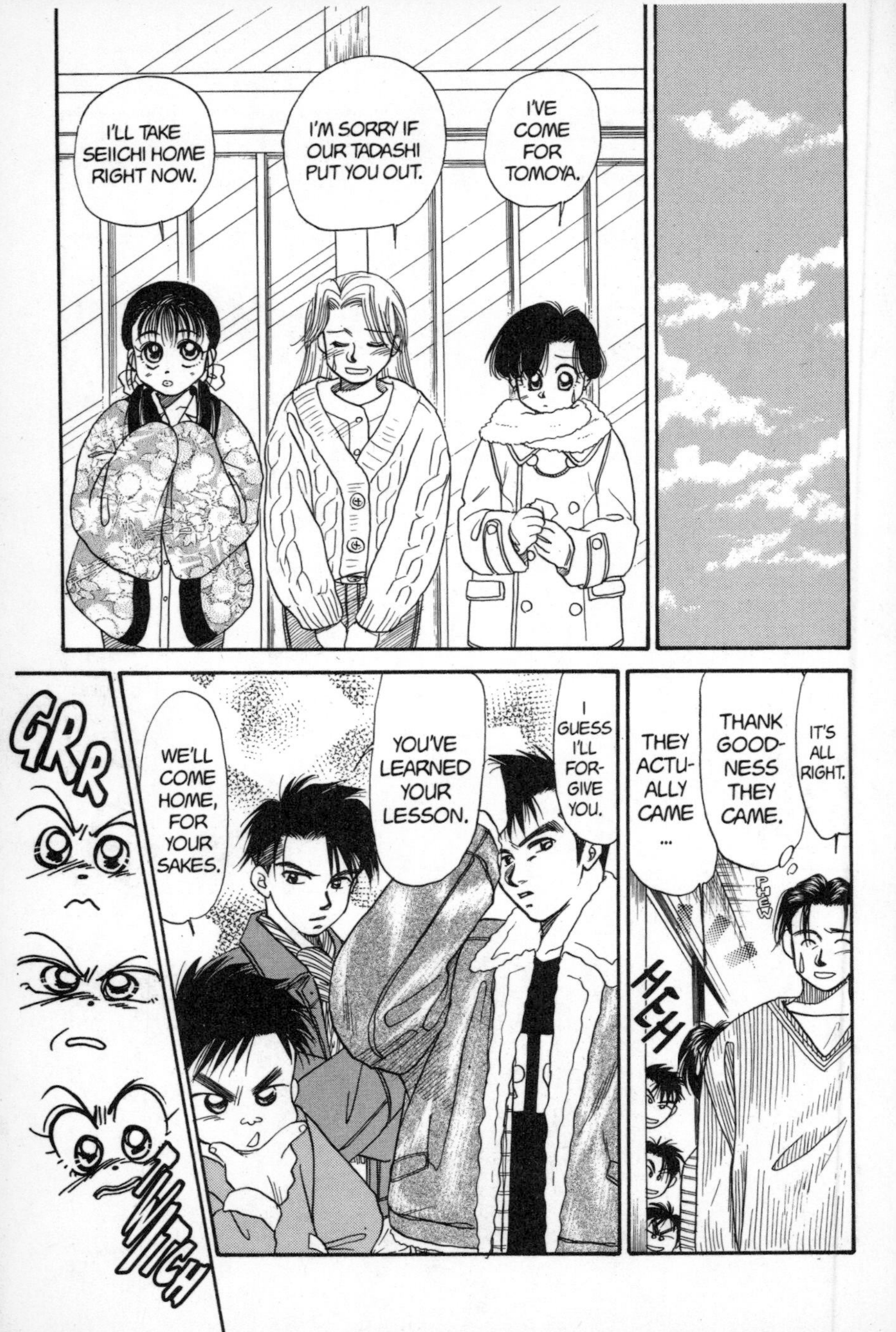
I'VE COME FOR TOMOYA.
I'M SORRY IF OUR TADASHI PUT YOU OUT.
I'LL TAKE SEIICHI HOME RIGHT NOW.
IT'S ALL RIGHT.
THANK GOOD-NESS THEY CAME.
THEY ACTU-ALLY CAME ...
PHEW
HEH
I GUESS I'LL FOR-GIVE YOU.
YOU'VE LEARNED YOUR LESSON.
WE'LL COME HOME, FOR YOUR SAKES.
GRR
TWITCH

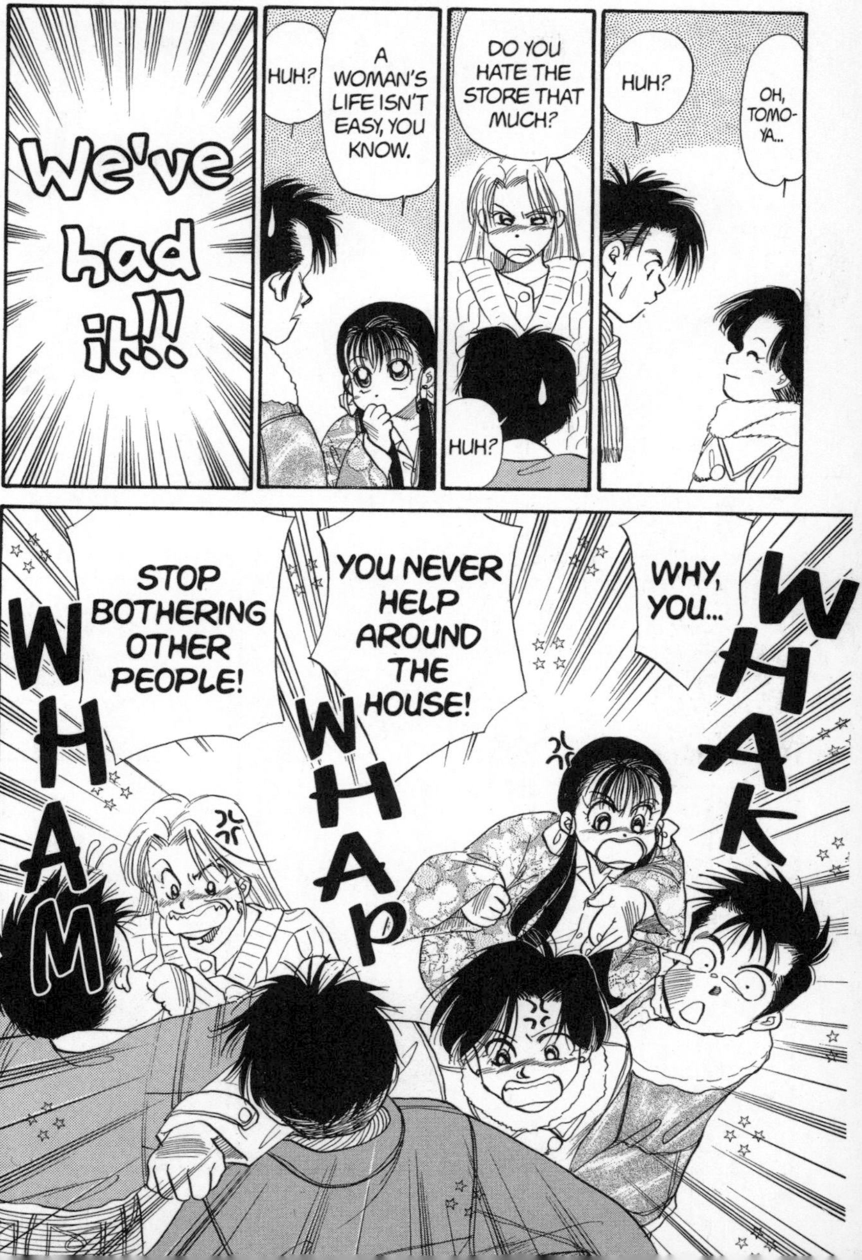
OH, TOMO-YA...
HUH?
DO YOU HATE THE STORE THAT MUCH?
HUH?
A WOMAN'S LIFE ISN'T EASY, YOU KNOW.
HUH?
We've had it!!
WHY, YOU...
WHAK
YOU NEVER HELP AROUND THE HOUSE!
WHAP
STOP BOTHERING OTHER PEOPLE!
WHAM

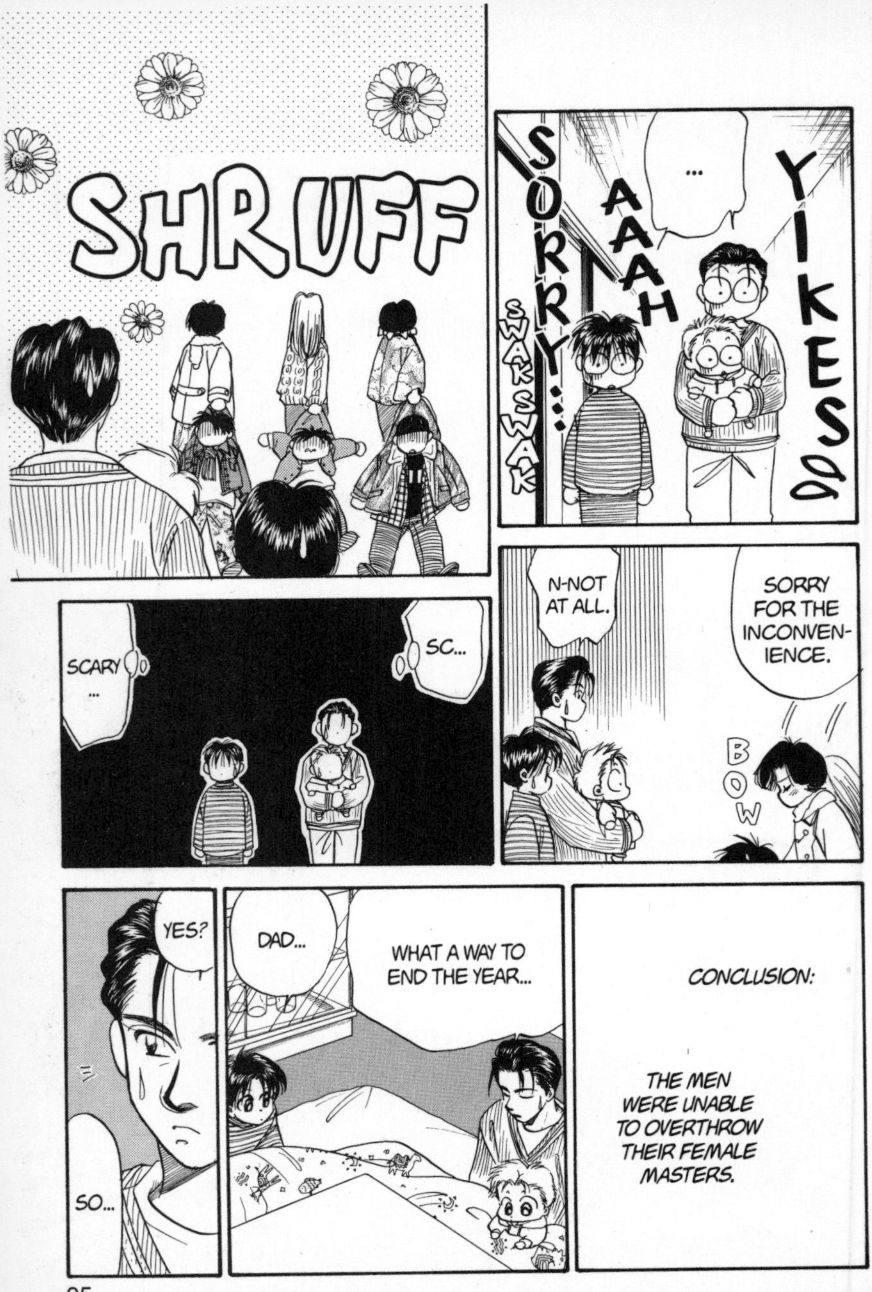
YIKES
...
AAAAH
SORRY...
SWAKSWAK
SHRUFF
SORRY FOR THE INCONVENIENCE.
BOW
N-NOT AT ALL.
SC...
SCARY...
CONCLUSION:
THE MEN WERE UNABLE TO OVERTHROW THEIR FEMALE MASTERS.
WHAT A WAY TO END THE YEAR...
DAD...
YES?
SO...

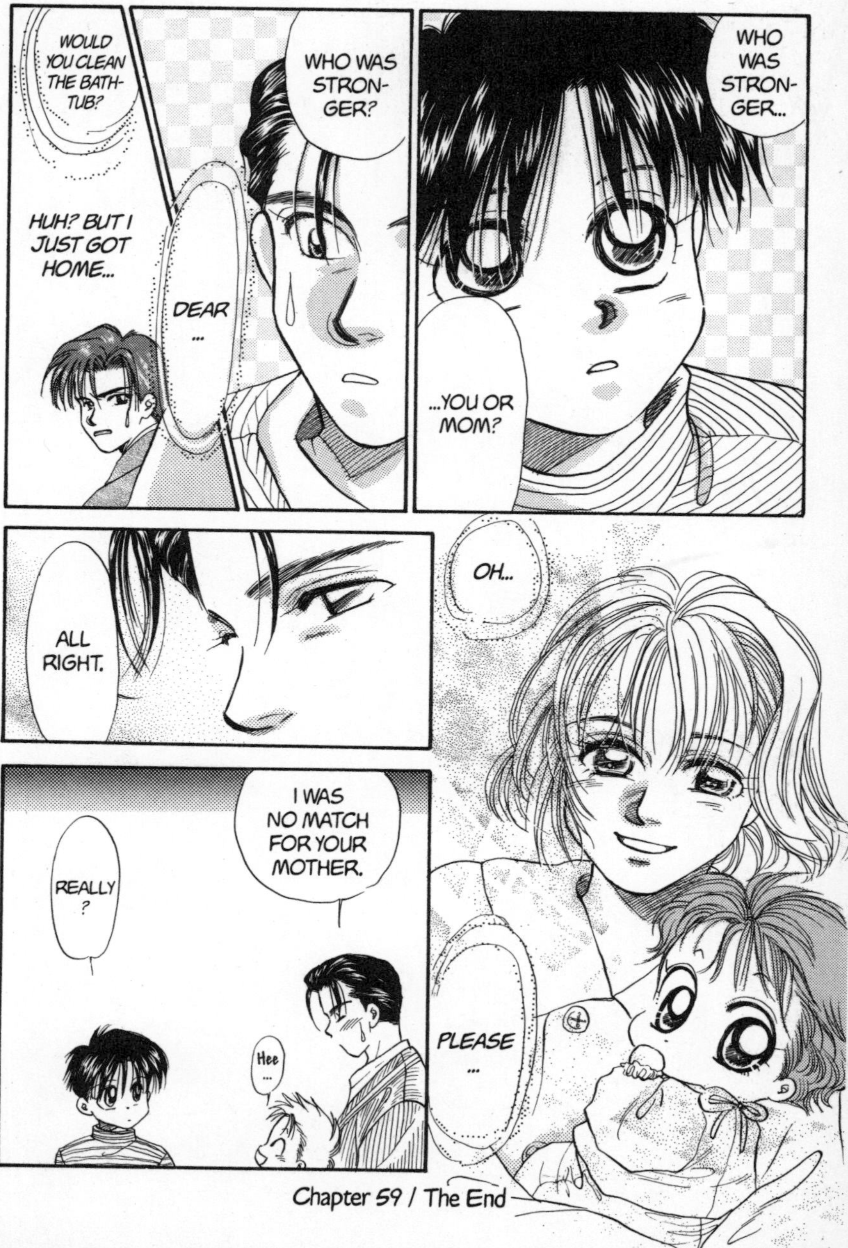
WHO WAS STRON-GER...
...YOU OR MOM?
WHO WAS STRON-GER?
DEAR ...
WOULD YOU CLEAN THE BATH-TUB?
HUH? BUT I JUST GOT HOME...
OH...
PLEASE ...
ALL RIGHT.
I WAS NO MATCH FOR YOUR MOTHER.
REALLY ?
Hee ...

Chapter 59 / The End

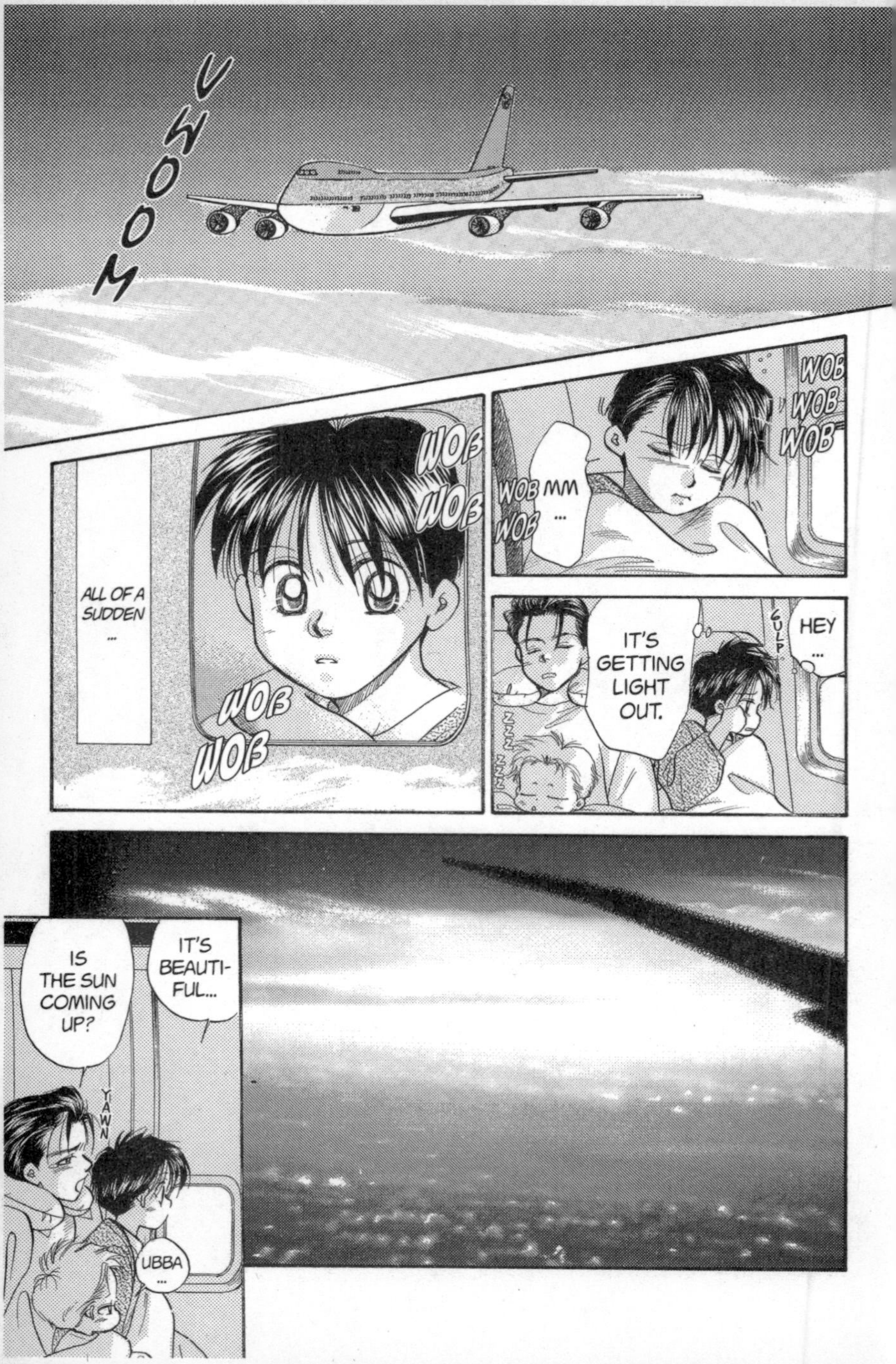
VWOOOM
WOB WOB WOB
MM ...
WOB WOB
HEY ...
GULP
IT'S GETTING LIGHT OUT.
ZZZ ZZZ
WOB WOB
ALL OF A SUDDEN ...
WOB WOB
IT'S BEAUTIFUL...
IS THE SUN COMING UP?
YAWN
UBBA ...

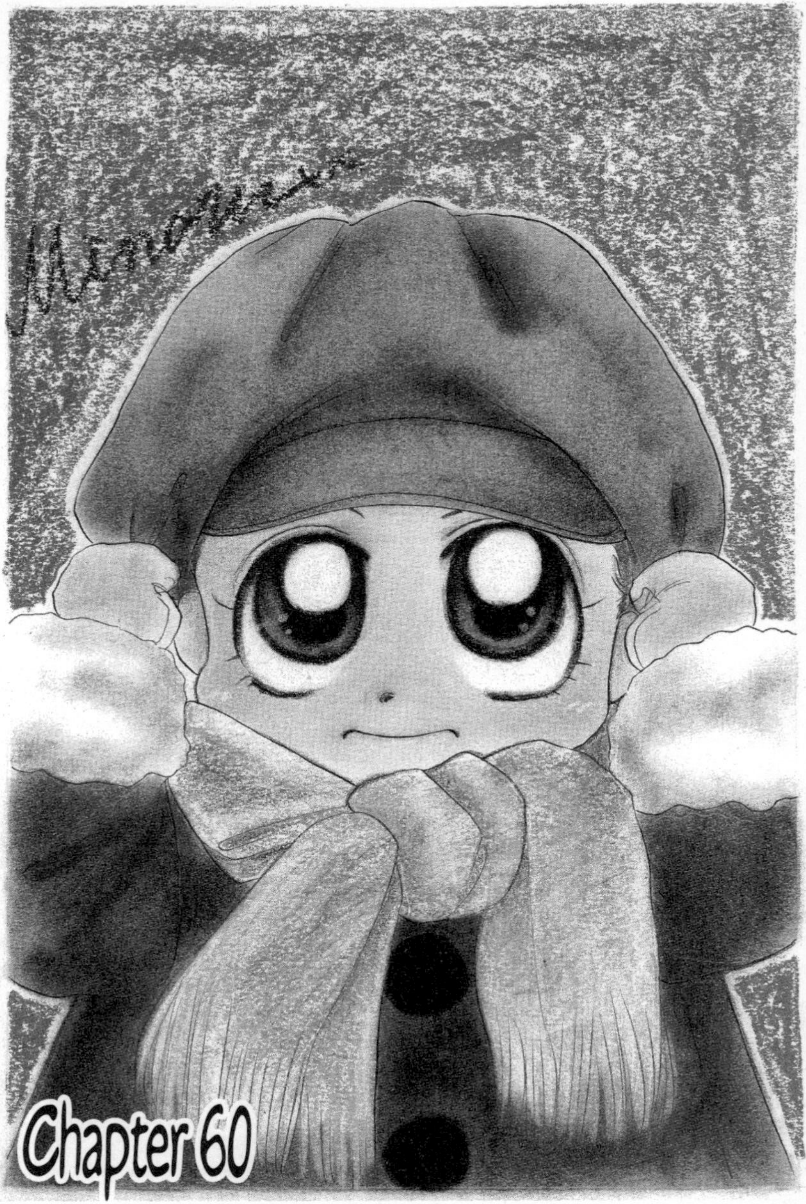
Chapter 60

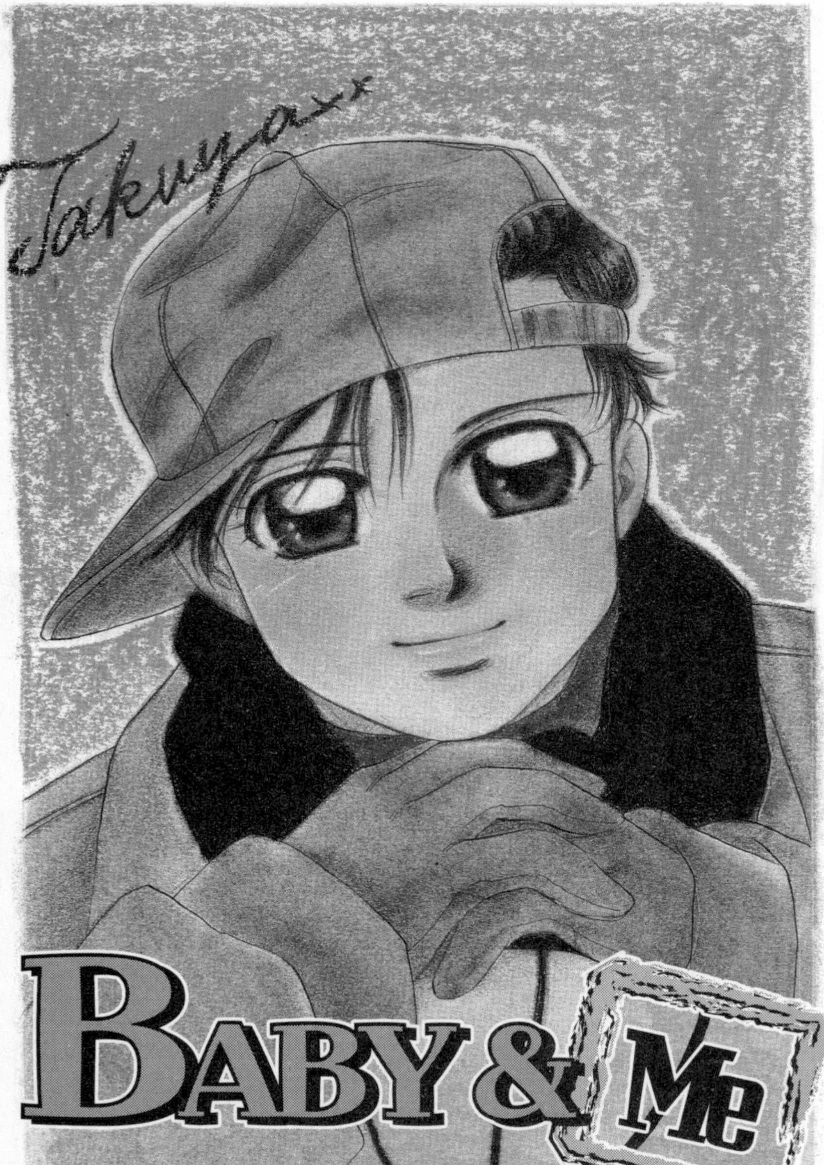
Takuya
BABY & Me

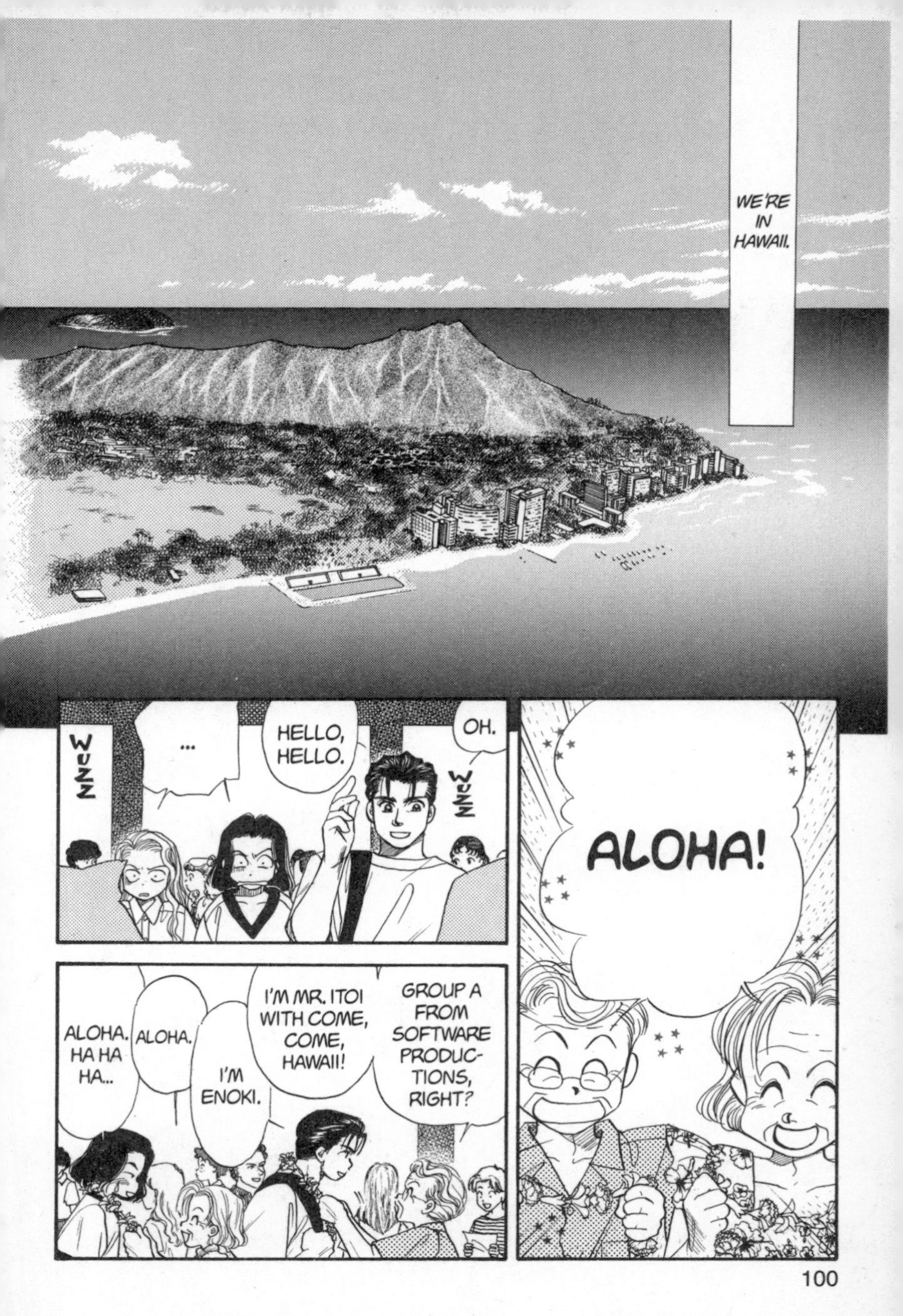
WE'RE IN HAWAII.
ALOHA!
OH.
WUZZ
HELLO, HELLO.
...
WUZZ
GROUP A FROM SOFTWARE PRODUC-TIONS, RIGHT?
I'M MR. ITOI WITH COME, COME, HAWAII!
I'M ENOKI.
ALOHA.
ALOHA. HA HA HA...

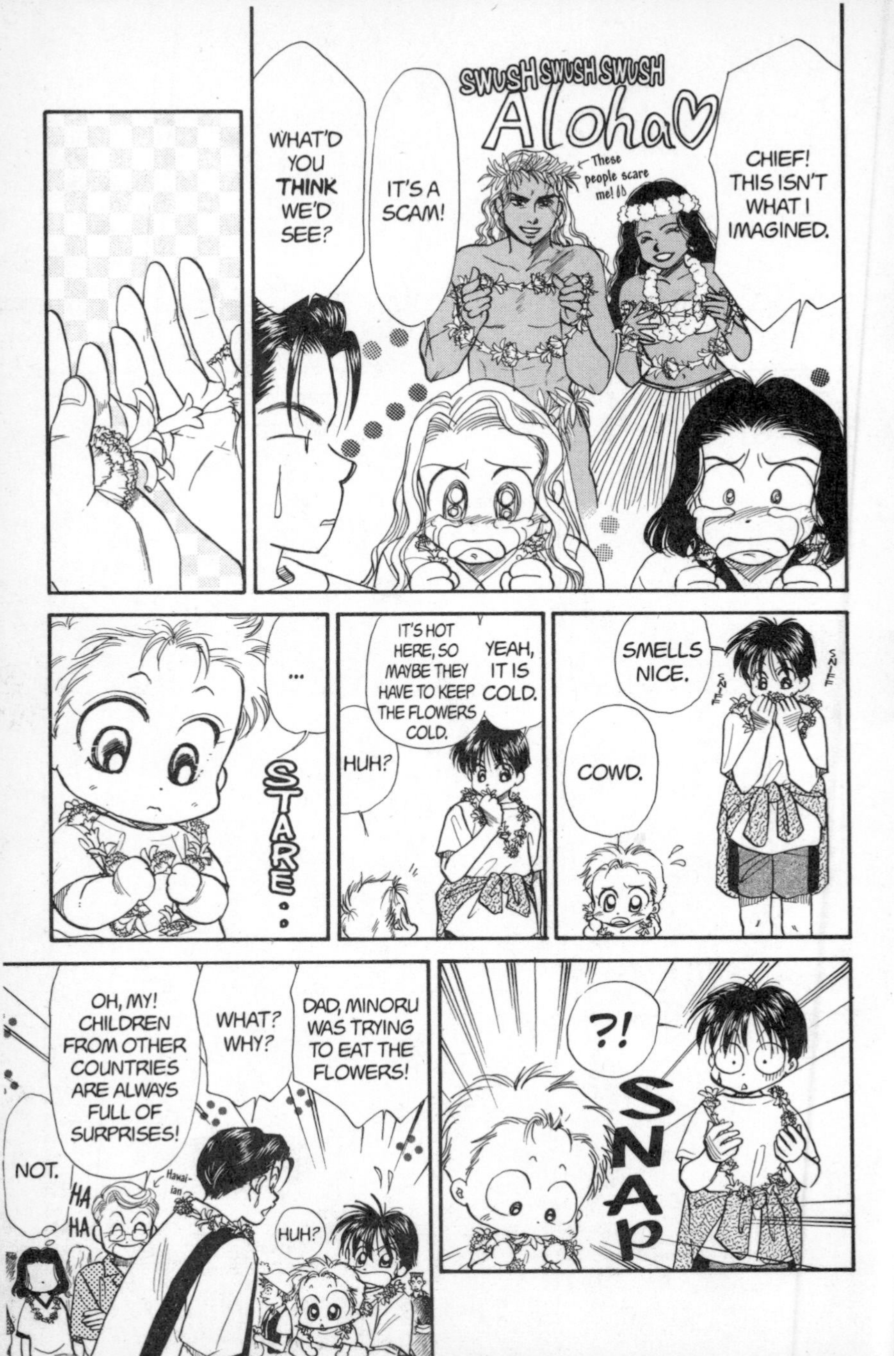
SWUSH SWUSH SWUSH
Aloha♡
These people scare me!
CHIEF! THIS ISN'T WHAT I IMAGINED.
IT'S A SCAM!
WHAT'D YOU THINK WE'D SEE?
SMELLS NICE.
SNIFF
SNIFF
COWD.
YEAH, IT IS COLD.
IT'S HOT HERE, SO MAYBE THEY HAVE TO KEEP THE FLOWERS COLD.
HUH?
...
STARE..
?!
SNAP
DAD, MINORU WAS TRYING TO EAT THE FLOWERS!
WHAT? WHY?
OH, MY! CHILDREN FROM OTHER COUNTRIES ARE ALWAYS FULL OF SURPRISES!
Hawaiian
HA HA
NOT.
HUH?

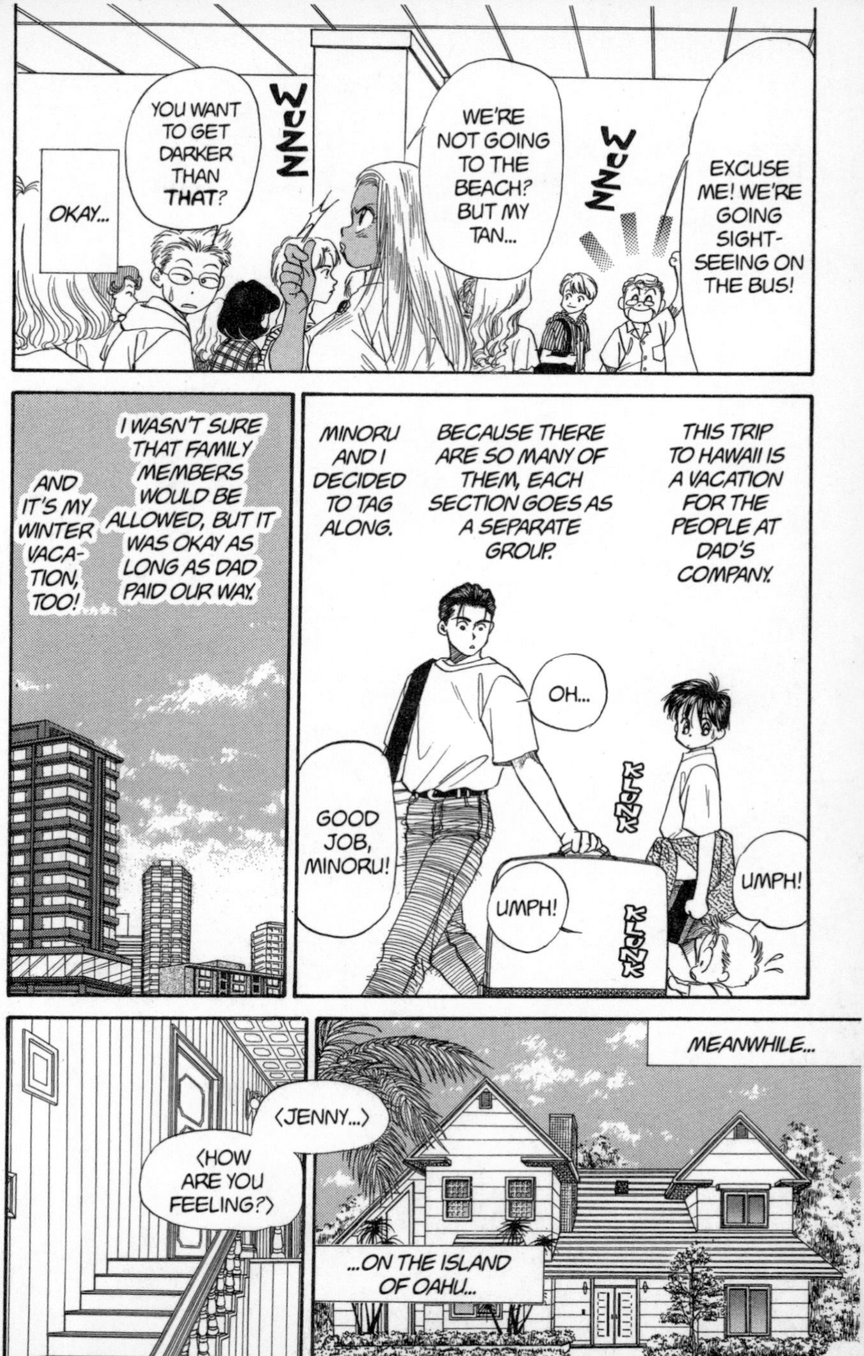
EXCUSE ME! WE'RE GOING SIGHT-SEEING ON THE BUS!
WUZZ
WE'RE NOT GOING TO THE BEACH? BUT MY TAN...
WUZZ
YOU WANT TO GET DARKER THAN THAT?
OKAY...
THIS TRIP TO HAWAII IS A VACATION FOR THE PEOPLE AT DAD'S COMPANY.
BECAUSE THERE ARE SO MANY OF THEM, EACH SECTION GOES AS A SEPARATE GROUP.
MINORU AND I DECIDED TO TAG ALONG.
OH...
KLUNK
UMPH!
KLUNK
UMPH!
GOOD JOB, MINORU!
I WASN'T SURE THAT FAMILY MEMBERS WOULD BE ALLOWED, BUT IT WAS OKAY AS LONG AS DAD PAID OUR WAY.
AND IT'S MY WINTER VACA-TION, TOO!
MEANWHILE...
...ON THE ISLAND OF OAHU...
⟨JENNY...⟩
⟨HOW ARE YOU FEELING?⟩

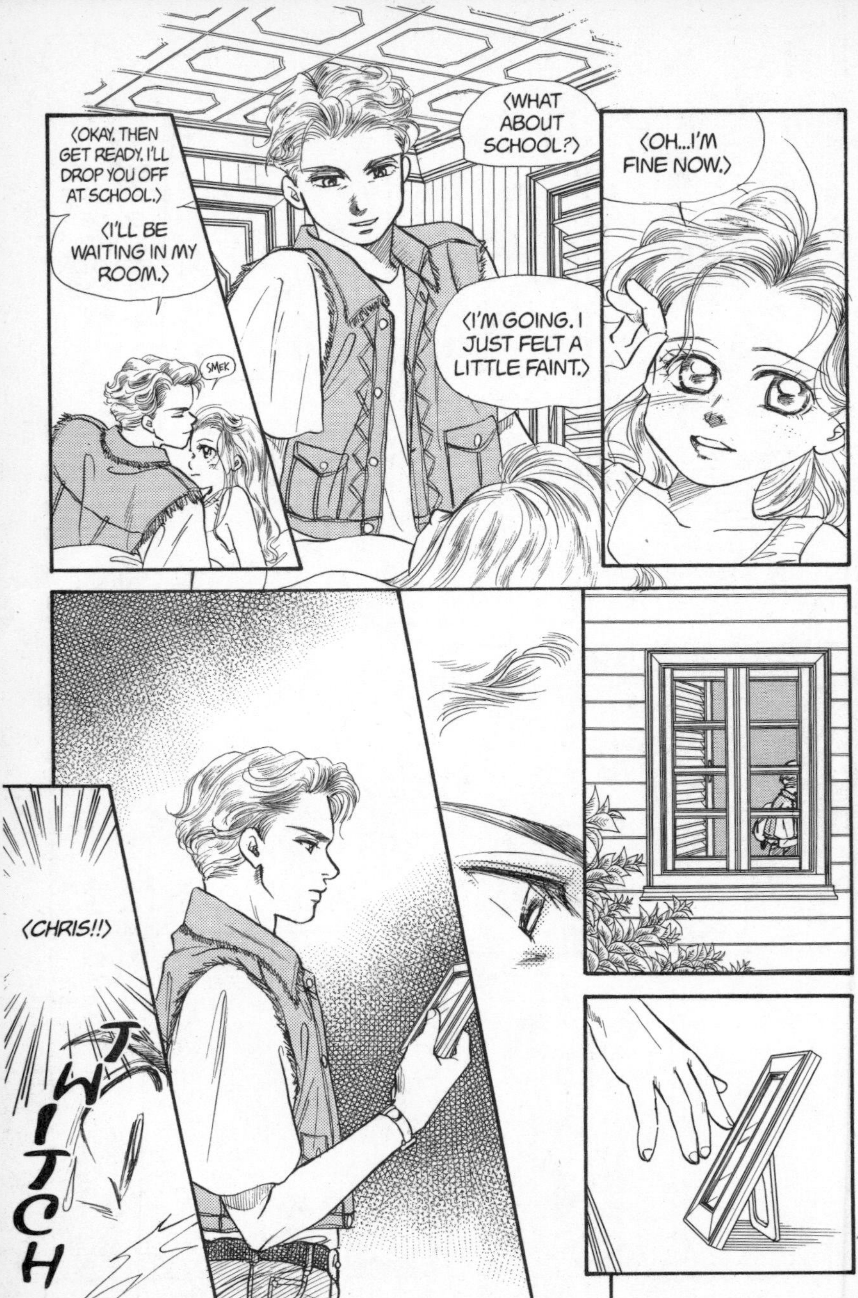

⟨OH...I'M FINE NOW.⟩
⟨WHAT ABOUT SCHOOL?⟩
⟨I'M GOING. I JUST FELT A LITTLE FAINT.⟩
⟨OKAY. THEN GET READY. I'LL DROP YOU OFF AT SCHOOL.⟩
⟨I'LL BE WAITING IN MY ROOM.⟩
SMEK
⟨CHRIS!!⟩
TWITCH

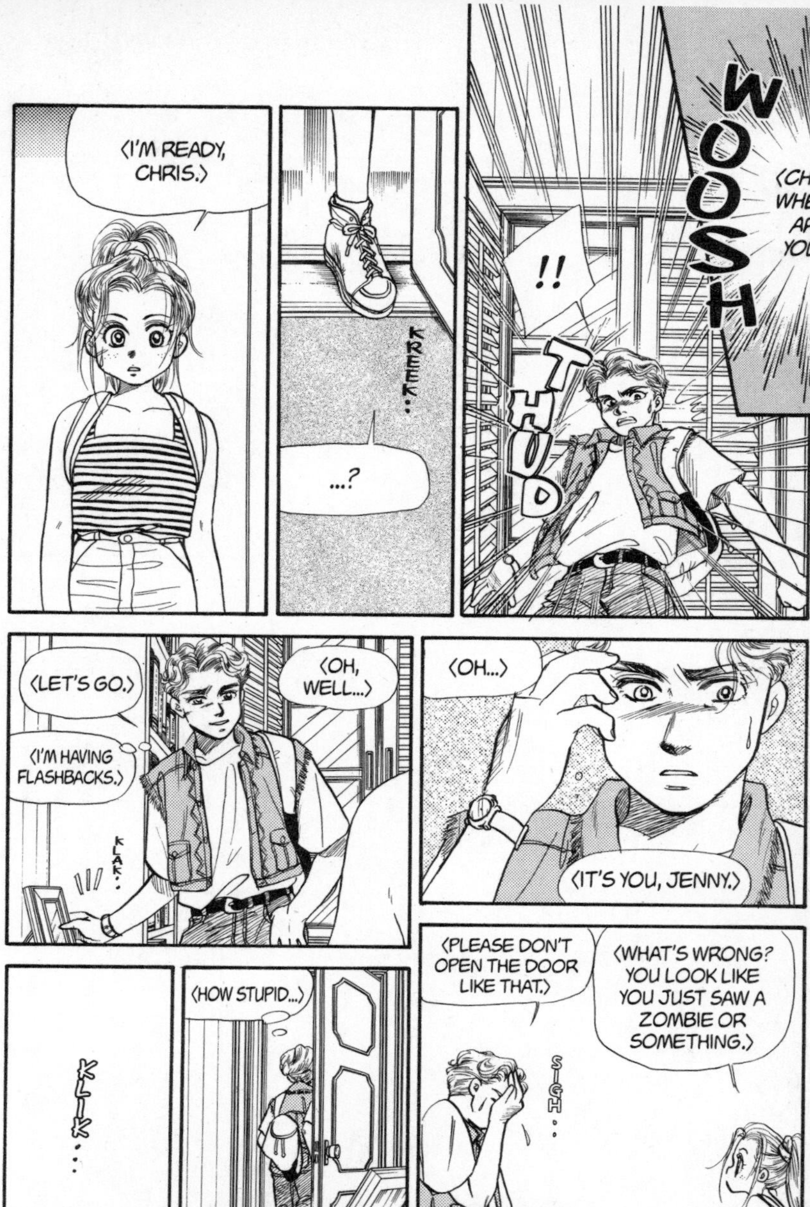
WOOSH
〈CHRIS, WHERE ARE YOU?〉
!!
THUD
KREEK..
...?
〈I'M READY, CHRIS.〉
〈OH...〉
〈IT'S YOU, JENNY.〉
〈OH, WELL...〉
〈LET'S GO.〉
〈I'M HAVING FLASHBACKS.〉
KLAK..
〈WHAT'S WRONG? YOU LOOK LIKE YOU JUST SAW A ZOMBIE OR SOMETHING.〉
〈PLEASE DON'T OPEN THE DOOR LIKE THAT.〉
SIGH..
〈HOW STUPID...〉
KLIK...

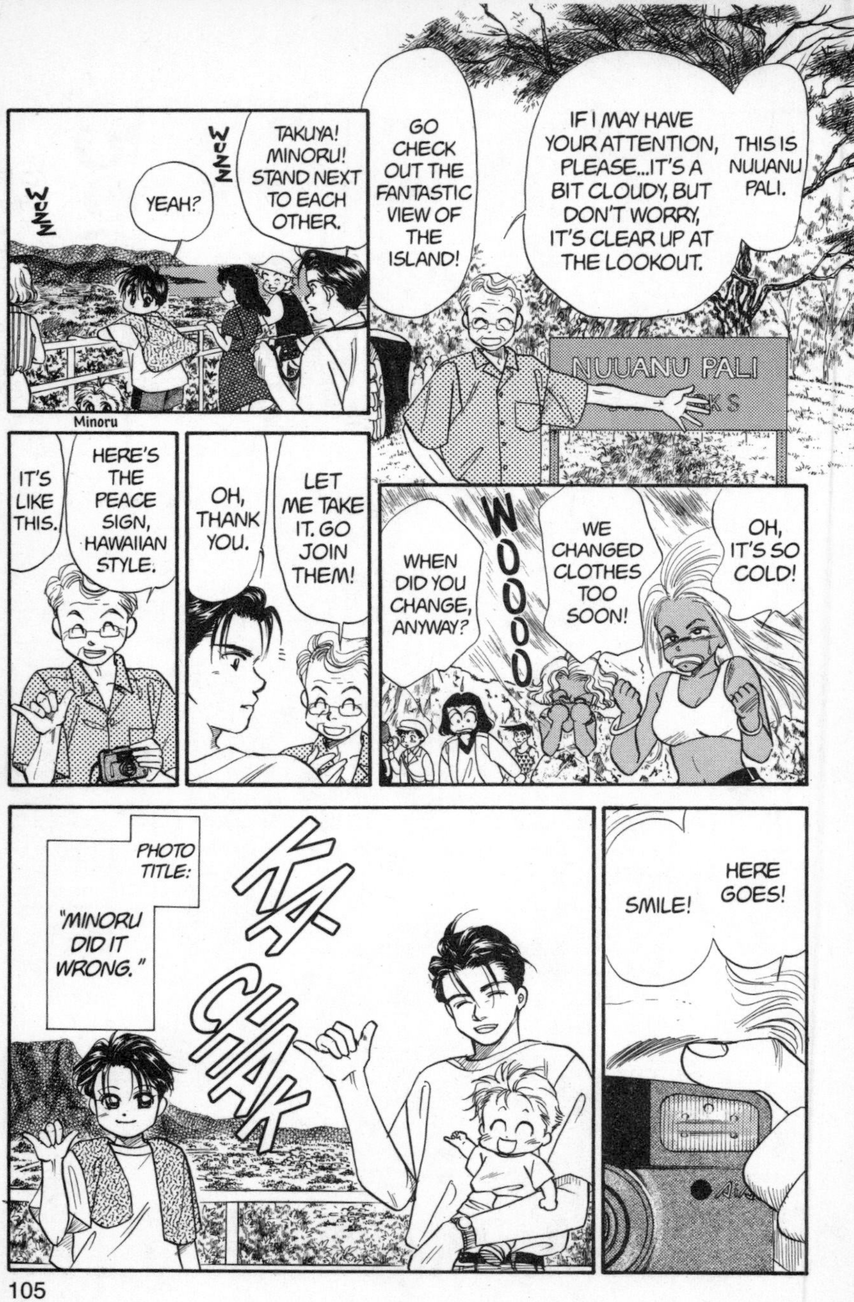
THIS IS NUUANU PALI.
IF I MAY HAVE YOUR ATTENTION, PLEASE...IT'S A BIT CLOUDY, BUT DON'T WORRY, IT'S CLEAR UP AT THE LOOKOUT.
GO CHECK OUT THE FANTASTIC VIEW OF THE ISLAND!
NUUANU PALI
TAKUYA! MINORU! STAND NEXT TO EACH OTHER.
WUZZ
YEAH?
WUZZ
Minoru
OH, IT'S SO COLD!
WE CHANGED CLOTHES TOO SOON!
WOOOOO
WHEN DID YOU CHANGE, ANYWAY?
LET ME TAKE IT. GO JOIN THEM!
OH, THANK YOU.
HERE'S THE PEACE SIGN, HAWAIIAN STYLE.
IT'S LIKE THIS.
HERE GOES!
SMILE!
KA-CHAK
PHOTO TITLE: "MINORU DID IT WRONG."

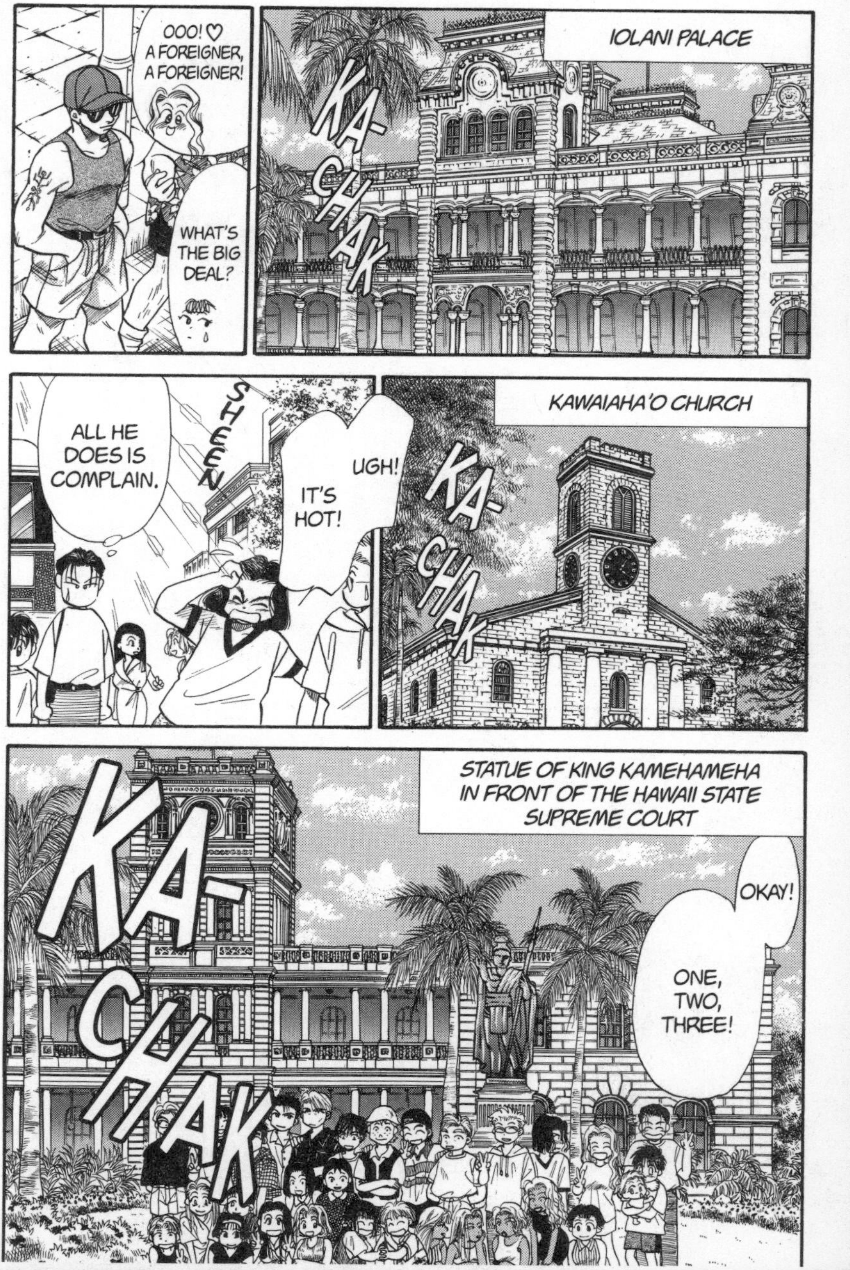
IOLANI PALACE
KA-CHAK
OOO! ♡ A FOREIGNER, A FOREIGNER!
WHAT'S THE BIG DEAL?
KAWAIAHA'O CHURCH
KA-CHAK
UGH!
IT'S HOT!
SHEEN
ALL HE DOES IS COMPLAIN.
STATUE OF KING KAMEHAMEHA IN FRONT OF THE HAWAII STATE SUPREME COURT
OKAY!
ONE, TWO, THREE!
KA-CHAK

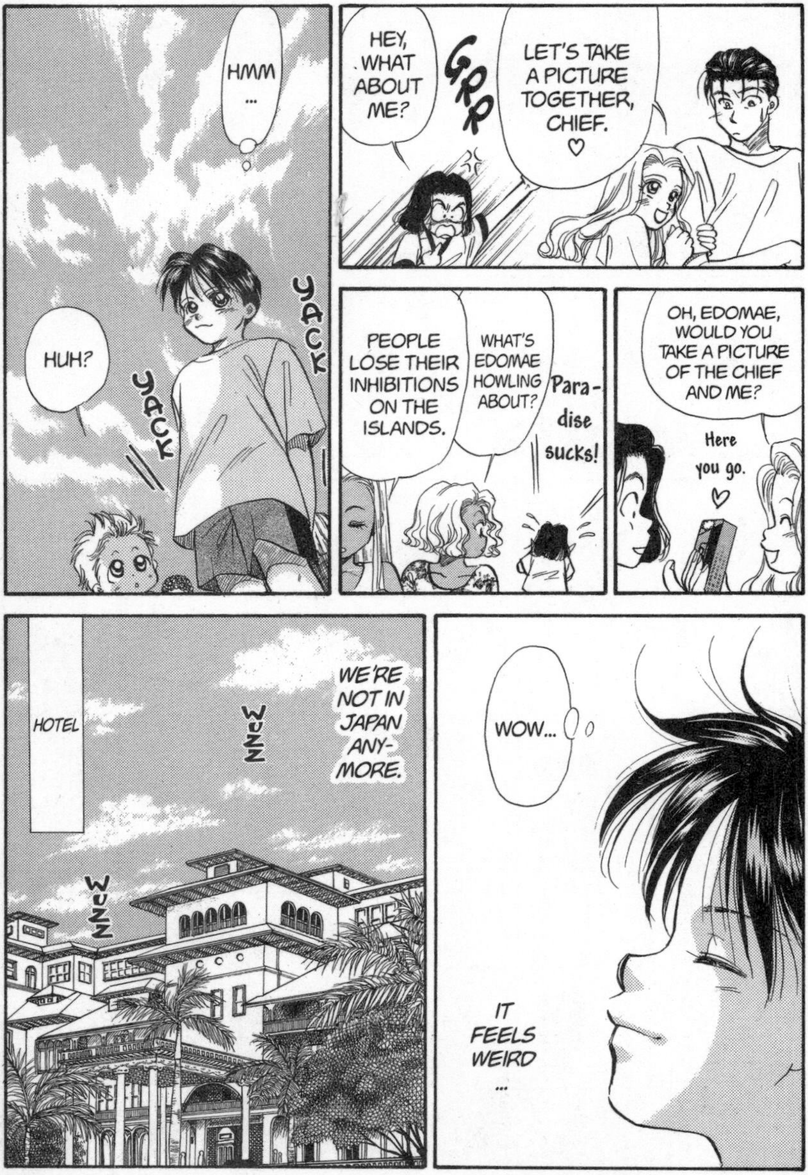
LET'S TAKE A PICTURE TOGETHER, CHIEF. ♡
GRR
HEY, WHAT ABOUT ME?
OH, EDOMAE, WOULD YOU TAKE A PICTURE OF THE CHIEF AND ME?
Here you go. ♡
Paradise sucks!
WHAT'S EDOMAE HOWLING ABOUT?
PEOPLE LOSE THEIR INHIBITIONS ON THE ISLANDS.
YACK
YACK
HMM ...
HUH?
WOW...
IT FEELS WEIRD ...
WE'RE NOT IN JAPAN ANYMORE.
WUZZ
WUZZ
HOTEL

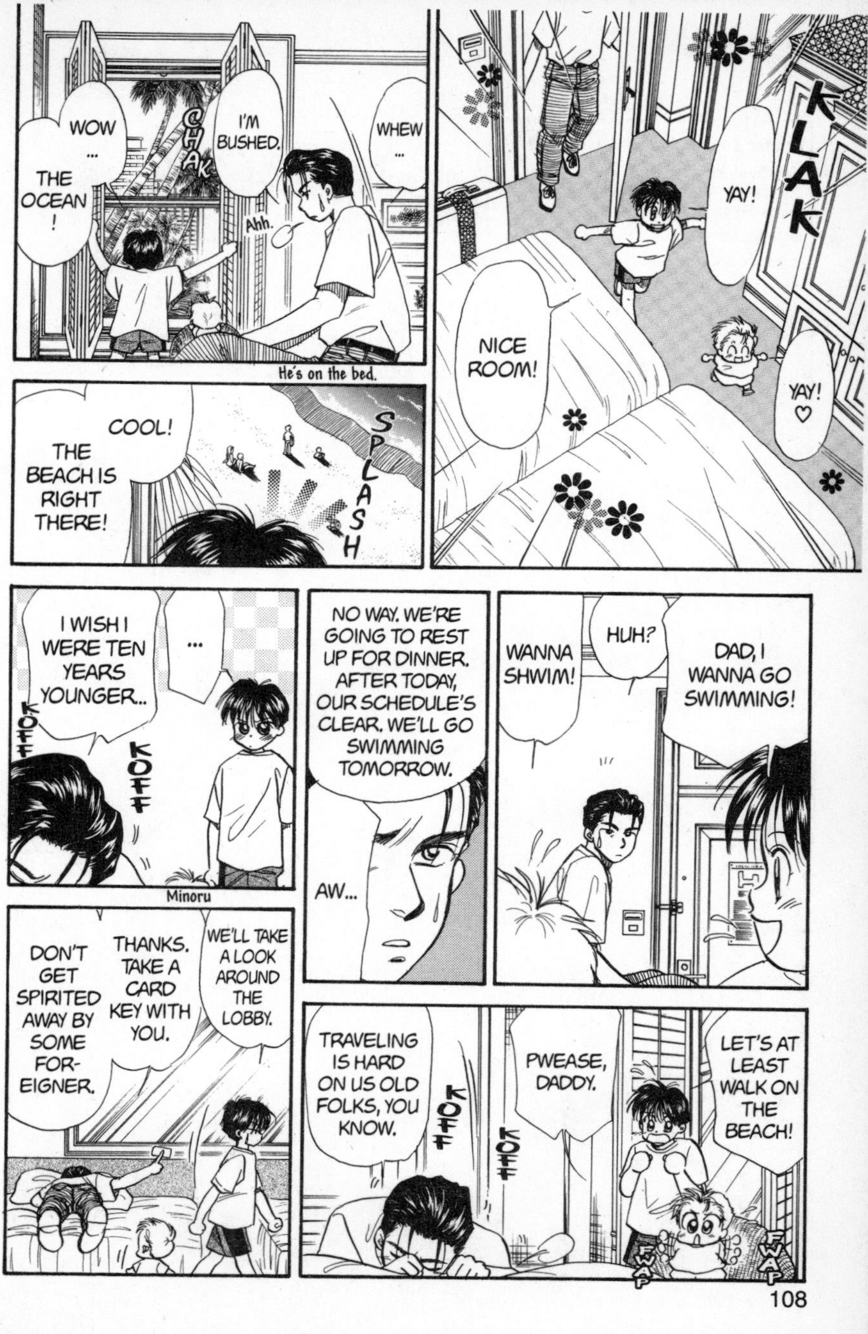
KLAK
YAY!
YAY! ♡
NICE ROOM!
WHEW...
Ahh.
I'M BUSHED.
CHAK
WOW... THE OCEAN!
He's on the bed.
SPLASH
COOL! THE BEACH IS RIGHT THERE!
DAD, I WANNA GO SWIMMING!
HUH?
WANNA SHWIM!
NO WAY. WE'RE GOING TO REST UP FOR DINNER. AFTER TODAY, OUR SCHEDULE'S CLEAR. WE'LL GO SWIMMING TOMORROW.
AW...
...
I WISH I WERE TEN YEARS YOUNGER...
KOFF
KOFF
Minoru
LET'S AT LEAST WALK ON THE BEACH!
FWAP
FWAP
PWEASE, DADDY.
KOFF
TRAVELING IS HARD ON US OLD FOLKS, YOU KNOW.
KOFF
WE'LL TAKE A LOOK AROUND THE LOBBY.
THANKS. TAKE A CARD KEY WITH YOU.
DON'T GET SPIRITED AWAY BY SOME FOR-EIGNER.

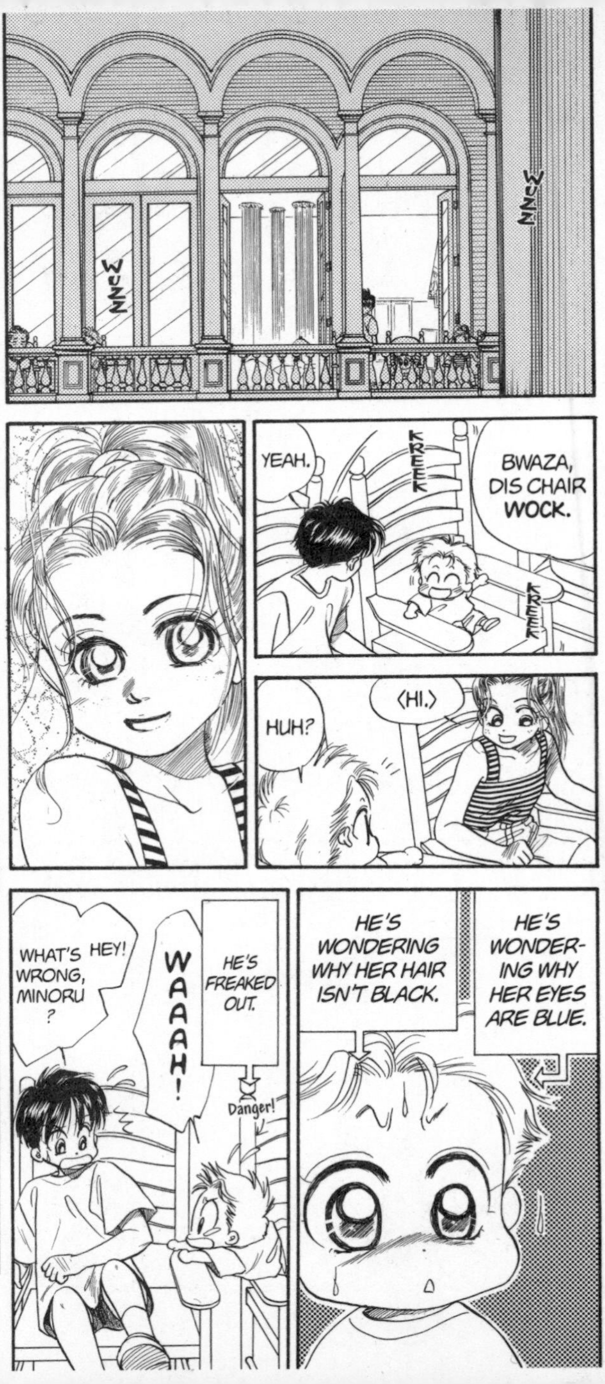
WUZZ
BWAZA, DIS CHAIR WOCK.
KREEK
YEAH.
KREEK
<HI.>
HUH?
HE'S WONDERING WHY HER EYES ARE BLUE.
HE'S WONDERING WHY HER HAIR ISN'T BLACK.
HE'S FREAKED OUT.
Danger!
WAAAAH!
HEY!
WHAT'S WRONG, MINORU?

Author's Note: Part 4
(Continued from Part 3)

Some people don't go to bars because they think cocktails are for snobs. Well, I have some advice for those people. (I'm talking to the grownups, of course.) If you've never had a cocktail before, and if you're a light drinker, go to a bar and order a "Kahlúa and cream." It has a smooth, sweet taste. It looks and tastes a lot like coffee with milk.

After that, try a rum- or liqueur-based cocktail from the menu. They're very nice. Cocktails made with gin, vodka, and tequila are too strong for beginners (in my opinion).

I especially recommend frozen drinks. They're like shaved ice, nice and cold. I really like frozen daiquiris, especially peach and strawberry. They're good and sweet.

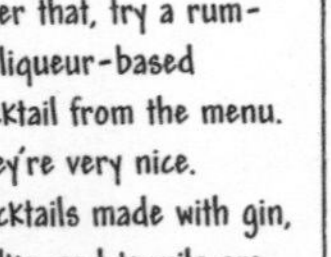
You can drink through this or scoop with it.

After that, take a look at the menu and order something that sounds interesting. It's so much fun when you find out what you ordered.

If the edge of your glass is covered with salt, you're supposed to lick off a little salt with each sip. Don't wipe the salt off.

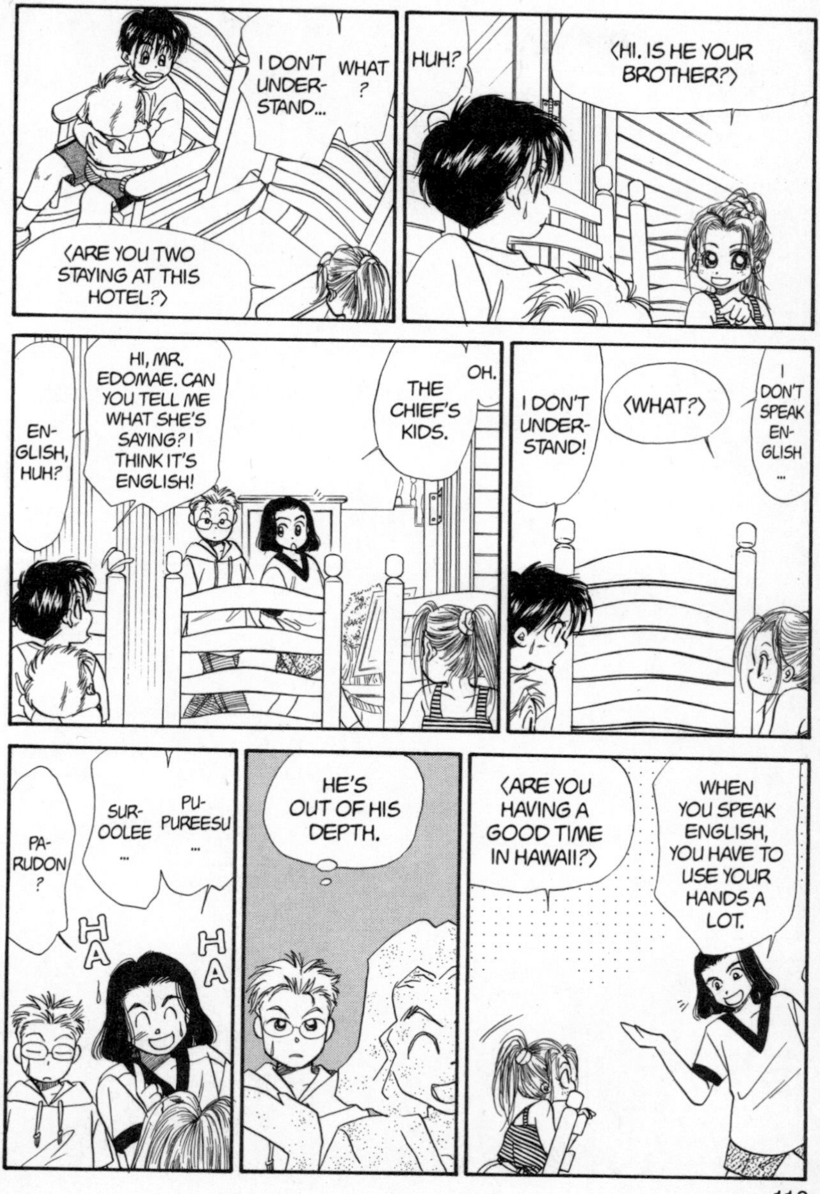
〈HI. IS HE YOUR BROTHER?〉
HUH?
WHAT?
I DON'T UNDERSTAND...
〈ARE YOU TWO STAYING AT THIS HOTEL?〉
I DON'T SPEAK ENGLISH...
〈WHAT?〉
I DON'T UNDERSTAND!
OH.
THE CHIEF'S KIDS.
HI, MR. EDOMAE. CAN YOU TELL ME WHAT SHE'S SAYING? I THINK IT'S ENGLISH!
ENGLISH, HUH?
WHEN YOU SPEAK ENGLISH, YOU HAVE TO USE YOUR HANDS A LOT.
〈ARE YOU HAVING A GOOD TIME IN HAWAII?〉
HE'S OUT OF HIS DEPTH.
PUPUREESU...
SUROOLEE...
PARUDON?
HA
HA

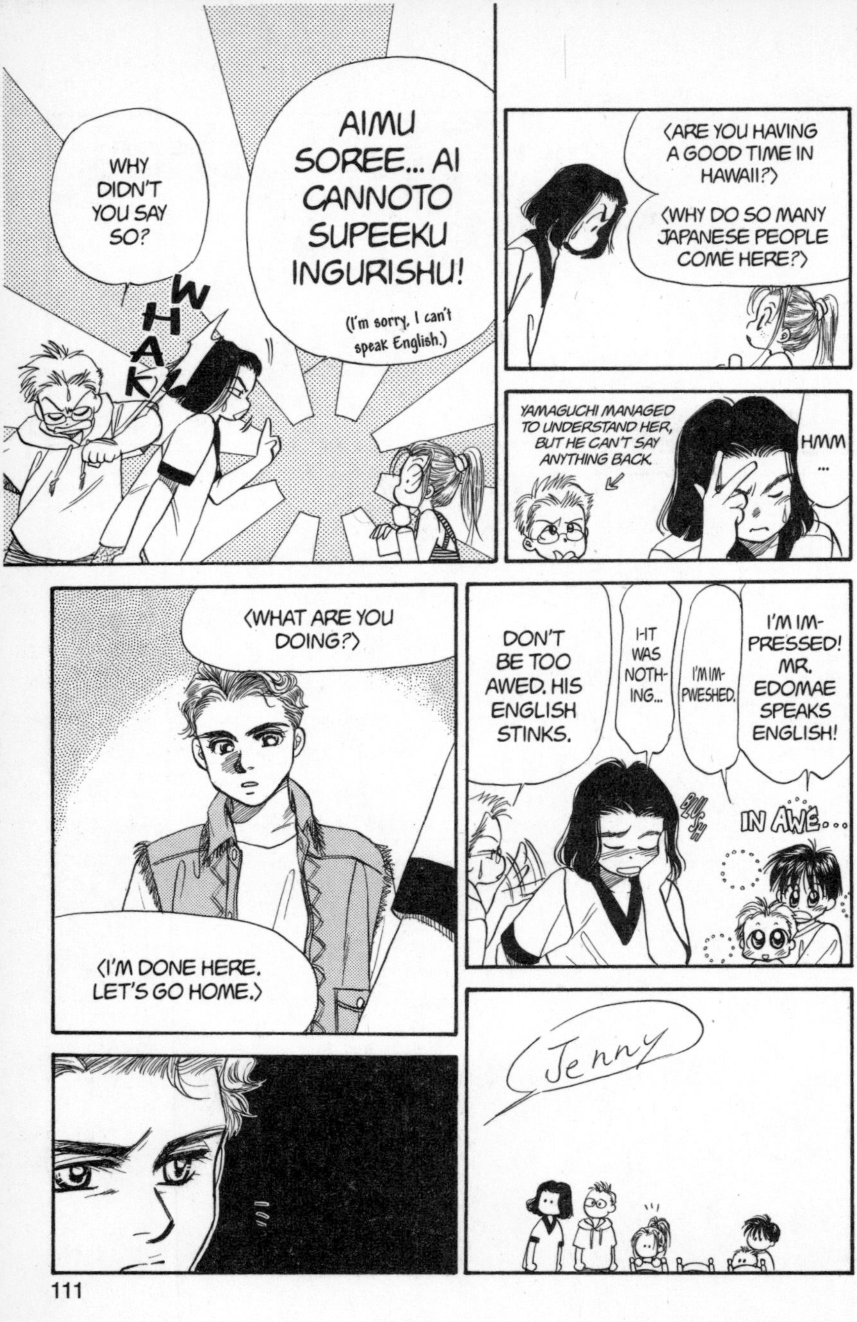
〈ARE YOU HAVING A GOOD TIME IN HAWAII?〉
〈WHY DO SO MANY JAPANESE PEOPLE COME HERE?〉
YAMAGUCHI MANAGED TO UNDERSTAND HER, BUT HE CAN'T SAY ANYTHING BACK.
HMM ...
AIMU SOREE... AI CANNOTO SUPEEKU INGURISHU!
(I'm sorry, I can't speak English.)
WHY DIDN'T YOU SAY SO?
WHAK
I'M IM-PRESSED! MR. EDOMAE SPEAKS ENGLISH!
I'M IM-PWESHED.
I-IT WAS NOTH-ING...
DON'T BE TOO AWED. HIS ENGLISH STINKS.
BLUSH
IN AWE...
〈WHAT ARE YOU DOING?〉
〈I'M DONE HERE. LET'S GO HOME.〉
Jenny

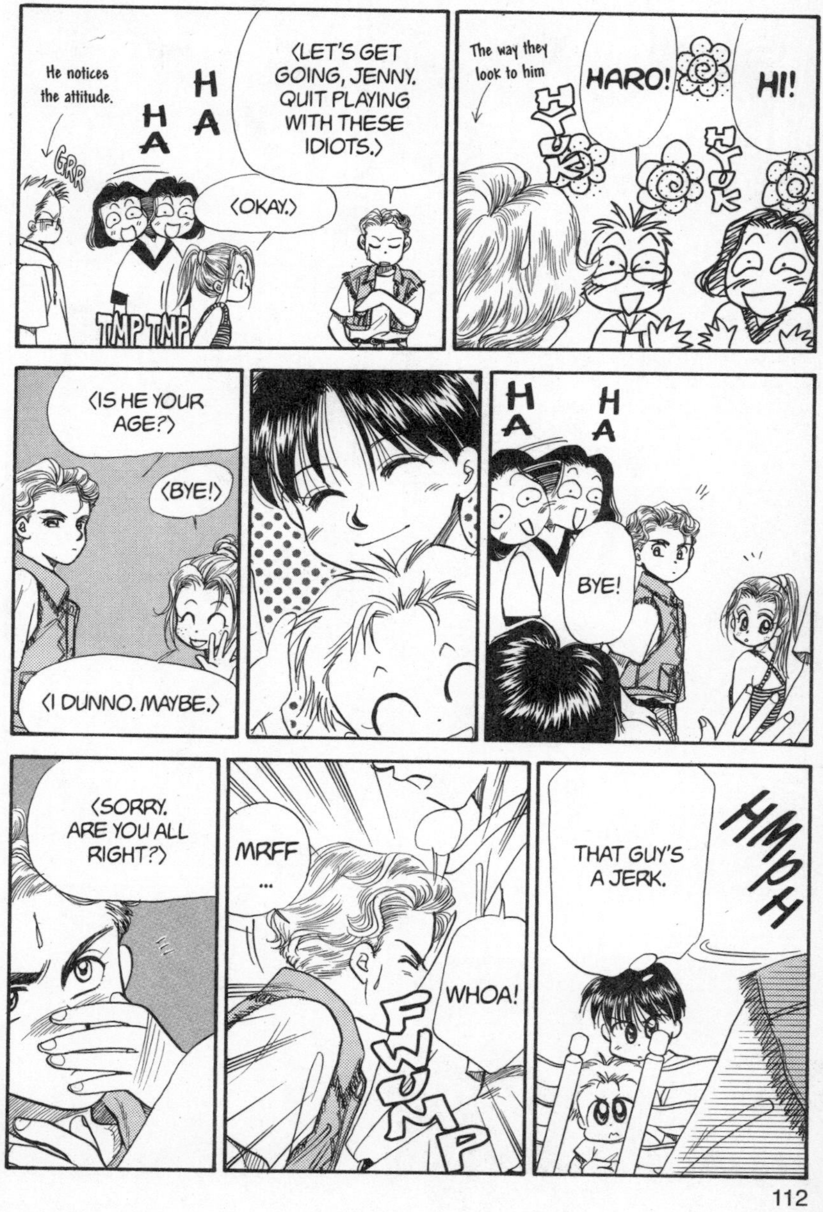
HI!
HARO!
HYUK HYUK
HYUK
The way they look to him
⟨LET'S GET GOING, JENNY. QUIT PLAYING WITH THESE IDIOTS.⟩
H A H A
⟨OKAY.⟩
He notices the attitude.
GRR
TMP TMP
H A H A
BYE!
⟨IS HE YOUR AGE?⟩
⟨BYE!⟩
⟨I DUNNO. MAYBE.⟩
HMPH
THAT GUY'S A JERK.
MRFF ...
WHOA!
FWUMP
⟨SORRY. ARE YOU ALL RIGHT?⟩

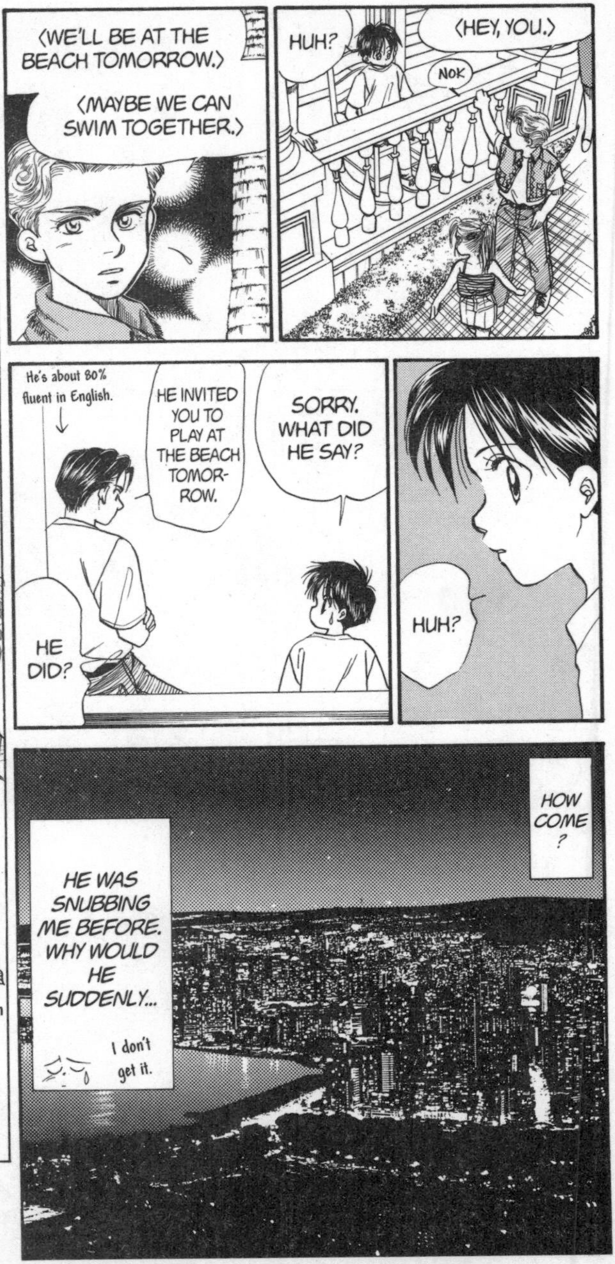
〈HEY, YOU.〉
HUH?
NOK
〈WE'LL BE AT THE BEACH TOMORROW.〉
〈MAYBE WE CAN SWIM TOGETHER.〉
HUH?
SORRY. WHAT DID HE SAY?
HE INVITED YOU TO PLAY AT THE BEACH TOMOR-ROW.
He's about 80% fluent in English.
HE DID?
HOW COME?
HE WAS SNUBBING ME BEFORE. WHY WOULD HE SUDDENLY...
I don't get it.

Author's Note: Part 5

This chapter, which takes place in Hawaii, was a New Year's Special, so I had 50 pages to work with.

My editor said, "Since we have 50 pages, why don't you do a story set somewhere exotic?" It was decided that there would be some foreign characters, too. But even though I had 50 pages, it still wasn't enough for me. I had to delete a lot of scenes. *Sigh...*

Please read this chapter as a Baby and Me extra.

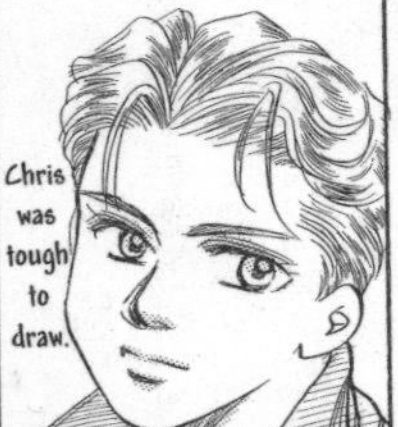
Chris was tough to draw.

Peach boy

=

Momotaro,

the fairy-tale baby who was found in a giant peach.

BOING

I'm not sure what Chris meant by that. Only he knows for sure.

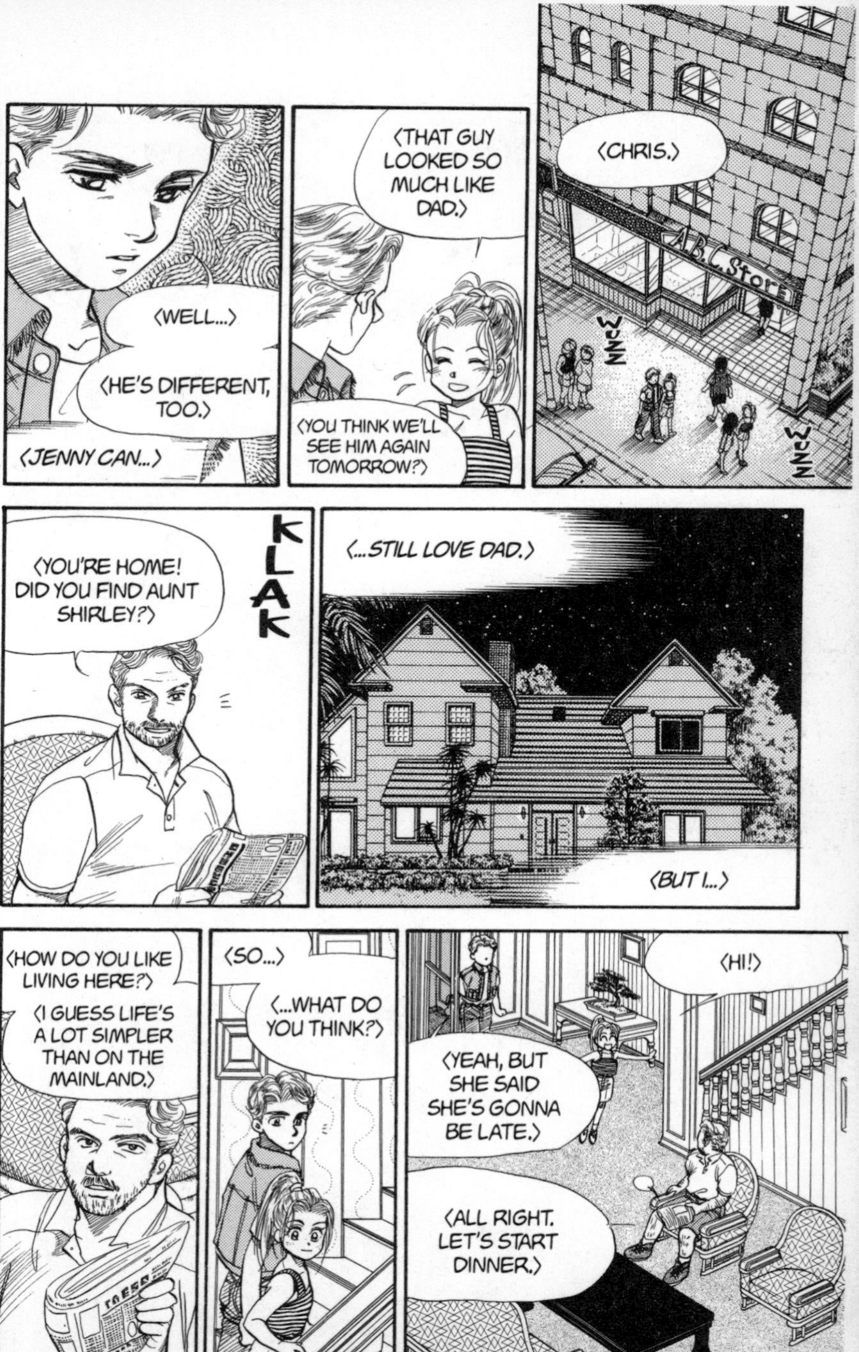
〈CHRIS.〉
WUZN
WUZN
〈THAT GUY LOOKED SO MUCH LIKE DAD.〉
〈YOU THINK WE'LL SEE HIM AGAIN TOMORROW?〉
〈WELL...〉
〈HE'S DIFFERENT, TOO.〉
〈JENNY CAN...〉
〈...STILL LOVE DAD.〉
〈BUT I...〉
KLAK
〈YOU'RE HOME! DID YOU FIND AUNT SHIRLEY?〉
〈HI!〉
〈YEAH, BUT SHE SAID SHE'S GONNA BE LATE.〉
〈ALL RIGHT. LET'S START DINNER.〉
〈SO...〉
〈...WHAT DO YOU THINK?〉
〈HOW DO YOU LIKE LIVING HERE?〉
〈I GUESS LIFE'S A LOT SIMPLER THAN ON THE MAINLAND.〉

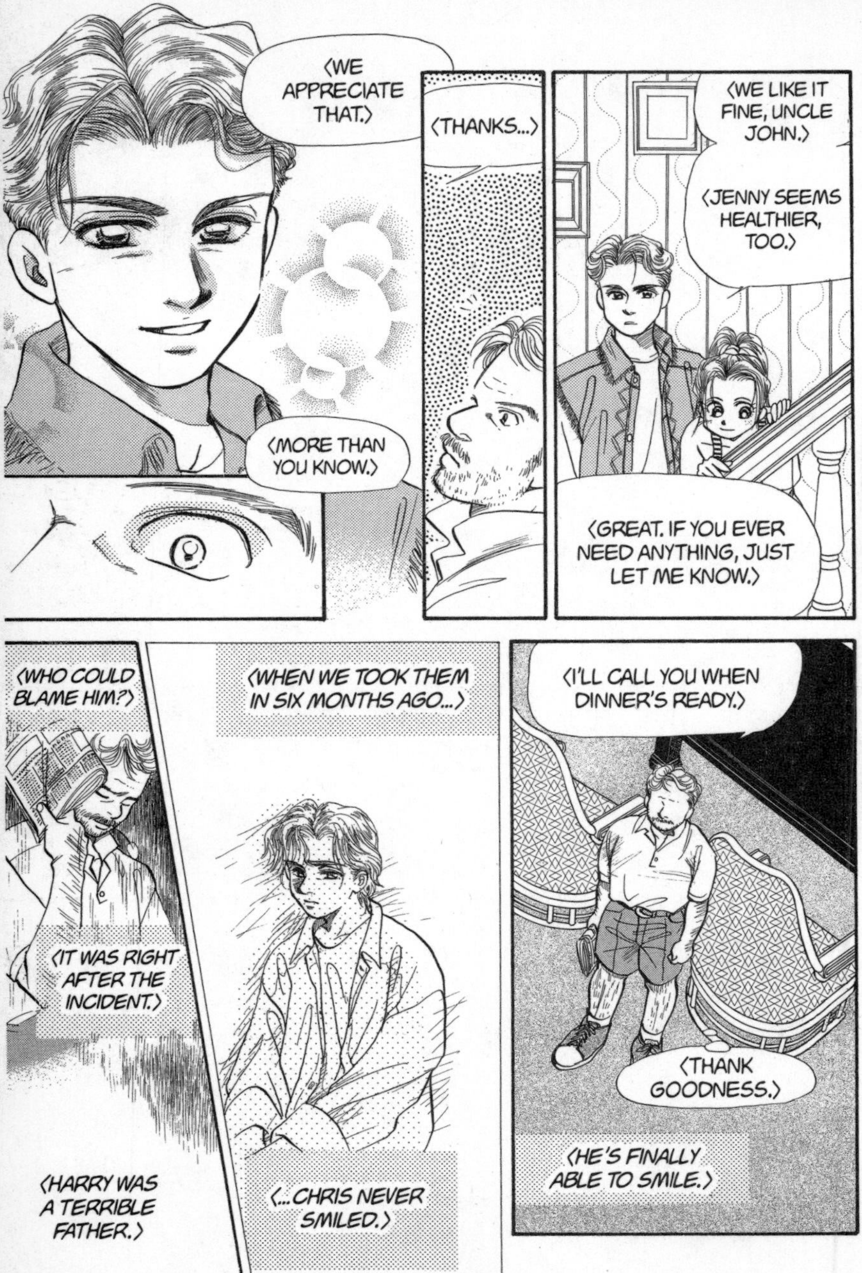
〈WE LIKE IT FINE, UNCLE JOHN.〉
〈JENNY SEEMS HEALTHIER, TOO.〉
〈GREAT. IF YOU EVER NEED ANYTHING, JUST LET ME KNOW.〉
〈THANKS...〉
〈WE APPRECIATE THAT.〉
〈MORE THAN YOU KNOW.〉
〈I'LL CALL YOU WHEN DINNER'S READY.〉
〈THANK GOODNESS.〉
〈HE'S FINALLY ABLE TO SMILE.〉
〈WHEN WE TOOK THEM IN SIX MONTHS AGO...〉
〈...CHRIS NEVER SMILED.〉
〈WHO COULD BLAME HIM?〉
〈IT WAS RIGHT AFTER THE INCIDENT.〉
〈HARRY WAS A TERRIBLE FATHER.〉

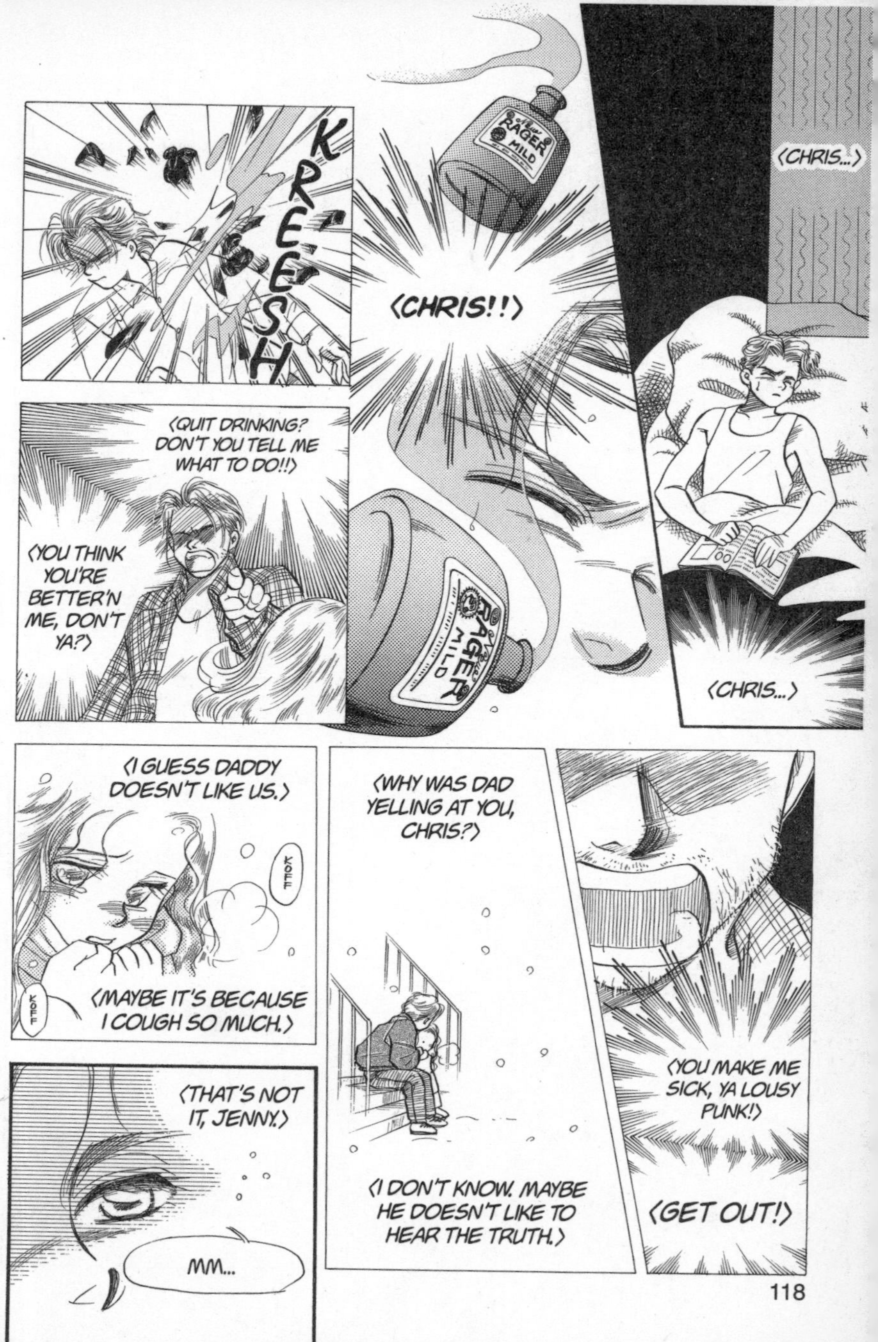
〈CHRIS...〉
〈CHRIS...〉
RAGER MILD
〈CHRIS!!〉
RAGER MILD
KREESH
〈QUIT DRINKING? DON'T YOU TELL ME WHAT TO DO!!〉
〈YOU THINK YOU'RE BETTER'N ME, DON'T YA?〉
〈YOU MAKE ME SICK, YA LOUSY PUNK!〉
〈GET OUT!〉
〈WHY WAS DAD YELLING AT YOU, CHRIS?〉
〈I DON'T KNOW. MAYBE HE DOESN'T LIKE TO HEAR THE TRUTH.〉
〈I GUESS DADDY DOESN'T LIKE US.〉
KOFF
KOFF
〈MAYBE IT'S BECAUSE I COUGH SO MUCH.〉
〈THAT'S NOT IT, JENNY.〉
MM...

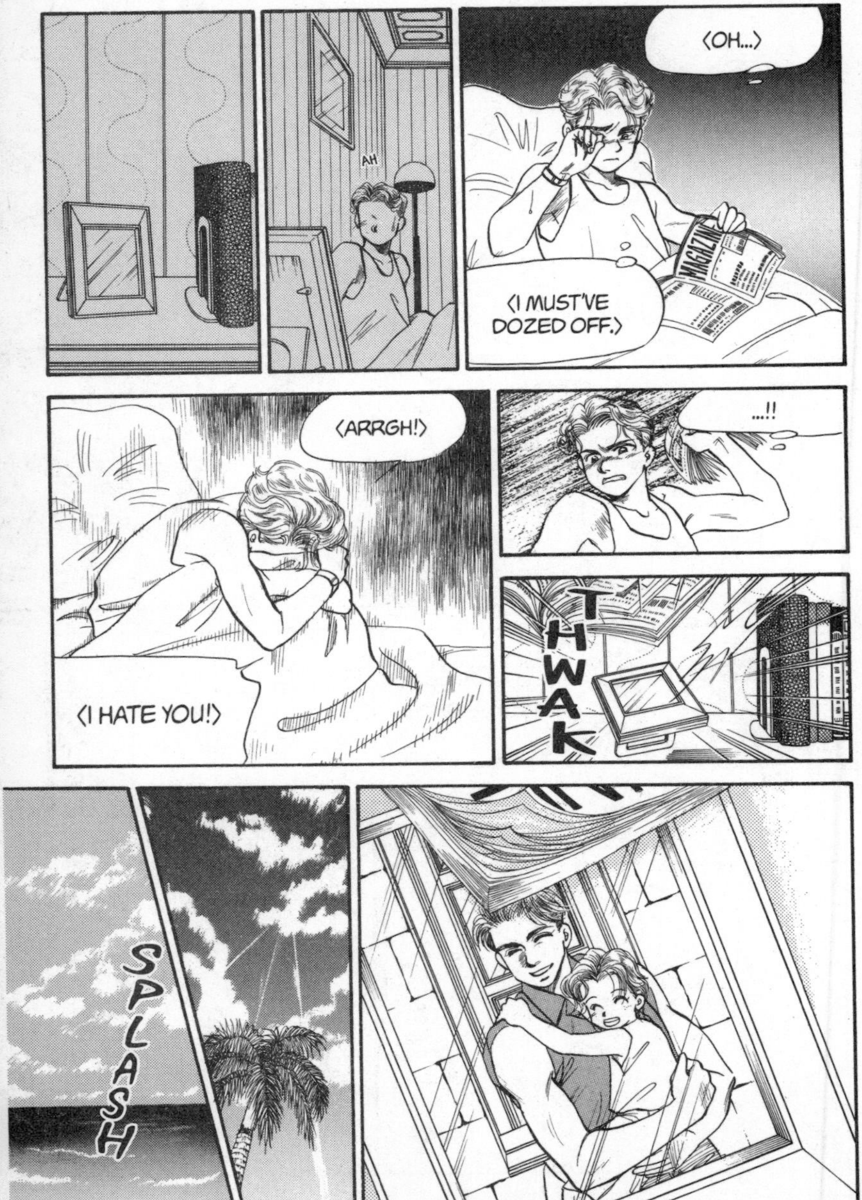
〈OH...〉
〈I MUST'VE DOZED OFF.〉
AH
...!!
THWAK
〈ARRGH!〉
〈I HATE YOU!〉
SPLASH

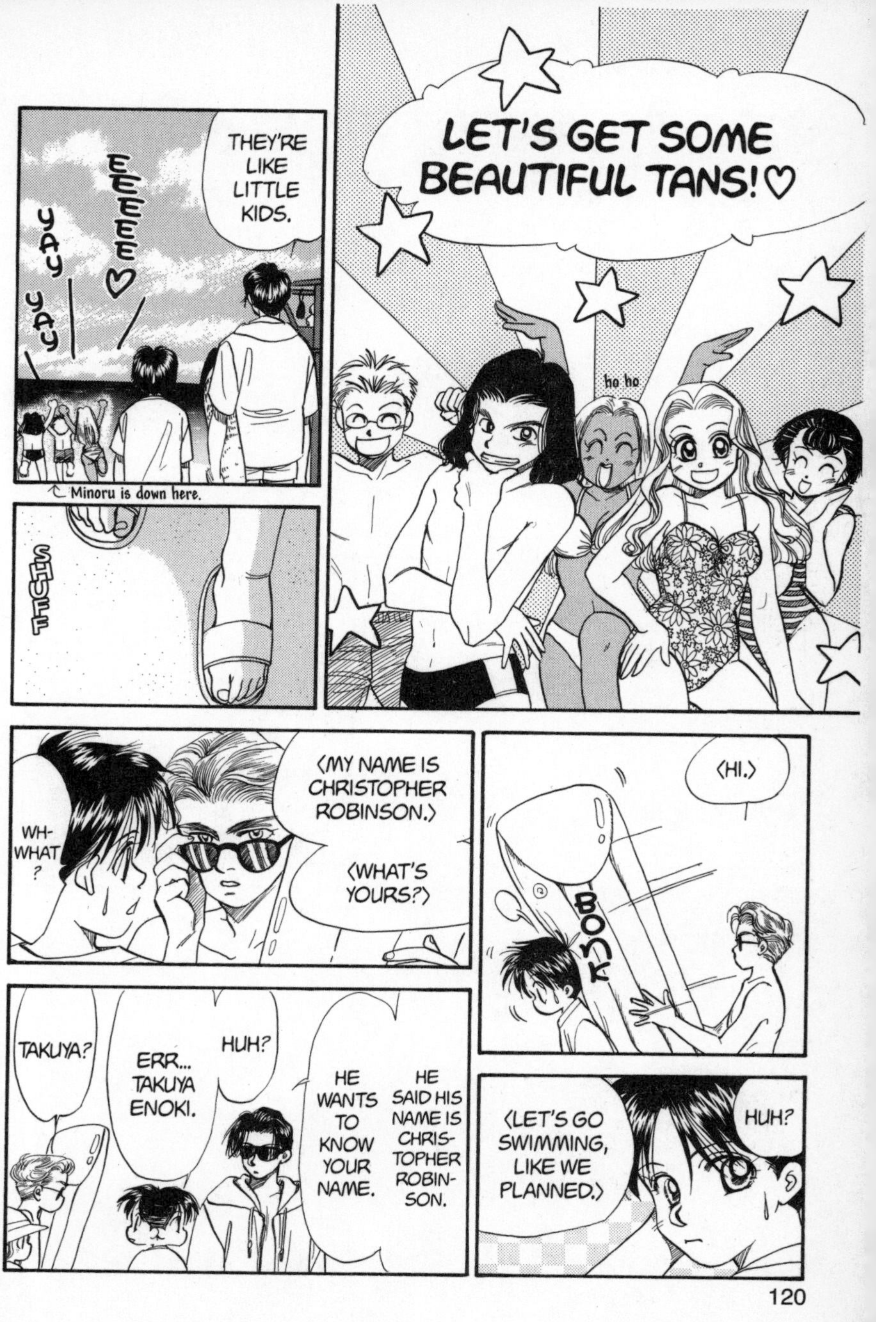
LET'S GET SOME BEAUTIFUL TANS! ♡
ho ho
THEY'RE LIKE LITTLE KIDS.
EEEEEE ♡
YAY
YAY
Minoru is down here.
SHUFF
⟨HI.⟩
BONK
⟨LET'S GO SWIMMING, LIKE WE PLANNED.⟩
HUH?
⟨MY NAME IS CHRISTOPHER ROBINSON.⟩
⟨WHAT'S YOURS?⟩
WH- WHAT ?
HE SAID HIS NAME IS CHRIS-TOPHER ROBIN-SON.
HE WANTS TO KNOW YOUR NAME.
HUH?
ERR... TAKUYA ENOKI.
TAKUYA?

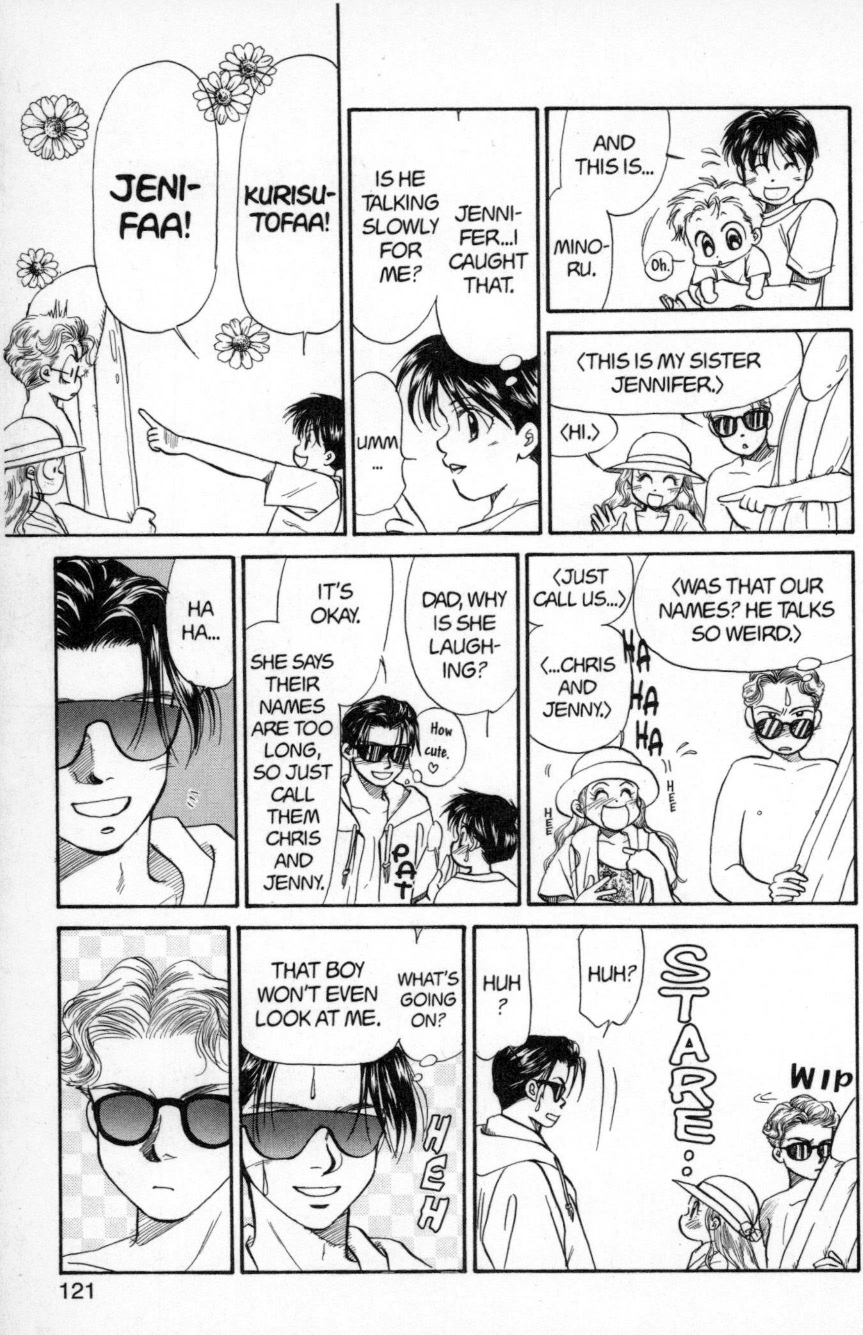
AND THIS IS...
MINO-RU.
Oh.
⟨THIS IS MY SISTER JENNIFER.⟩
⟨HI.⟩
JENNI-FER...I CAUGHT THAT.
IS HE TALKING SLOWLY FOR ME?
UMM...
KURISU-TOFAA!
JENI-FAA!
⟨WAS THAT OUR NAMES? HE TALKS SO WEIRD.⟩
⟨JUST CALL US...⟩
⟨...CHRIS AND JENNY.⟩
HA HA HA
HEE HEE
DAD, WHY IS SHE LAUGHING?
IT'S OKAY.
SHE SAYS THEIR NAMES ARE TOO LONG, SO JUST CALL THEM CHRIS AND JENNY.
How cute. ♡
PAT
HA HA...
HUH?
HUH?
STARE..
Wip
WHAT'S GOING ON?
THAT BOY WON'T EVEN LOOK AT ME.
HEH

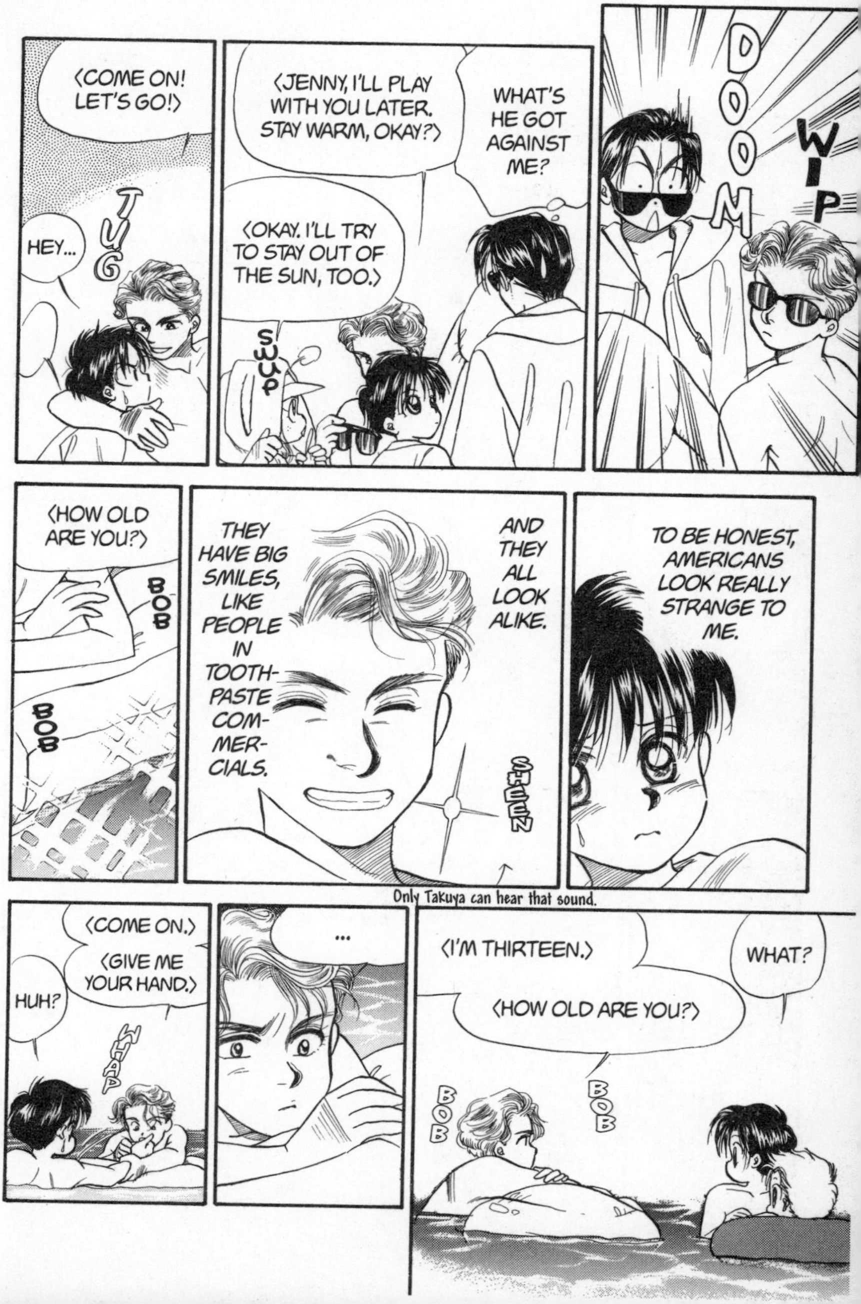
DOOM
WIP
WHAT'S HE GOT AGAINST ME?
〈JENNY, I'LL PLAY WITH YOU LATER. STAY WARM, OKAY?〉
〈OKAY. I'LL TRY TO STAY OUT OF THE SUN, TOO.〉
SWUP
〈COME ON! LET'S GO!〉
TUG
HEY...
TO BE HONEST, AMERICANS LOOK REALLY STRANGE TO ME.
AND THEY ALL LOOK ALIKE.
THEY HAVE BIG SMILES, LIKE PEOPLE IN TOOTH-PASTE COM-MER-CIALS.
SHEEN
〈HOW OLD ARE YOU?〉
BOB
BOB
Only Takuya can hear that sound.
WHAT?
〈I'M THIRTEEN.〉
〈HOW OLD ARE YOU?〉
BOB
BOB
...
〈COME ON.〉
〈GIVE ME YOUR HAND.〉
HUH?
WHAP

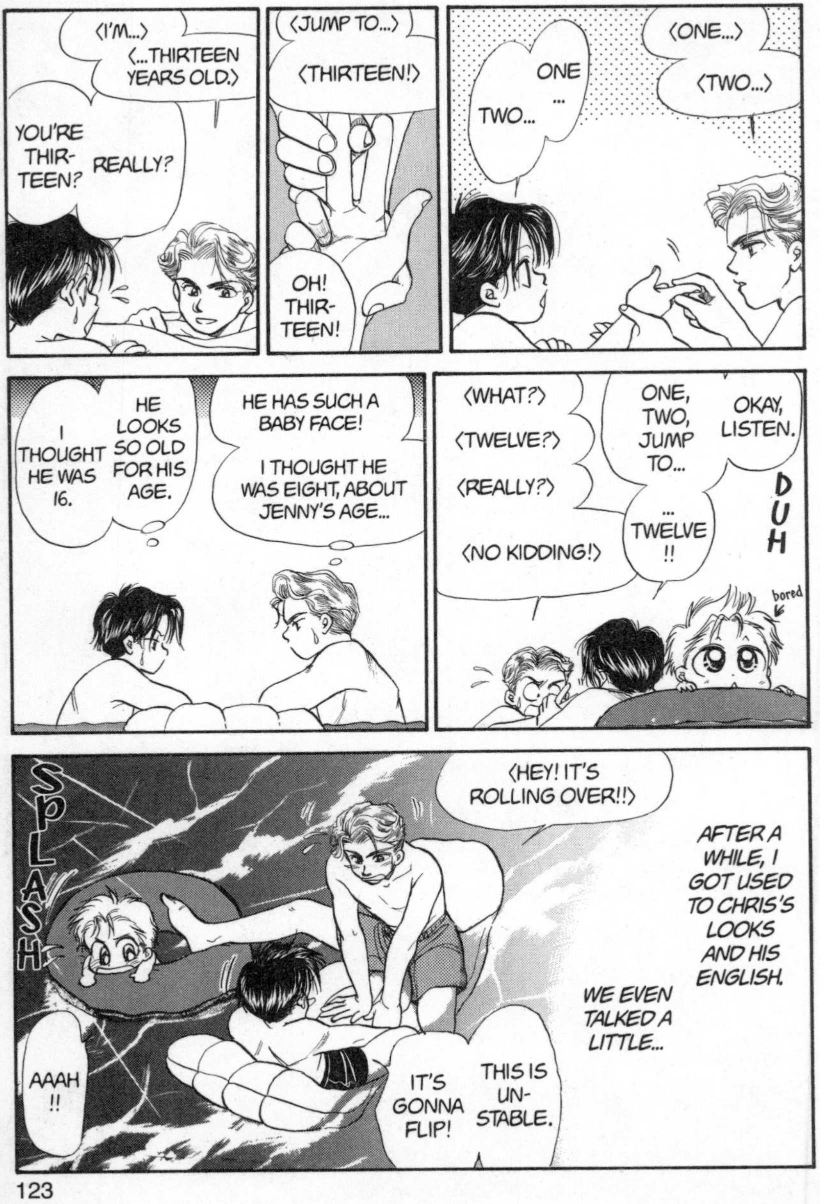
⟨ONE...⟩
⟨TWO...⟩
ONE ... TWO...
⟨JUMP TO...⟩
⟨THIRTEEN!⟩
OH! THIRTEEN!
⟨I'M...⟩
⟨...THIRTEEN YEARS OLD.⟩
REALLY?
YOU'RE THIRTEEN?
OKAY, LISTEN.
ONE, TWO, JUMP TO...
... TWELVE !!
DUH
⟨WHAT?⟩
⟨TWELVE?⟩
⟨REALLY?⟩
⟨NO KIDDING!⟩
bored
HE HAS SUCH A BABY FACE!
I THOUGHT HE WAS EIGHT, ABOUT JENNY'S AGE...
HE LOOKS SO OLD FOR HIS AGE.
I THOUGHT HE WAS 16.
AFTER A WHILE, I GOT USED TO CHRIS'S LOOKS AND HIS ENGLISH.
WE EVEN TALKED A LITTLE...
⟨HEY! IT'S ROLLING OVER!!⟩
THIS IS UNSTABLE.
IT'S GONNA FLIP!
AAAH !!
SPLASH

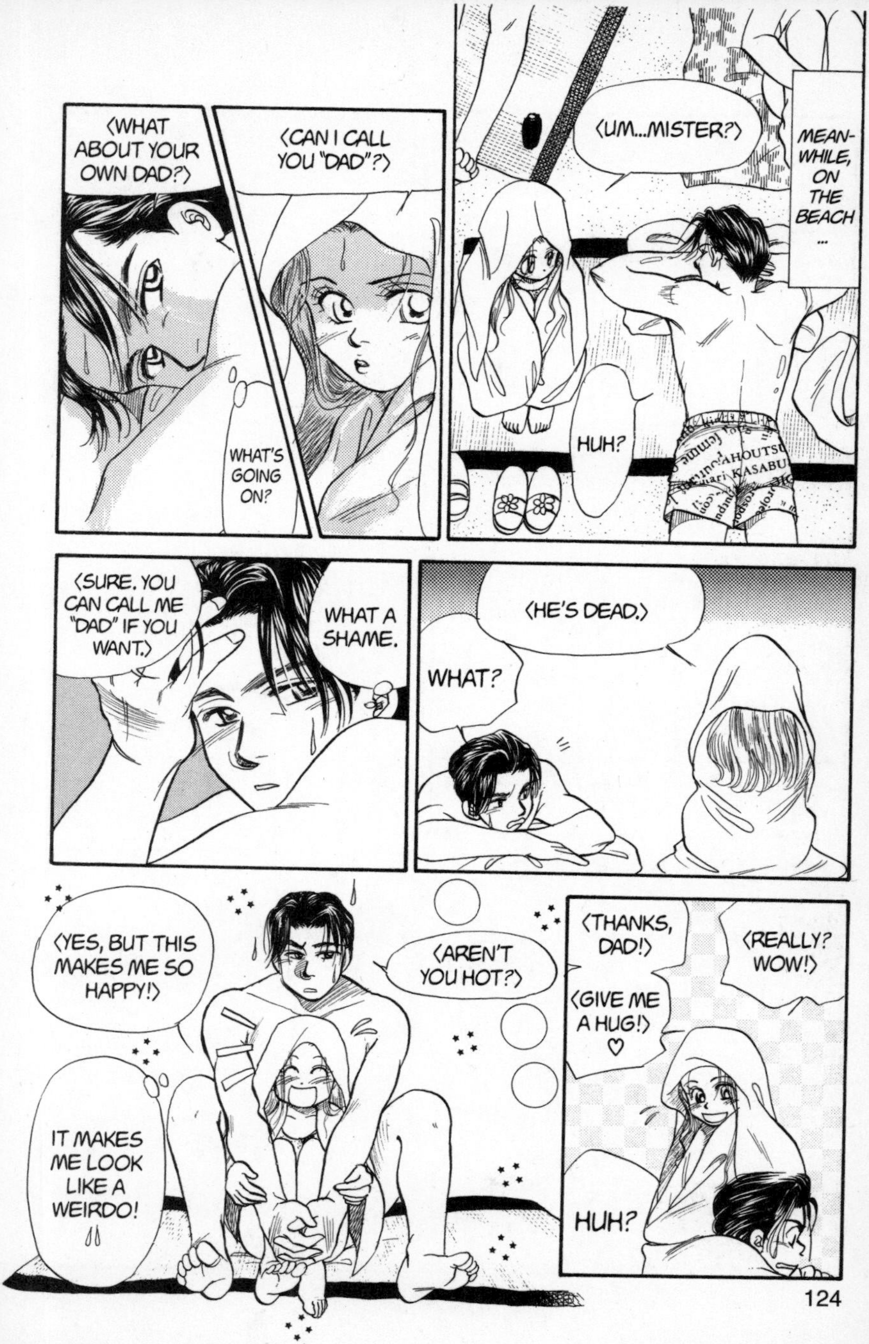
MEAN-WHILE, ON THE BEACH...
⟨UM...MISTER?⟩
HUH?
⟨CAN I CALL YOU "DAD"?⟩
⟨WHAT ABOUT YOUR OWN DAD?⟩
WHAT'S GOING ON?
⟨HE'S DEAD.⟩
WHAT?
WHAT A SHAME.
⟨SURE. YOU CAN CALL ME "DAD" IF YOU WANT.⟩
⟨REALLY? WOW!⟩
⟨THANKS, DAD!⟩
⟨GIVE ME A HUG!⟩ ♡
HUH?
⟨AREN'T YOU HOT?⟩
⟨YES, BUT THIS MAKES ME SO HAPPY!⟩
IT MAKES ME LOOK LIKE A WEIRDO!

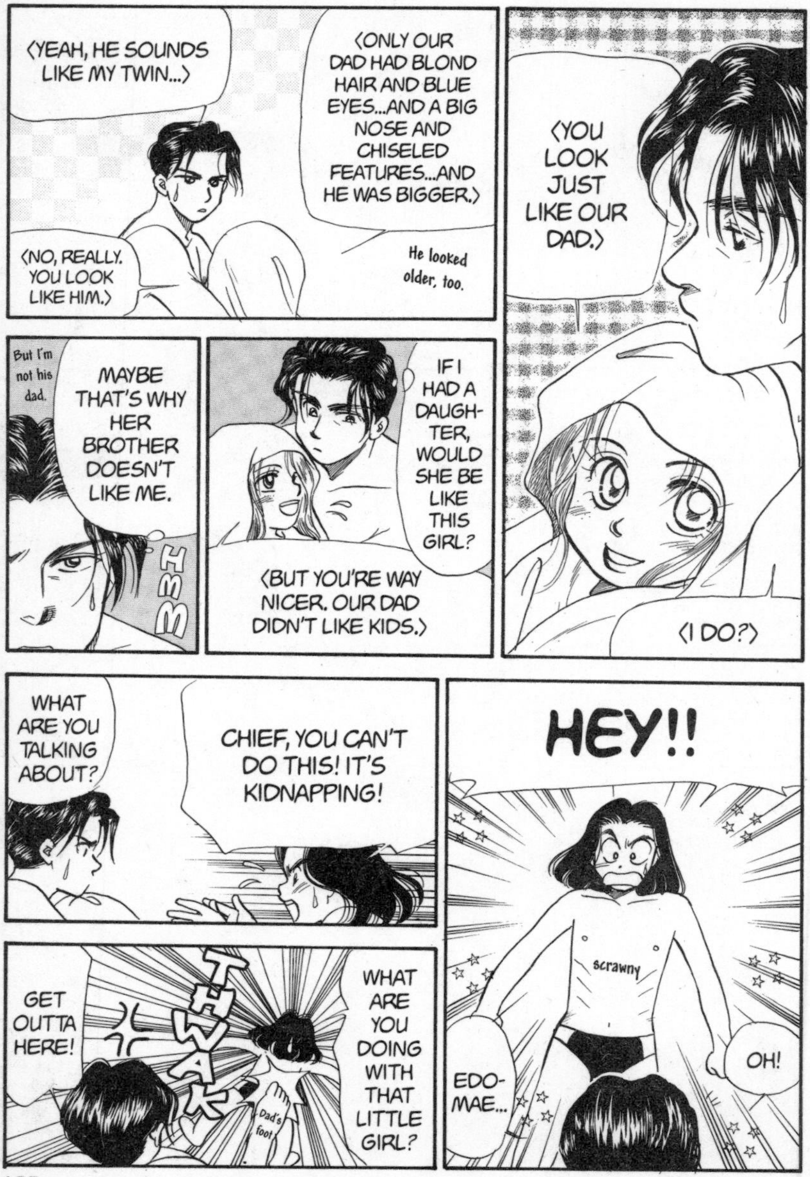

〈YOU LOOK JUST LIKE OUR DAD.〉
〈I DO?〉
〈ONLY OUR DAD HAD BLOND HAIR AND BLUE EYES...AND A BIG NOSE AND CHISELED FEATURES...AND HE WAS BIGGER.〉
〈YEAH, HE SOUNDS LIKE MY TWIN...〉
He looked older, too.
〈NO, REALLY. YOU LOOK LIKE HIM.〉
IF I HAD A DAUGHTER, WOULD SHE BE LIKE THIS GIRL?
〈BUT YOU'RE WAY NICER. OUR DAD DIDN'T LIKE KIDS.〉
MAYBE THAT'S WHY HER BROTHER DOESN'T LIKE ME.
But I'm not his dad.
HMM
HEY!!
scrawny
OH!
EDO-MAE...
CHIEF, YOU CAN'T DO THIS! IT'S KIDNAPPING!
WHAT ARE YOU TALKING ABOUT?
WHAT ARE YOU DOING WITH THAT LITTLE GIRL?
THWAK
Dad's foot
GET OUTTA HERE!

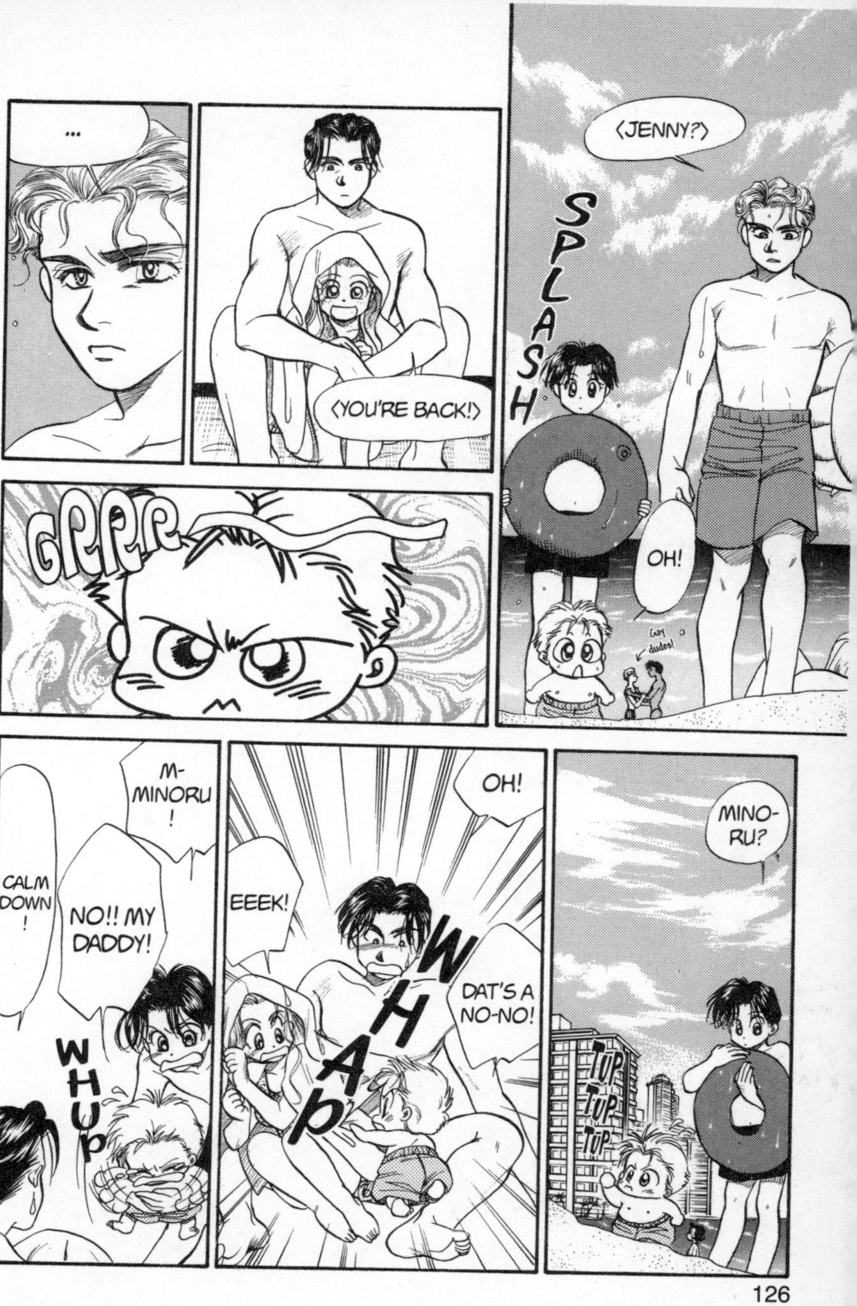
〈JENNY?〉
SPLASH
OH!
Gay dudes!
〈YOU'RE BACK!〉
...
GRRR
MINO-RU?
TUP TUP TUP
OH!
EEEK!
WHAP
DAT'S A NO-NO!
M-MINORU!
NO!! MY DADDY!
CALM DOWN!
WHUP

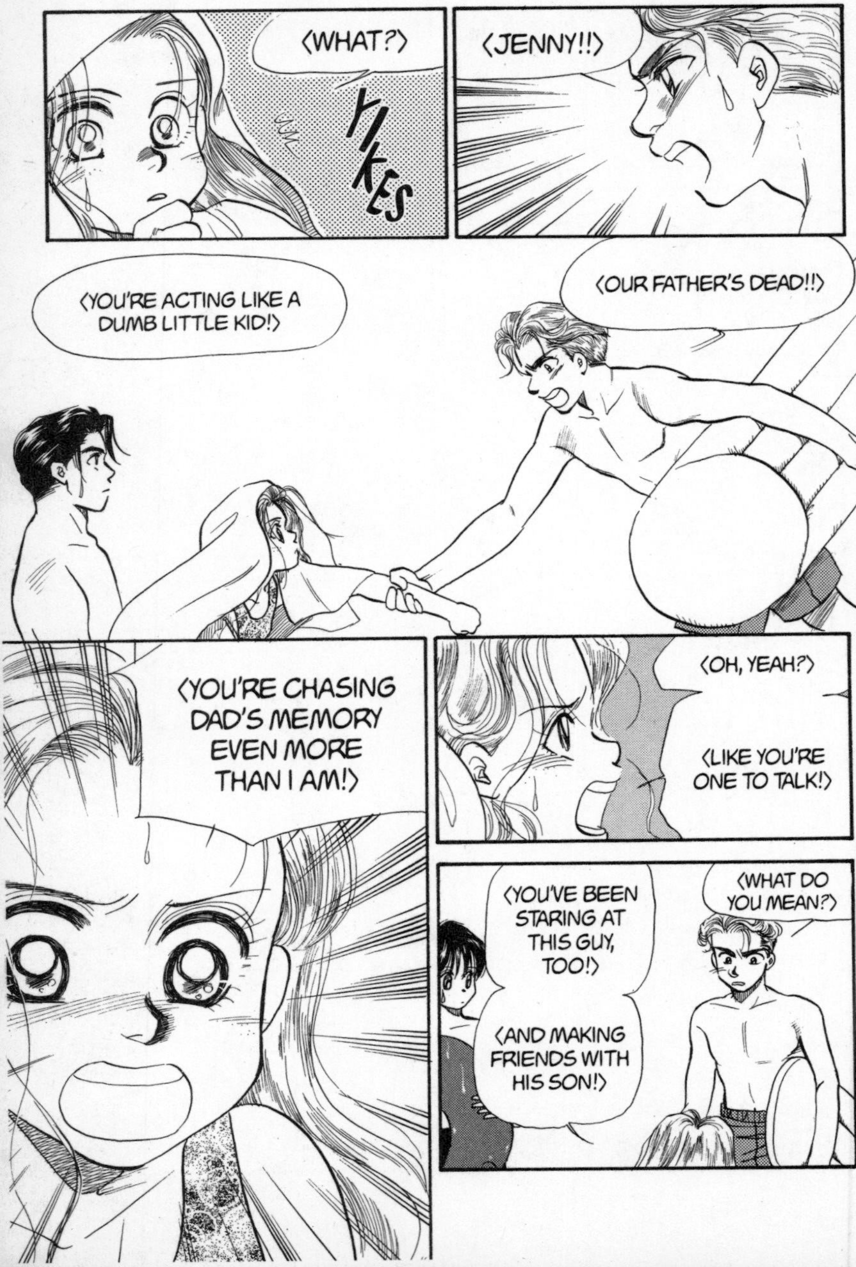
〈JENNY!!〉
〈WHAT?〉
YIKES
〈OUR FATHER'S DEAD!!〉
〈YOU'RE ACTING LIKE A DUMB LITTLE KID!〉
〈OH, YEAH?〉
〈LIKE YOU'RE ONE TO TALK!〉
〈WHAT DO YOU MEAN?〉
〈YOU'VE BEEN STARING AT THIS GUY, TOO!〉
〈AND MAKING FRIENDS WITH HIS SON!〉
〈YOU'RE CHASING DAD'S MEMORY EVEN MORE THAN I AM!〉

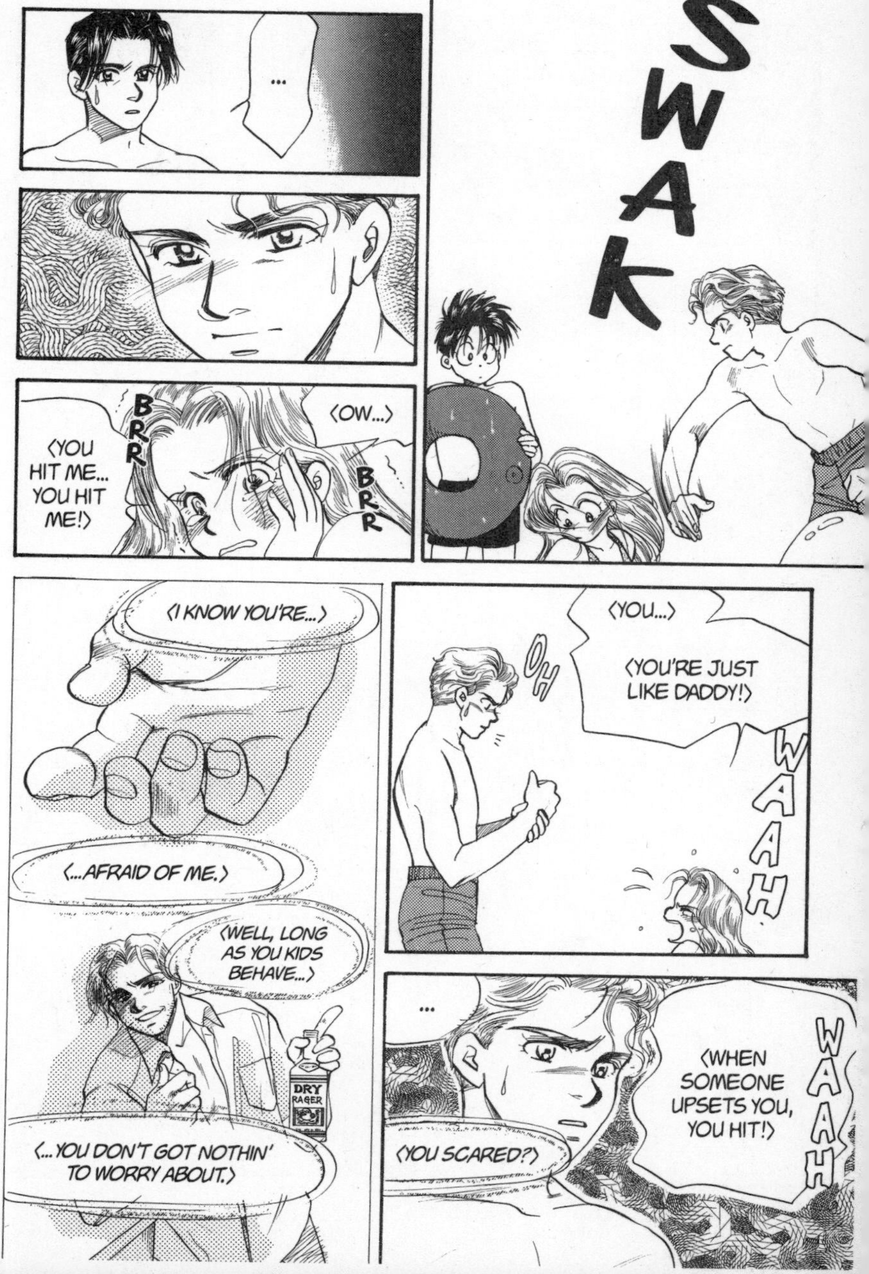
SWAK
...
〈OW...〉
BRR
〈YOU HIT ME... YOU HIT ME!〉
BRR
〈YOU...〉
OH
〈YOU'RE JUST LIKE DADDY!〉
WAAH
WAAH
〈WHEN SOMEONE UPSETS YOU, YOU HIT!〉
...
〈YOU SCARED?〉
〈I KNOW YOU'RE...〉
〈...AFRAID OF ME.〉
〈WELL, LONG AS YOU KIDS BEHAVE...〉
DRY RAGER
〈...YOU DON'T GOT NOTHIN' TO WORRY ABOUT.〉

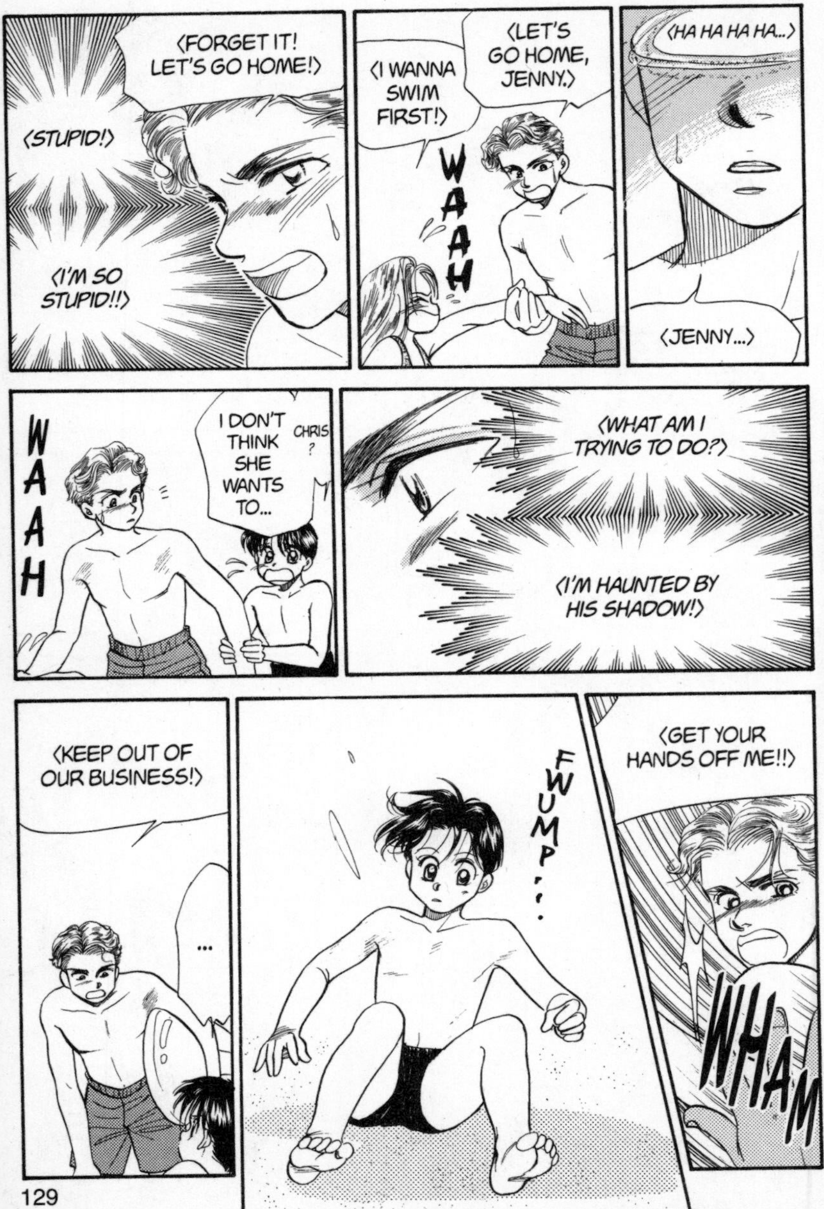

⟨HA HA HA HA...⟩
⟨JENNY...⟩
⟨LET'S GO HOME, JENNY.⟩
⟨I WANNA SWIM FIRST!⟩
WAAH
⟨FORGET IT! LET'S GO HOME!⟩
⟨STUPID!⟩
⟨I'M SO STUPID!!⟩
⟨WHAT AM I TRYING TO DO?⟩
⟨I'M HAUNTED BY HIS SHADOW!⟩
CHRIS ?
I DON'T THINK SHE WANTS TO...
WAAH
⟨GET YOUR HANDS OFF ME!!⟩
WHAM
FWUMP...
⟨KEEP OUT OF OUR BUSINESS!⟩
...

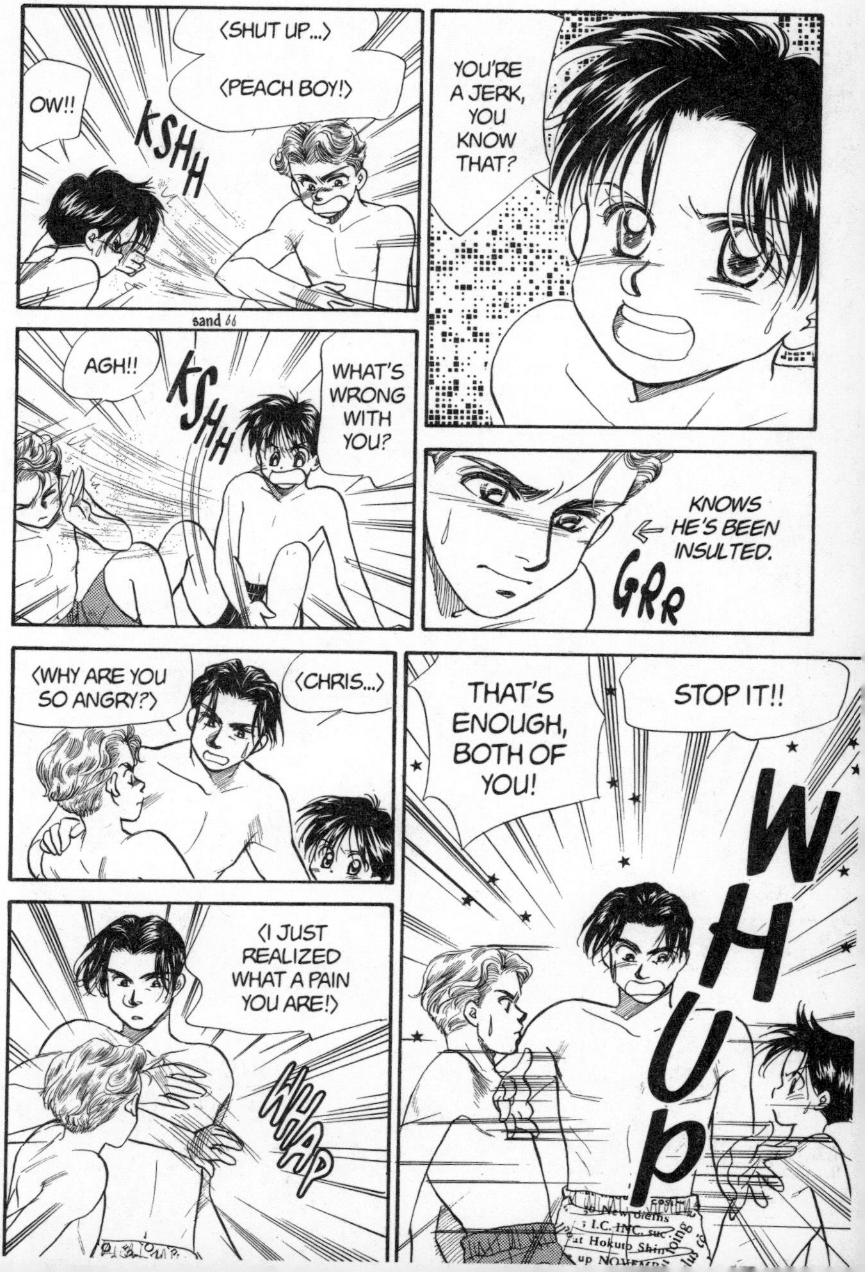
<SHUT UP...>
<PEACH BOY!>
OW!!
KSHH
YOU'RE A JERK, YOU KNOW THAT?
AGH!!
KSHH
WHAT'S WRONG WITH YOU?
KNOWS HE'S BEEN INSULTED.
GRR
<WHY ARE YOU SO ANGRY?>
<CHRIS...>
<I JUST REALIZED WHAT A PAIN YOU ARE!>
WHAP
THAT'S ENOUGH, BOTH OF YOU!
STOP IT!!
WHUP

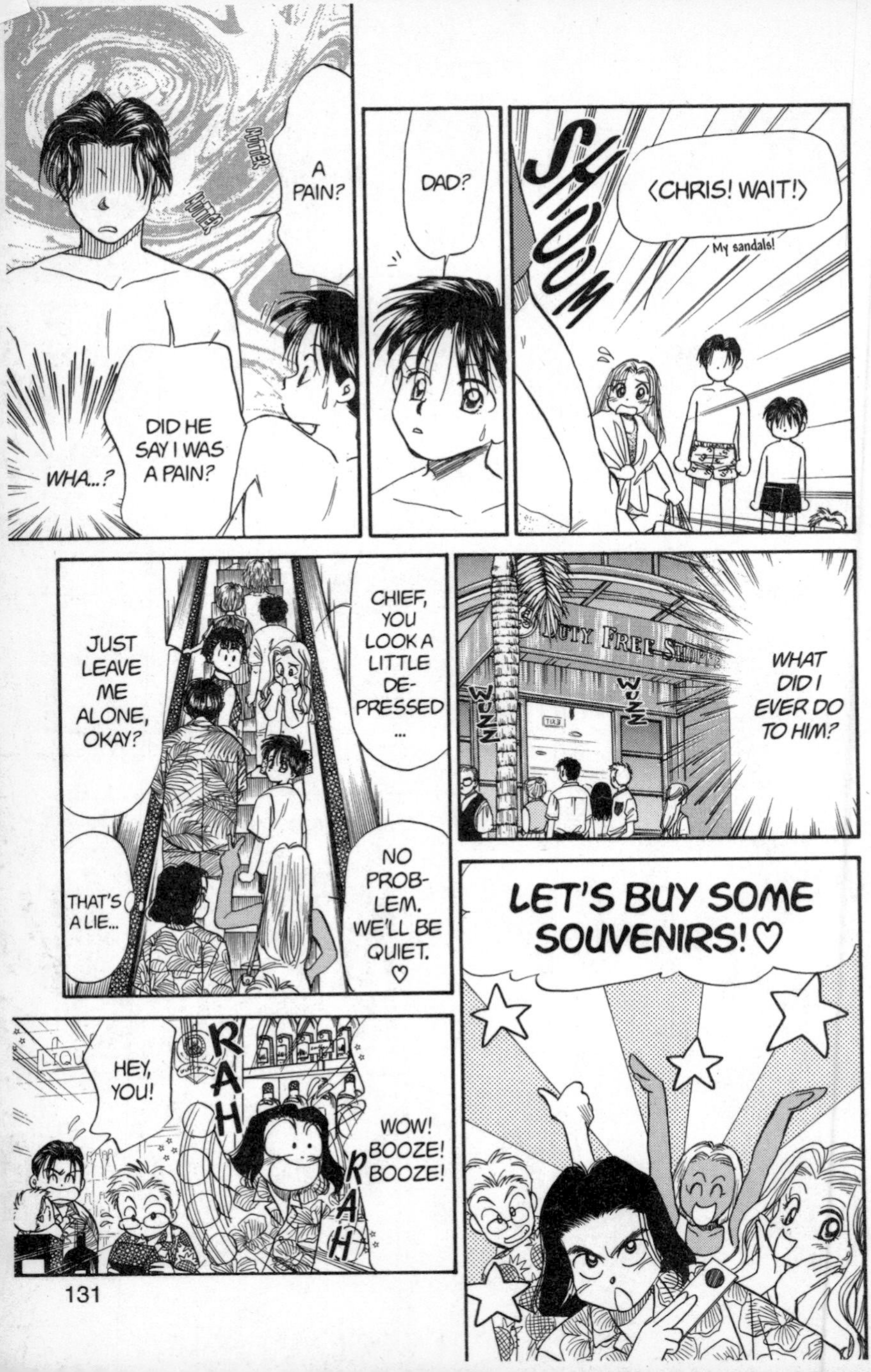
SHOOOM
⟨CHRIS! WAIT!⟩
My sandals!
DAD?
A PAIN?
MUTTER
MUTTER
DID HE SAY I WAS A PAIN?
WHA...?
WHAT DID I EVER DO TO HIM?
WUZZ
WUZZ
CHIEF, YOU LOOK A LITTLE DE-PRESSED ...
JUST LEAVE ME ALONE, OKAY?
NO PROB-LEM. WE'LL BE QUIET. ♡
THAT'S A LIE...
LET'S BUY SOME SOUVENIRS! ♡
WOW! BOOZE! BOOZE!
RAH
RAH
HEY, YOU!

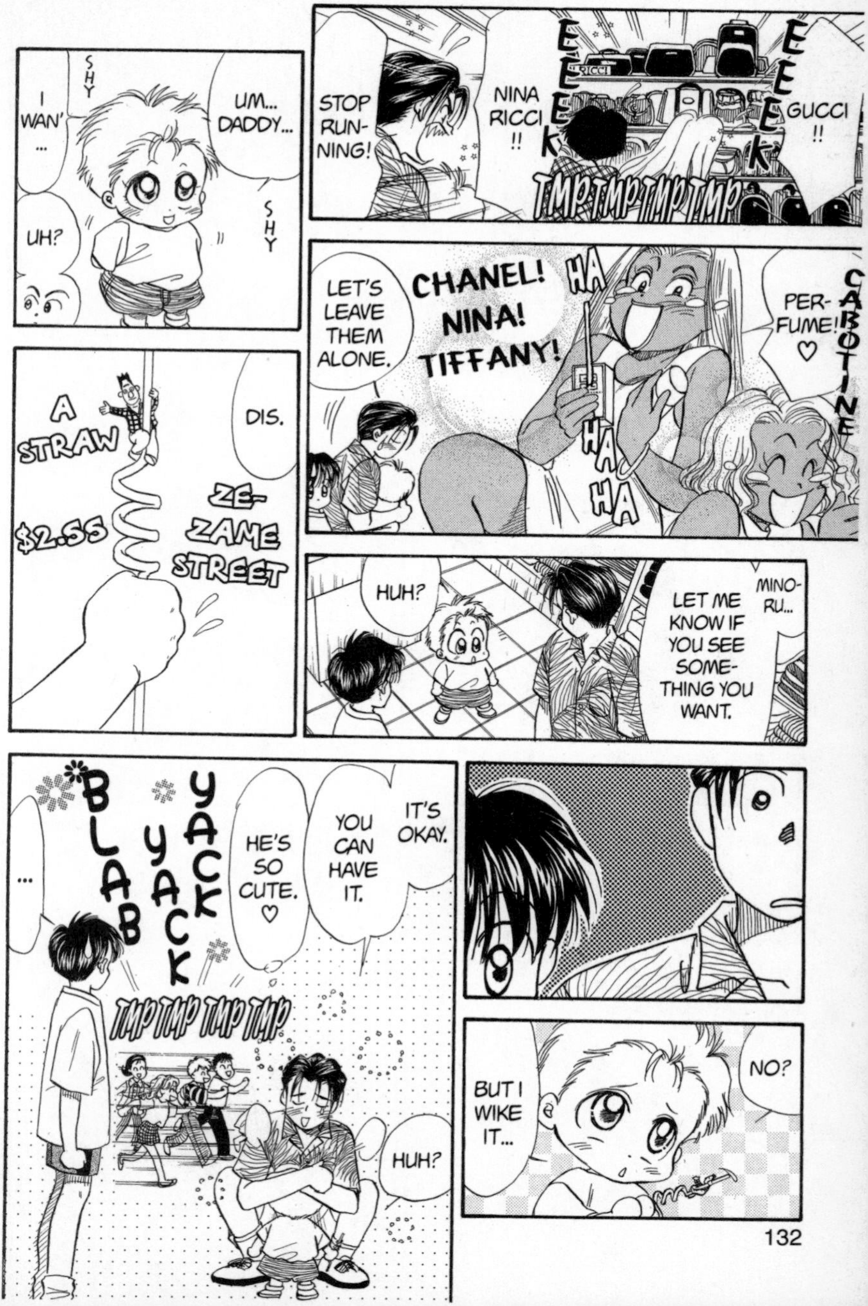
GUCCI !!
EEEEK
EEEEK
NINA RICCI !!
STOP RUN-NING!
TMPTMPTMPTMP
PER-FUME! ♡
CABOTINE
HA HA HA
CHANEL! NINA! TIFFANY!
LET'S LEAVE THEM ALONE.
MINO-RU...
LET ME KNOW IF YOU SEE SOME-THING YOU WANT.
HUH?
UM... DADDY...
SHY
SHY
I WAN' ...
UH?
DIS.
ZE-ZAME STREET
A STRAW
$2.55
NO?
BUT I WIKE IT...
IT'S OKAY.
YOU CAN HAVE IT.
HE'S SO CUTE. ♡
YACK YACK
BLAB
...
HUH?
TMPTMPTMPTMP

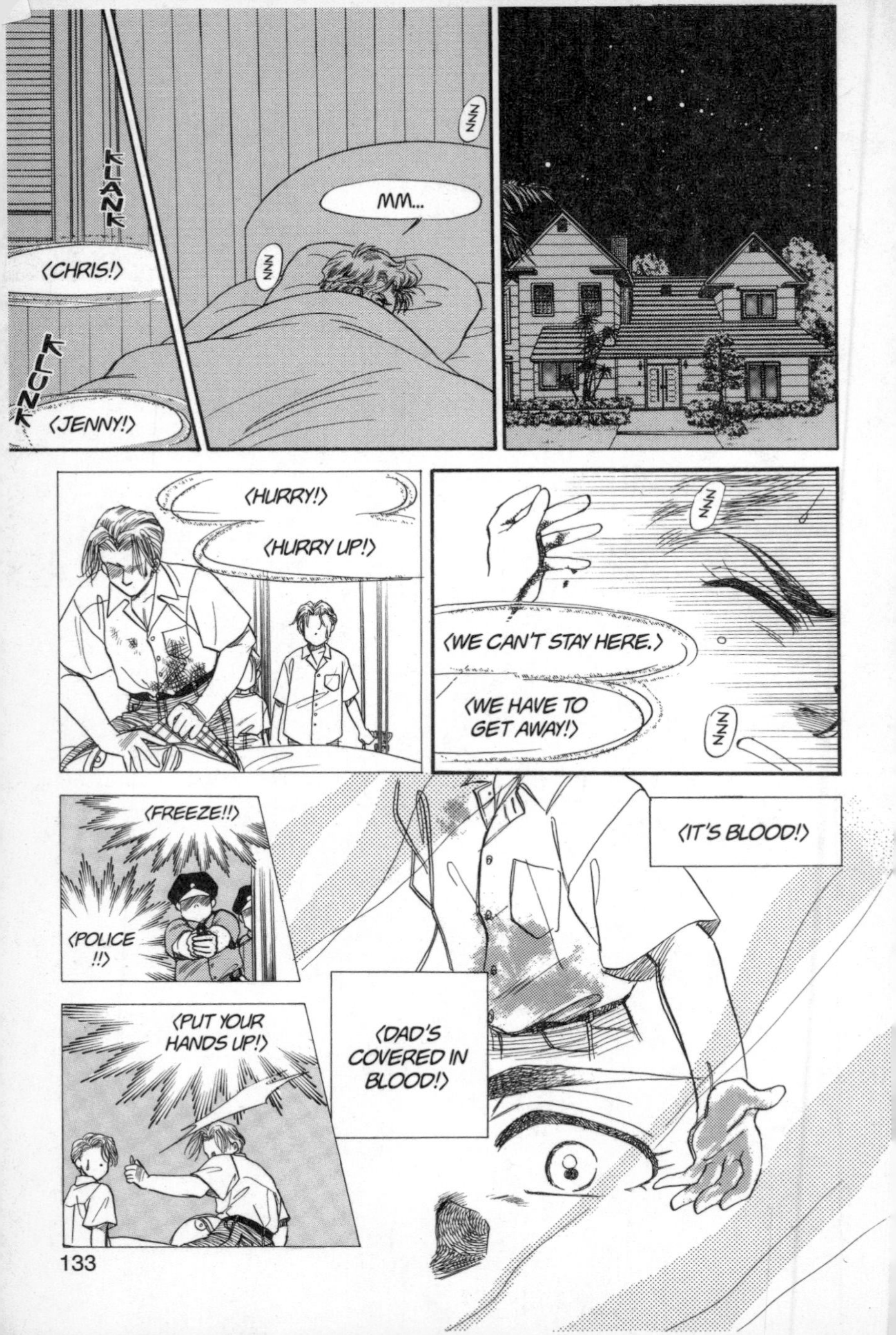
ZZZ
MM...
ZZZ
KLANK
<CHRIS!>
KLUNK
<JENNY!>
ZZZ
<WE CAN'T STAY HERE.>
<WE HAVE TO GET AWAY!>
ZZZ
<HURRY!>
<HURRY UP!>
<IT'S BLOOD!>
<DAD'S COVERED IN BLOOD!>
<FREEZE!!>
<POLICE!!>
<PUT YOUR HANDS UP!>

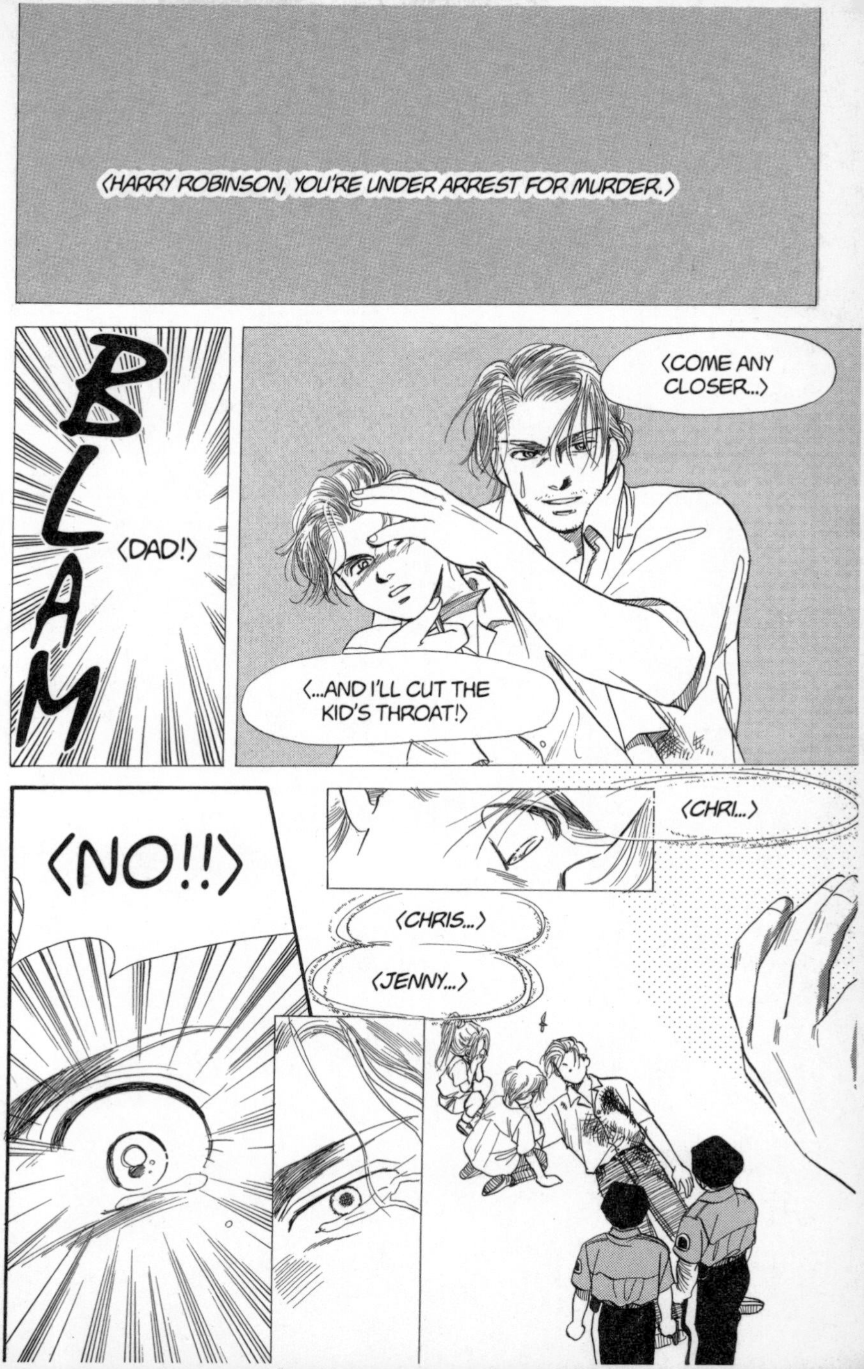
〈HARRY ROBINSON, YOU'RE UNDER ARREST FOR MURDER.〉
〈COME ANY CLOSER...〉
〈...AND I'LL CUT THE KID'S THROAT!〉
BLAM
〈DAD!〉
〈CHRI...〉
〈CHRIS...〉
〈JENNY...〉
〈NO!!〉

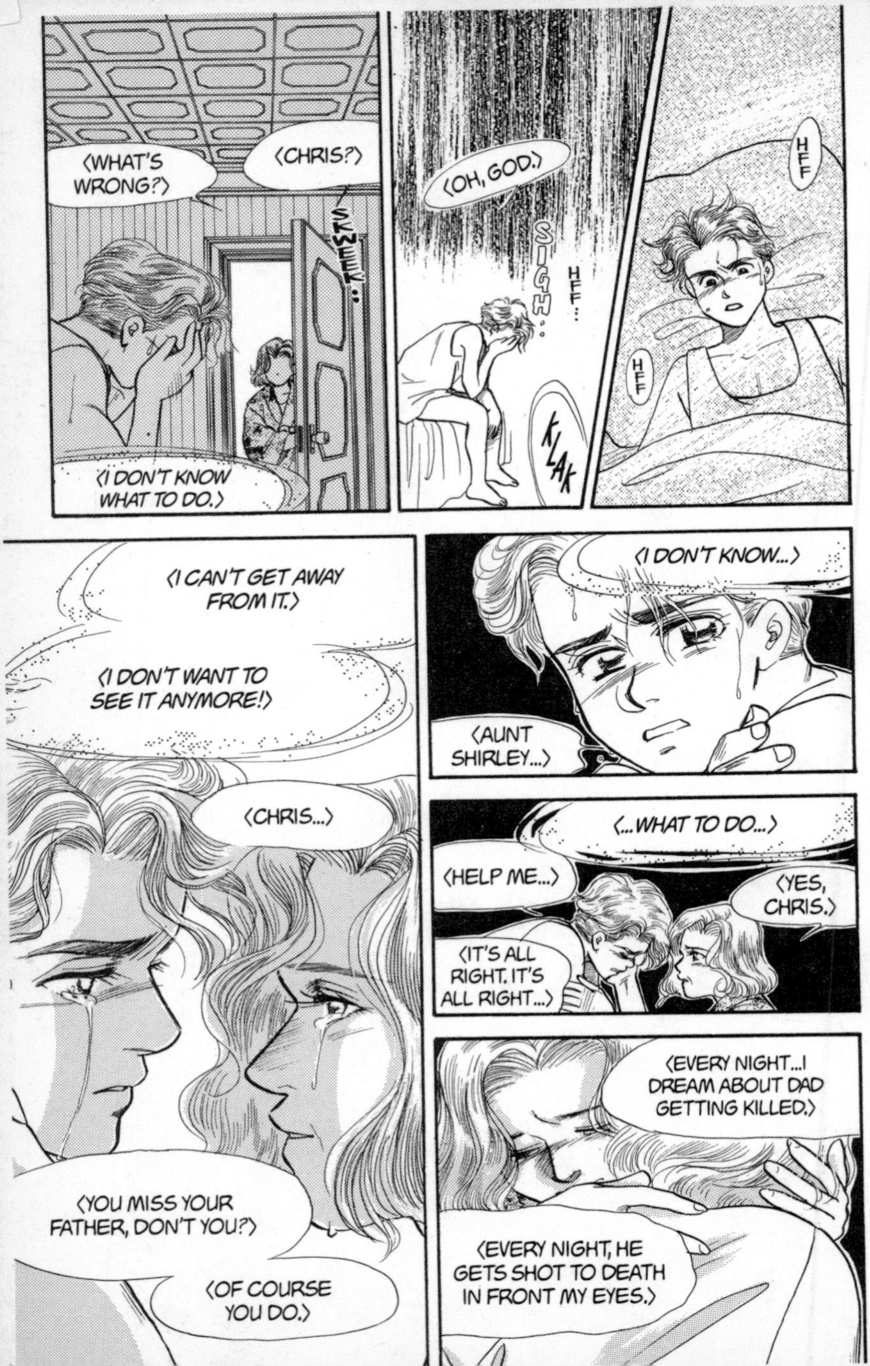
HFF
HFF
⟨OH, GOD.⟩
SIGH..
HFF..
KLAK
⟨CHRIS?⟩
SKWEEK..
⟨WHAT'S WRONG?⟩
⟨I DON'T KNOW WHAT TO DO.⟩
⟨I DON'T KNOW...⟩
⟨AUNT SHIRLEY...⟩
⟨...WHAT TO DO...⟩
⟨YES, CHRIS.⟩
⟨HELP ME...⟩
⟨IT'S ALL RIGHT. IT'S ALL RIGHT...⟩
⟨EVERY NIGHT...I DREAM ABOUT DAD GETTING KILLED.⟩
⟨EVERY NIGHT, HE GETS SHOT TO DEATH IN FRONT MY EYES.⟩
⟨I CAN'T GET AWAY FROM IT.⟩
⟨I DON'T WANT TO SEE IT ANYMORE!⟩
⟨CHRIS...⟩
⟨YOU MISS YOUR FATHER, DON'T YOU?⟩
⟨OF COURSE YOU DO.⟩

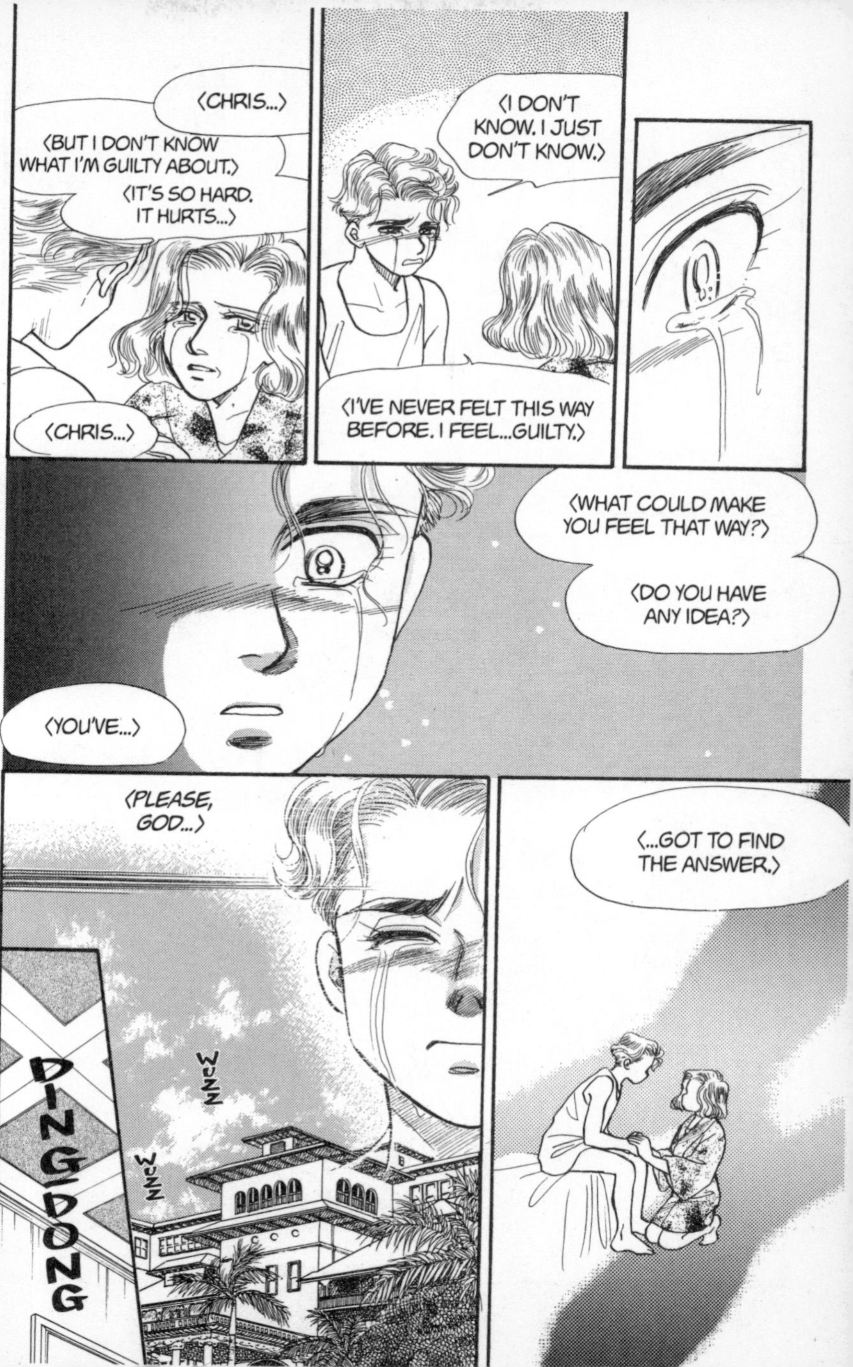
⟨I DON'T KNOW. I JUST DON'T KNOW.⟩
⟨I'VE NEVER FELT THIS WAY BEFORE. I FEEL...GUILTY.⟩
⟨CHRIS...⟩
⟨BUT I DON'T KNOW WHAT I'M GUILTY ABOUT.⟩
⟨IT'S SO HARD. IT HURTS...⟩
⟨CHRIS...⟩
⟨WHAT COULD MAKE YOU FEEL THAT WAY?⟩
⟨DO YOU HAVE ANY IDEA?⟩
⟨YOU'VE...⟩
⟨...GOT TO FIND THE ANSWER.⟩
⟨PLEASE, GOD...⟩
WUZZ
WUZZ
DING DONG

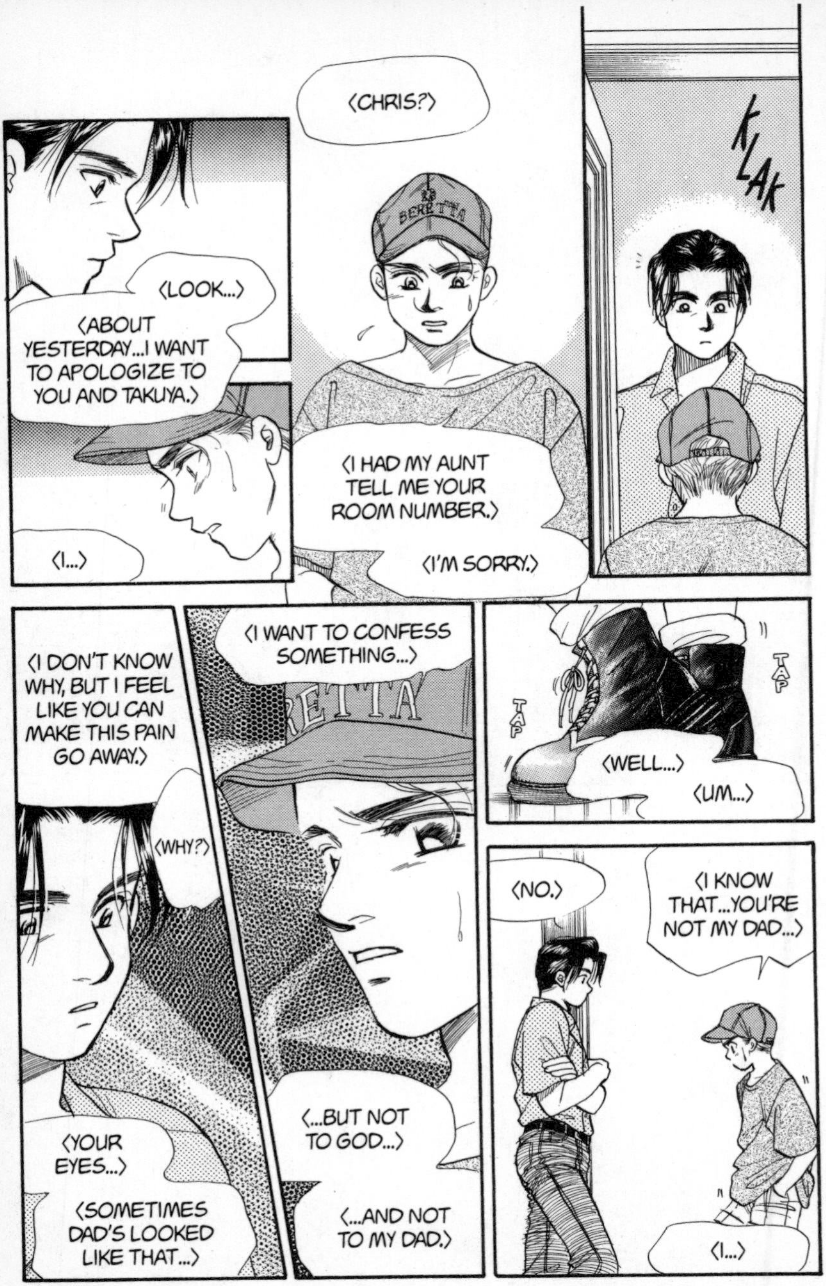
KLAK
〈CHRIS?〉
〈I HAD MY AUNT TELL ME YOUR ROOM NUMBER.〉
〈I'M SORRY.〉
〈LOOK...〉
〈ABOUT YESTERDAY...I WANT TO APOLOGIZE TO YOU AND TAKUYA.〉
〈I...〉
TAP
TAP
〈WELL...〉
〈UM...〉
〈I KNOW THAT...YOU'RE NOT MY DAD...〉
〈NO.〉
〈I...〉
〈I WANT TO CONFESS SOMETHING...〉
〈...BUT NOT TO GOD...〉
〈...AND NOT TO MY DAD.〉
〈I DON'T KNOW WHY, BUT I FEEL LIKE YOU CAN MAKE THIS PAIN GO AWAY.〉
〈WHY?〉
〈YOUR EYES...〉
〈SOMETIMES DAD'S LOOKED LIKE THAT...〉

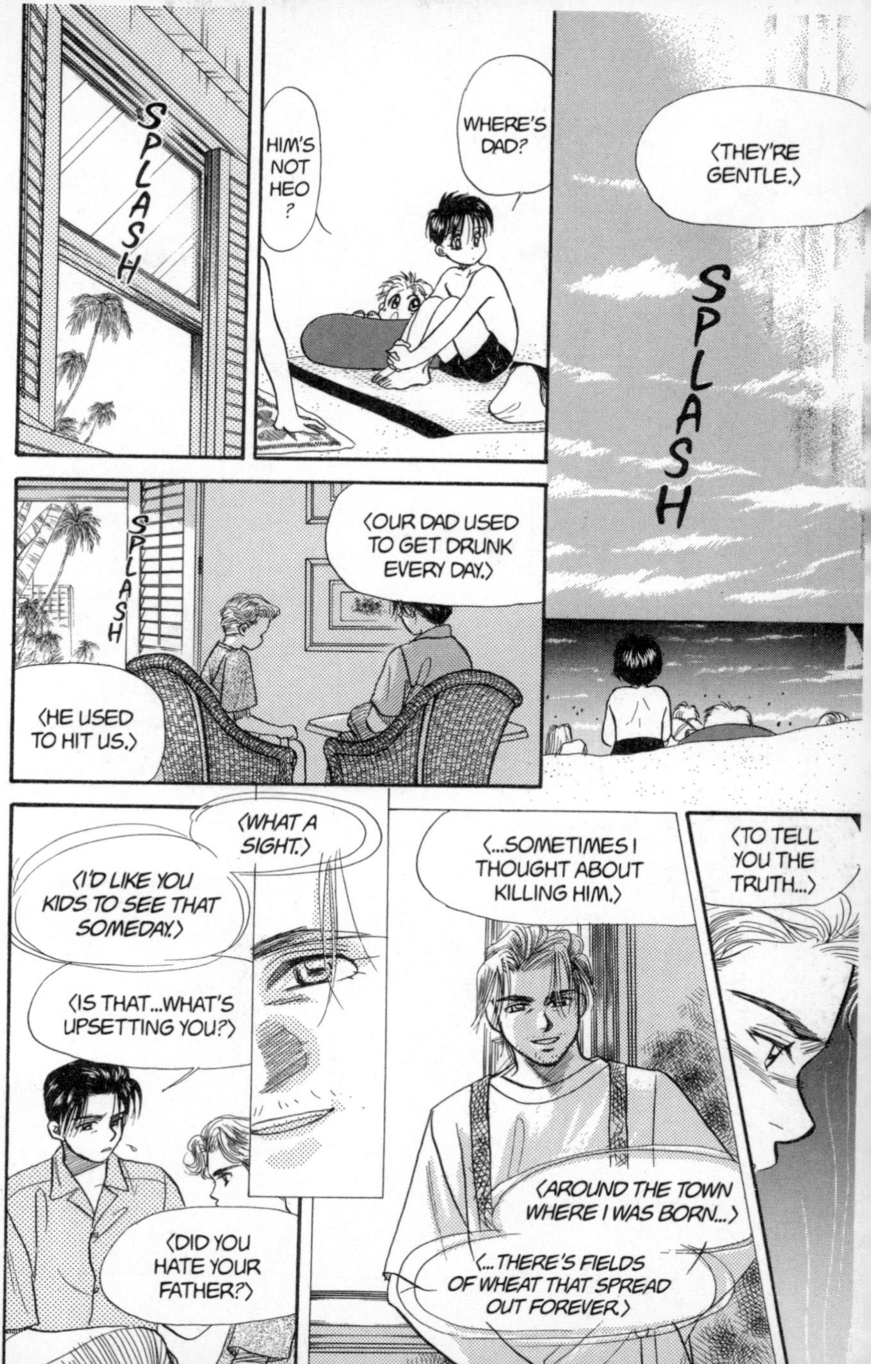
〈THEY'RE GENTLE.〉
SPLASH
WHERE'S DAD?
HIM'S NOT HEO?
SPLASH
〈OUR DAD USED TO GET DRUNK EVERY DAY.〉
SPLASH
〈HE USED TO HIT US.〉
〈TO TELL YOU THE TRUTH...〉
〈...SOMETIMES I THOUGHT ABOUT KILLING HIM.〉
〈AROUND THE TOWN WHERE I WAS BORN...〉
〈...THERE'S FIELDS OF WHEAT THAT SPREAD OUT FOREVER.〉
〈WHAT A SIGHT.〉
〈I'D LIKE YOU KIDS TO SEE THAT SOMEDAY.〉
〈IS THAT...WHAT'S UPSETTING YOU?〉
〈DID YOU HATE YOUR FATHER?〉

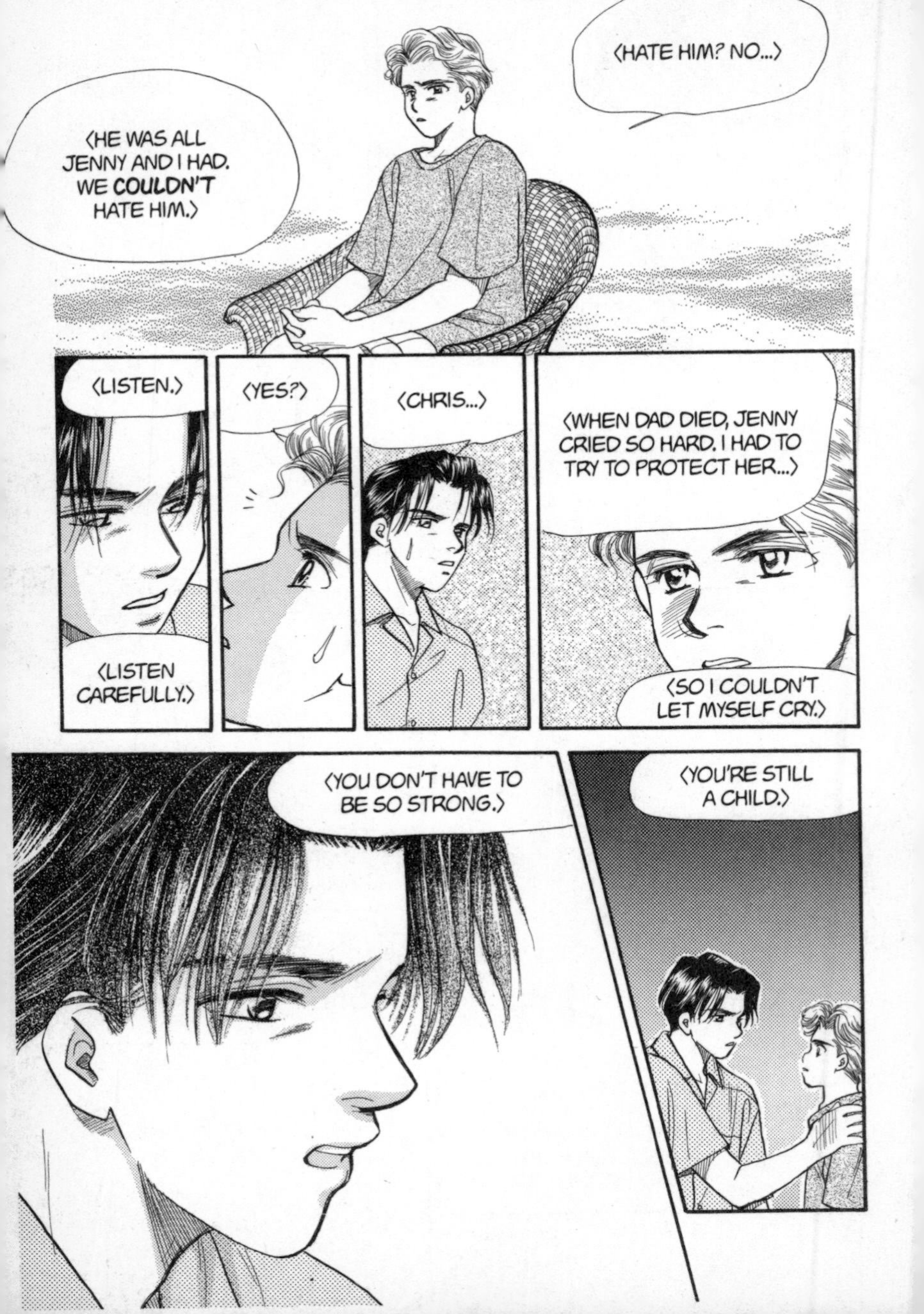
⟨HATE HIM? NO...⟩
⟨HE WAS ALL JENNY AND I HAD. WE **COULDN'T** HATE HIM.⟩
⟨WHEN DAD DIED, JENNY CRIED SO HARD. I HAD TO TRY TO PROTECT HER...⟩
⟨SO I COULDN'T LET MYSELF CRY.⟩
⟨CHRIS...⟩
⟨YES?⟩
⟨LISTEN.⟩
⟨LISTEN CAREFULLY.⟩
⟨YOU'RE STILL A CHILD.⟩
⟨YOU DON'T HAVE TO BE SO STRONG.⟩

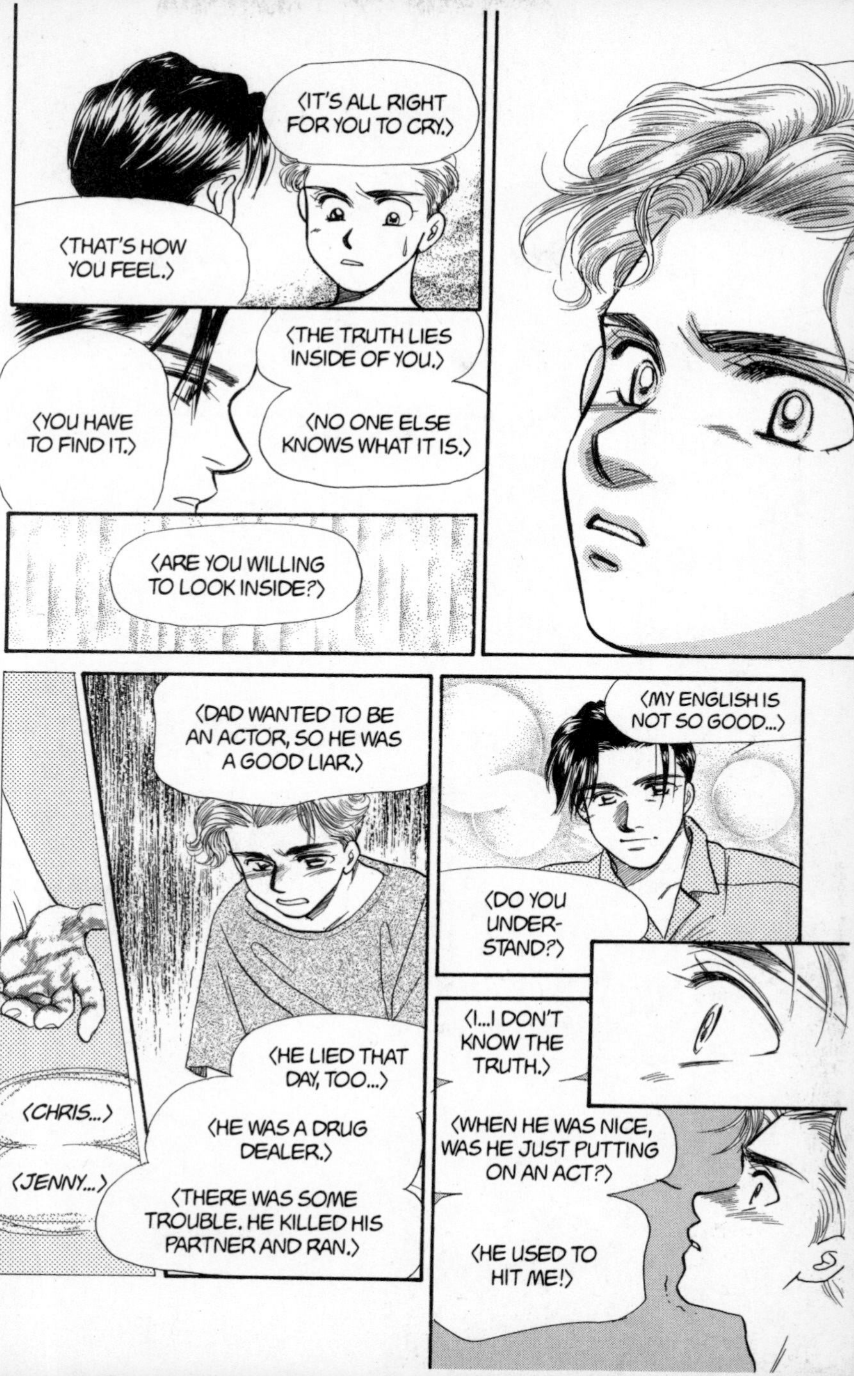
〈IT'S ALL RIGHT FOR YOU TO CRY.〉
〈THAT'S HOW YOU FEEL.〉
〈THE TRUTH LIES INSIDE OF YOU.〉
〈NO ONE ELSE KNOWS WHAT IT IS.〉
〈YOU HAVE TO FIND IT.〉
〈ARE YOU WILLING TO LOOK INSIDE?〉
〈MY ENGLISH IS NOT SO GOOD...〉
〈DO YOU UNDER-STAND?〉
〈I...I DON'T KNOW THE TRUTH.〉
〈WHEN HE WAS NICE, WAS HE JUST PUTTING ON AN ACT?〉
〈HE USED TO HIT ME!〉
〈DAD WANTED TO BE AN ACTOR, SO HE WAS A GOOD LIAR.〉
〈HE LIED THAT DAY, TOO...〉
〈HE WAS A DRUG DEALER.〉
〈THERE WAS SOME TROUBLE. HE KILLED HIS PARTNER AND RAN.〉
〈CHRIS...〉
〈JENNY...〉

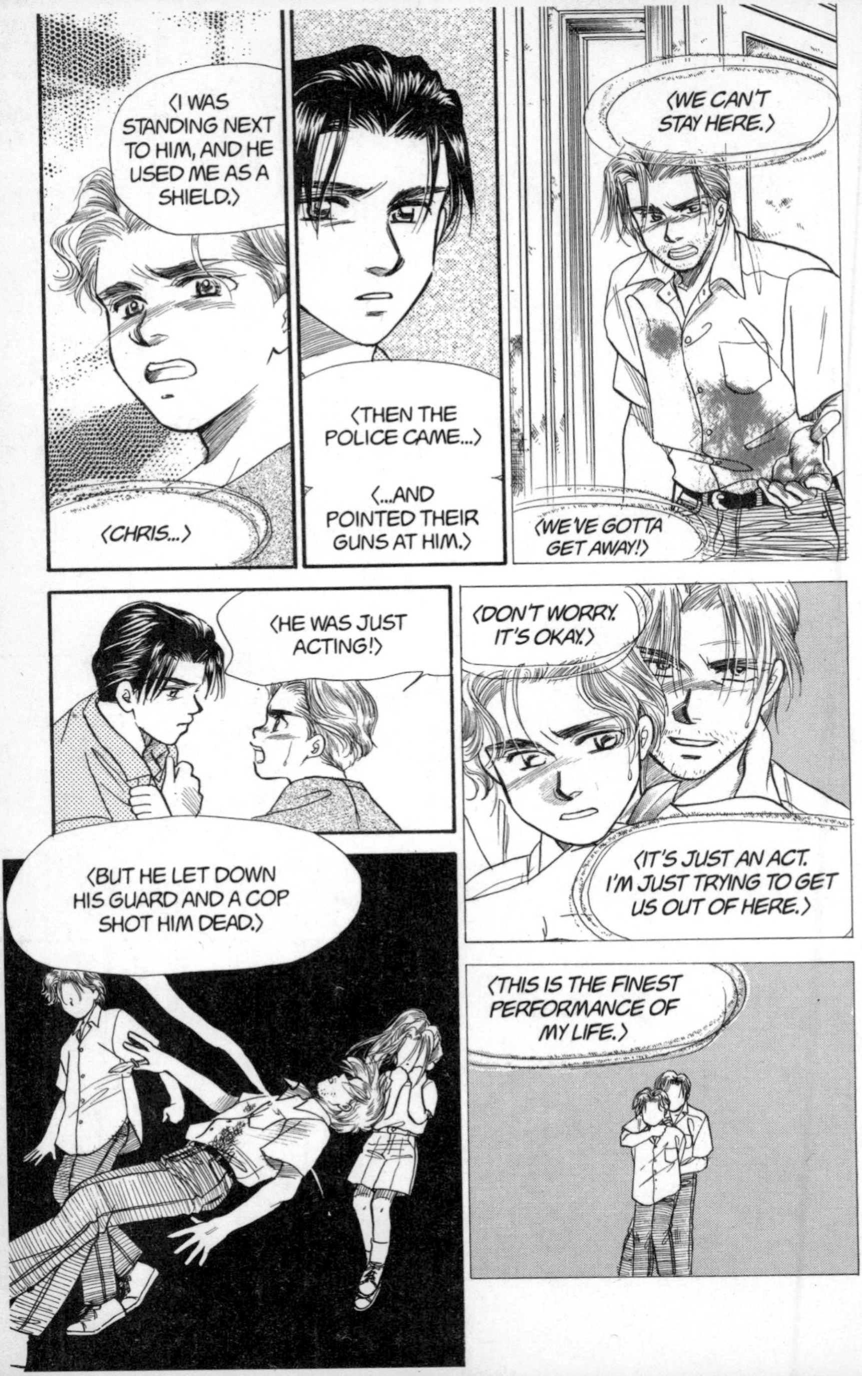
⟨WE CAN'T STAY HERE.⟩
⟨WE'VE GOTTA GET AWAY!⟩
⟨THEN THE POLICE CAME...⟩
⟨...AND POINTED THEIR GUNS AT HIM.⟩
⟨I WAS STANDING NEXT TO HIM, AND HE USED ME AS A SHIELD.⟩
⟨CHRIS...⟩
⟨DON'T WORRY. IT'S OKAY.⟩
⟨IT'S JUST AN ACT. I'M JUST TRYING TO GET US OUT OF HERE.⟩
⟨HE WAS JUST ACTING!⟩
⟨THIS IS THE FINEST PERFORMANCE OF MY LIFE.⟩
⟨BUT HE LET DOWN HIS GUARD AND A COP SHOT HIM DEAD.⟩

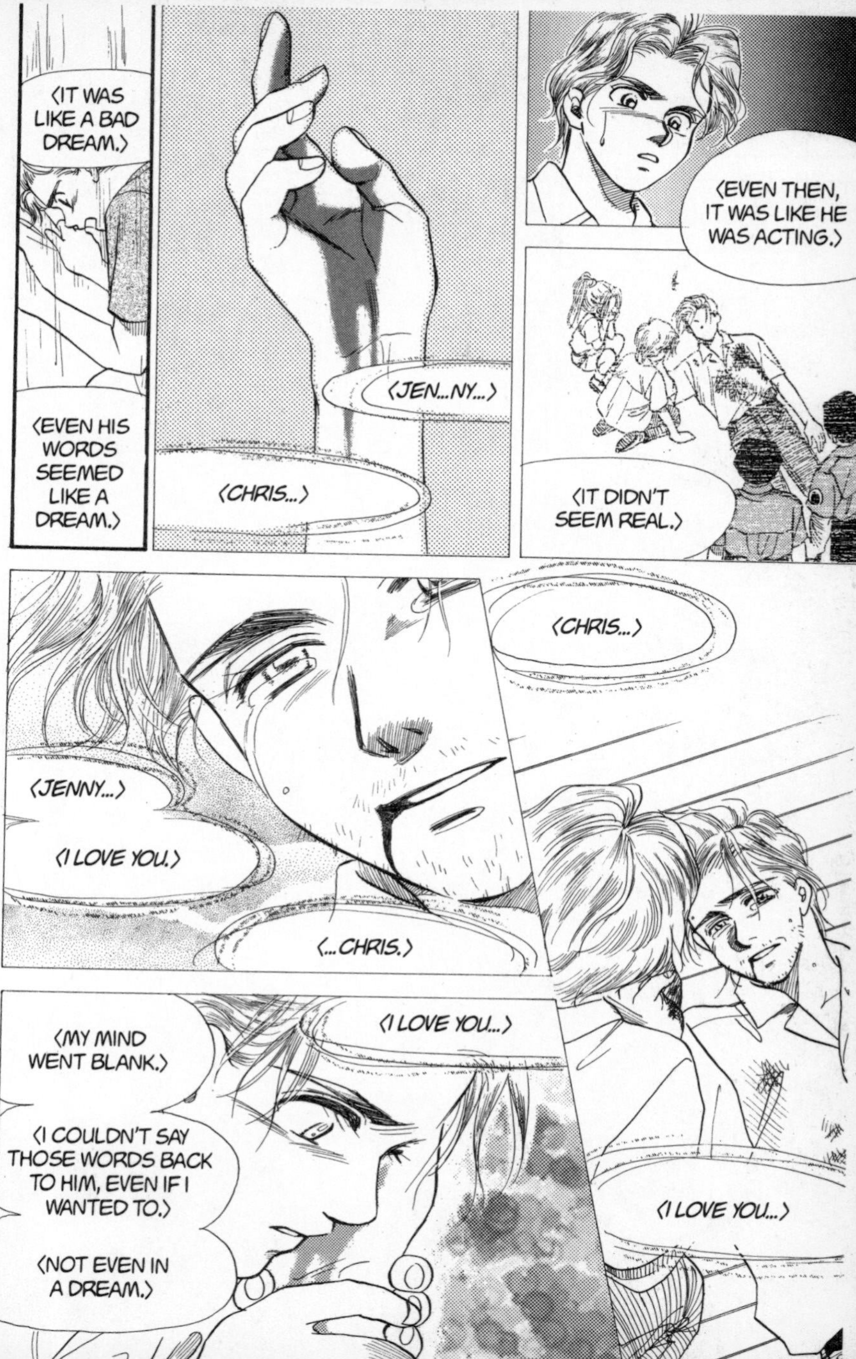

⟨EVEN THEN, IT WAS LIKE HE WAS ACTING.⟩
⟨IT DIDN'T SEEM REAL.⟩
⟨JEN...NY...⟩
⟨CHRIS...⟩
⟨IT WAS LIKE A BAD DREAM.⟩
⟨EVEN HIS WORDS SEEMED LIKE A DREAM.⟩
⟨CHRIS...⟩
⟨I LOVE YOU...⟩
⟨JENNY...⟩
⟨I LOVE YOU.⟩
⟨...CHRIS.⟩
⟨I LOVE YOU...⟩
⟨MY MIND WENT BLANK.⟩
⟨I COULDN'T SAY THOSE WORDS BACK TO HIM, EVEN IF I WANTED TO.⟩
⟨NOT EVEN IN A DREAM.⟩

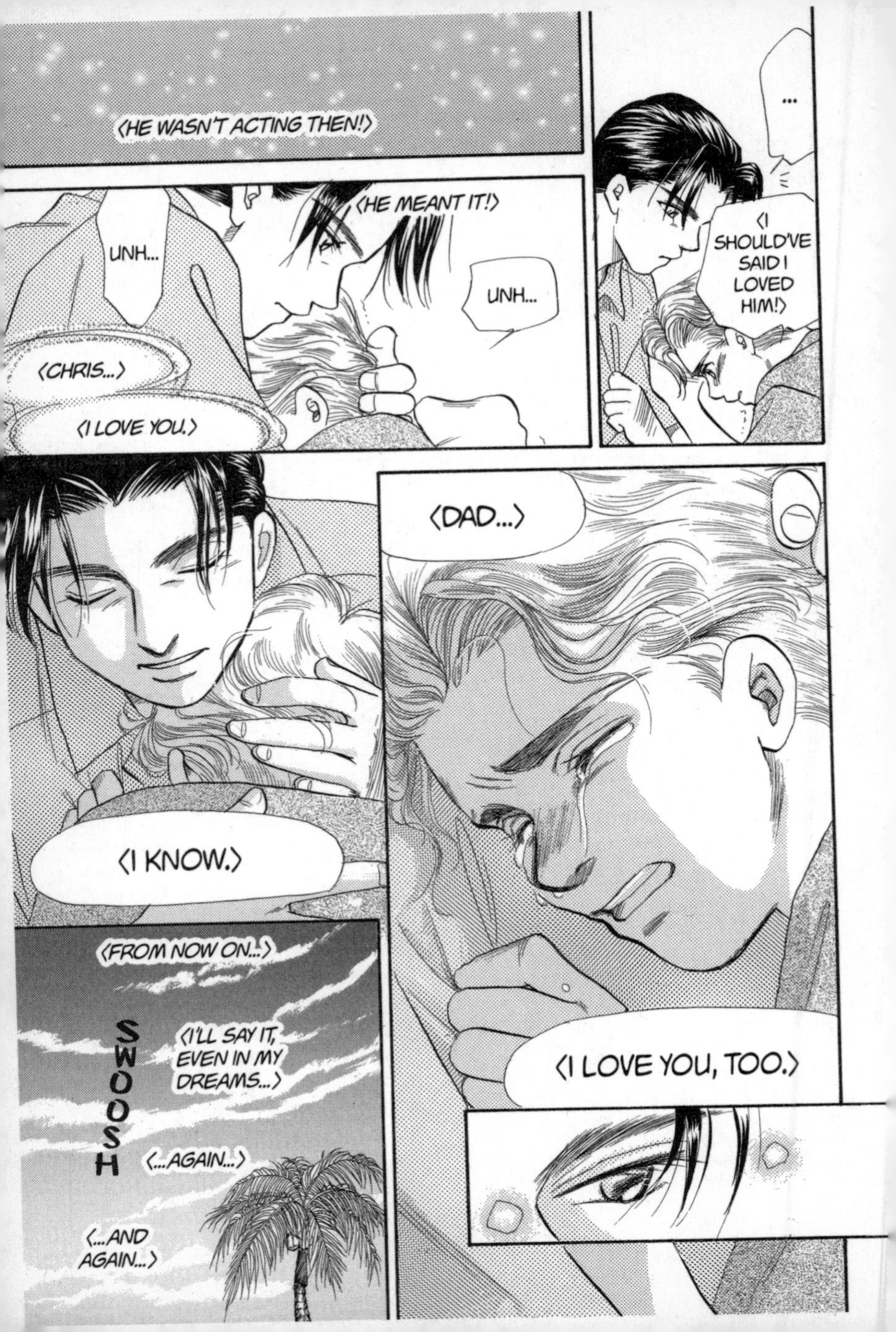
...
〈I SHOULD'VE SAID I LOVED HIM!〉
〈HE WASN'T ACTING THEN!〉
〈HE MEANT IT!〉
UNH...
UNH...
〈CHRIS...〉
〈I LOVE YOU.〉
〈DAD...〉
〈I LOVE YOU, TOO.〉
〈I KNOW.〉
〈FROM NOW ON...〉
〈I'LL SAY IT, EVEN IN MY DREAMS...〉
SWOOSH
〈...AGAIN...〉
〈...AND AGAIN...〉

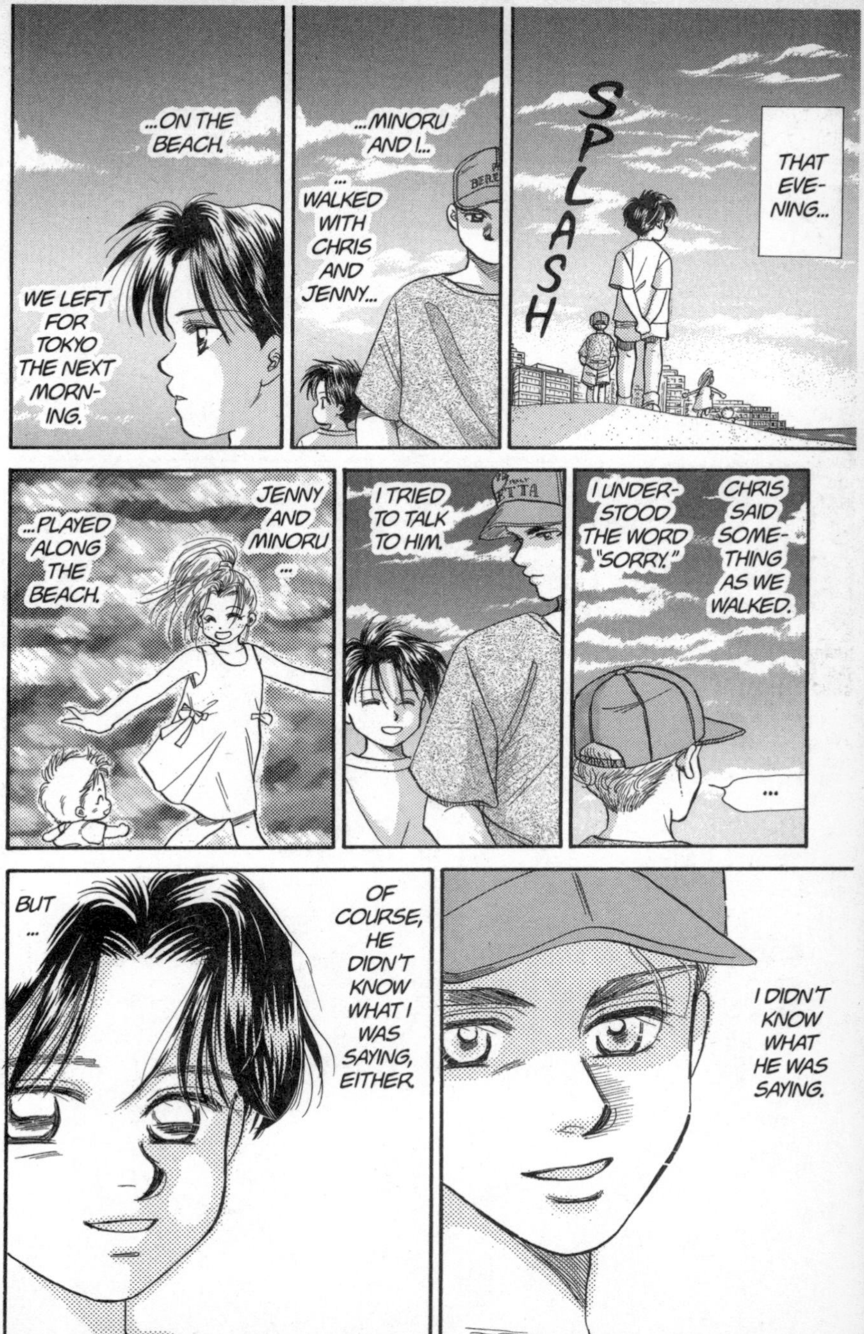
THAT EVENING...
SPLASH
...MINORU AND I...
...WALKED WITH CHRIS AND JENNY...
...ON THE BEACH.
WE LEFT FOR TOKYO THE NEXT MORNING.
CHRIS SAID SOMETHING AS WE WALKED.
I UNDERSTOOD THE WORD "SORRY."
...
I TRIED TO TALK TO HIM.
JENNY AND MINORU ...
...PLAYED ALONG THE BEACH.
I DIDN'T KNOW WHAT HE WAS SAYING.
BUT ...
OF COURSE, HE DIDN'T KNOW WHAT I WAS SAYING, EITHER.

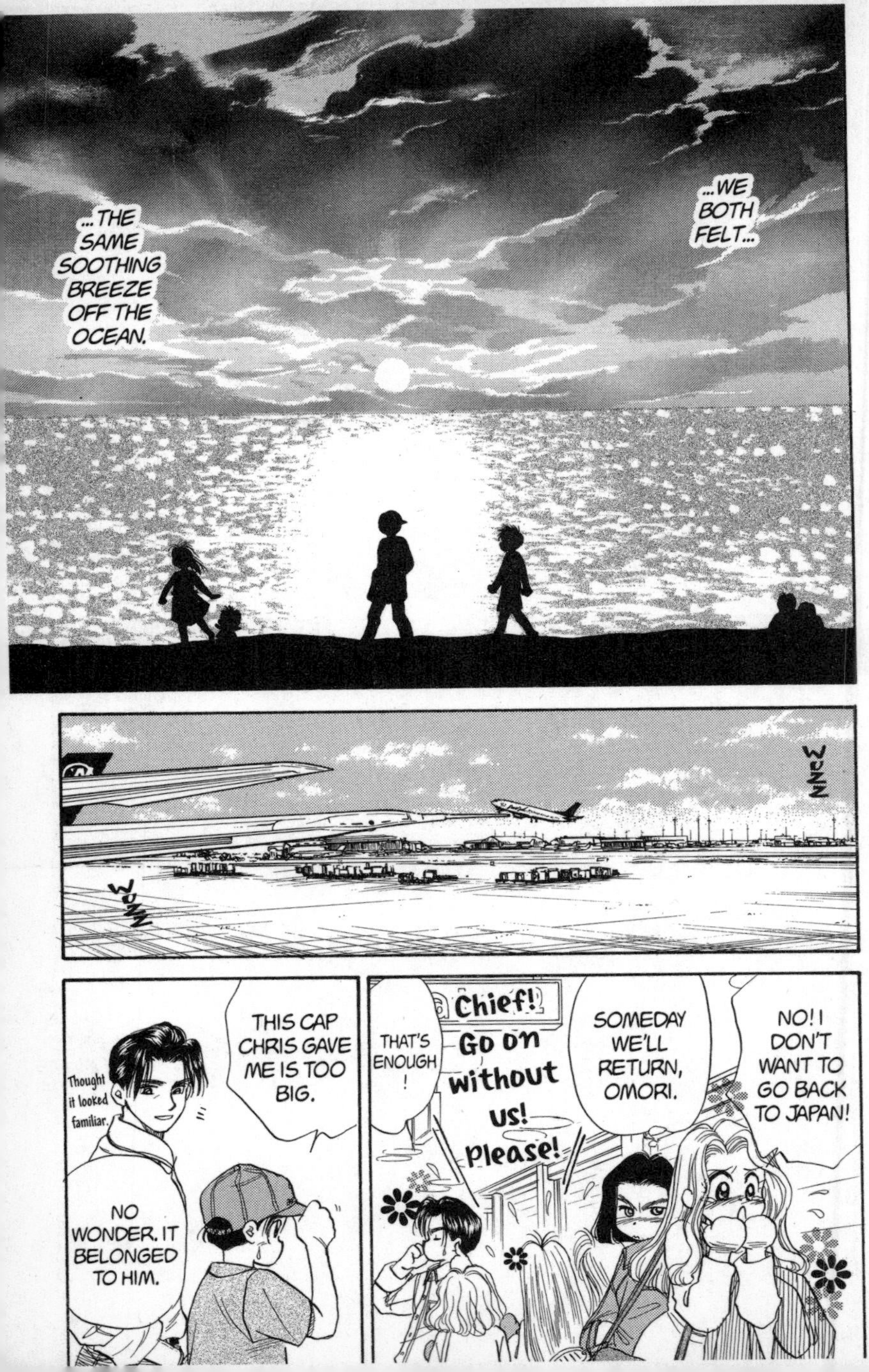
...WE BOTH FELT...
...THE SAME SOOTHING BREEZE OFF THE OCEAN.
WUZN
WUZN
NO! I DON'T WANT TO GO BACK TO JAPAN!
SOMEDAY WE'LL RETURN, OMORI.
Chief! Go on without us! Please!
THAT'S ENOUGH!
THIS CAP CHRIS GAVE ME IS TOO BIG.
Thought it looked familiar.
NO WONDER. IT BELONGED TO HIM.

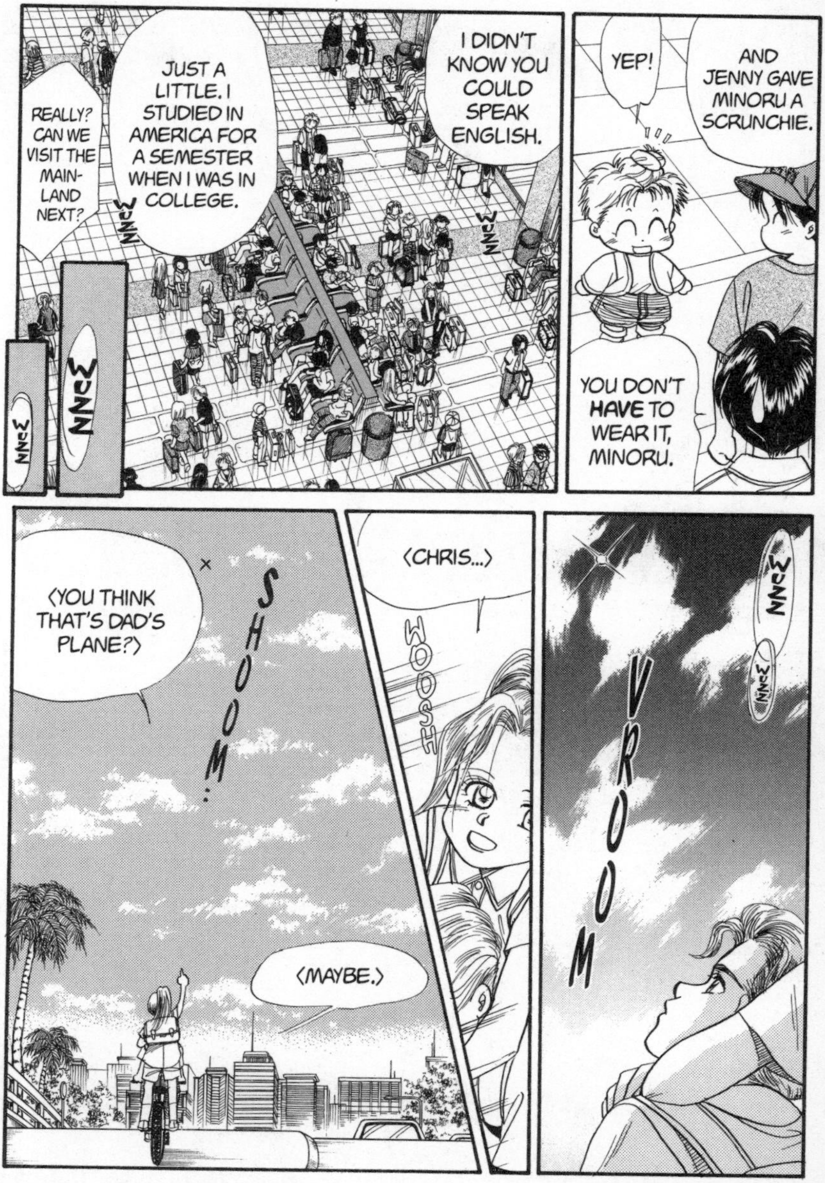
AND JENNY GAVE MINORU A SCRUNCHIE.
YEP!
YOU DON'T **HAVE** TO WEAR IT, MINORU.
I DIDN'T KNOW YOU COULD SPEAK ENGLISH.
WUZZ
JUST A LITTLE. I STUDIED IN AMERICA FOR A SEMESTER WHEN I WAS IN COLLEGE.
WUZZ
REALLY? CAN WE VISIT THE MAINLAND NEXT?
WUZZ
WUZZ
WUZZ
VROOOOM
WUZZ
⟨CHRIS...⟩
WOOSH
⟨YOU THINK THAT'S DAD'S PLANE?⟩
SHOOOM!
⟨MAYBE.⟩

Chapter 60 / The End

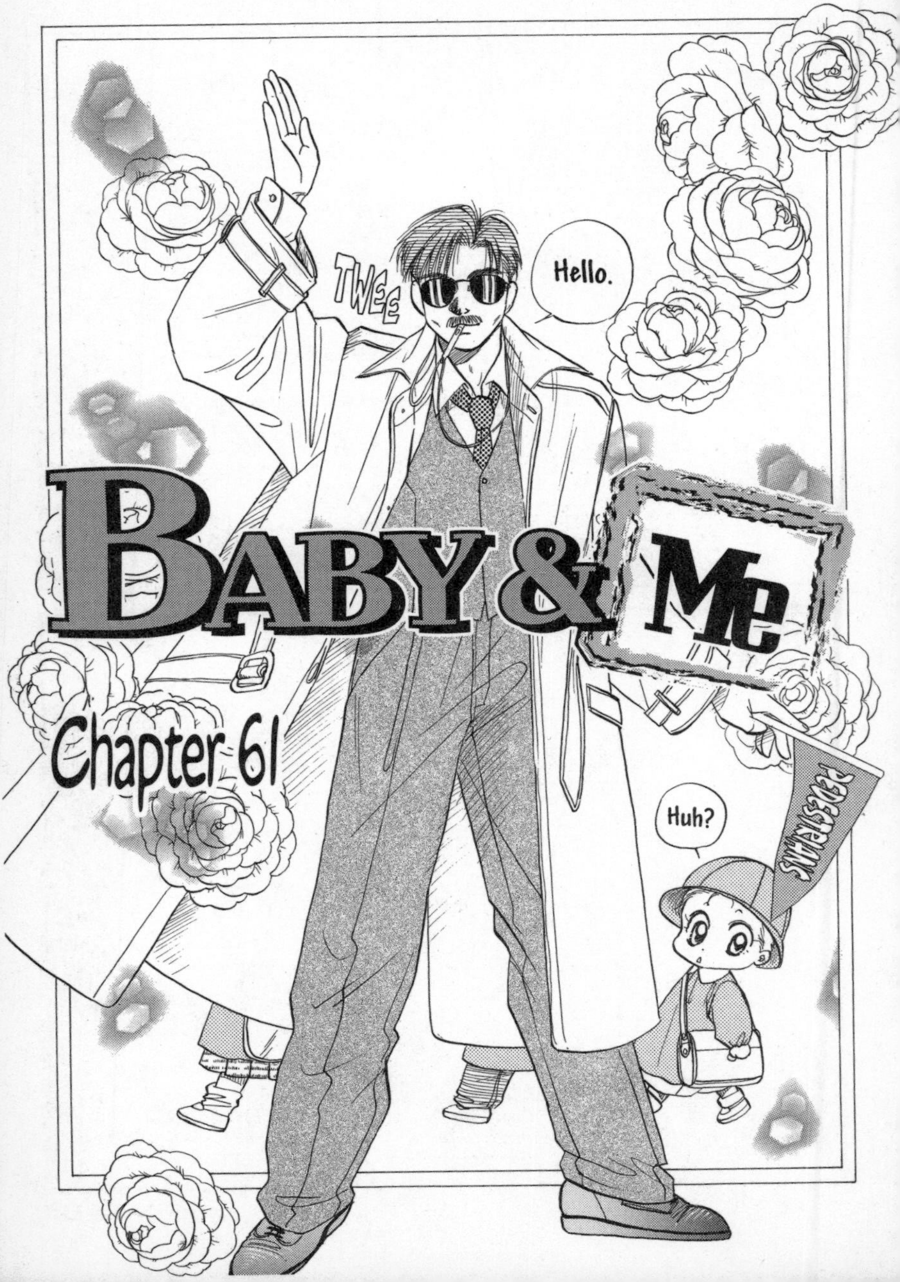
Hello.
TWEE
BABY & Me
Chapter 61
Huh?
PEDESTRIANS

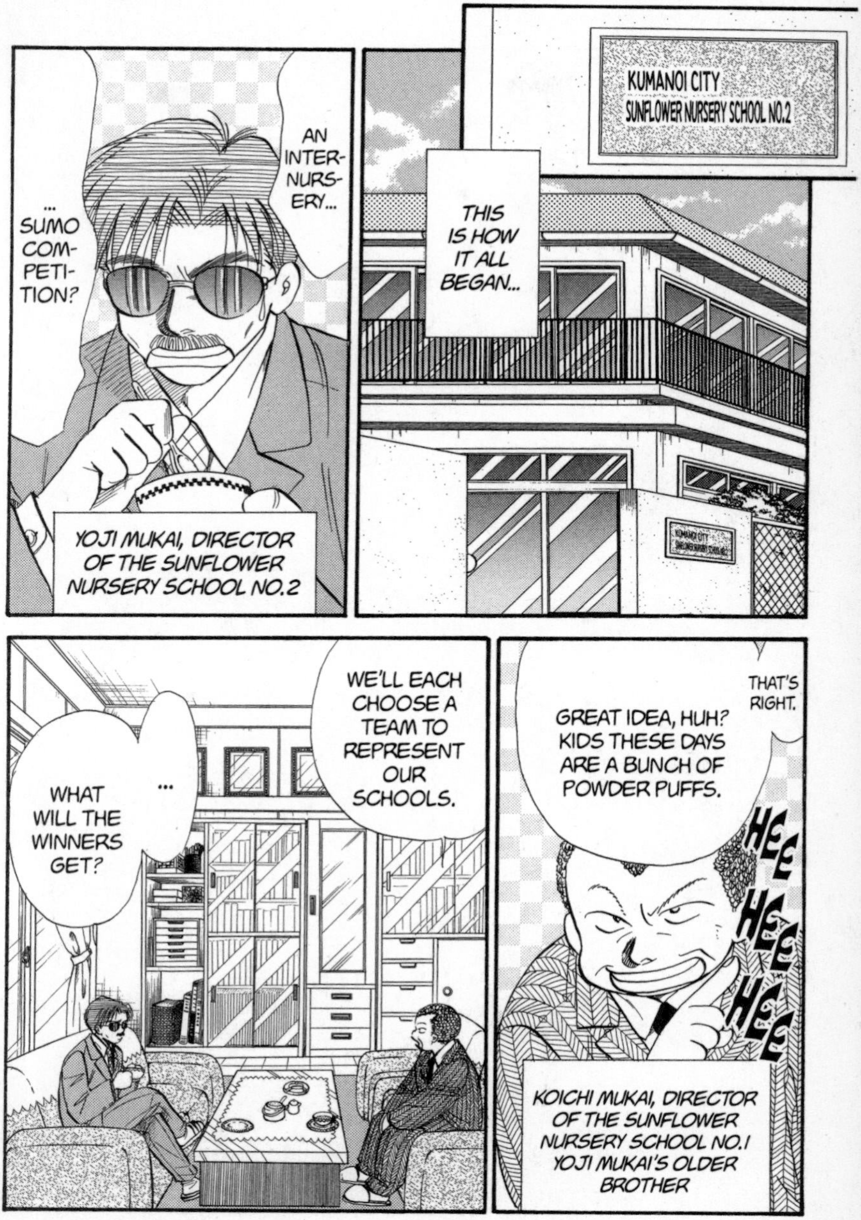
KUMANOI CITY
SUNFLOWER NURSERY SCHOOL NO.2
THIS IS HOW IT ALL BEGAN...
AN INTER-NURSERY...
... SUMO COMPETITION?
YOJI MUKAI, DIRECTOR OF THE SUNFLOWER NURSERY SCHOOL NO.2
THAT'S RIGHT.
GREAT IDEA, HUH? KIDS THESE DAYS ARE A BUNCH OF POWDER PUFFS.
HEE HEE HEE
KOICHI MUKAI, DIRECTOR OF THE SUNFLOWER NURSERY SCHOOL NO.1 YOJI MUKAI'S OLDER BROTHER
WE'LL EACH CHOOSE A TEAM TO REPRESENT OUR SCHOOLS.
...
WHAT WILL THE WINNERS GET?

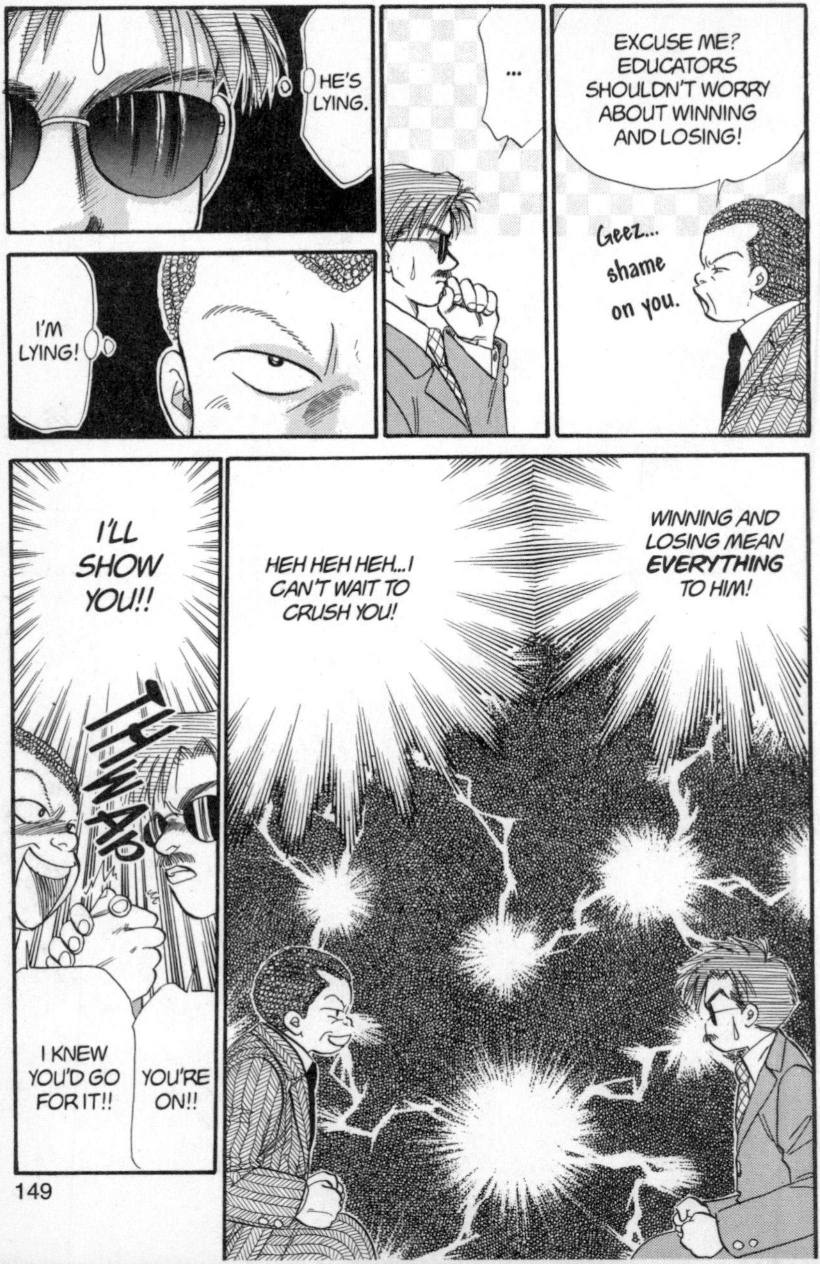
EXCUSE ME? EDUCATORS SHOULDN'T WORRY ABOUT WINNING AND LOSING!
Geez... shame on you.
...
HE'S LYING.
I'M LYING!
WINNING AND LOSING MEAN **EVERYTHING** TO HIM!
HEH HEH HEH...I CAN'T WAIT TO CRUSH YOU!
I'LL SHOW YOU!!
THWAP
YOU'RE ON!!
I KNEW YOU'D GO FOR IT!!

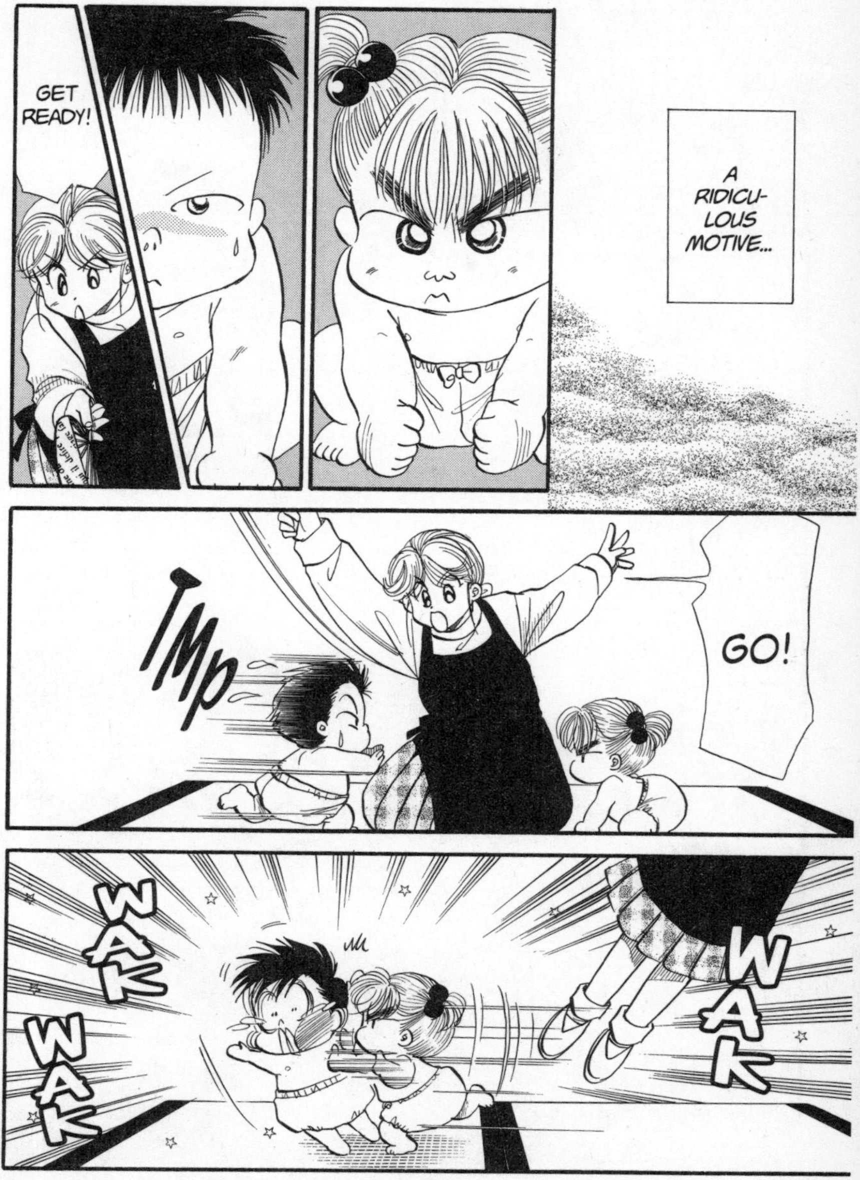
A RIDICU-
LOUS
MOTIVE...
GET
READY!
GO!
TMP
WAK
WAK
WAK

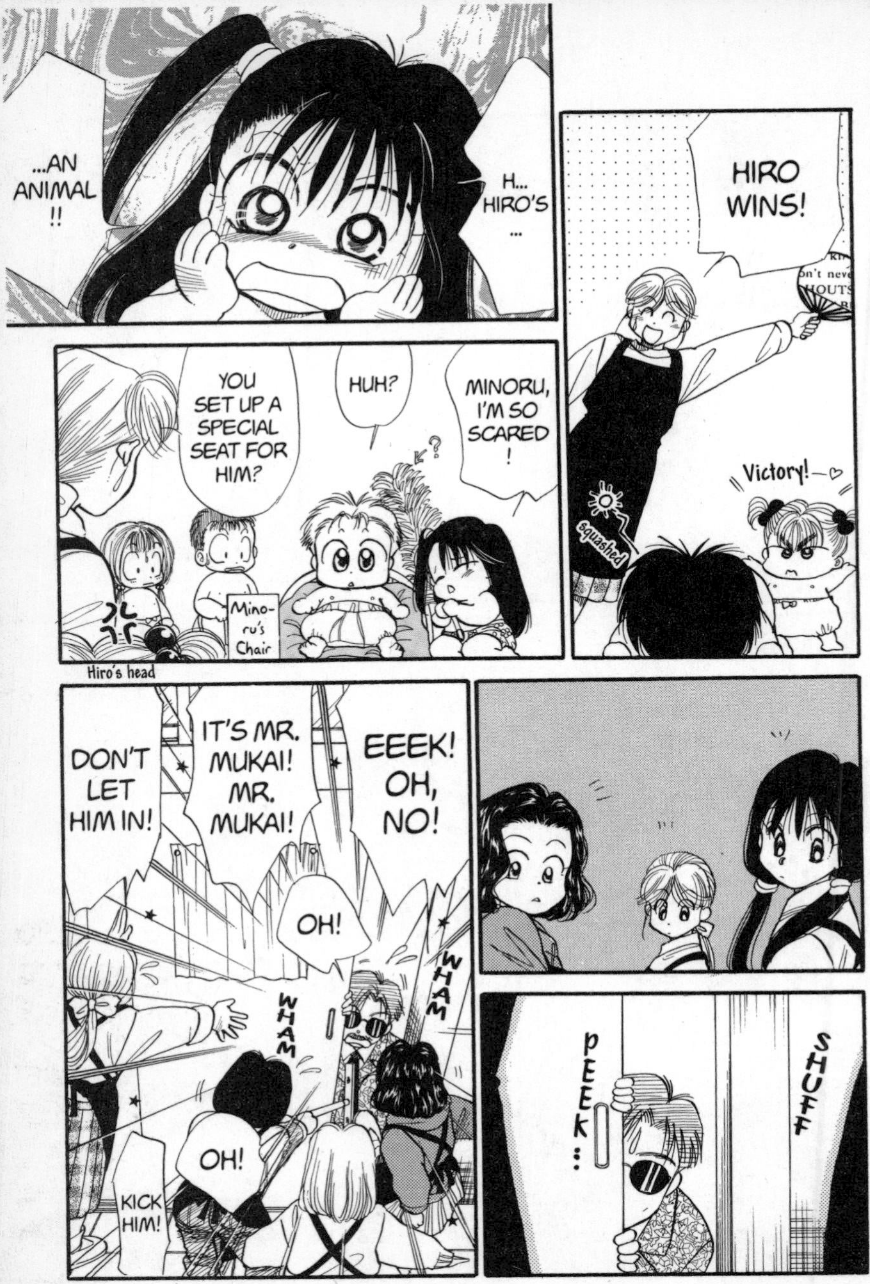
H... HIRO'S ...
...AN ANIMAL !!
HIRO WINS!
Victory!
squashed
MINORU, I'M SO SCARED !
HUH?
YOU SET UP A SPECIAL SEAT FOR HIM?
Mino-ru's Chair
Hiro's head
SHUFF
PEEK...
EEEK! OH, NO!
IT'S MR. MUKAI! MR. MUKAI!
DON'T LET HIM IN!
OH!
WHAM
WHAM
OH!
KICK HIM!

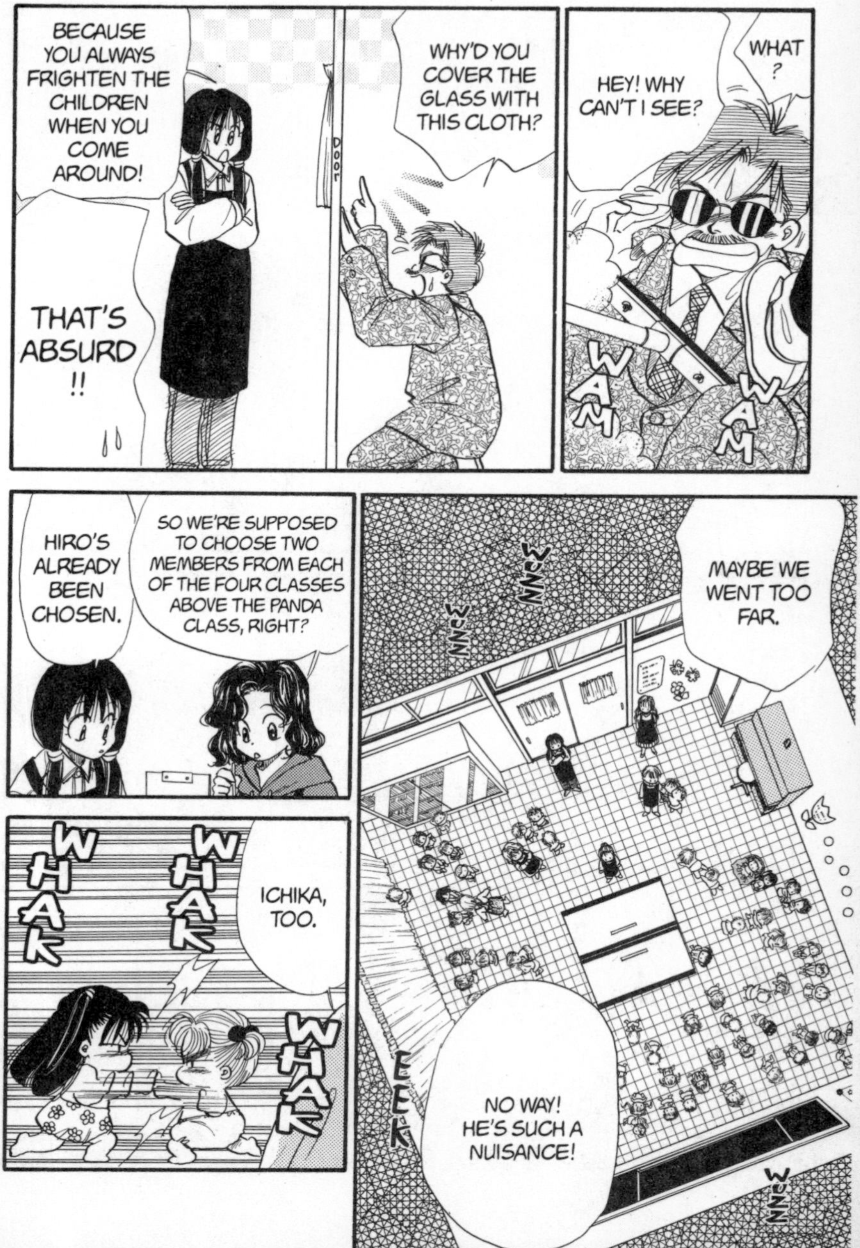
WHAT?
HEY! WHY CAN'T I SEE?
WAM
WAM
WHY'D YOU COVER THE GLASS WITH THIS CLOTH?
DOOR
BECAUSE YOU ALWAYS FRIGHTEN THE CHILDREN WHEN YOU COME AROUND!
THAT'S ABSURD!!
MAYBE WE WENT TOO FAR.
WNN
WNN
NO WAY! HE'S SUCH A NUISANCE!
EEEK
WNN
SO WE'RE SUPPOSED TO CHOOSE TWO MEMBERS FROM EACH OF THE FOUR CLASSES ABOVE THE PANDA CLASS, RIGHT?
HIRO'S ALREADY BEEN CHOSEN.
ICHIKA, TOO.
WHAK
WHAK
WHAK

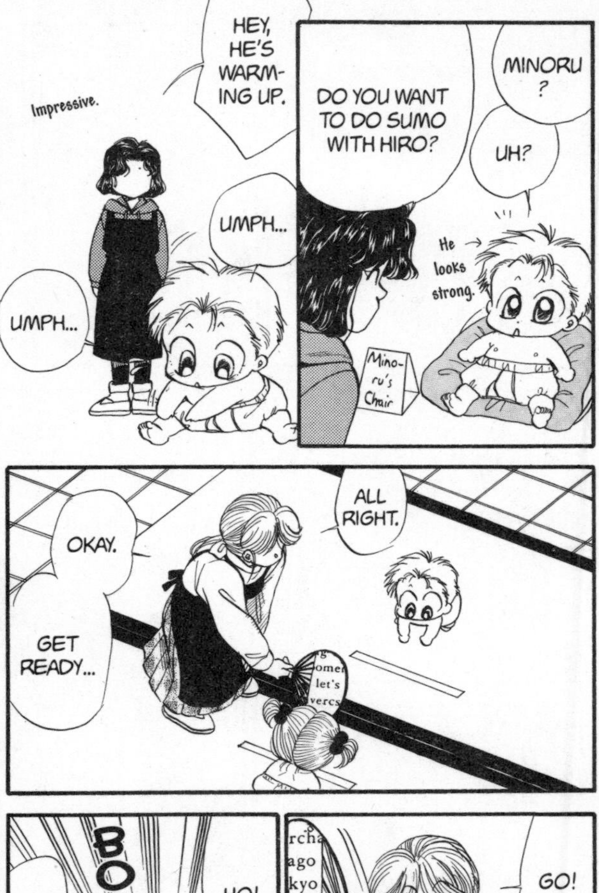
MINORU?
DO YOU WANT TO DO SUMO WITH HIRO?
UH?
He looks strong.
Mino-ru's Chair
HEY, HE'S WARMING UP.
Impressive.
UMPH...
UMPH...
ALL RIGHT.
OKAY.
GET READY...
GO!
TUP TUP TUP
HO!
BOOM
OOF!

Author's Note: Part 6

A Small Advertisement

Marimo Ragawa's Book of Illustrations: Baby and Me Upside Down Toy Box, published by Hakusensha...Only 1,600 yen! Please buy one! ♡

The book may be hard to find in rural areas. A lot of people wrote to say they couldn't find one anywhere. But you can order it through your local bookstore! It's simple and easy to do!

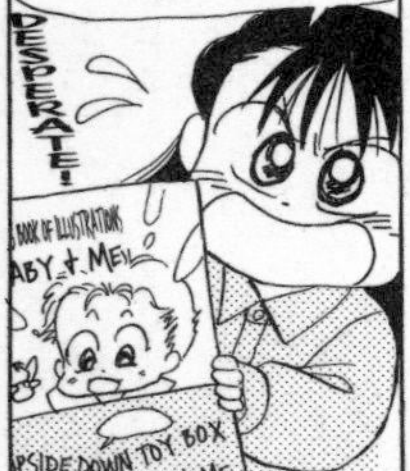
DESPERATE!
BOOK OF ILLUSTRATIONS
BABY + ME
UPSIDE DOWN TOY BOX
BABY + ME

There's a Baby and Me Card Gallery on sale, too. Ragawa is very happy because both are selling better than expected.

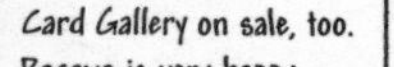
Whew! Just one more author's note to write. But first I'll take a break.

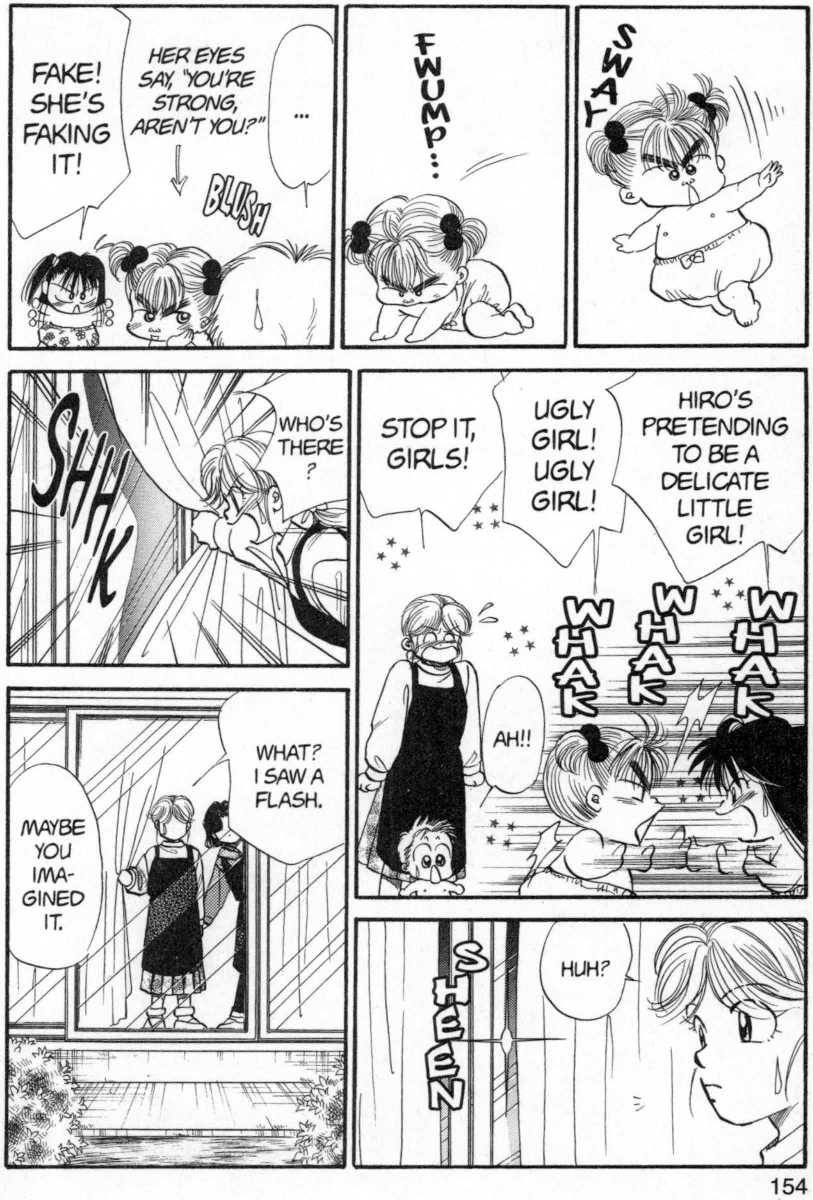
SWAY
FWUMP...
...
HER EYES SAY, "YOU'RE STRONG, AREN'T YOU?"
BLUSH
FAKE! SHE'S FAKING IT!
HIRO'S PRETENDING TO BE A DELICATE LITTLE GIRL!
UGLY GIRL! UGLY GIRL!
STOP IT, GIRLS!
WHAK
WHAK
WHAK
AH!!
SHEEN
HUH?
WHO'S THERE?
SHHK
WHAT? I SAW A FLASH.
MAYBE YOU IMAGINED IT.

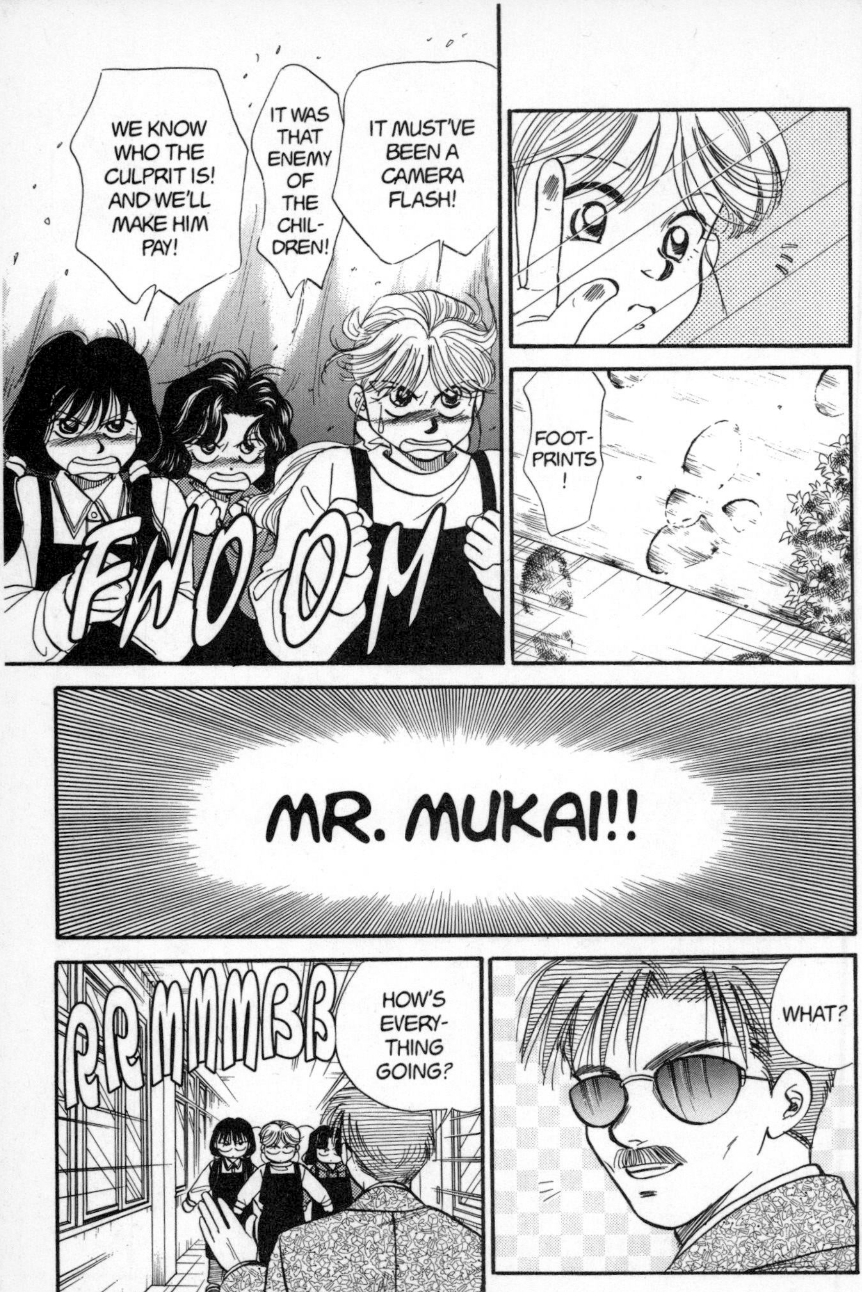
FOOT-PRINTS!
IT MUST'VE BEEN A CAMERA FLASH!
IT WAS THAT ENEMY OF THE CHIL-DREN!
WE KNOW WHO THE CULPRIT IS! AND WE'LL MAKE HIM PAY!
FWOOM
MR. MUKAI!!
WHAT?
HOW'S EVERY-THING GOING?
RRMMMBB

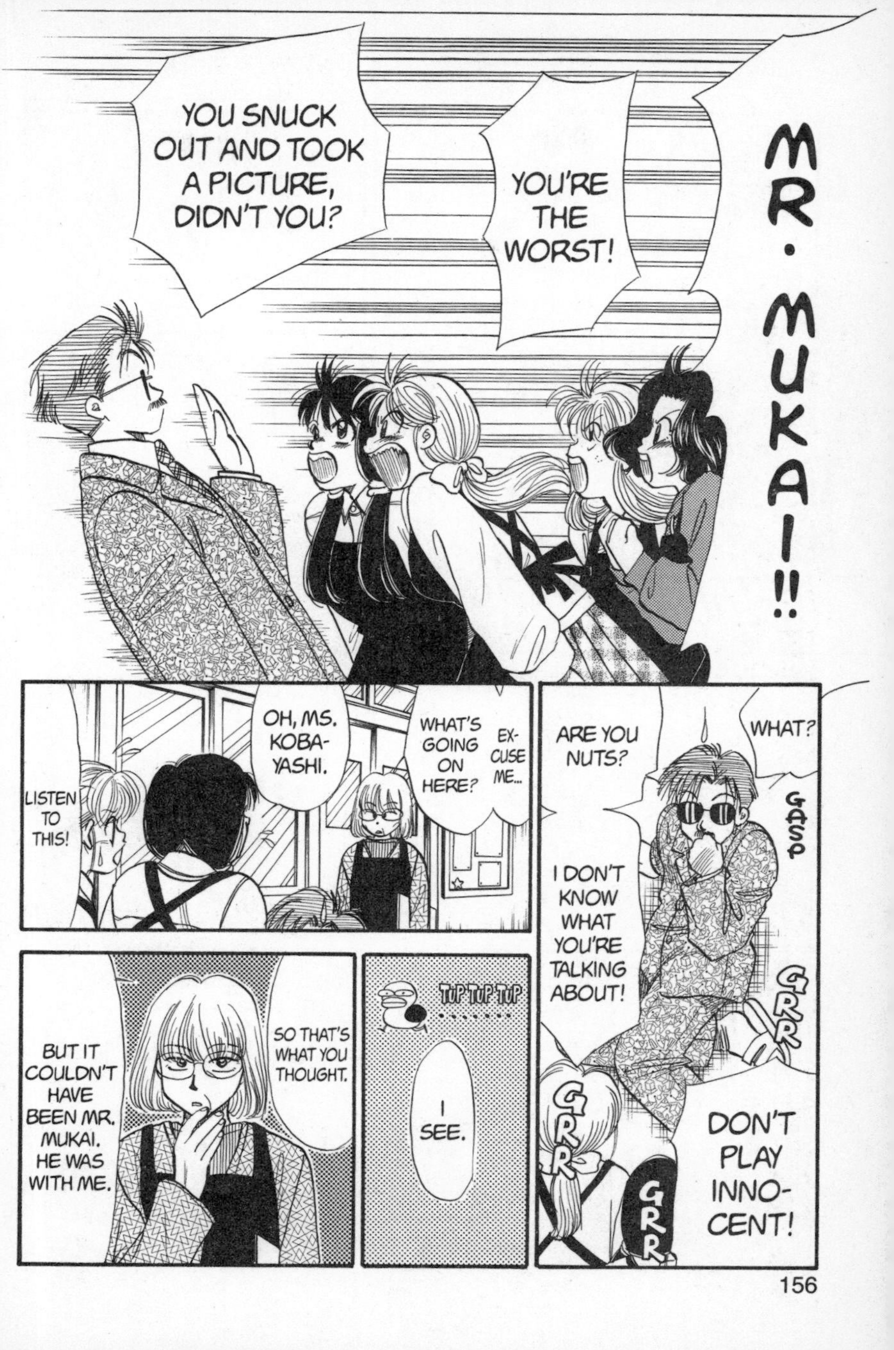
MR. MUKAI!!
YOU'RE THE WORST!
YOU SNUCK OUT AND TOOK A PICTURE, DIDN'T YOU?
WHAT?
GASP
ARE YOU NUTS?
I DON'T KNOW WHAT YOU'RE TALKING ABOUT!
GRR
GRR
GRR
DON'T PLAY INNO-CENT!
EX-CUSE ME...
WHAT'S GOING ON HERE?
OH, MS. KOBA-YASHI.
LISTEN TO THIS!
TUP TUP TUP
I SEE.
SO THAT'S WHAT YOU THOUGHT.
BUT IT COULDN'T HAVE BEEN MR. MUKAI. HE WAS WITH ME.

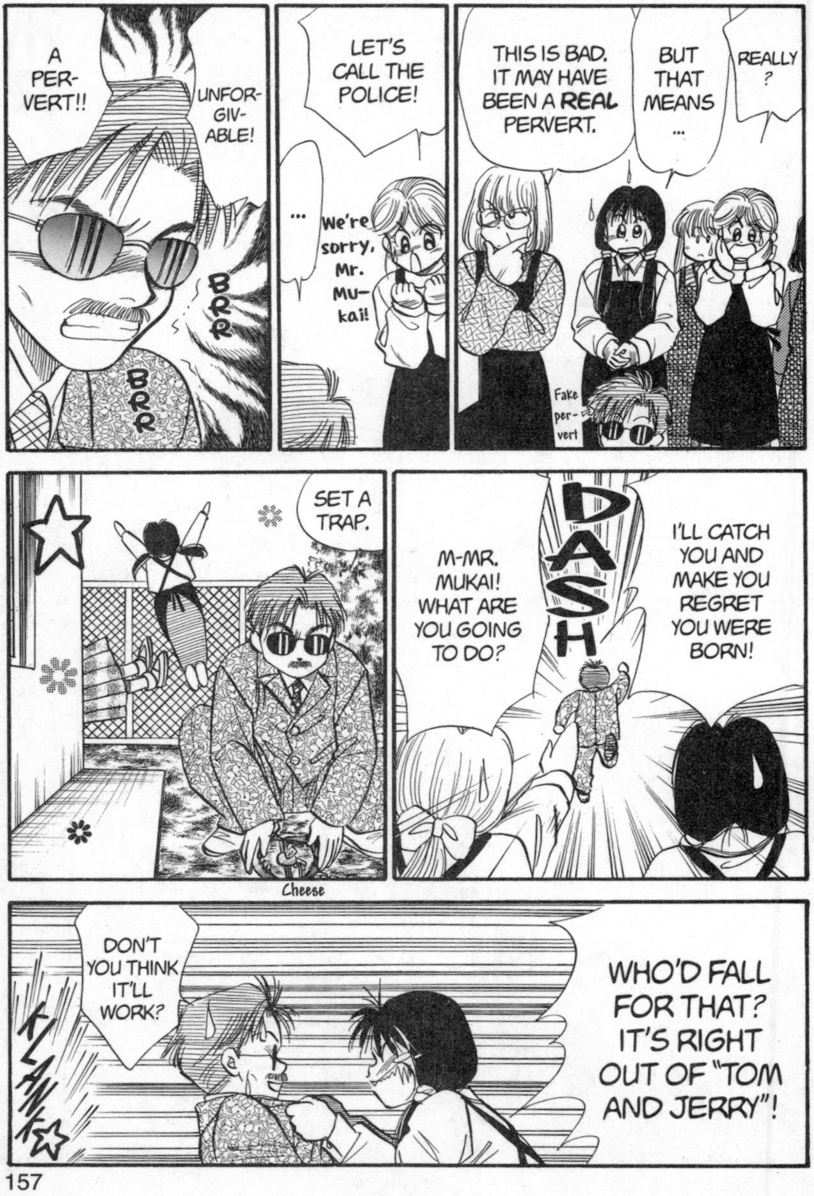
REALLY?
BUT THAT MEANS ...
THIS IS BAD. IT MAY HAVE BEEN A **REAL** PERVERT.
Fake pervert
LET'S CALL THE POLICE!
We're sorry, Mr. Mukai!
...
UNFORGIVABLE!
A PERVERT!!
BRR
BRR
I'LL CATCH YOU AND MAKE YOU REGRET YOU WERE BORN!
DASH
M-MR. MUKAI! WHAT ARE YOU GOING TO DO?
SET A TRAP.
Cheese
WHO'D FALL FOR THAT? IT'S RIGHT OUT OF "TOM AND JERRY"!
DON'T YOU THINK IT'LL WORK?
KLANK

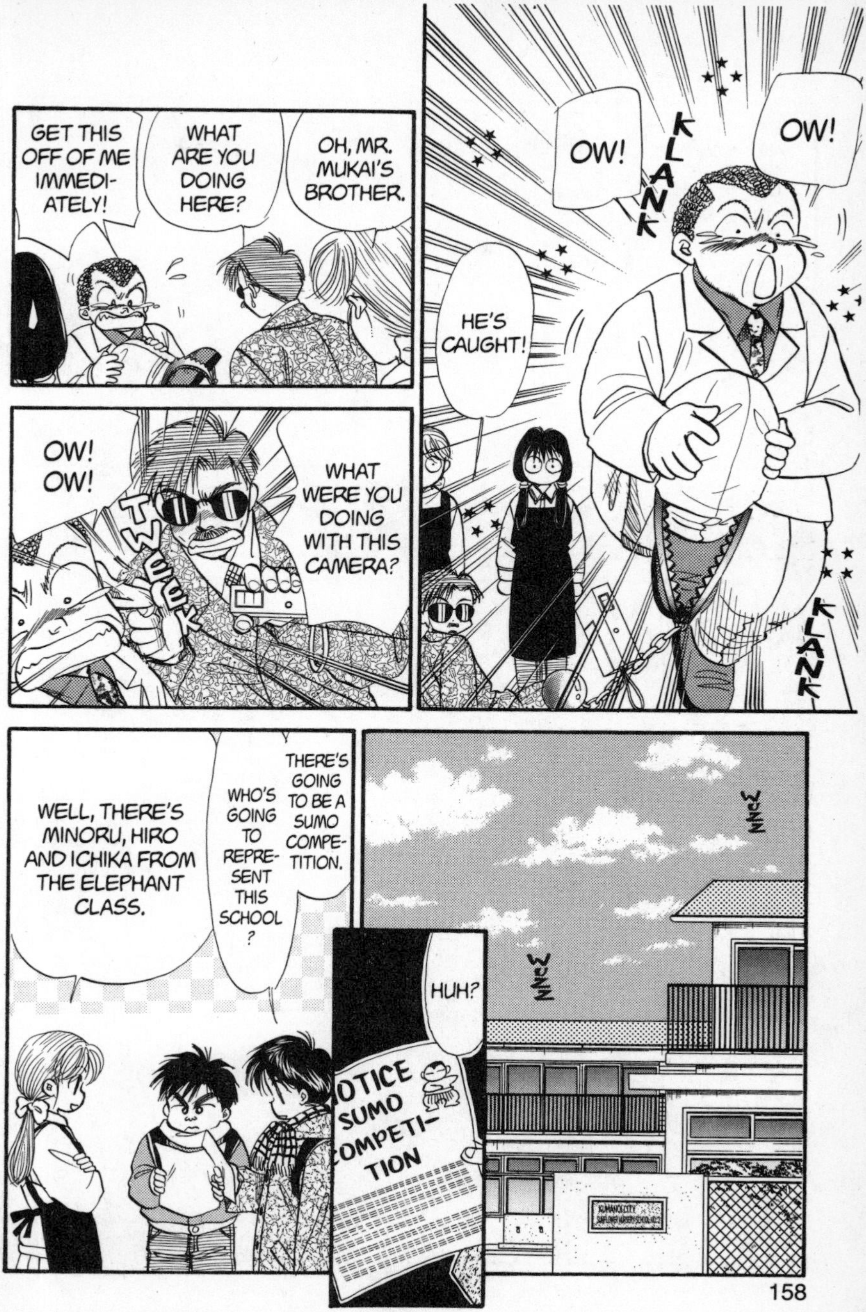
OW!
KLANK
OW!
HE'S CAUGHT!
KLANK
OH, MR. MUKAI'S BROTHER.
WHAT ARE YOU DOING HERE?
GET THIS OFF OF ME IMMEDIATELY!
WHAT WERE YOU DOING WITH THIS CAMERA?
TWEEK
OW! OW!
WUZZ
WUZZ
HUH?
OTICE SUMO COMPETITION
THERE'S GOING TO BE A SUMO COMPETITION.
WHO'S GOING TO REPRESENT THIS SCHOOL?
WELL, THERE'S MINORU, HIRO AND ICHIKA FROM THE ELEPHANT CLASS.

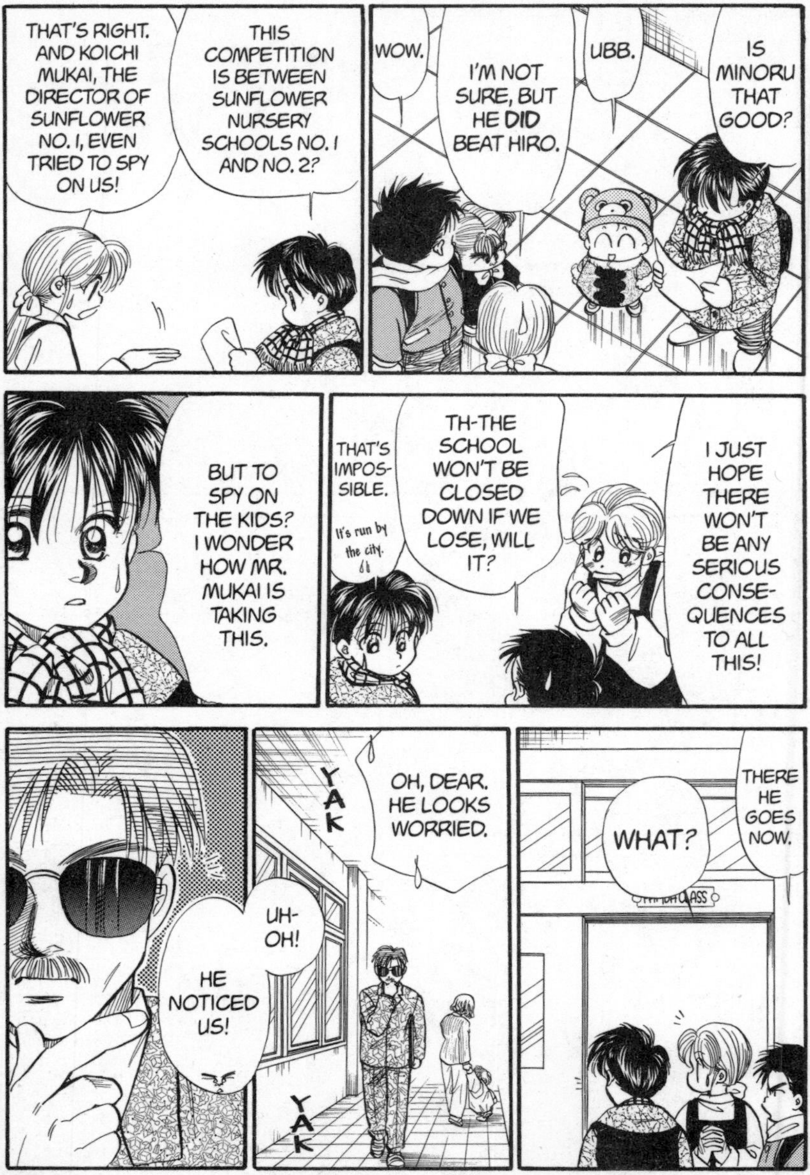
IS MINORU THAT GOOD?
UBB.
I'M NOT SURE, BUT HE DID BEAT HIRO.
WOW.
THIS COMPETITION IS BETWEEN SUNFLOWER NURSERY SCHOOLS NO. 1 AND NO. 2?
THAT'S RIGHT. AND KOICHI MUKAI, THE DIRECTOR OF SUNFLOWER NO. 1, EVEN TRIED TO SPY ON US!
I JUST HOPE THERE WON'T BE ANY SERIOUS CONSEQUENCES TO ALL THIS!
TH-THE SCHOOL WON'T BE CLOSED DOWN IF WE LOSE, WILL IT?
THAT'S IMPOSSIBLE.
It's run by the city.
BUT TO SPY ON THE KIDS? I WONDER HOW MR. MUKAI IS TAKING THIS.
THERE HE GOES NOW.
WHAT?
OH, DEAR. HE LOOKS WORRIED.
YAK
YAK
UH-OH!
HE NOTICED US!

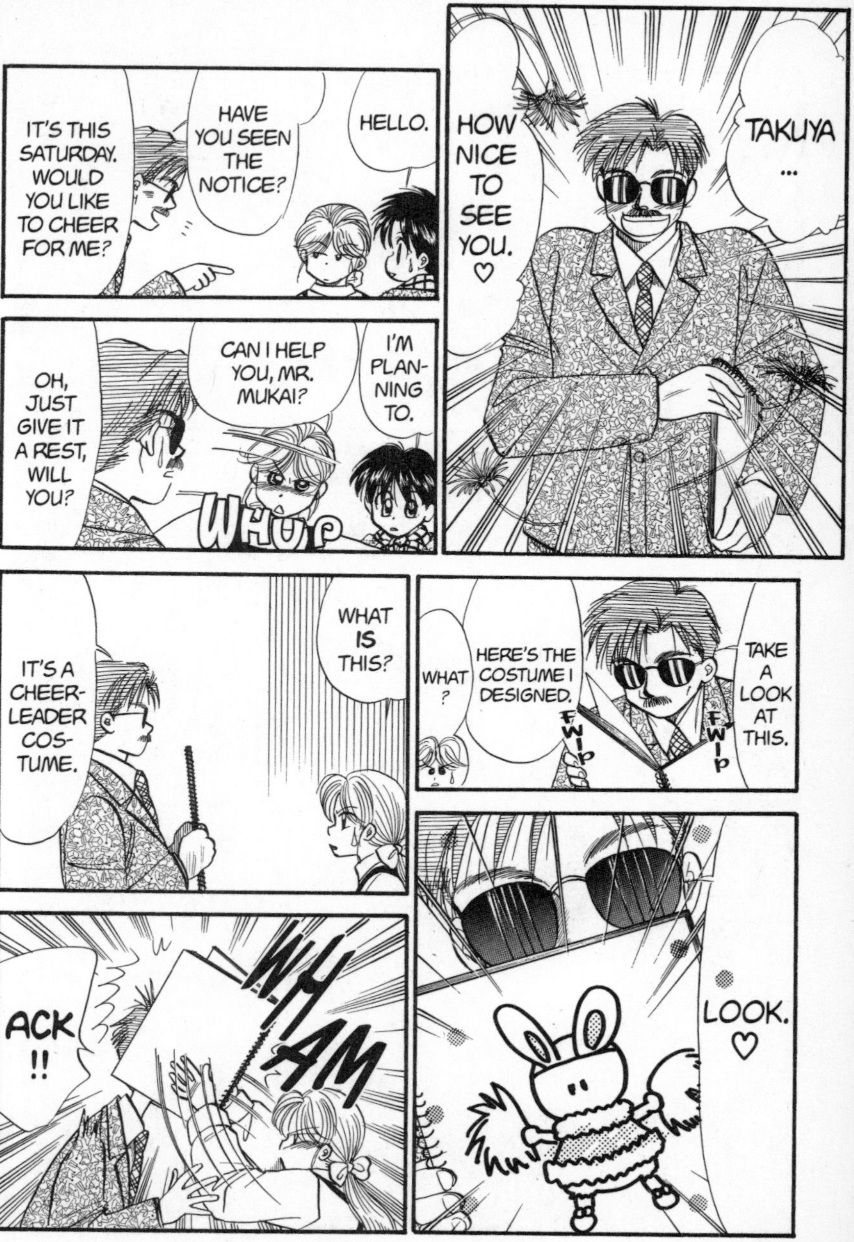
TAKUYA ...
HOW NICE TO SEE YOU. ♡
HELLO.
HAVE YOU SEEN THE NOTICE?
IT'S THIS SATURDAY. WOULD YOU LIKE TO CHEER FOR ME?
I'M PLAN-NING TO.
CAN I HELP YOU, MR. MUKAI?
WHUP
OH, JUST GIVE IT A REST, WILL YOU?
TAKE A LOOK AT THIS.
FWIP
FWIP
HERE'S THE COSTUME I DESIGNED.
WHAT ?
LOOK. ♡
WHAT IS THIS?
IT'S A CHEER-LEADER COS-TUME.
WHAM
ACK !!

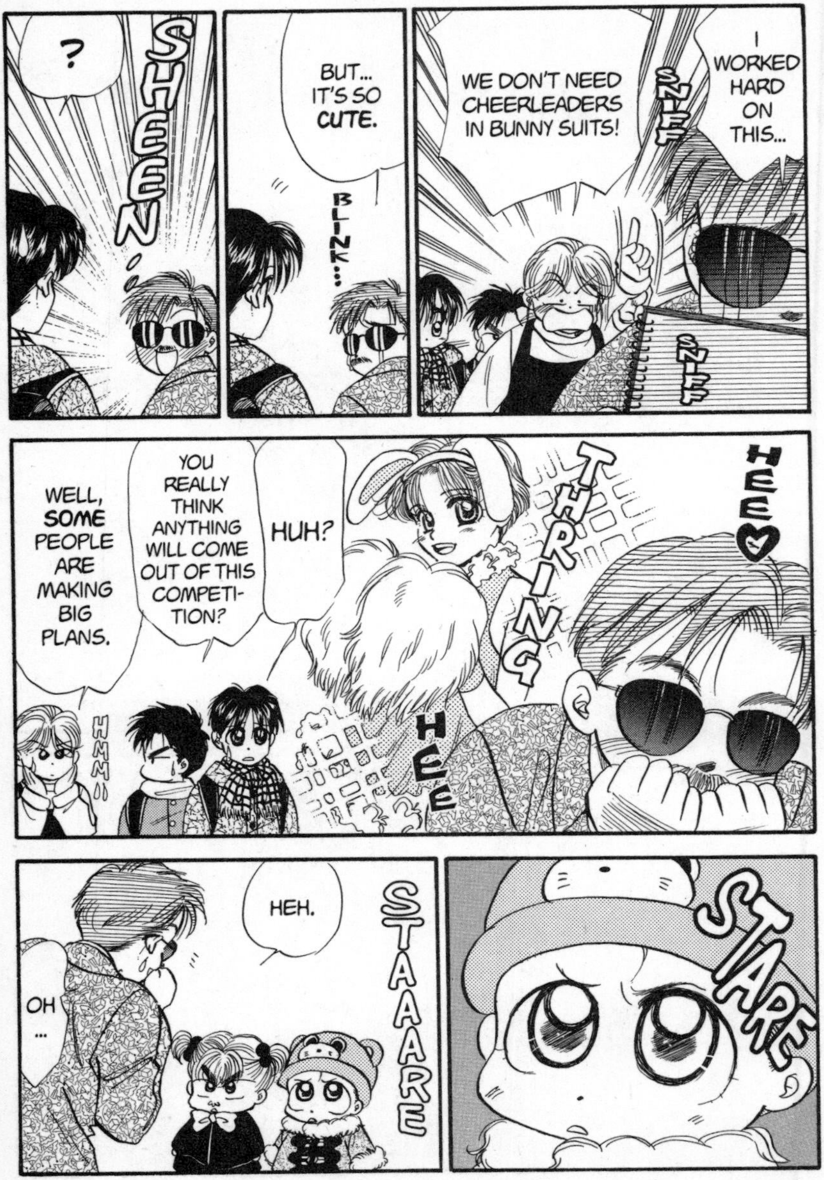
I WORKED HARD ON THIS...
SNIFF
WE DON'T NEED CHEERLEADERS IN BUNNY SUITS!
SNIFF
BUT... IT'S SO CUTE.
BLINK...
SHEEN
?
HEE♥
THRING
HEE HEE
HUH?
YOU REALLY THINK ANYTHING WILL COME OUT OF THIS COMPETITION?
WELL, SOME PEOPLE ARE MAKING BIG PLANS.
HMM
STARE
STAAAARE
HEH.
OH ...

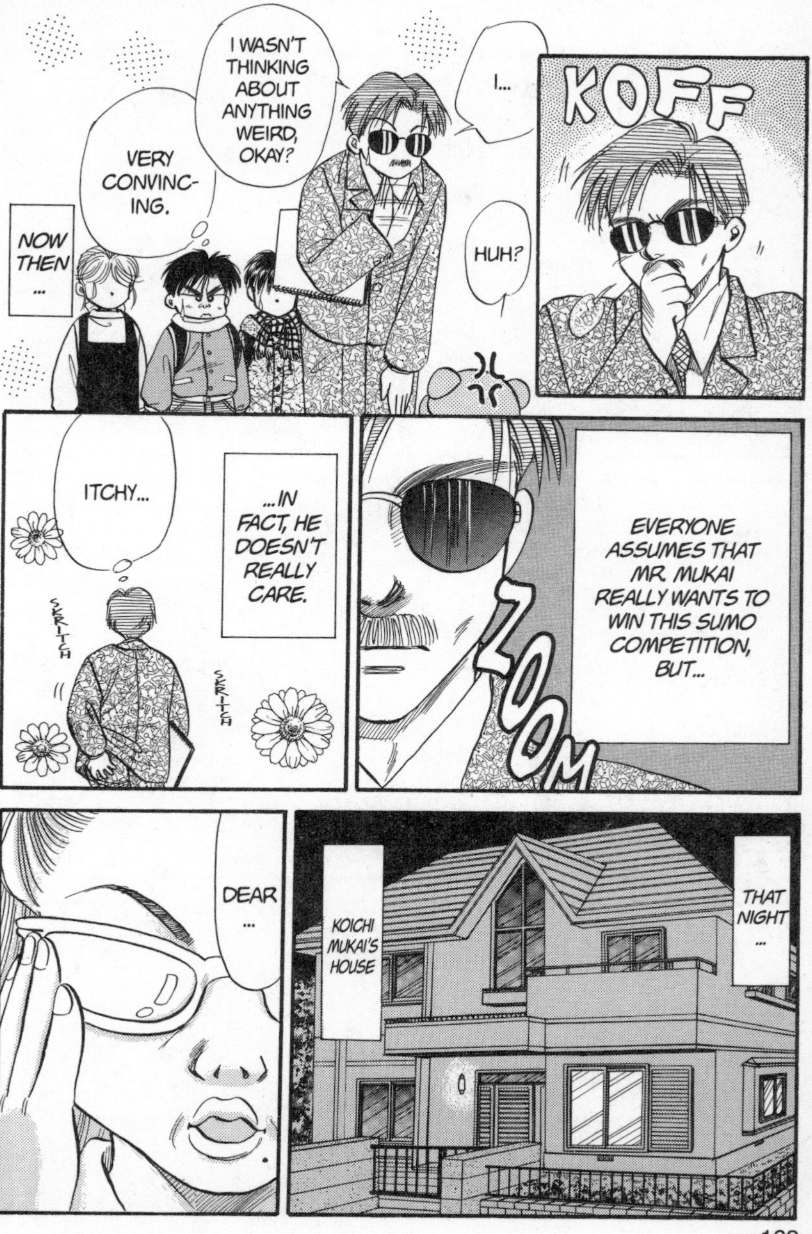
KOFF
I...
I WASN'T THINKING ABOUT ANYTHING WEIRD, OKAY?
HUH?
VERY CONVINCING.
NOW THEN ...
EVERYONE ASSUMES THAT MR. MUKAI REALLY WANTS TO WIN THIS SUMO COMPETITION, BUT...
ZOOM
...IN FACT, HE DOESN'T REALLY CARE.
ITCHY...
SKRITCH
SKRITCH
THAT NIGHT ...
KOICHI MUKAI'S HOUSE
DEAR ...

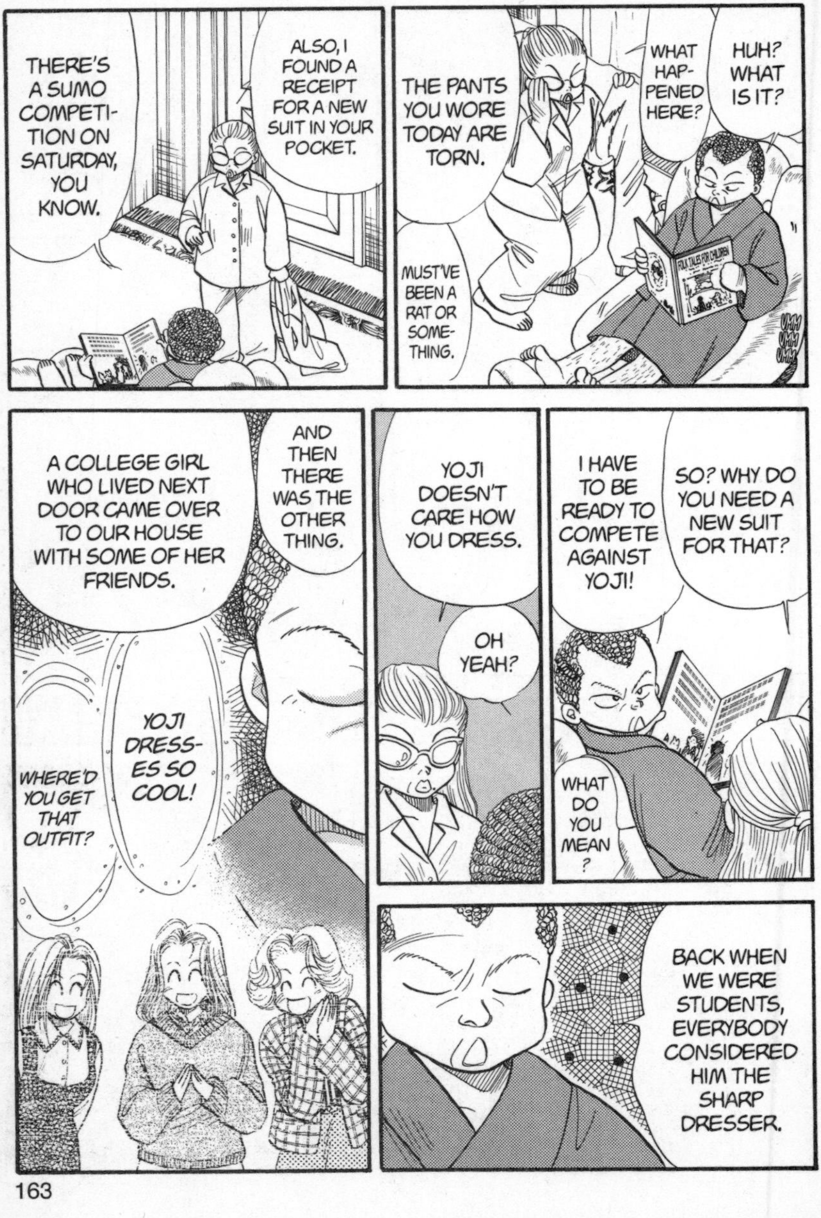
HUH? WHAT IS IT?
WHAT HAPPENED HERE?
THE PANTS YOU WORE TODAY ARE TORN.
MUST'VE BEEN A RAT OR SOMETHING.
ALSO, I FOUND A RECEIPT FOR A NEW SUIT IN YOUR POCKET.
THERE'S A SUMO COMPETITION ON SATURDAY, YOU KNOW.
FOLK TALES FOR CHILDREN
SO? WHY DO YOU NEED A NEW SUIT FOR THAT?
I HAVE TO BE READY TO COMPETE AGAINST YOJI!
WHAT DO YOU MEAN?
YOJI DOESN'T CARE HOW YOU DRESS.
OH YEAH?
BACK WHEN WE WERE STUDENTS, EVERYBODY CONSIDERED HIM THE SHARP DRESSER.
AND THEN THERE WAS THE OTHER THING.
A COLLEGE GIRL WHO LIVED NEXT DOOR CAME OVER TO OUR HOUSE WITH SOME OF HER FRIENDS.
YOJI DRESSES SO COOL!
WHERE'D YOU GET THAT OUTFIT?

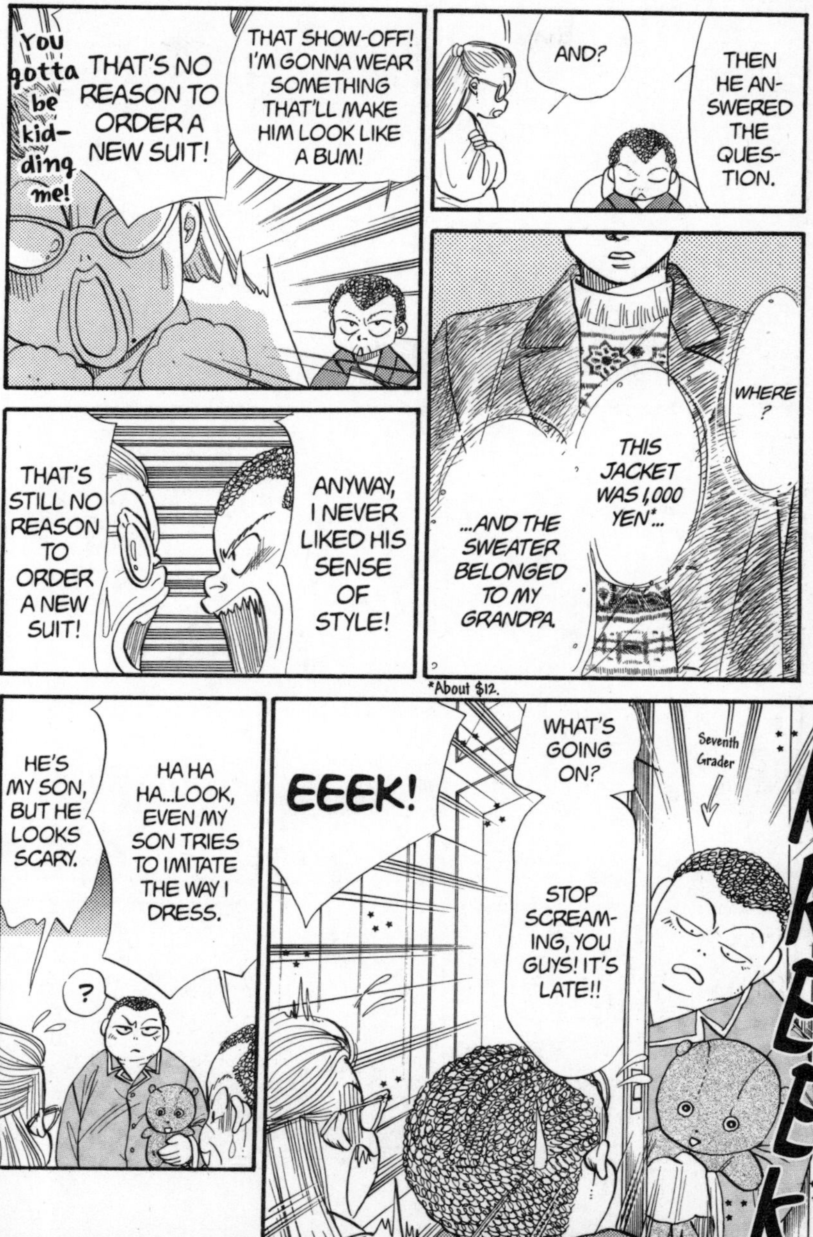
THEN HE ANSWERED THE QUESTION.
AND?
THAT SHOW-OFF! I'M GONNA WEAR SOMETHING THAT'LL MAKE HIM LOOK LIKE A BUM!
THAT'S NO REASON TO ORDER A NEW SUIT!
You gotta be kidding me!
WHERE?
THIS JACKET WAS 1,000 YEN*...
...AND THE SWEATER BELONGED TO MY GRANDPA.
ANYWAY, I NEVER LIKED HIS SENSE OF STYLE!
THAT'S STILL NO REASON TO ORDER A NEW SUIT!
KREEEK
Seventh Grader
WHAT'S GOING ON?
STOP SCREAMING, YOU GUYS! IT'S LATE!!
EEEK!
HA HA HA...LOOK, EVEN MY SON TRIES TO IMITATE THE WAY I DRESS.
HE'S MY SON, BUT HE LOOKS SCARY.
?

*About $12.

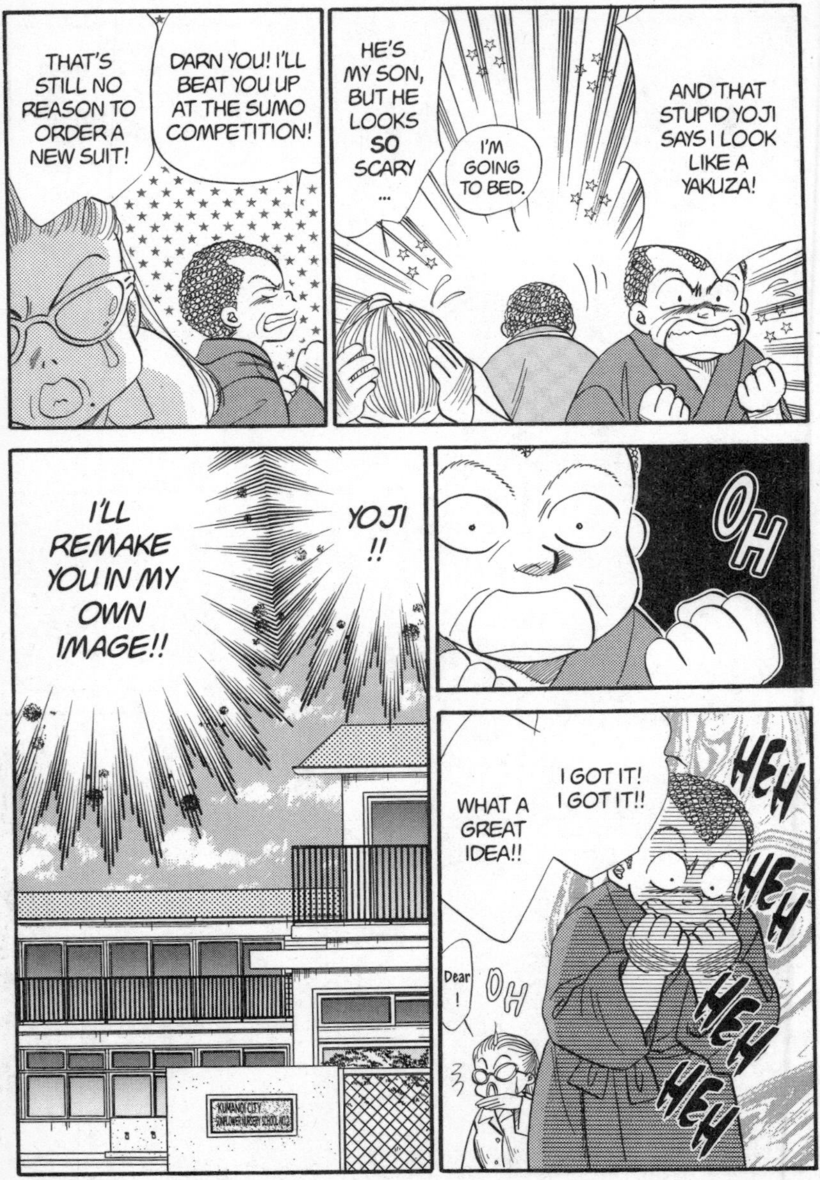
AND THAT STUPID YOJI SAYS I LOOK LIKE A YAKUZA!
I'M GOING TO BED.
HE'S MY SON, BUT HE LOOKS SO SCARY ...
DARN YOU! I'LL BEAT YOU UP AT THE SUMO COMPETITION!
THAT'S STILL NO REASON TO ORDER A NEW SUIT!
OH
HEH HEH HEH HEH
I GOT IT! I GOT IT!!
WHAT A GREAT IDEA!!
OH
Dear!
YOJI !!
I'LL REMAKE YOU IN MY OWN IMAGE!!
KUMANOI CITY SUNFLOWER NURSERY SCHOOL NO.2

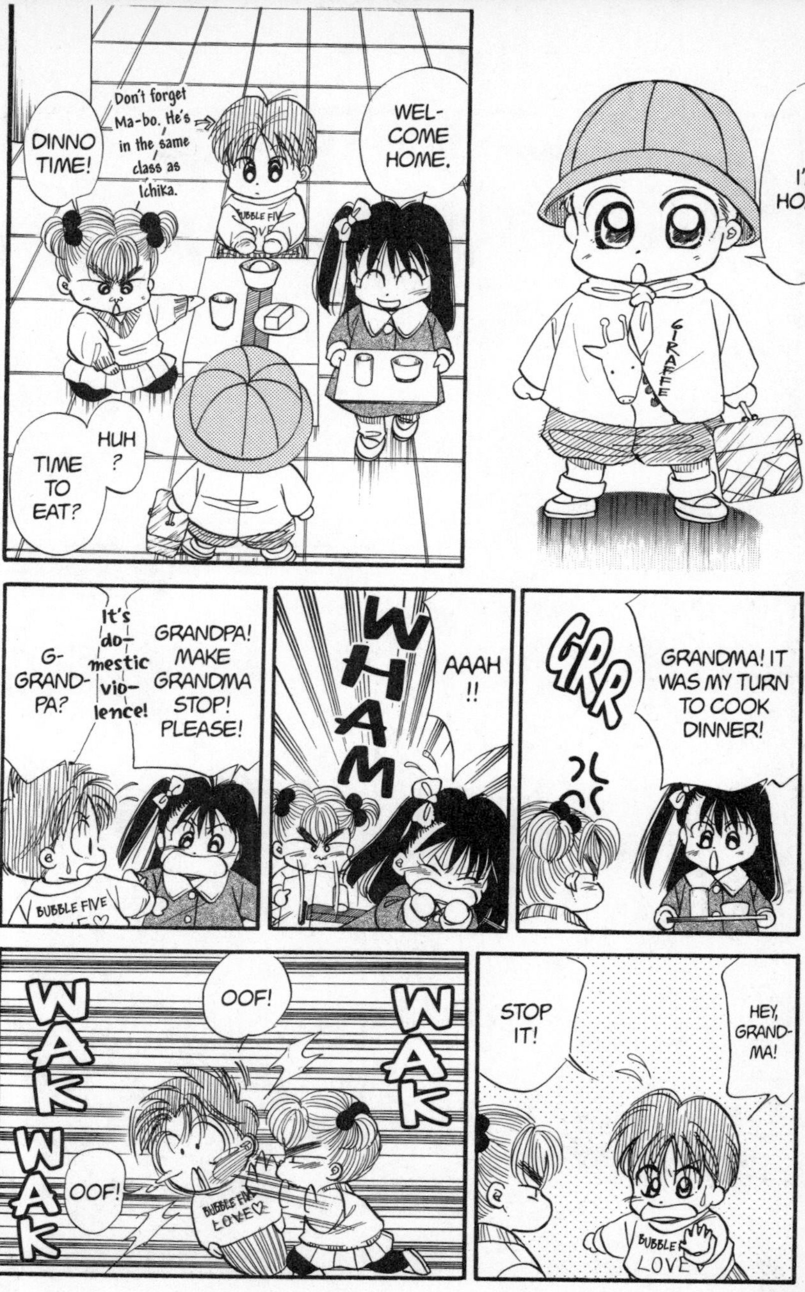
I'M HOME.
WEL-COME HOME.
Don't forget Ma-bo. He's in the same class as Ichika.
DINNO TIME!
HUH? TIME TO EAT?
GRR
GRANDMA! IT WAS MY TURN TO COOK DINNER!
WHAM
AAAH!!
GRANDPA! MAKE GRANDMA STOP! PLEASE!
It's do-mestic vio-lence!
G-GRAND-PA?
HEY, GRAND-MA!
STOP IT!
WAK
OOF!
WAK
WAK
OOF!
WAK

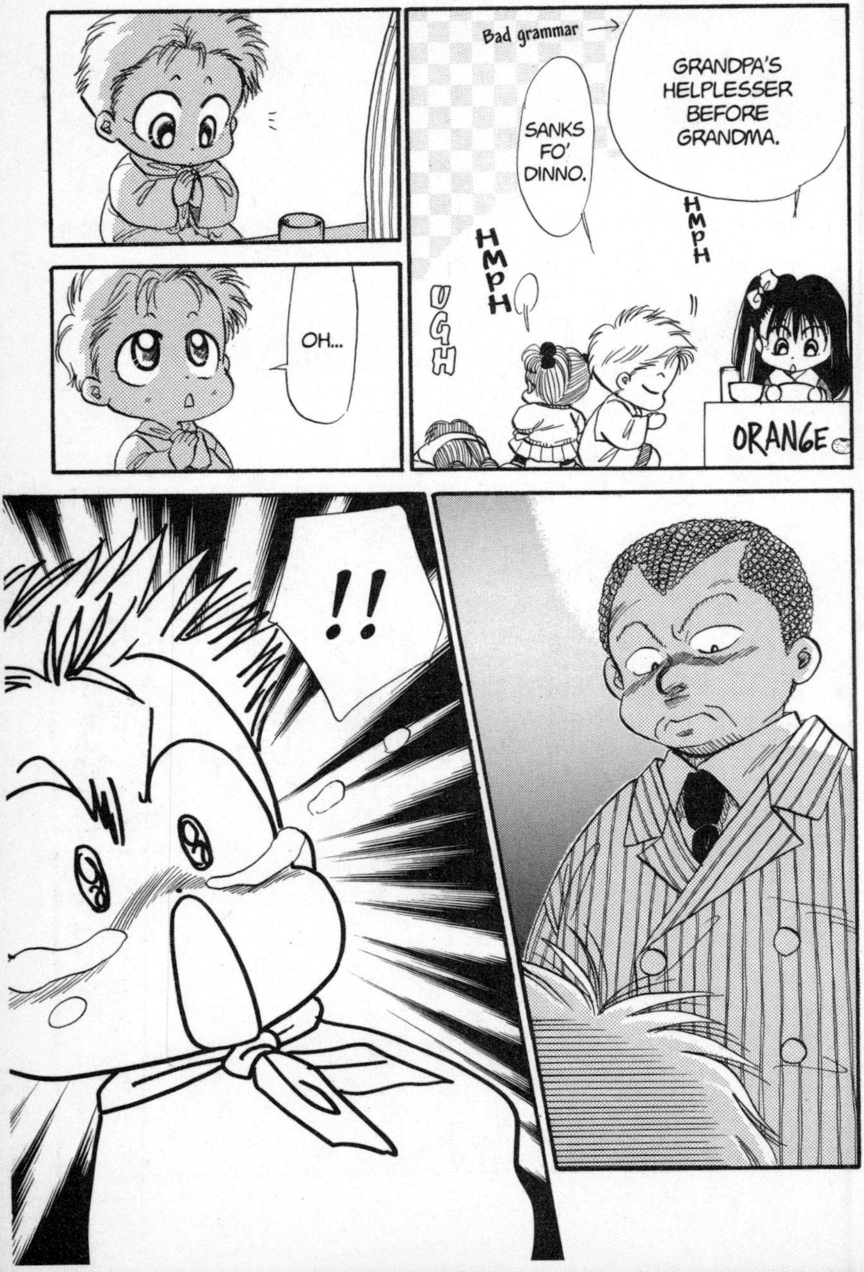
GRANDPA'S HELPLESSER BEFORE GRANDMA.
Bad grammar
HMPH
SANKS FO' DINNO.
HMPH
UGH
ORANGE
OH...
!!

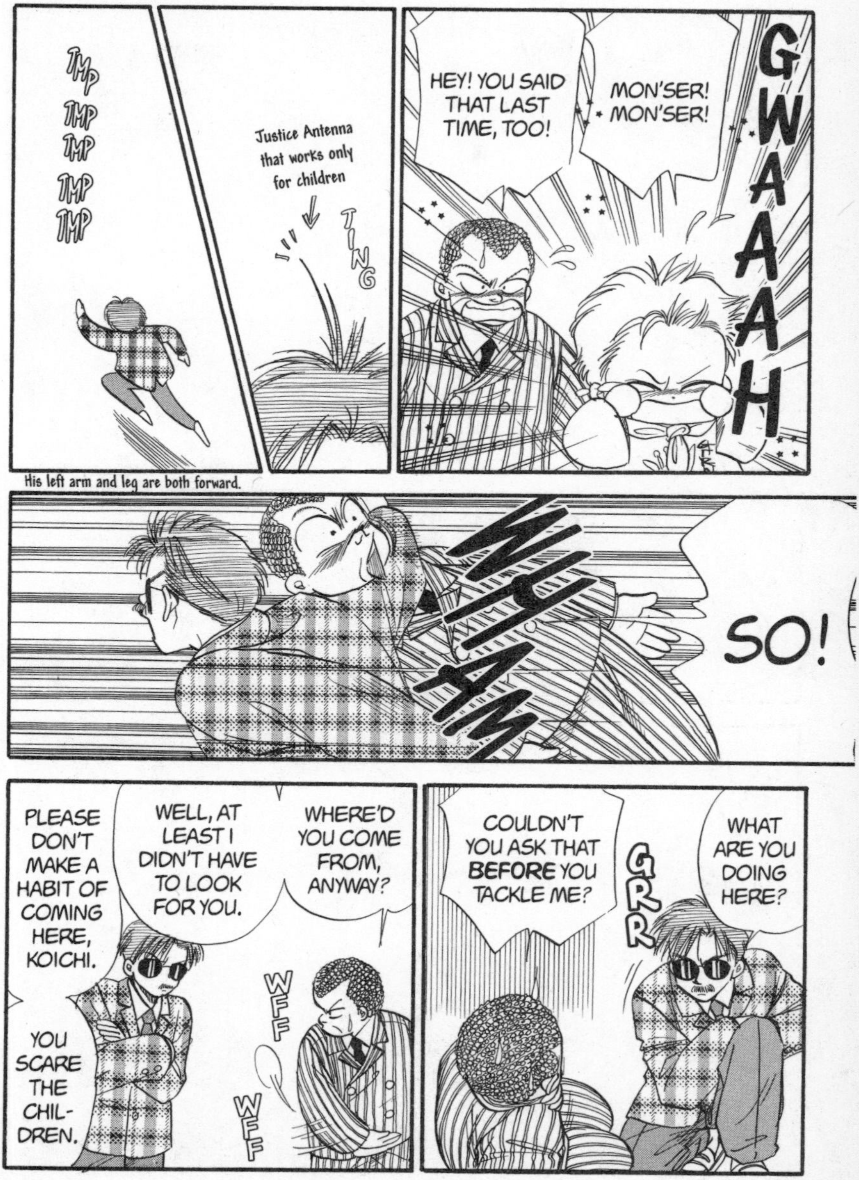
GWAAAH
MON'SER! MON'SER!
HEY! YOU SAID THAT LAST TIME, TOO!
TING
Justice Antenna that works only for children
TMP TMP TMP TMP TMP
His left arm and leg are both forward.
SO!
WHAM
WHAT ARE YOU DOING HERE?
GRR
COULDN'T YOU ASK THAT **BEFORE** YOU TACKLE ME?
WHERE'D YOU COME FROM, ANYWAY?
WFF
WFF
WELL, AT LEAST I DIDN'T HAVE TO LOOK FOR YOU.
PLEASE DON'T MAKE A HABIT OF COMING HERE, KOICHI.
YOU SCARE THE CHIL-DREN.

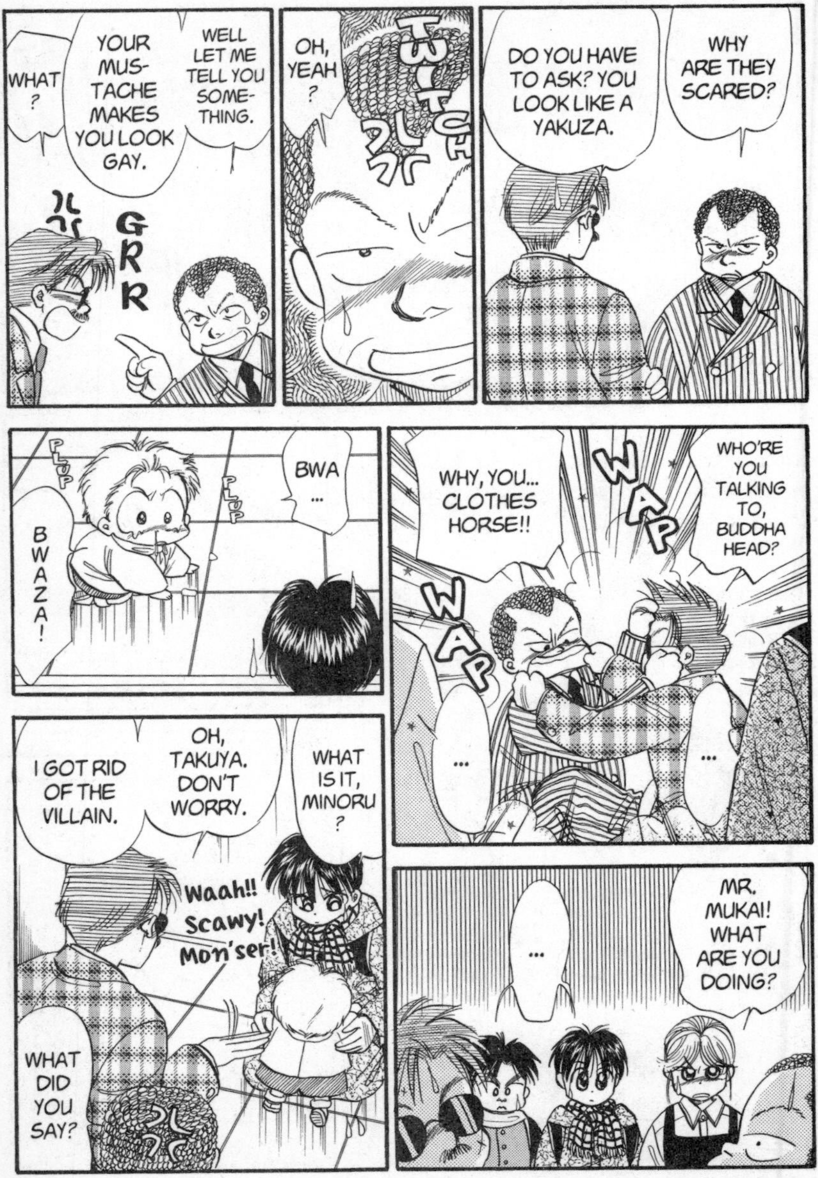

WHY ARE THEY SCARED?
DO YOU HAVE TO ASK? YOU LOOK LIKE A YAKUZA.
OH, YEAH?
TWITCH
WELL LET ME TELL YOU SOMETHING.
YOUR MUSTACHE MAKES YOU LOOK GAY.
WHAT?
GRR
WHO'RE YOU TALKING TO, BUDDHA HEAD?
WAP
WHY, YOU... CLOTHES HORSE!!
WAP
...
...
BWA...
PLUP
PLUP
BWAZA!
WHAT IS IT, MINORU?
OH, TAKUYA. DON'T WORRY.
I GOT RID OF THE VILLAIN.
Waah!! Scawy! Mon'ser!
WHAT DID YOU SAY?
MR. MUKAI! WHAT ARE YOU DOING?
...

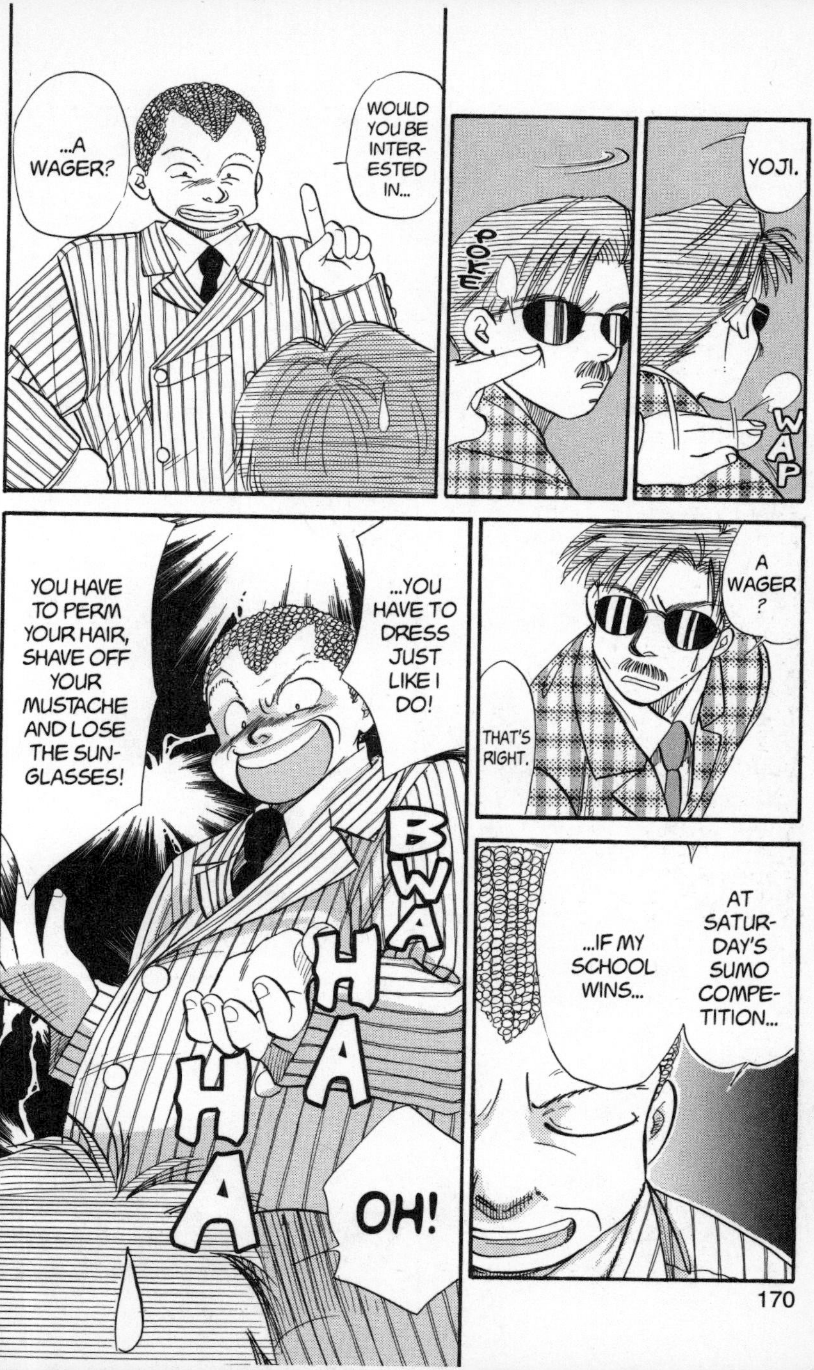
YOJI.
WAP
POKE
WOULD YOU BE INTERESTED IN...
...A WAGER?
A WAGER?
THAT'S RIGHT.
AT SATURDAY'S SUMO COMPETITION...
...IF MY SCHOOL WINS...
...YOU HAVE TO DRESS JUST LIKE I DO!
YOU HAVE TO PERM YOUR HAIR, SHAVE OFF YOUR MUSTACHE AND LOSE THE SUNGLASSES!
BWAHAHAHA
OH!

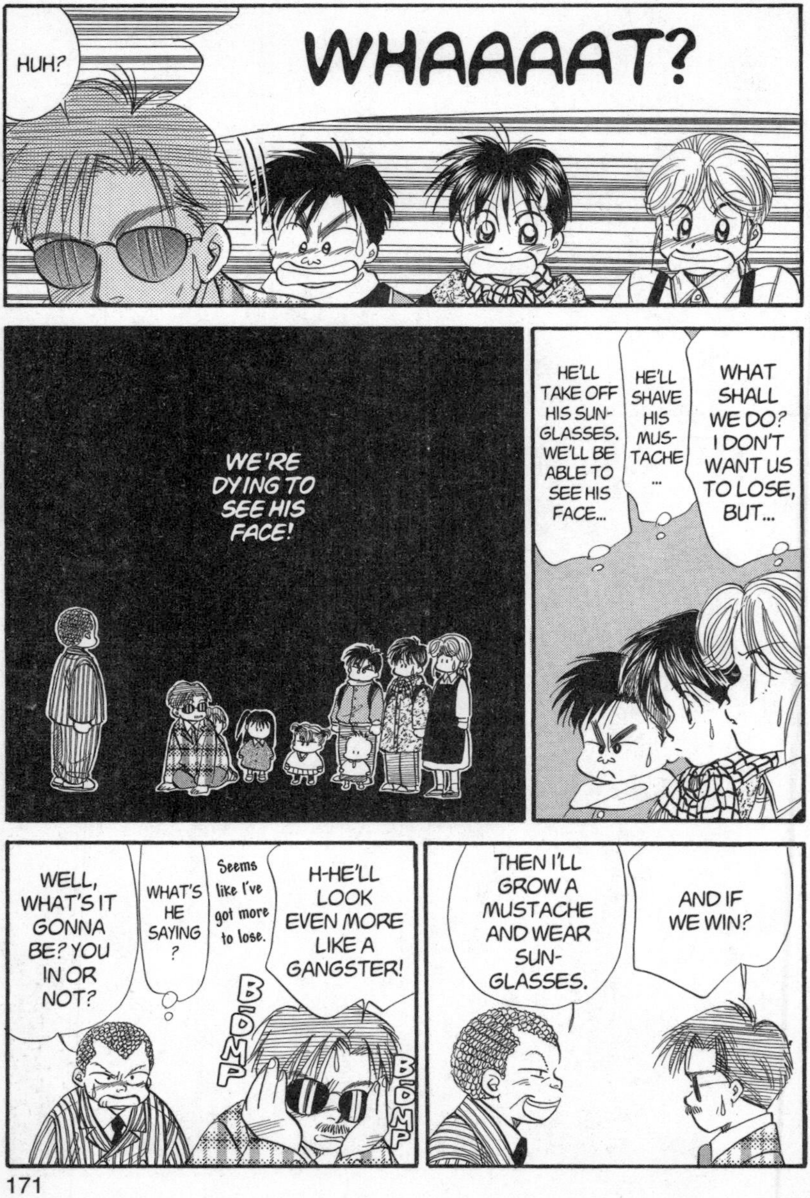
WHAAAAT?
HUH?
WHAT SHALL WE DO? I DON'T WANT US TO LOSE, BUT...
HE'LL SHAVE HIS MUSTACHE...
HE'LL TAKE OFF HIS SUNGLASSES. WE'LL BE ABLE TO SEE HIS FACE...
WE'RE DYING TO SEE HIS FACE!
AND IF WE WIN?
THEN I'LL GROW A MUSTACHE AND WEAR SUNGLASSES.
H-HE'LL LOOK EVEN MORE LIKE A GANGSTER!
BDOMP
BDOMP
Seems like I've got more to lose.
WHAT'S HE SAYING?
WELL, WHAT'S IT GONNA BE? YOU IN OR NOT?

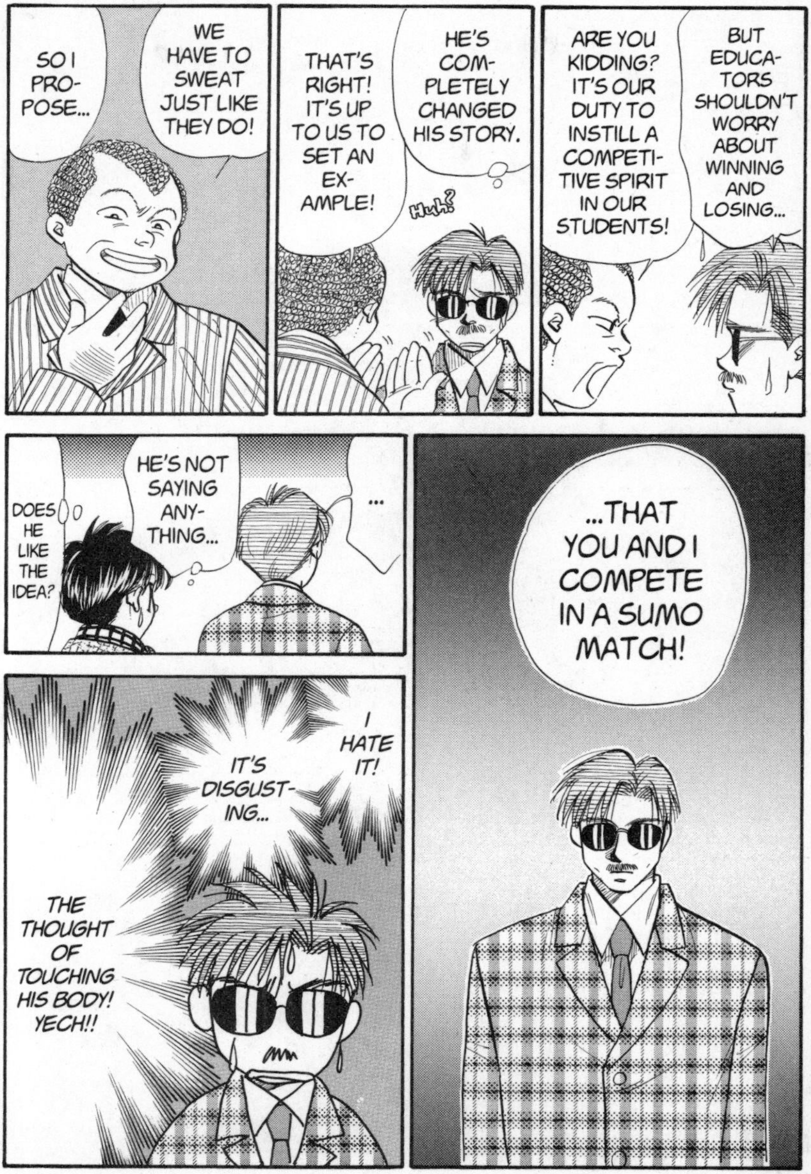
BUT EDUCATORS SHOULDN'T WORRY ABOUT WINNING AND LOSING...
ARE YOU KIDDING? IT'S OUR DUTY TO INSTILL A COMPETITIVE SPIRIT IN OUR STUDENTS!
HE'S COMPLETELY CHANGED HIS STORY.
THAT'S RIGHT! IT'S UP TO US TO SET AN EXAMPLE!
HUH?
WE HAVE TO SWEAT JUST LIKE THEY DO!
SO I PROPOSE...
...THAT YOU AND I COMPETE IN A SUMO MATCH!
...
HE'S NOT SAYING ANYTHING...
DOES HE LIKE THE IDEA?
I HATE IT!
IT'S DISGUSTING...
THE THOUGHT OF TOUCHING HIS BODY! YECH!!

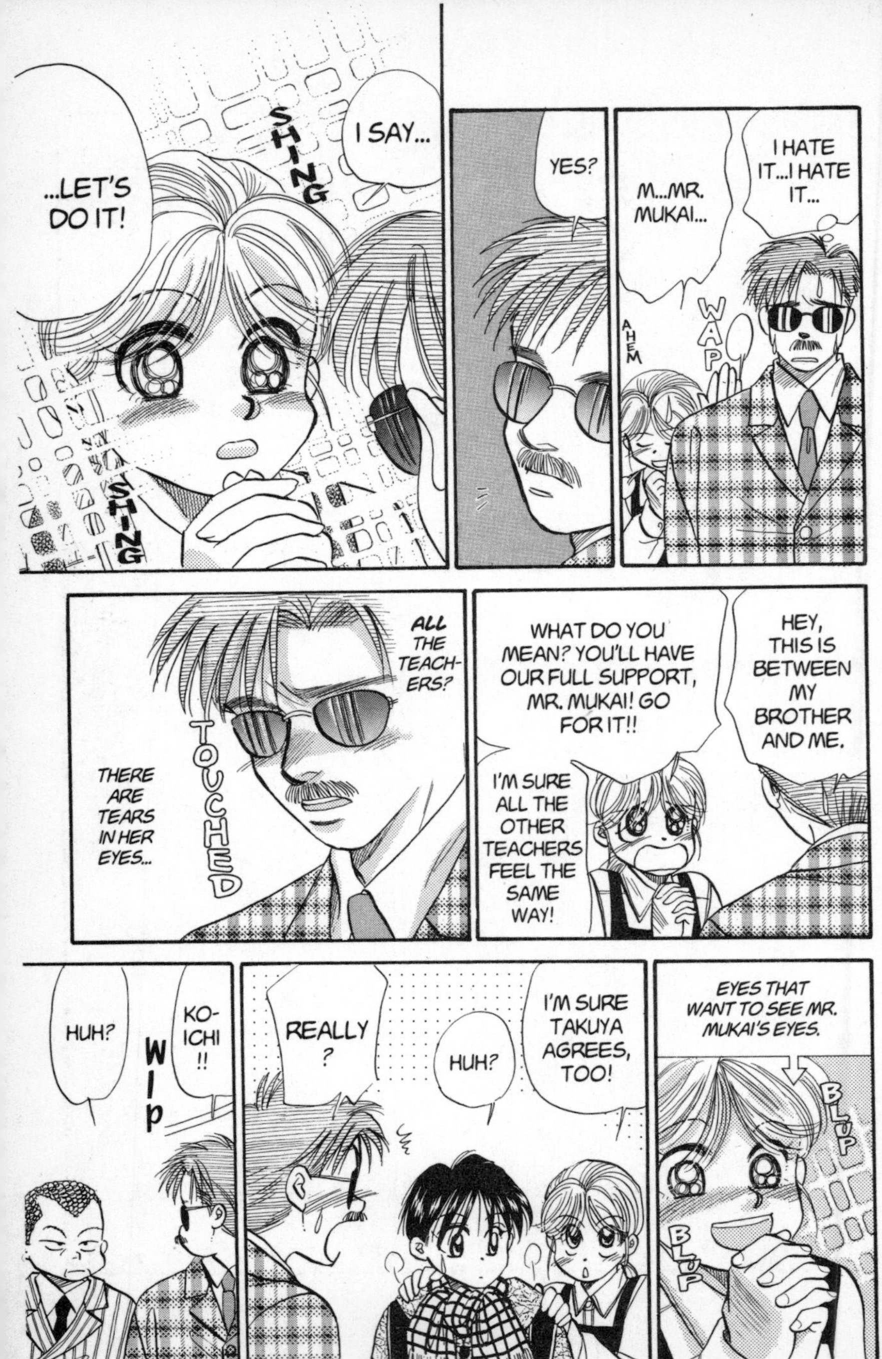
I HATE IT...I HATE IT...
M...MR. MUKAI...
WAP
AHEM
YES?
I SAY...
SHING
...LET'S DO IT!
SHING
HEY, THIS IS BETWEEN MY BROTHER AND ME.
WHAT DO YOU MEAN? YOU'LL HAVE OUR FULL SUPPORT, MR. MUKAI! GO FOR IT!!
I'M SURE ALL THE OTHER TEACHERS FEEL THE SAME WAY!
ALL THE TEACHERS?
TOUCHED
THERE ARE TEARS IN HER EYES...
EYES THAT WANT TO SEE MR. MUKAI'S EYES.
BLUP
BLUP
I'M SURE TAKUYA AGREES, TOO!
HUH?
REALLY?
KO-ICHI!!
WIP
HUH?

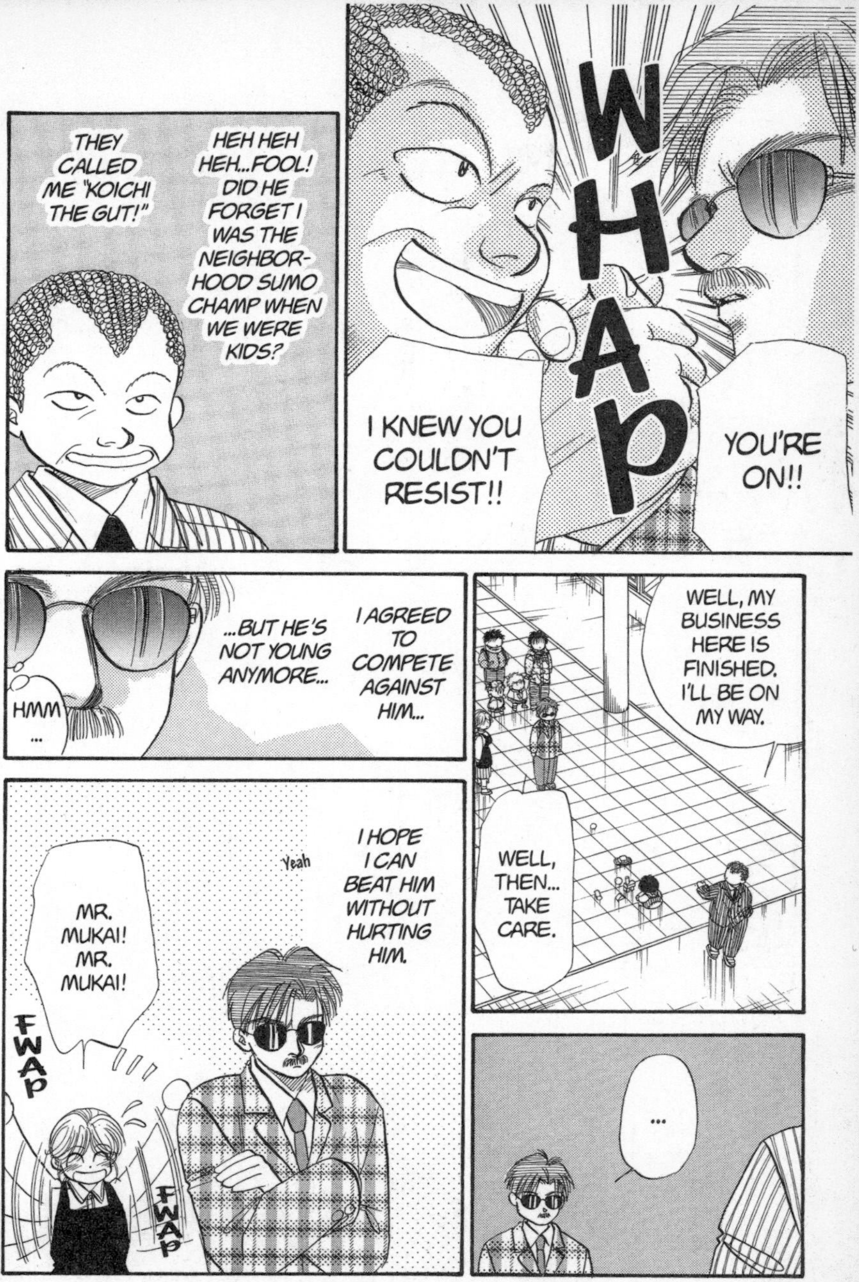
WHAP
YOU'RE ON!!
I KNEW YOU COULDN'T RESIST!!
HEH HEH HEH...FOOL! DID HE FORGET I WAS THE NEIGHBOR-HOOD SUMO CHAMP WHEN WE WERE KIDS?
THEY CALLED ME "KOICHI THE GUT!"
WELL, MY BUSINESS HERE IS FINISHED. I'LL BE ON MY WAY.
WELL, THEN... TAKE CARE.
I AGREED TO COMPETE AGAINST HIM...
...BUT HE'S NOT YOUNG ANYMORE...
HMM...
...
I HOPE I CAN BEAT HIM WITHOUT HURTING HIM.
Yeah
MR. MUKAI! MR. MUKAI!
FWAP
FWAP

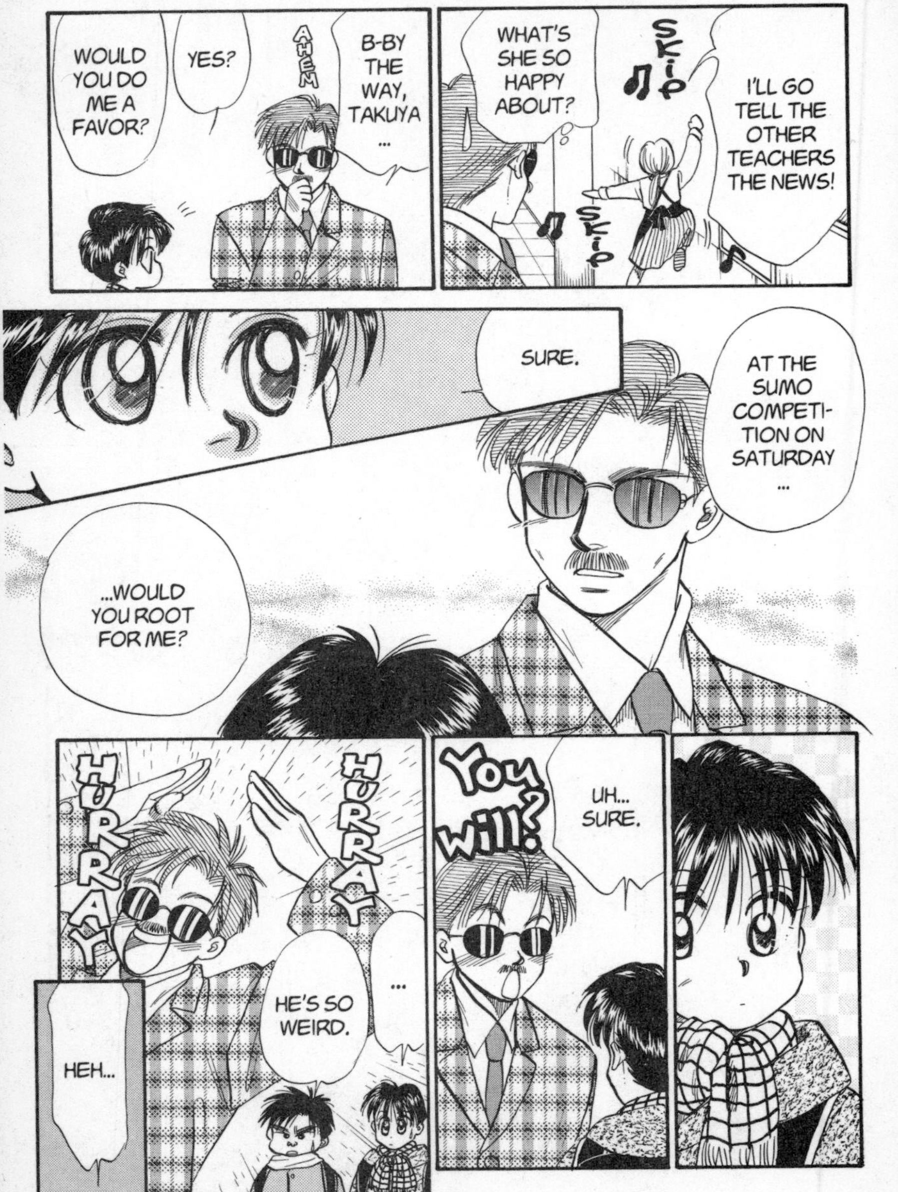
I'LL GO TELL THE OTHER TEACHERS THE NEWS!
SKIP
SKIP
WHAT'S SHE SO HAPPY ABOUT?
B-BY THE WAY, TAKUYA ...
AHEM
YES?
WOULD YOU DO ME A FAVOR?
SURE.
AT THE SUMO COMPETITION ON SATURDAY ...
...WOULD YOU ROOT FOR ME?
UH... SURE.
You will?
HURRAY
HURRAY
...
HE'S SO WEIRD.
HEH...

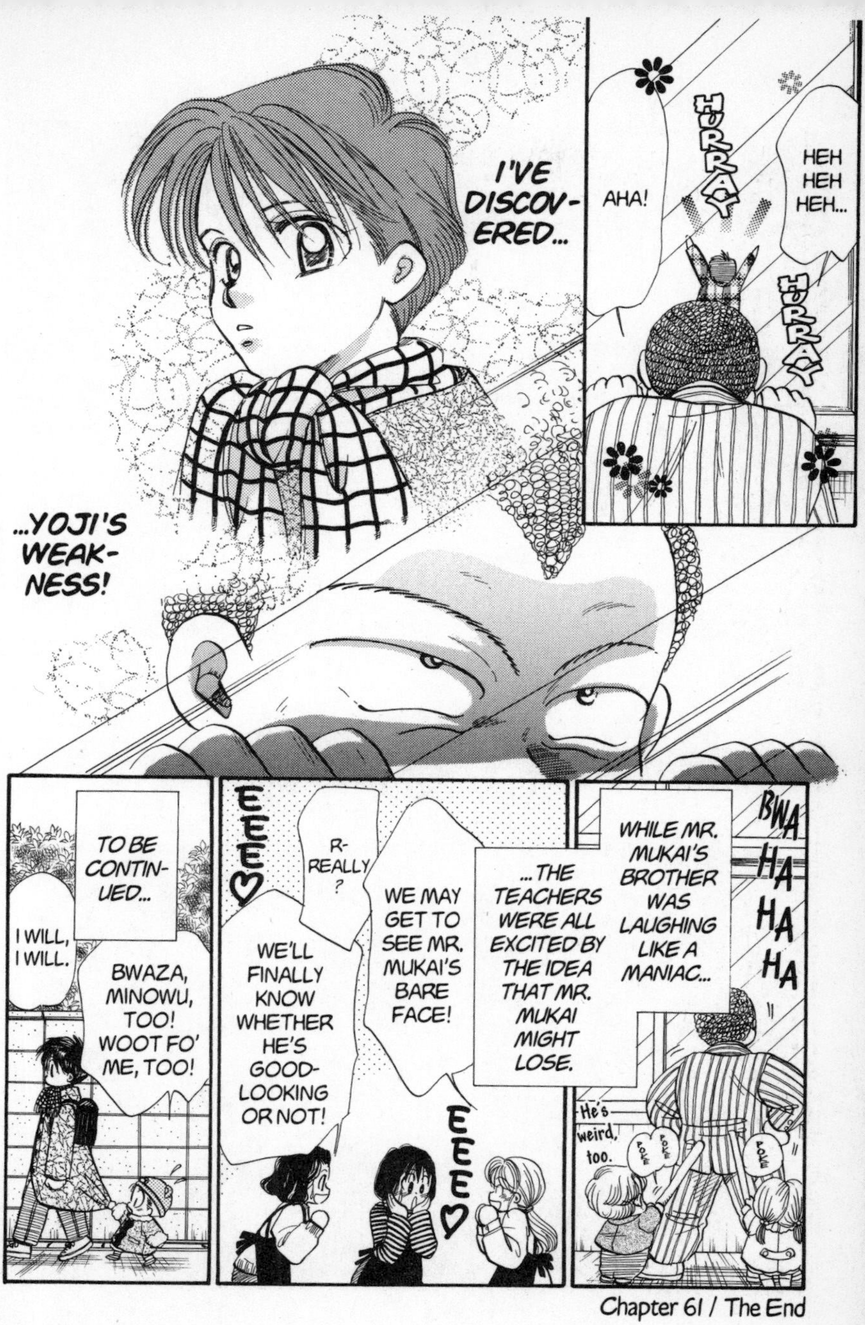
HEH HEH HEH...
HURRAY
AHA!
HURRAY
I'VE DISCOVERED...
...YOJI'S WEAKNESS!
BWAHAHAHAHA
WHILE MR. MUKAI'S BROTHER WAS LAUGHING LIKE A MANIAC...
...THE TEACHERS WERE ALL EXCITED BY THE IDEA THAT MR. MUKAI MIGHT LOSE.
He's weird, too.
POKE
POKE
POKE
EEE♥
R-REALLY?
WE MAY GET TO SEE MR. MUKAI'S BARE FACE!
WE'LL FINALLY KNOW WHETHER HE'S GOOD-LOOKING OR NOT!
EEE♥
TO BE CONTINUED...
BWAZA, MINOWU, TOO! WOOT FO' ME, TOO!
I WILL, I WILL.

Chapter 61 / The End

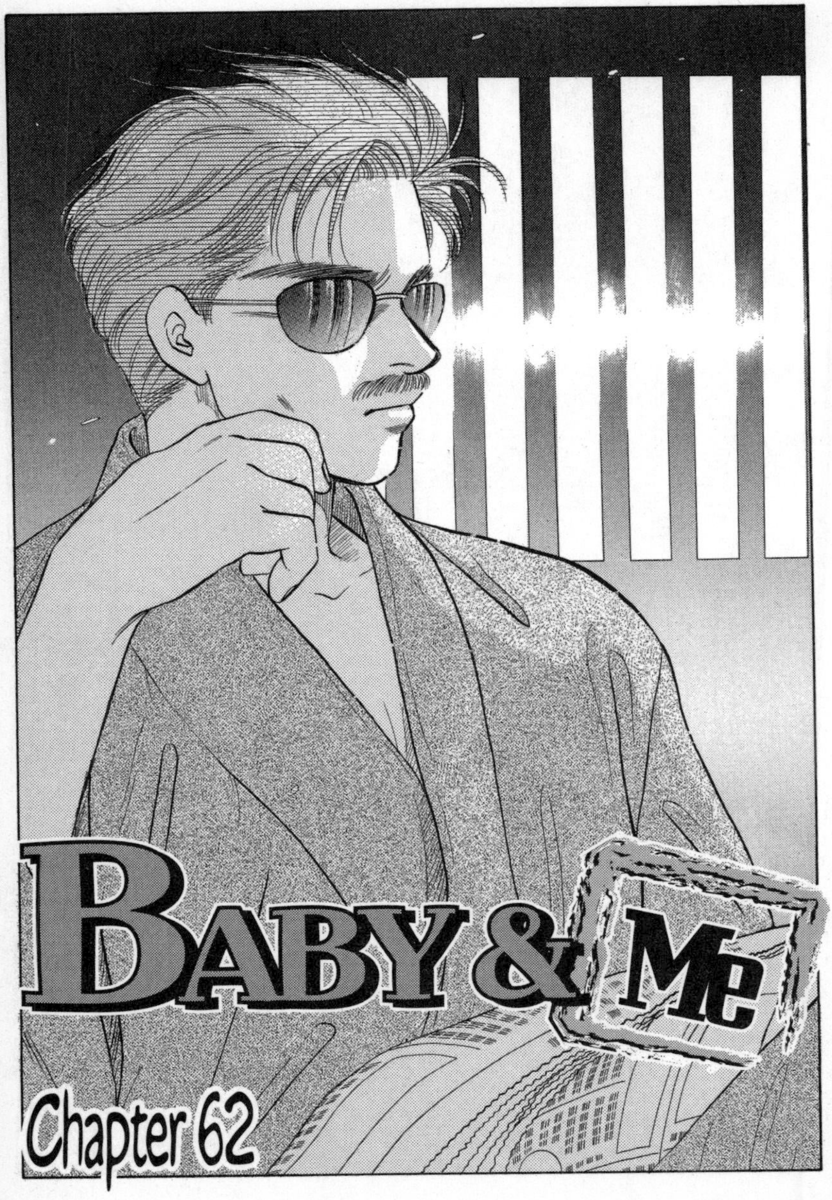
BABY & Me
Chapter 62

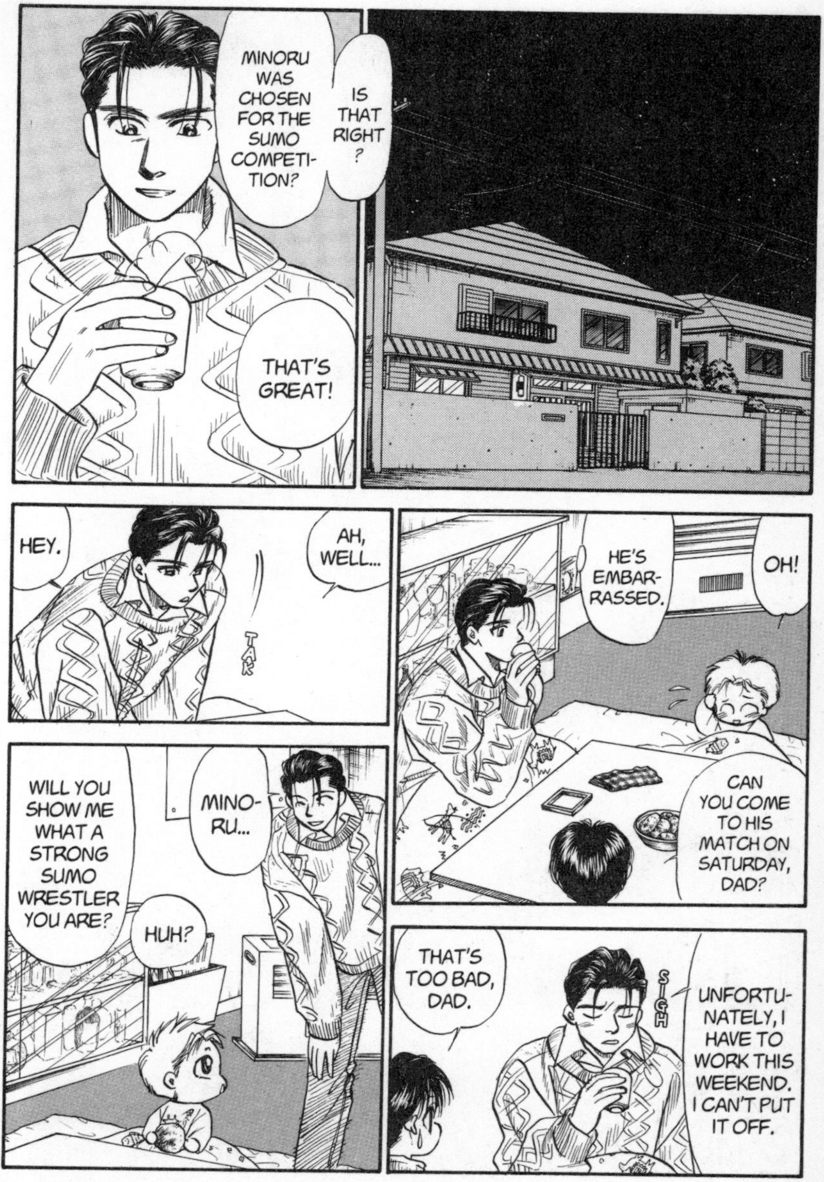
IS THAT RIGHT?
MINORU WAS CHOSEN FOR THE SUMO COMPETITION?
THAT'S GREAT!
OH!
HE'S EMBARRASSED.
CAN YOU COME TO HIS MATCH ON SATURDAY, DAD?
AH, WELL...
TAK
HEY.
UNFORTUNATELY, I HAVE TO WORK THIS WEEKEND. I CAN'T PUT IT OFF.
SIGH
THAT'S TOO BAD, DAD.
MINO-RU...
WILL YOU SHOW ME WHAT A STRONG SUMO WRESTLER YOU ARE?
HUH?

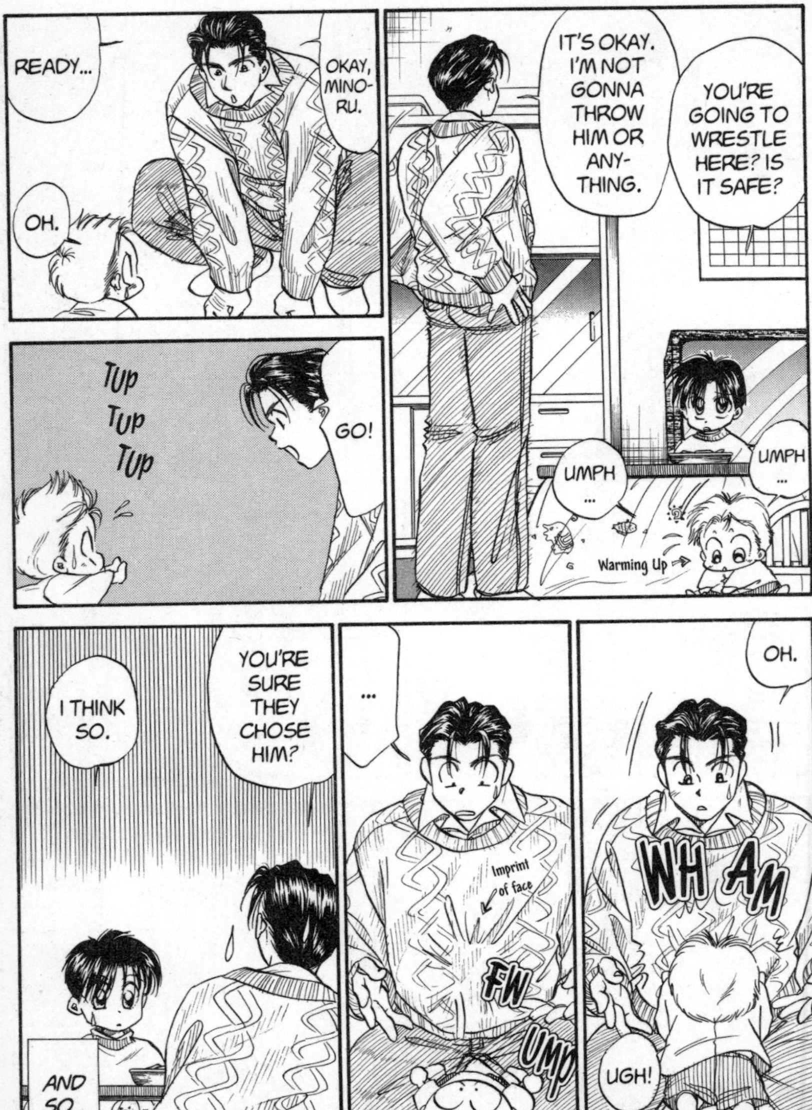
YOU'RE GOING TO WRESTLE HERE? IS IT SAFE?
IT'S OKAY. I'M NOT GONNA THROW HIM OR ANY-THING.
UMPH ...
UMPH ...
Warming Up
OKAY, MINO-RU.
READY...
OH.
GO!
TUP TUP TUP
OH.
WH AM
UGH!
...
Imprint of face
FW UMP
YOU'RE SURE THEY CHOSE HIM?
I THINK SO.
AND SO...

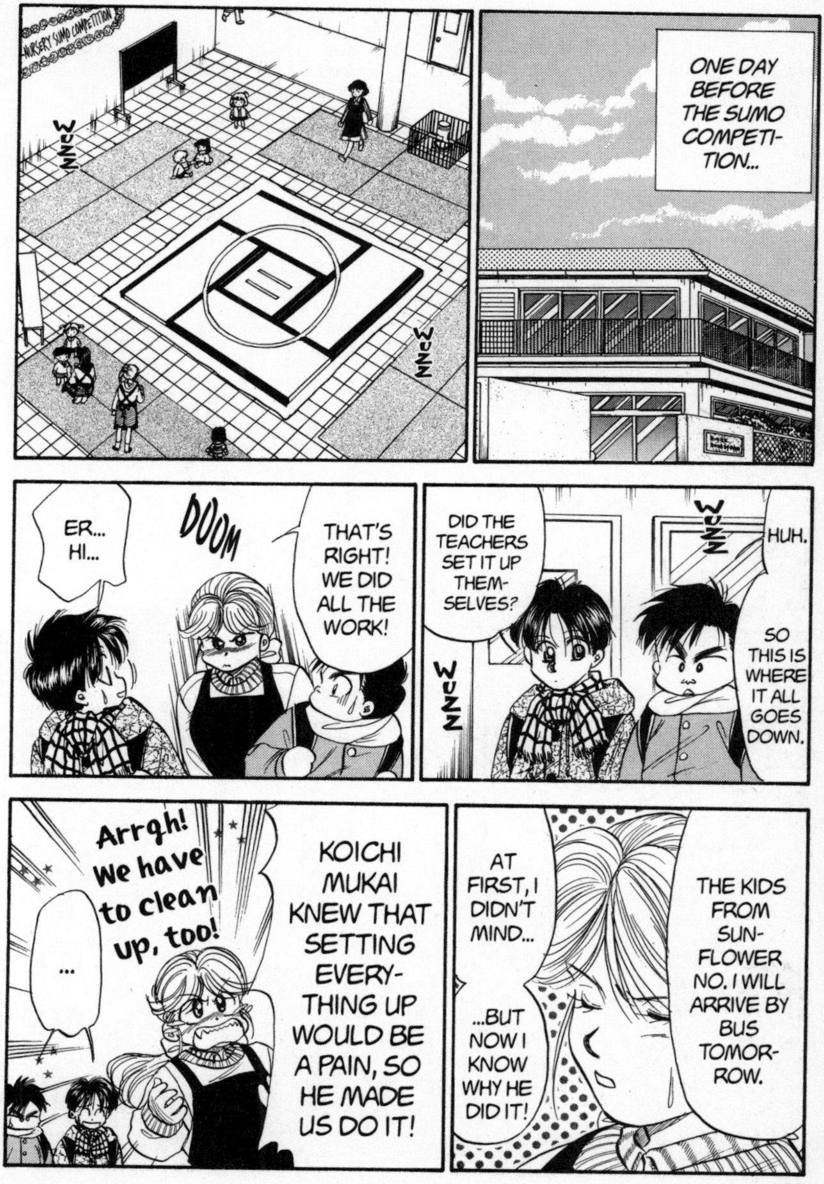
ONE DAY BEFORE THE SUMO COMPETITION...
NURSERY SUMO COMPETITION
WUZZ
WUZZ
HUH.
SO THIS IS WHERE IT ALL GOES DOWN.
WUZZ
DID THE TEACHERS SET IT UP THEMSELVES?
WUZZ
THAT'S RIGHT! WE DID ALL THE WORK!
DOOM
ER... HI...
THE KIDS FROM SUNFLOWER NO. I WILL ARRIVE BY BUS TOMORROW.
AT FIRST, I DIDN'T MIND...
...BUT NOW I KNOW WHY HE DID IT!
KOICHI MUKAI KNEW THAT SETTING EVERYTHING UP WOULD BE A PAIN, SO HE MADE US DO IT!
Arrgh! We have to clean up, too!
...

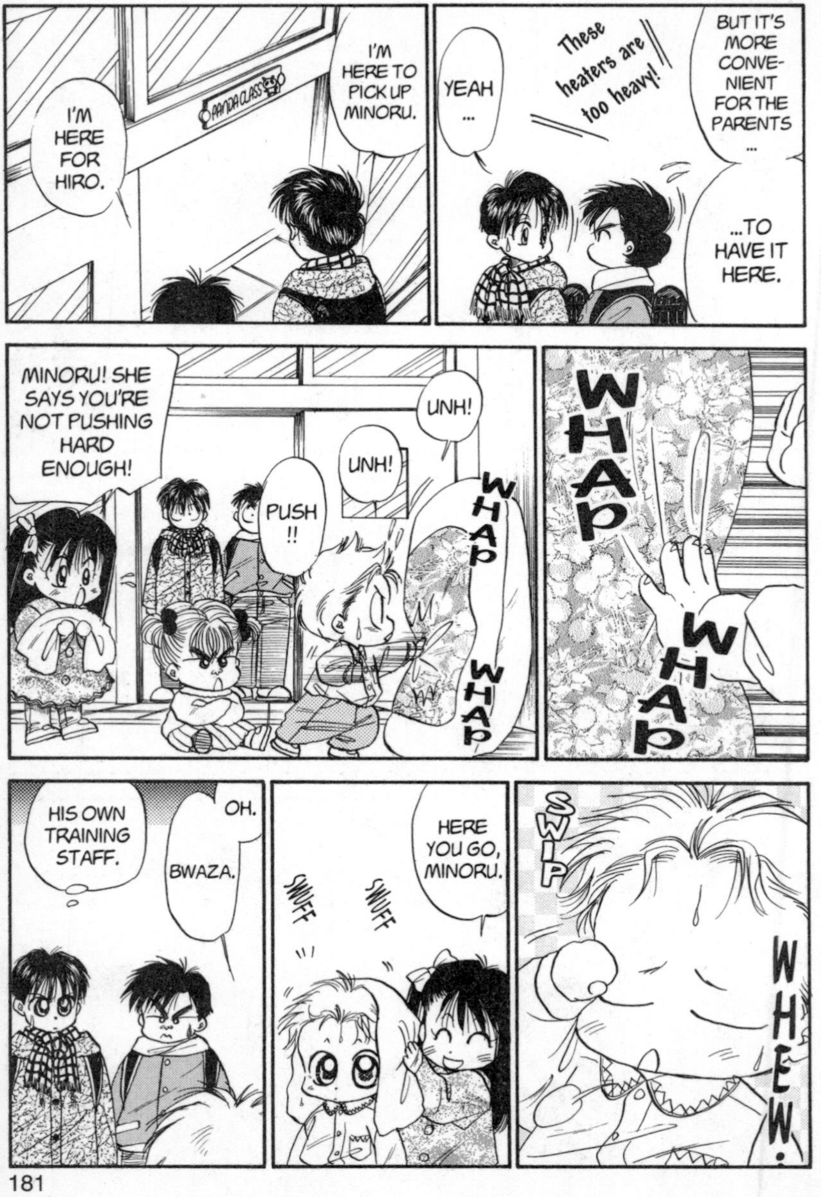
BUT IT'S MORE CONVENIENT FOR THE PARENTS ...
...TO HAVE IT HERE.
These heaters are too heavy!
YEAH ...
I'M HERE TO PICK UP MINORU.
PANDA CLASS
I'M HERE FOR HIRO.
WHAP
WHAP
UNH!
UNH!
WHAP
PUSH !!
MINORU! SHE SAYS YOU'RE NOT PUSHING HARD ENOUGH!
WHAP
SWIP
WHEW.
HERE YOU GO, MINORU.
SNIFF
SNIFF
OH.
BWAZA.
HIS OWN TRAINING STAFF.

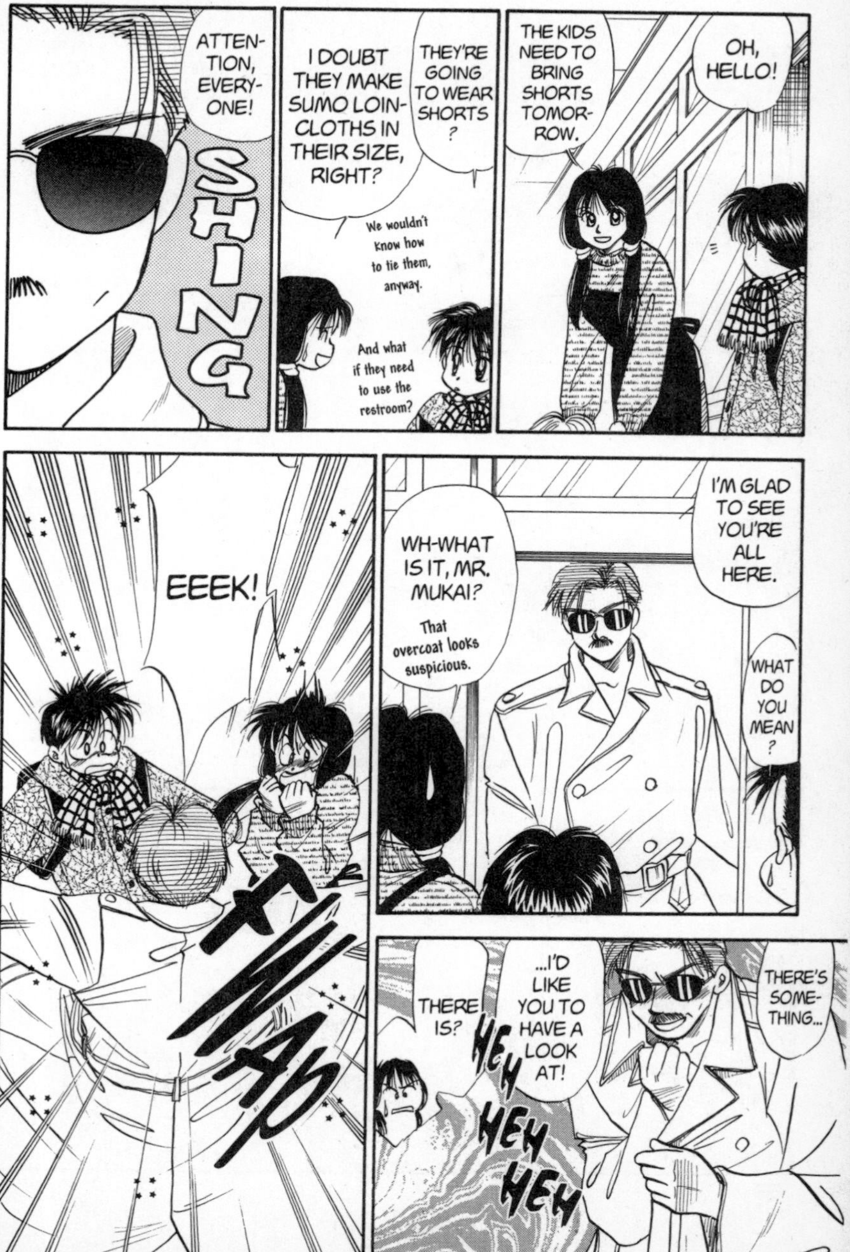
OH, HELLO!
THE KIDS NEED TO BRING SHORTS TOMORROW.
THEY'RE GOING TO WEAR SHORTS?
I DOUBT THEY MAKE SUMO LOIN-CLOTHS IN THEIR SIZE, RIGHT?
We wouldn't know how to tie them, anyway.
And what if they need to use the restroom?
ATTENTION, EVERYONE!
SHING
I'M GLAD TO SEE YOU'RE ALL HERE.
WHAT DO YOU MEAN?
WH-WHAT IS IT, MR. MUKAI?
That overcoat looks suspicious.
THERE'S SOMETHING...
...I'D LIKE YOU TO HAVE A LOOK AT!
THERE IS?
HEH HEH HEH HEH
EEEK!

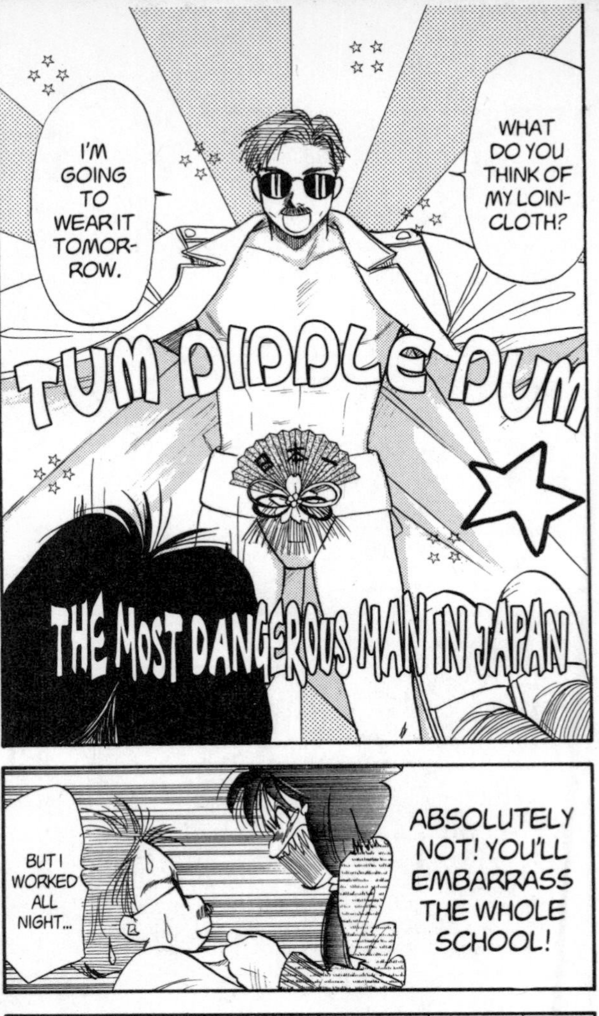
WHAT DO YOU THINK OF MY LOIN-CLOTH?
I'M GOING TO WEAR IT TOMORROW.
TUM DIDDLE DUM
THE MOST DANGEROUS MAN IN JAPAN
ABSOLUTELY NOT! YOU'LL EMBARRASS THE WHOLE SCHOOL!
BUT I WORKED ALL NIGHT...
YOU STAYED UP ALL NIGHT MAKING THAT ABOMINATION?
NO. THIS IS JUST SOMETHING EXTRA.
TAKUYA ...
ABOUT TOMORROW'S CHEERING...
YES?

Author's Note: Part 7

This is the last author's note of the volume.

Readers often ask me about my younger brother, but there's nothing special to say about him, so here's a picture he drew.

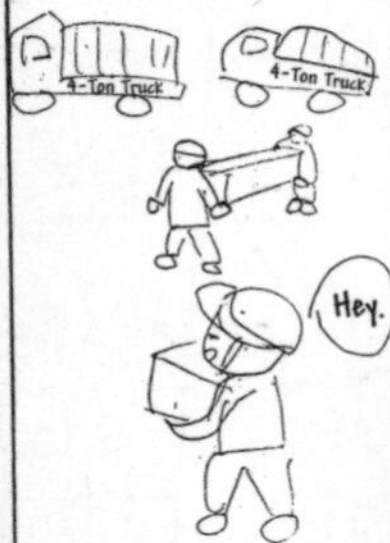
4-Ton Truck
4-Ton Truck
Hey.

Ha ha ha! What do you think? Can you believe a 21-year-old drew that?

It's terrible...

People write my name with the wrong *kanji* a lot. They get Takuya's name wrong, too. Sometimes the results can be very funny. I can't help but laugh.

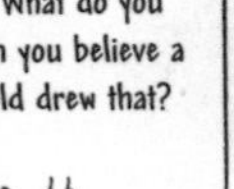
Hee hee

Okay, I'll see you again in Volume 12!

Ciao! ♡

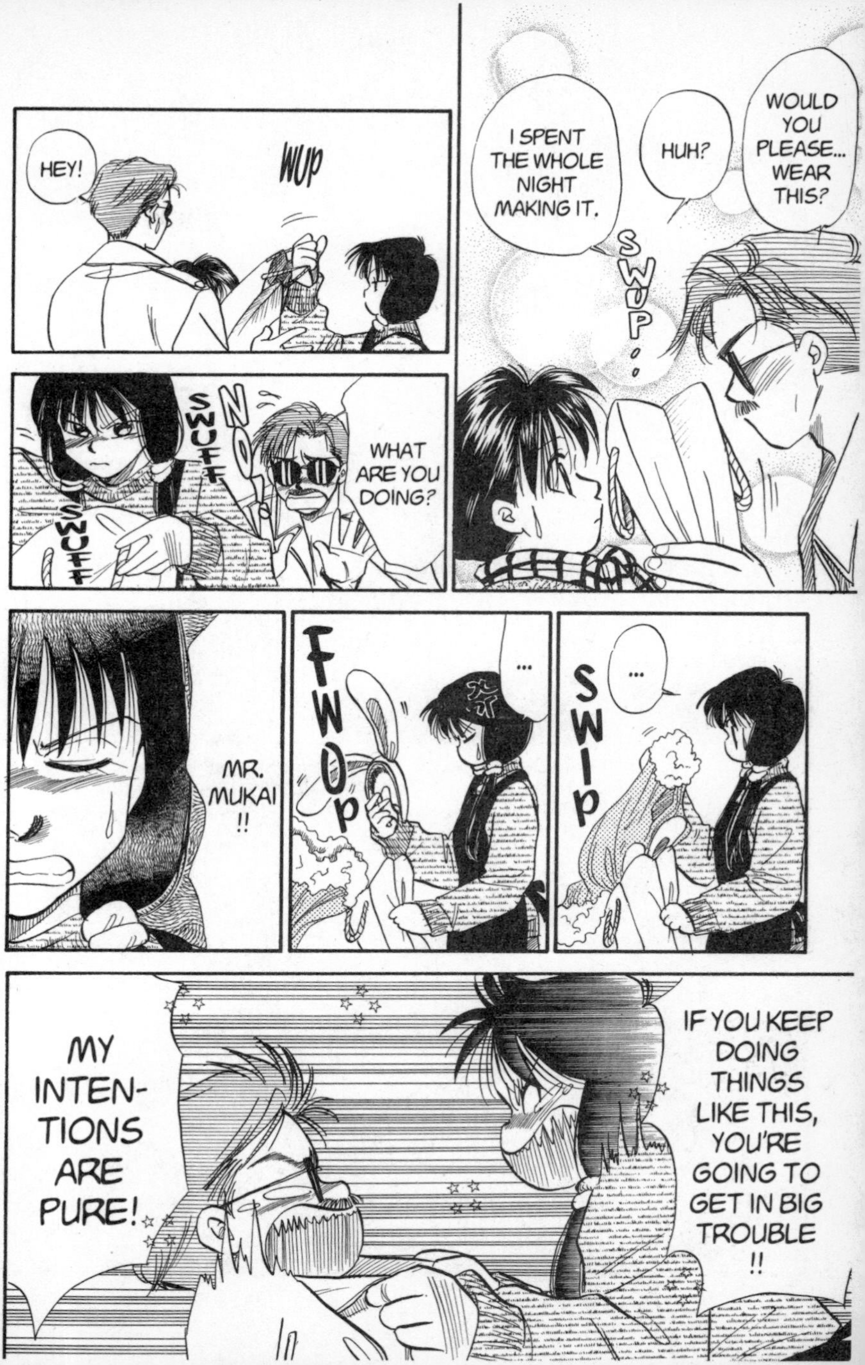
WOULD YOU PLEASE... WEAR THIS?
HUH?
I SPENT THE WHOLE NIGHT MAKING IT.
SWUP
HEY!
WUP
WHAT ARE YOU DOING?
NO
SWUFF
SWUFF
...
SWIP
...
FWOP
MR. MUKAI !!
IF YOU KEEP DOING THINGS LIKE THIS, YOU'RE GOING TO GET IN BIG TROUBLE !!
MY INTEN-TIONS ARE PURE!

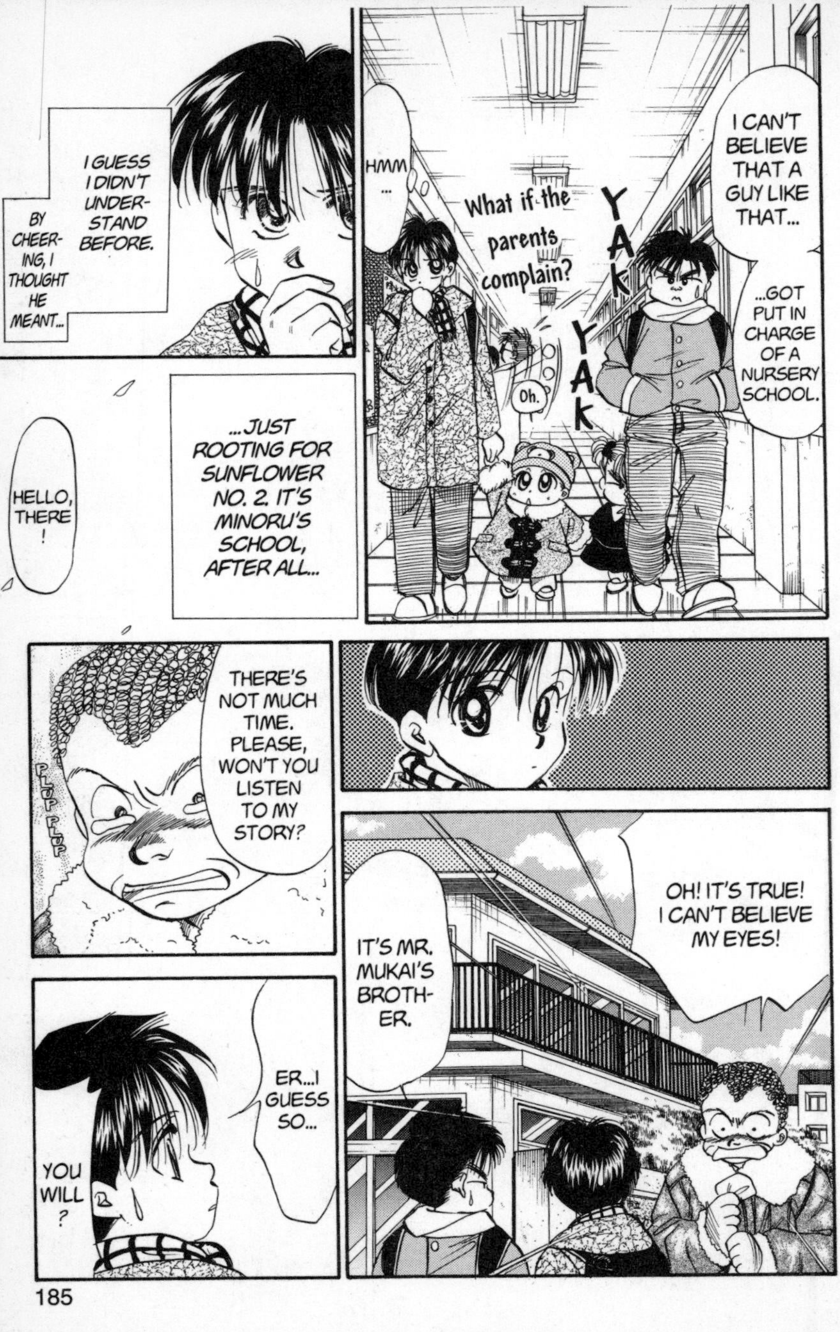
I CAN'T BELIEVE THAT A GUY LIKE THAT...
...GOT PUT IN CHARGE OF A NURSERY SCHOOL.
YAK YAK
What if the parents complain?
Oh.
HMM...
I GUESS I DIDN'T UNDERSTAND BEFORE.
BY CHEERING, I THOUGHT HE MEANT...
...JUST ROOTING FOR SUNFLOWER NO. 2. IT'S MINORU'S SCHOOL, AFTER ALL...
HELLO, THERE!
THERE'S NOT MUCH TIME. PLEASE, WON'T YOU LISTEN TO MY STORY?
PLOP PLOP
OH! IT'S TRUE! I CAN'T BELIEVE MY EYES!
IT'S MR. MUKAI'S BROTHER.
ER...I GUESS SO...
YOU WILL?

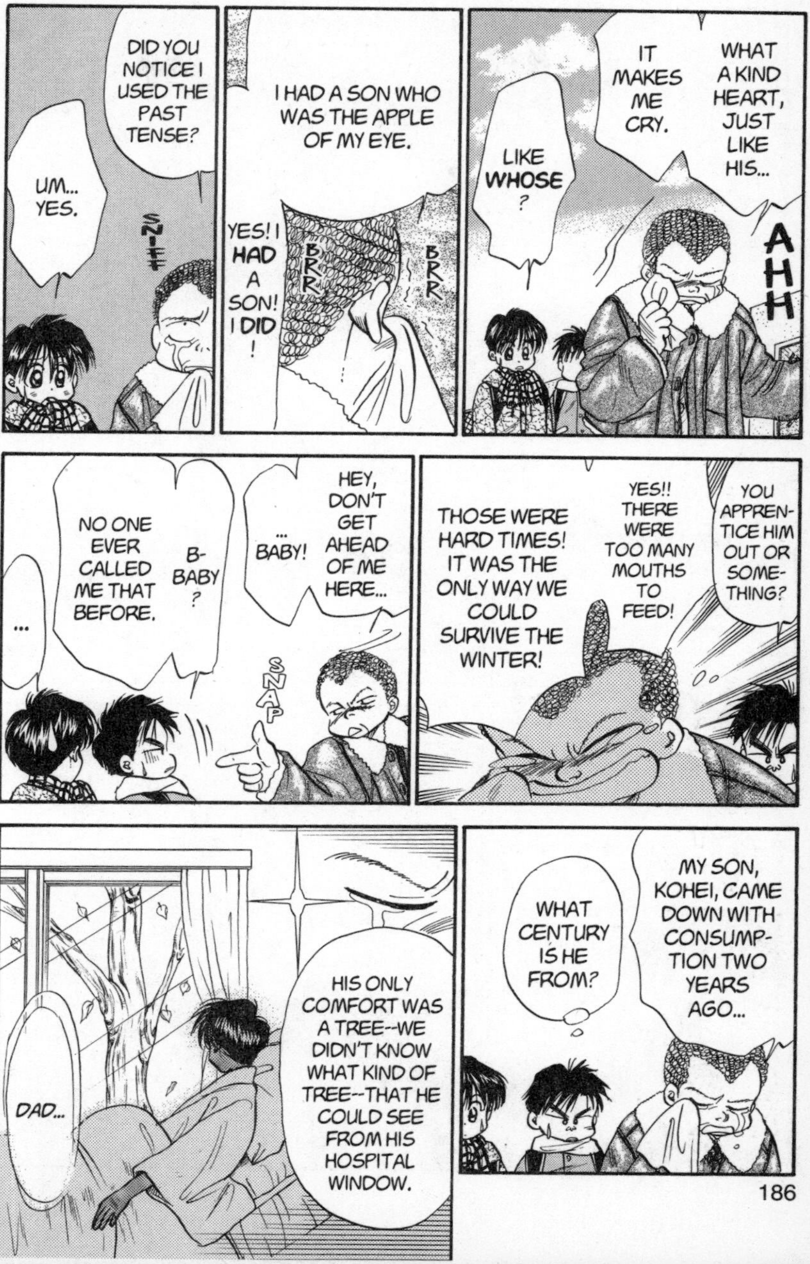
WHAT A KIND HEART, JUST LIKE HIS...
IT MAKES ME CRY.
AHH
LIKE WHOSE?
I HAD A SON WHO WAS THE APPLE OF MY EYE.
BRR
BRR
YES! I HAD A SON! I DID!
DID YOU NOTICE I USED THE PAST TENSE?
SNIFF
UM... YES.
YOU APPRENTICE HIM OUT OR SOMETHING?
YES!! THERE WERE TOO MANY MOUTHS TO FEED!
THOSE WERE HARD TIMES! IT WAS THE ONLY WAY WE COULD SURVIVE THE WINTER!
HEY, DON'T GET AHEAD OF ME HERE...
... BABY!
SNAP
B-BABY?
NO ONE EVER CALLED ME THAT BEFORE.
...
MY SON, KOHEI, CAME DOWN WITH CONSUMPTION TWO YEARS AGO...
WHAT CENTURY IS HE FROM?
HIS ONLY COMFORT WAS A TREE--WE DIDN'T KNOW WHAT KIND OF TREE--THAT HE COULD SEE FROM HIS HOSPITAL WINDOW.
DAD...

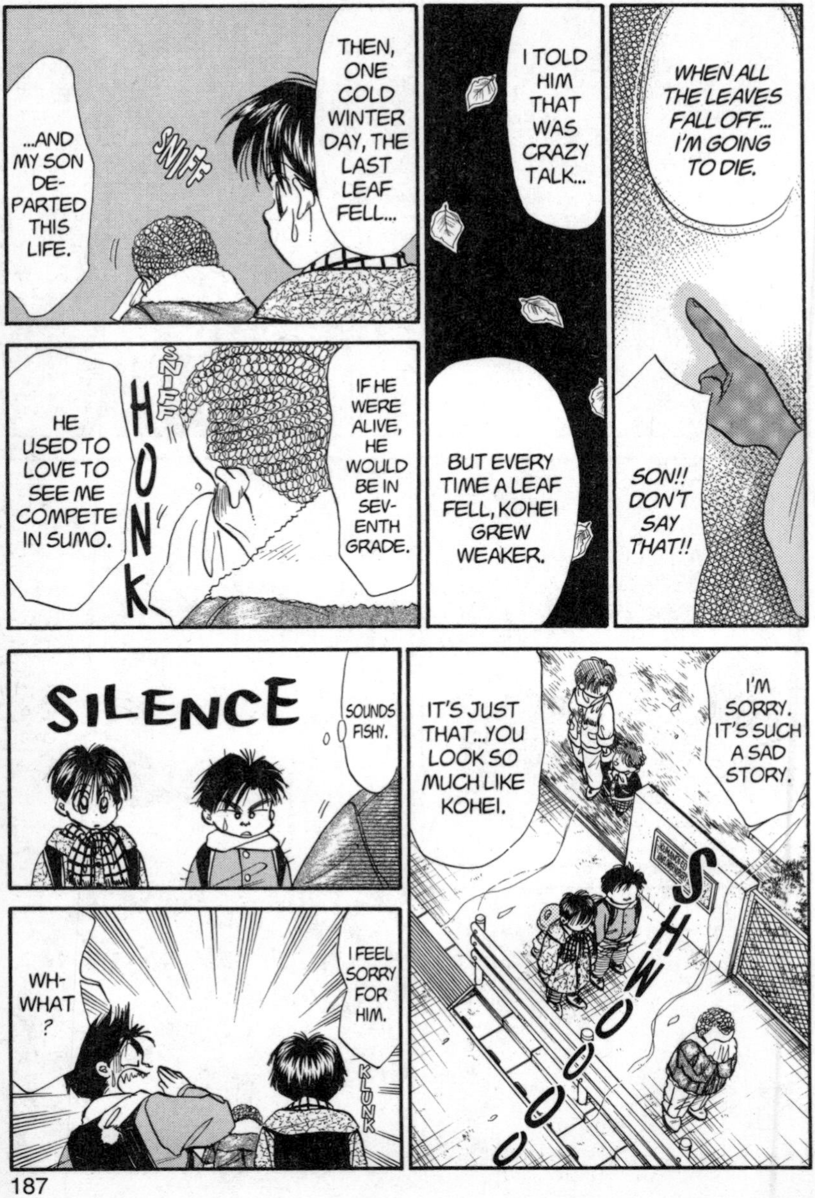
WHEN ALL THE LEAVES FALL OFF... I'M GOING TO DIE.
SON!! DON'T SAY THAT!!
I TOLD HIM THAT WAS CRAZY TALK...
BUT EVERY TIME A LEAF FELL, KOHEI GREW WEAKER.
THEN, ONE COLD WINTER DAY, THE LAST LEAF FELL...
SNIFF
...AND MY SON DE-PARTED THIS LIFE.
IF HE WERE ALIVE, HE WOULD BE IN SEV-ENTH GRADE.
SNIFF
HONK
HE USED TO LOVE TO SEE ME COMPETE IN SUMO.
I'M SORRY. IT'S SUCH A SAD STORY.
IT'S JUST THAT...YOU LOOK SO MUCH LIKE KOHEI.
SHWOOOOO
SOUNDS FISHY.
SILENCE
I FEEL SORRY FOR HIM.
KLUNK
WH-WHAT?

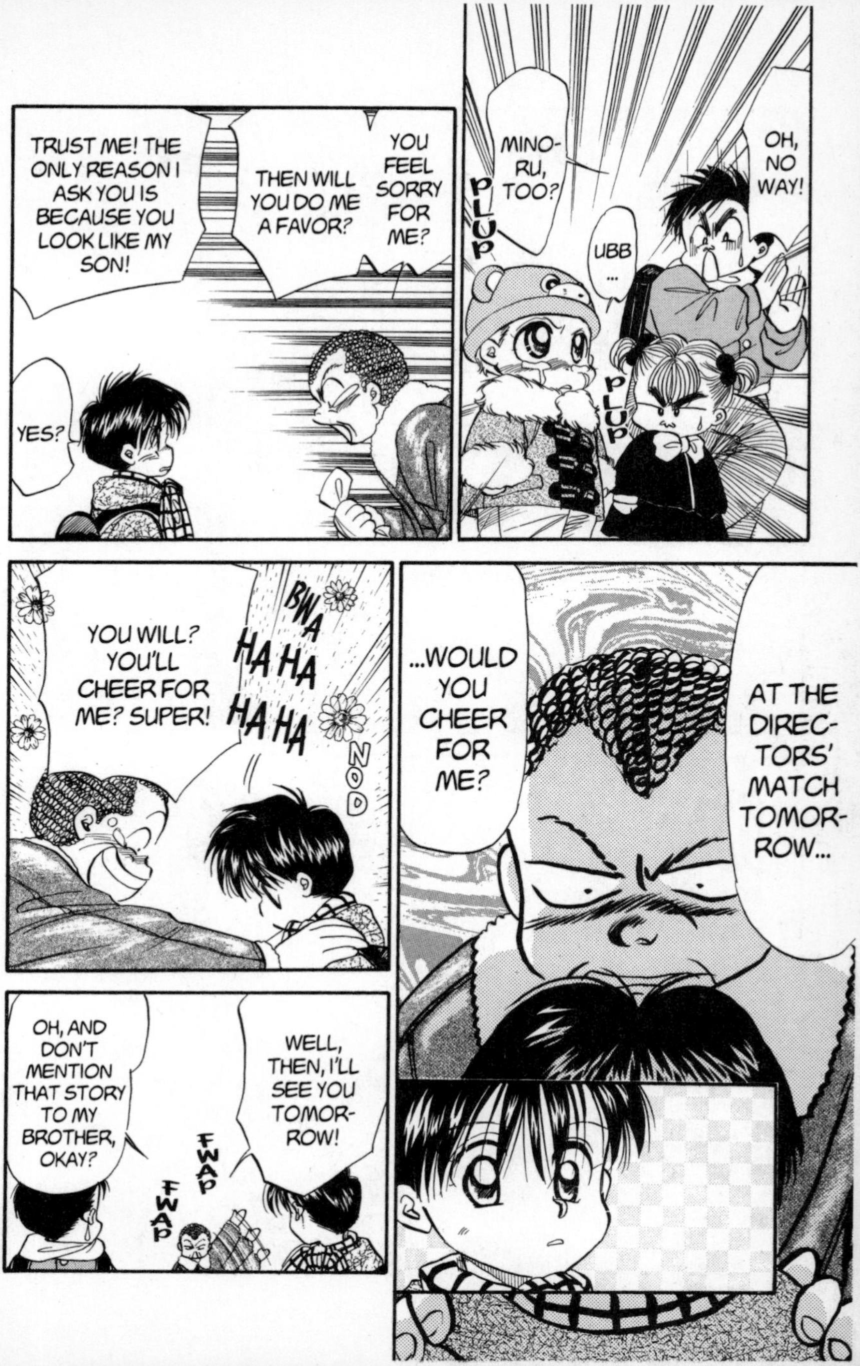
OH, NO WAY!
MINO-RU, TOO?
UBB ...
PLUP
PLUP
YOU FEEL SORRY FOR ME?
THEN WILL YOU DO ME A FAVOR?
TRUST ME! THE ONLY REASON I ASK YOU IS BECAUSE YOU LOOK LIKE MY SON!
YES?
AT THE DIREC-TORS' MATCH TOMOR-ROW...
...WOULD YOU CHEER FOR ME?
BWA HA HA HA HA
NOD
YOU WILL? YOU'LL CHEER FOR ME? SUPER!
WELL, THEN, I'LL SEE YOU TOMOR-ROW!
FWAP
FWAP
OH, AND DON'T MENTION THAT STORY TO MY BROTHER, OKAY?

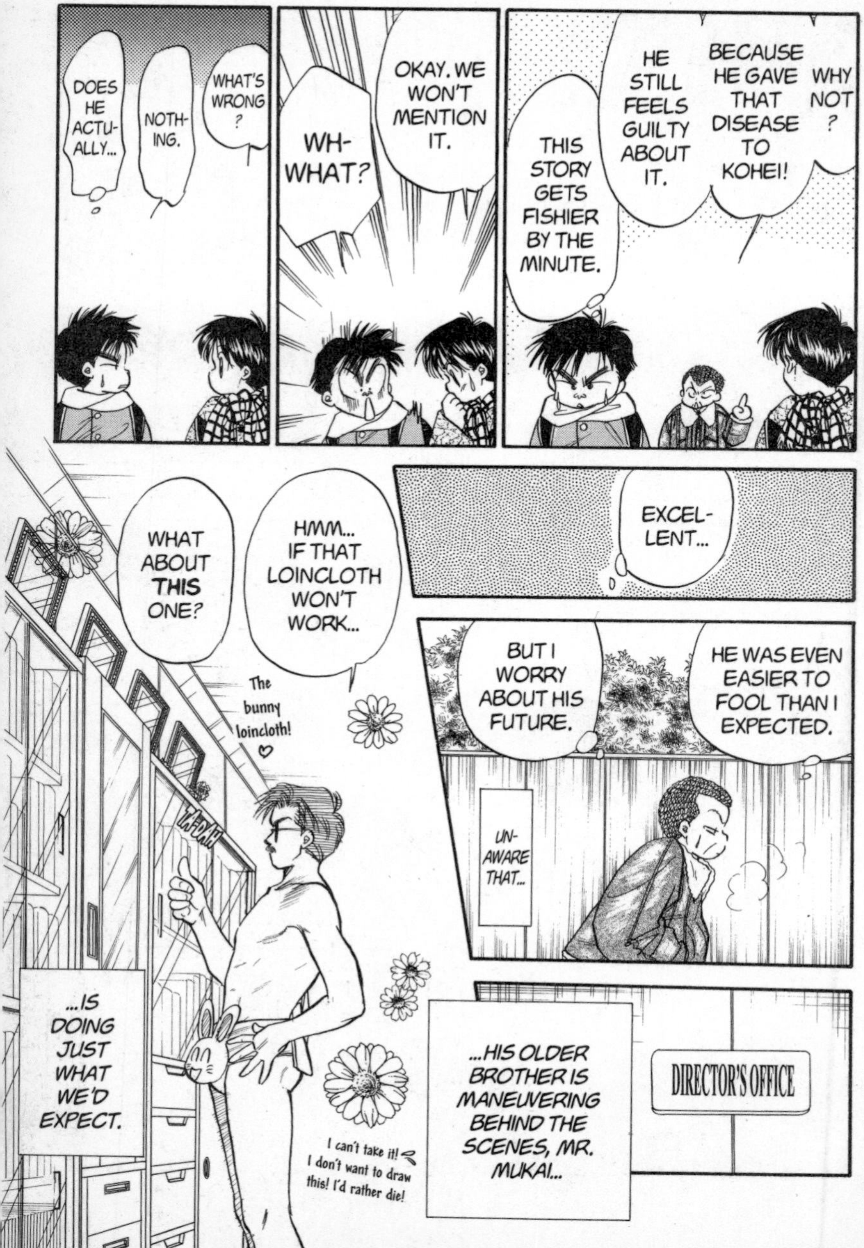
WHY NOT?
BECAUSE HE GAVE THAT DISEASE TO KOHEI!
HE STILL FEELS GUILTY ABOUT IT.
THIS STORY GETS FISHIER BY THE MINUTE.
OKAY. WE WON'T MENTION IT.
WH-WHAT?
WHAT'S WRONG?
NOTHING.
DOES HE ACTUALLY...
EXCELLENT...
HE WAS EVEN EASIER TO FOOL THAN I EXPECTED.
BUT I WORRY ABOUT HIS FUTURE.
UNAWARE THAT...
...HIS OLDER BROTHER IS MANEUVERING BEHIND THE SCENES, MR. MUKAI...
DIRECTOR'S OFFICE
HMM... IF THAT LOINCLOTH WON'T WORK...
WHAT ABOUT **THIS** ONE?
The bunny loincloth! ♡
TA-DAH
...IS DOING JUST WHAT WE'D EXPECT.
I can't take it! I don't want to draw this! I'd rather die!

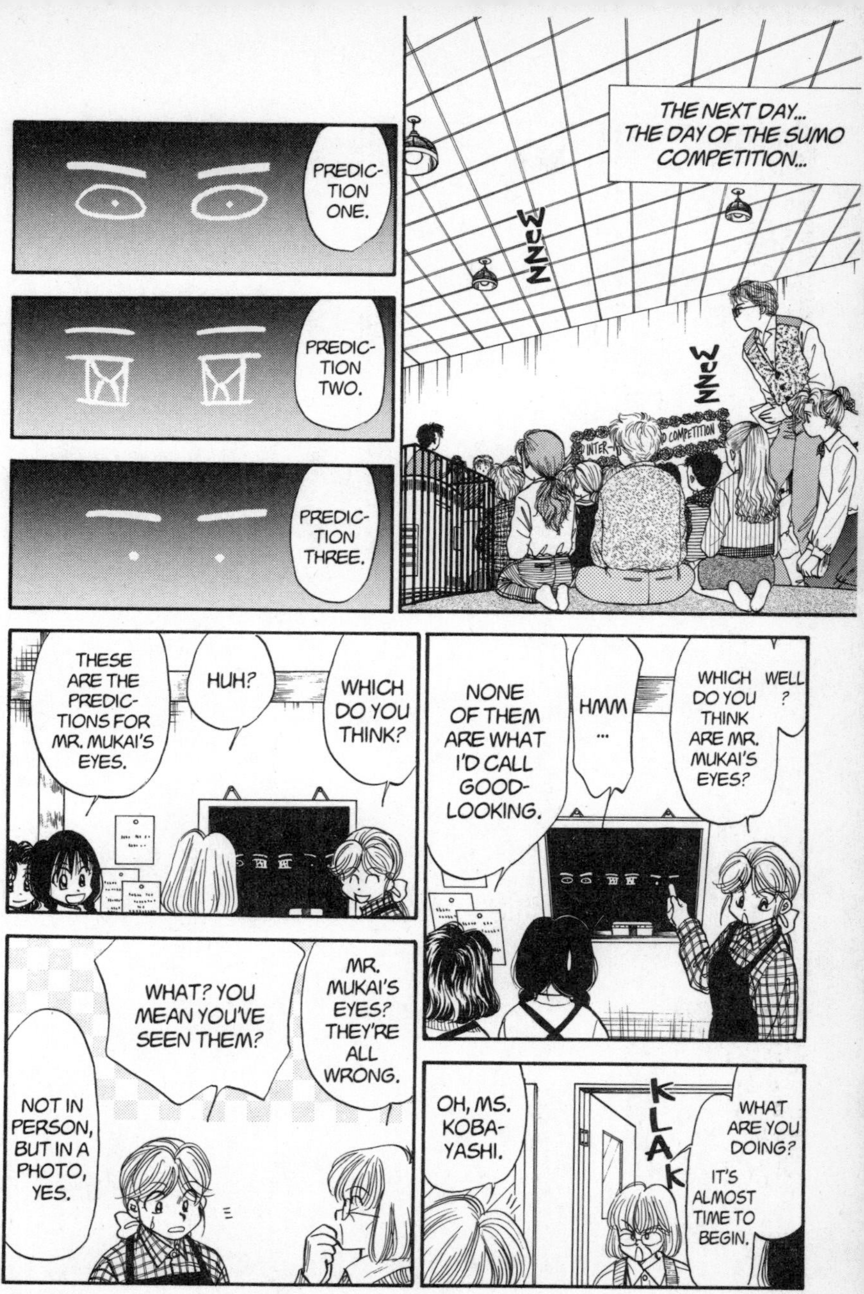
THE NEXT DAY... THE DAY OF THE SUMO COMPETITION...
WUZZ
WUZZ
PREDICTION ONE.
PREDICTION TWO.
PREDICTION THREE.
WELL?
WHICH DO YOU THINK ARE MR. MUKAI'S EYES?
HMM...
NONE OF THEM ARE WHAT I'D CALL GOOD-LOOKING.
WHICH DO YOU THINK?
HUH?
THESE ARE THE PREDICTIONS FOR MR. MUKAI'S EYES.
MR. MUKAI'S EYES? THEY'RE ALL WRONG.
WHAT? YOU MEAN YOU'VE SEEN THEM?
NOT IN PERSON, BUT IN A PHOTO, YES.
WHAT ARE YOU DOING?
IT'S ALMOST TIME TO BEGIN.
KLAK
OH, MS. KOBAYASHI.

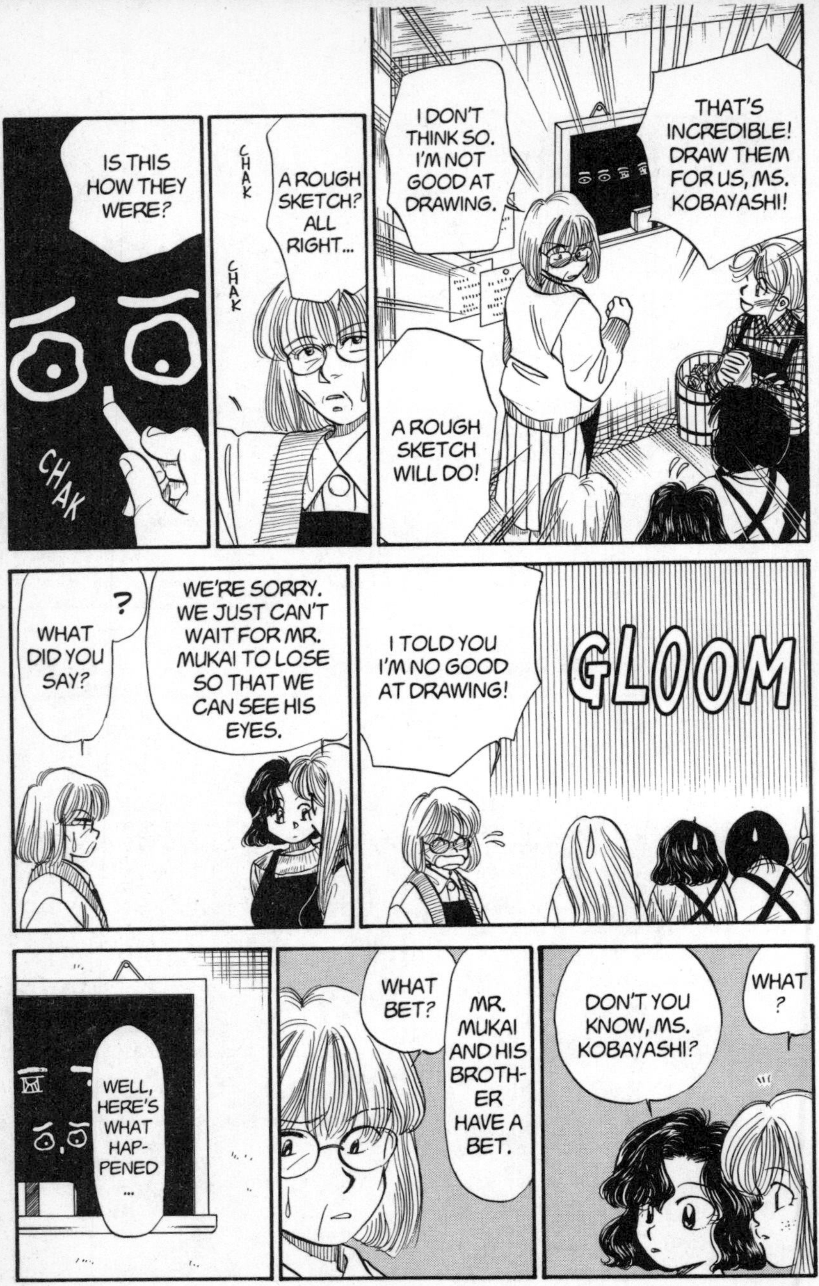
THAT'S INCREDIBLE! DRAW THEM FOR US, MS. KOBAYASHI!
I DON'T THINK SO. I'M NOT GOOD AT DRAWING.
A ROUGH SKETCH WILL DO!
CHAK
A ROUGH SKETCH? ALL RIGHT...
CHAK
IS THIS HOW THEY WERE?
CHAK
GLOOM
I TOLD YOU I'M NO GOOD AT DRAWING!
WE'RE SORRY. WE JUST CAN'T WAIT FOR MR. MUKAI TO LOSE SO THAT WE CAN SEE HIS EYES.
?
WHAT DID YOU SAY?
WHAT ?
DON'T YOU KNOW, MS. KOBAYASHI?
MR. MUKAI AND HIS BROTH-ER HAVE A BET.
WHAT BET?
WELL, HERE'S WHAT HAP-PENED ...

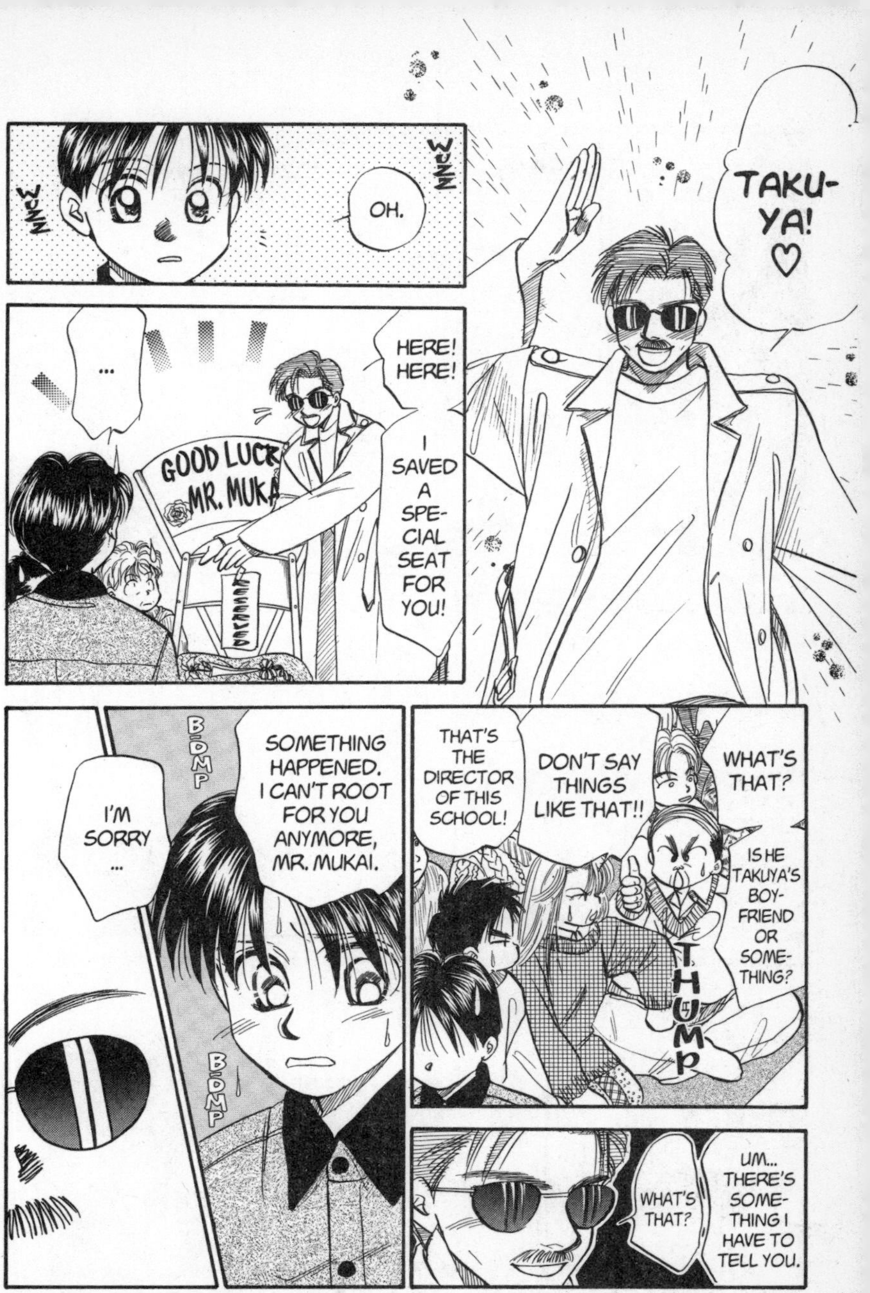
TAKU-YA! ♡
WUZN
OH.
WUZN
HERE! HERE!
I SAVED A SPE-CIAL SEAT FOR YOU!
GOOD LUCK MR. MUKA
...
WHAT'S THAT?
IS HE TAKUYA'S BOY-FRIEND OR SOME-THING?
DON'T SAY THINGS LIKE THAT!!
THAT'S THE DIRECTOR OF THIS SCHOOL!
THUMP
UM... THERE'S SOME-THING I HAVE TO TELL YOU.
WHAT'S THAT?
SOMETHING HAPPENED. I CAN'T ROOT FOR YOU ANYMORE, MR. MUKAI.
B-DMP
B-DMP
I'M SORRY ...

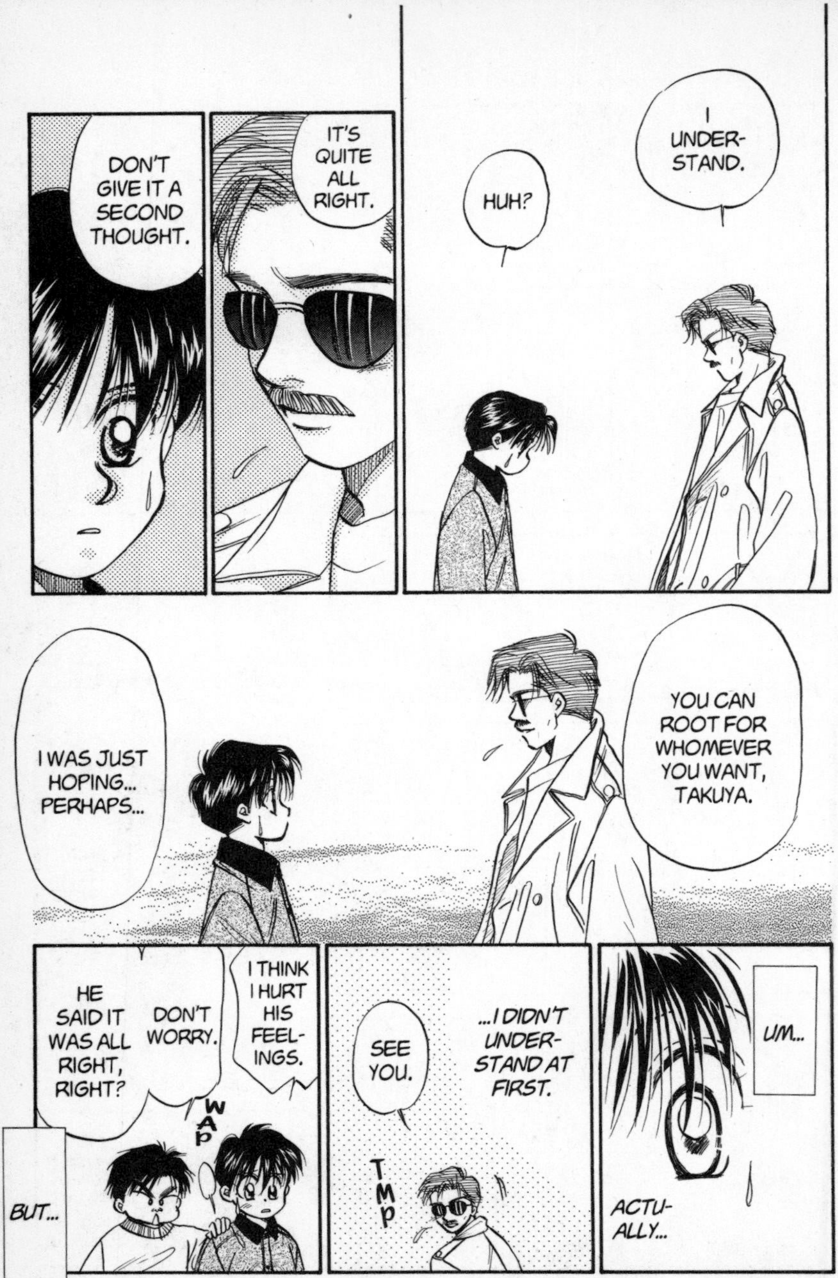
I UNDER-STAND.
HUH?
IT'S QUITE ALL RIGHT.
DON'T GIVE IT A SECOND THOUGHT.
YOU CAN ROOT FOR WHOMEVER YOU WANT, TAKUYA.
I WAS JUST HOPING... PERHAPS...
UM...
ACTU-ALLY...
...I DIDN'T UNDER-STAND AT FIRST.
SEE YOU.
TMP
I THINK I HURT HIS FEEL-INGS.
DON'T WORRY.
HE SAID IT WAS ALL RIGHT, RIGHT?
WAP
BUT...

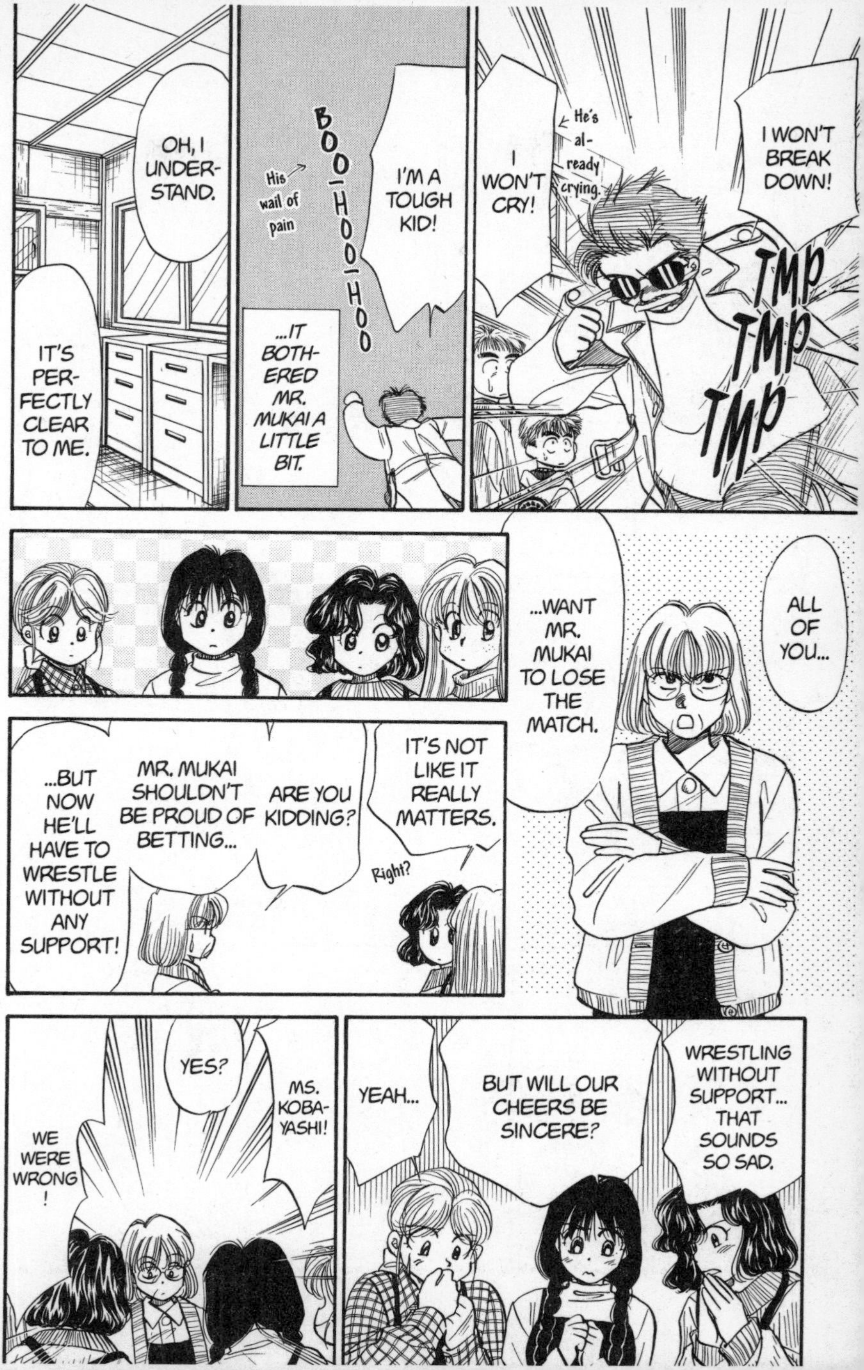
I WON'T BREAK DOWN!
I WON'T CRY!
He's already crying.
TMP TMP TMP
I'M A TOUGH KID!
BOO-HOO-HOO-HOO
His wail of pain
...IT BOTHERED MR. MUKAI A LITTLE BIT.
OH, I UNDERSTAND.
IT'S PERFECTLY CLEAR TO ME.
ALL OF YOU...
...WANT MR. MUKAI TO LOSE THE MATCH.
IT'S NOT LIKE IT REALLY MATTERS.
Right?
ARE YOU KIDDING?
MR. MUKAI SHOULDN'T BE PROUD OF BETTING...
...BUT NOW HE'LL HAVE TO WRESTLE WITHOUT ANY SUPPORT!
WRESTLING WITHOUT SUPPORT... THAT SOUNDS SO SAD.
BUT WILL OUR CHEERS BE SINCERE?
YEAH...
MS. KOBAYASHI!
YES?
WE WERE WRONG!

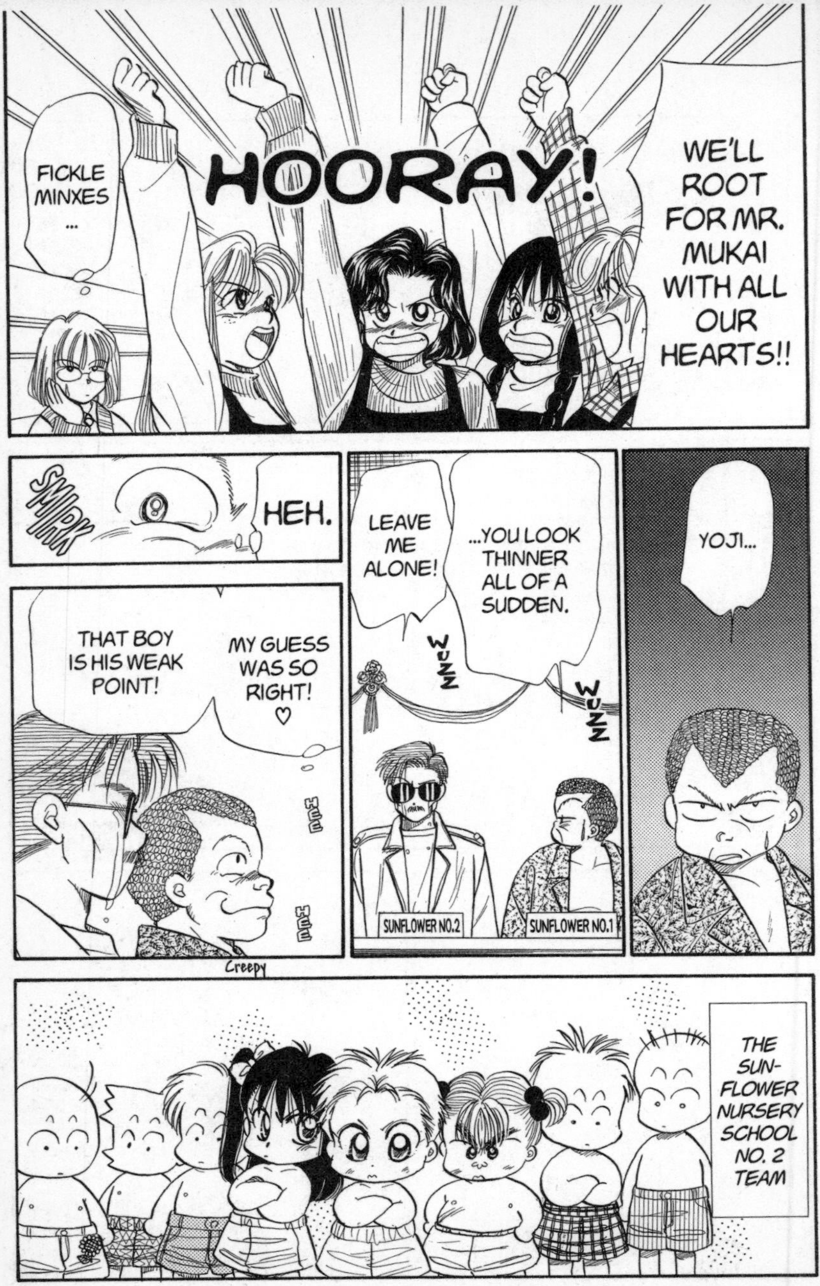
WE'LL ROOT FOR MR. MUKAI WITH ALL OUR HEARTS!!
HOORAY!
FICKLE MINXES ...
YOJI...
...YOU LOOK THINNER ALL OF A SUDDEN.
LEAVE ME ALONE!
WUZZ
WUZZ
SUNFLOWER NO.1
SUNFLOWER NO.2
HEH.
SMIRK
MY GUESS WAS SO RIGHT! ♡
THAT BOY IS HIS WEAK POINT!
HEE
HEE
Creepy
THE SUN-FLOWER NURSERY SCHOOL NO. 2 TEAM

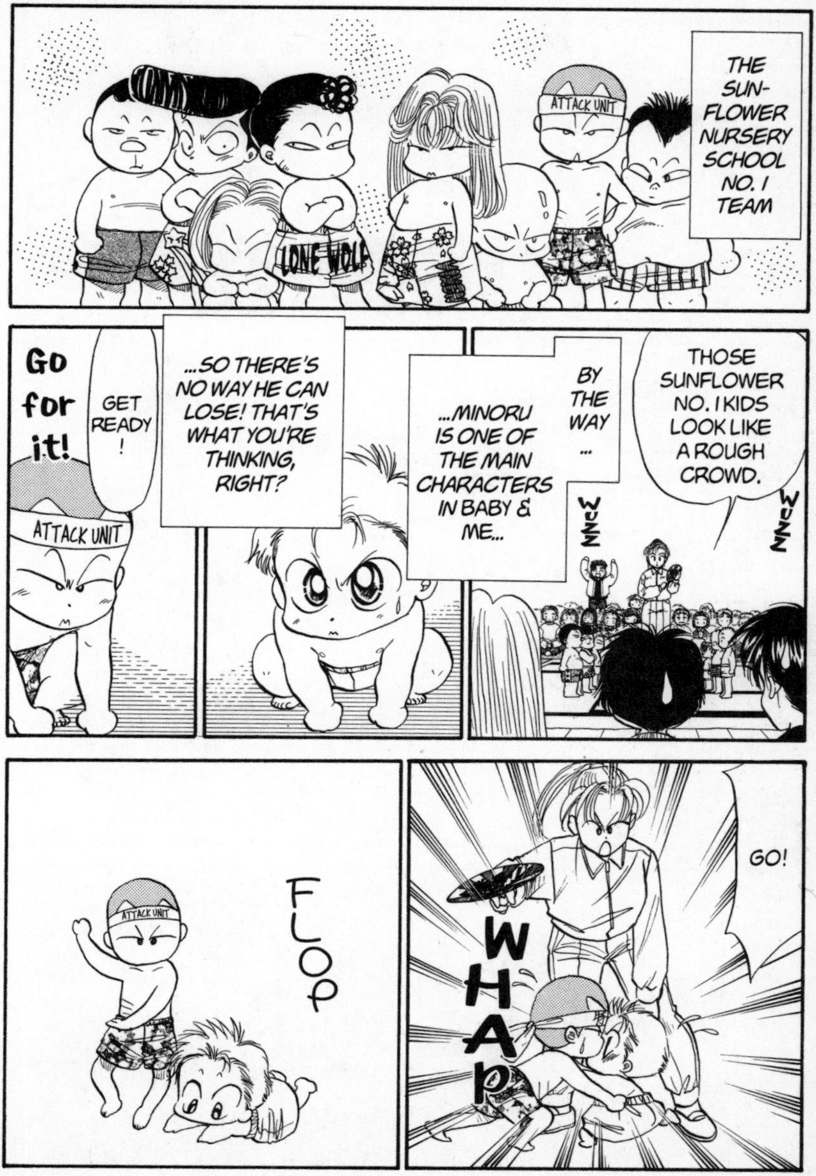
THE SUN-FLOWER NURSERY SCHOOL NO. 1 TEAM
ATTACK UNIT
LONE WOLF
THOSE SUNFLOWER NO. 1 KIDS LOOK LIKE A ROUGH CROWD.
WUZZ
WUZZ
BY THE WAY...
...MINORU IS ONE OF THE MAIN CHARACTERS IN BABY & ME...
...SO THERE'S NO WAY HE CAN LOSE! THAT'S WHAT YOU'RE THINKING, RIGHT?
GET READY!
Go for it!
ATTACK UNIT
GO!
WHAP
FLOP
ATTACK UNIT

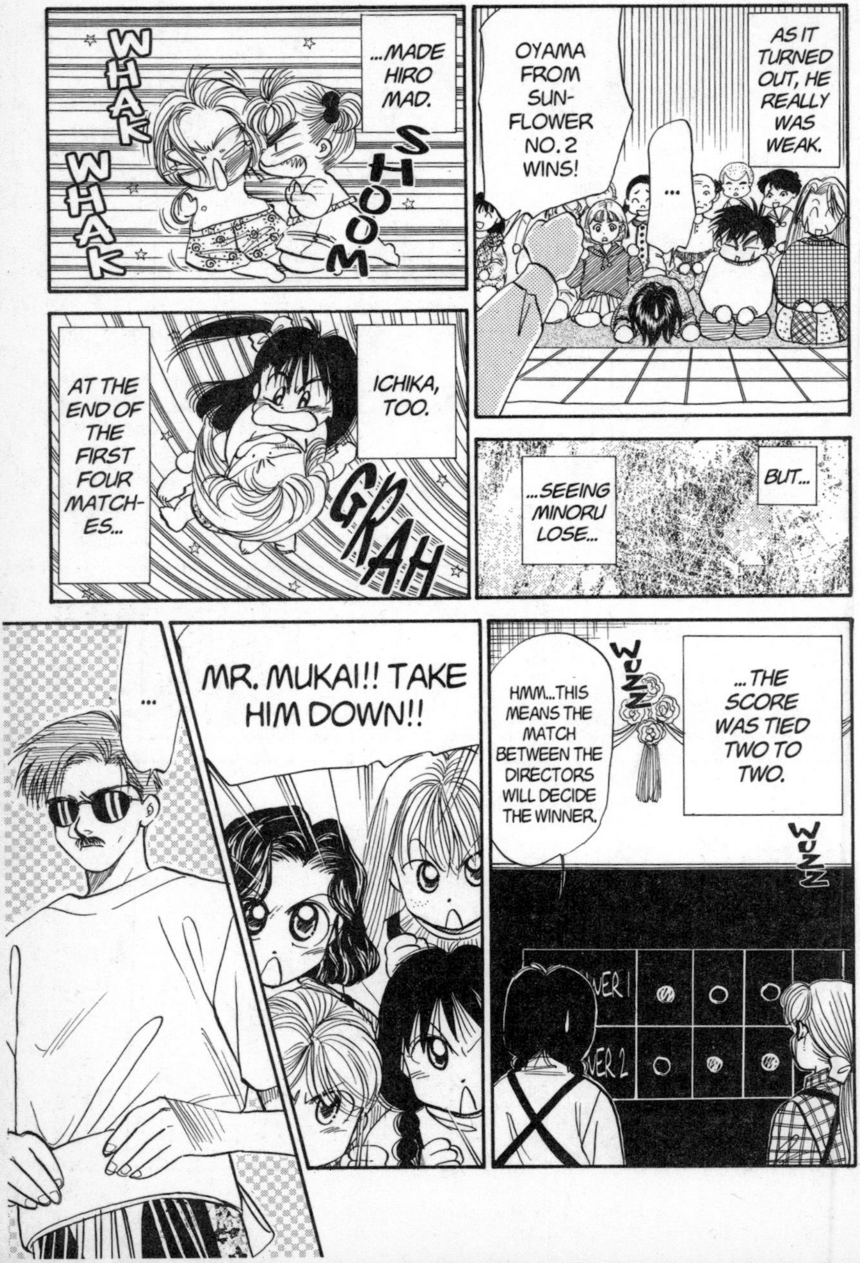
AS IT TURNED OUT, HE REALLY WAS WEAK.
OYAMA FROM SUN-FLOWER NO. 2 WINS!
...
BUT...
...SEEING MINORU LOSE...
...MADE HIRO MAD.
SHOOM
WHAK WHAK
ICHIKA, TOO.
GRAH
AT THE END OF THE FIRST FOUR MATCH-ES...
...THE SCORE WAS TIED TWO TO TWO.
WUZZ
HMM...THIS MEANS THE MATCH BETWEEN THE DIRECTORS WILL DECIDE THE WINNER.
WUZZ
MR. MUKAI!! TAKE HIM DOWN!!
...

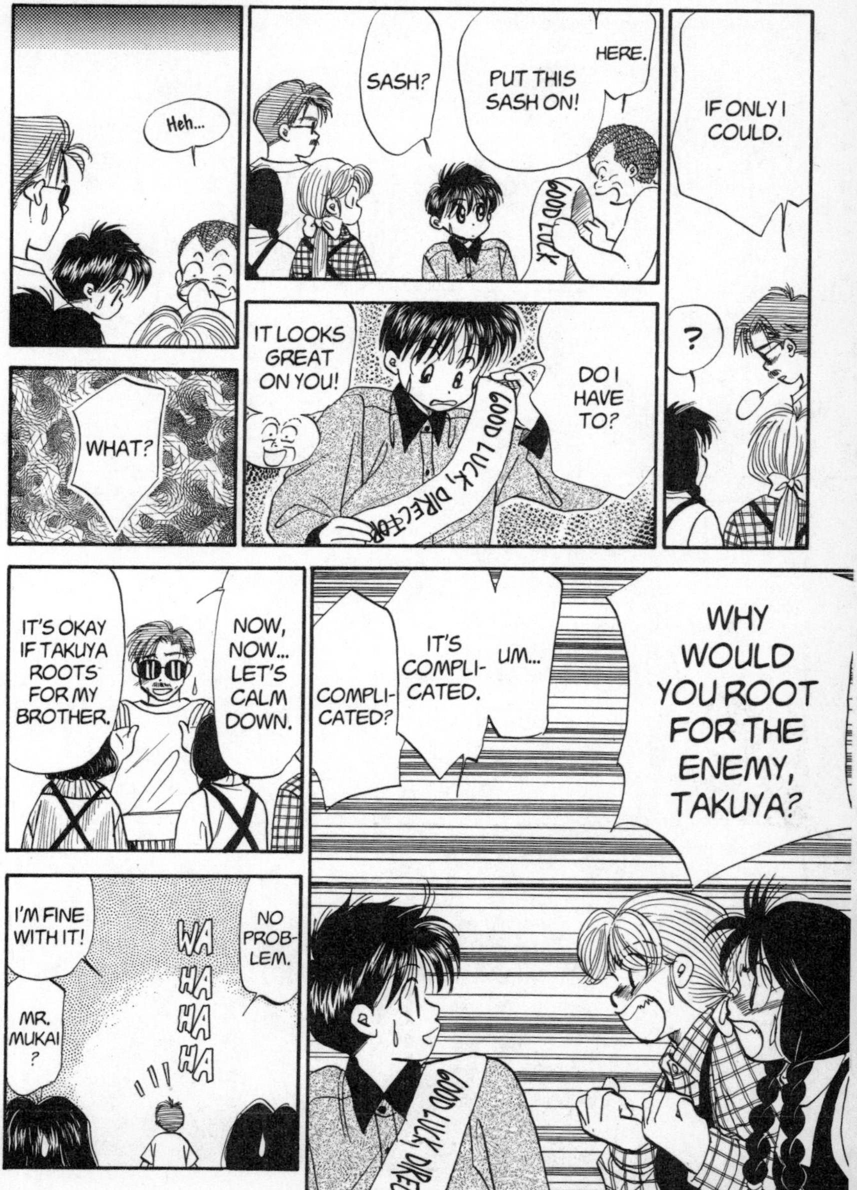
IF ONLY I COULD.
HERE.
PUT THIS SASH ON!
SASH?
GOOD LUCK
Heh...
?
DO I HAVE TO?
IT LOOKS GREAT ON YOU!
GOOD LUCK, DIRECTOR
WHAT?
WHY WOULD YOU ROOT FOR THE ENEMY, TAKUYA?
UM...
IT'S COMPLI-CATED.
COMPLI-CATED?
GOOD LUCK, DIRECTOR NO. 1
NOW, NOW... LET'S CALM DOWN.
IT'S OKAY IF TAKUYA ROOTS FOR MY BROTHER.
NO PROB-LEM.
I'M FINE WITH IT!
WA HA HA HA HA
MR. MUKAI?

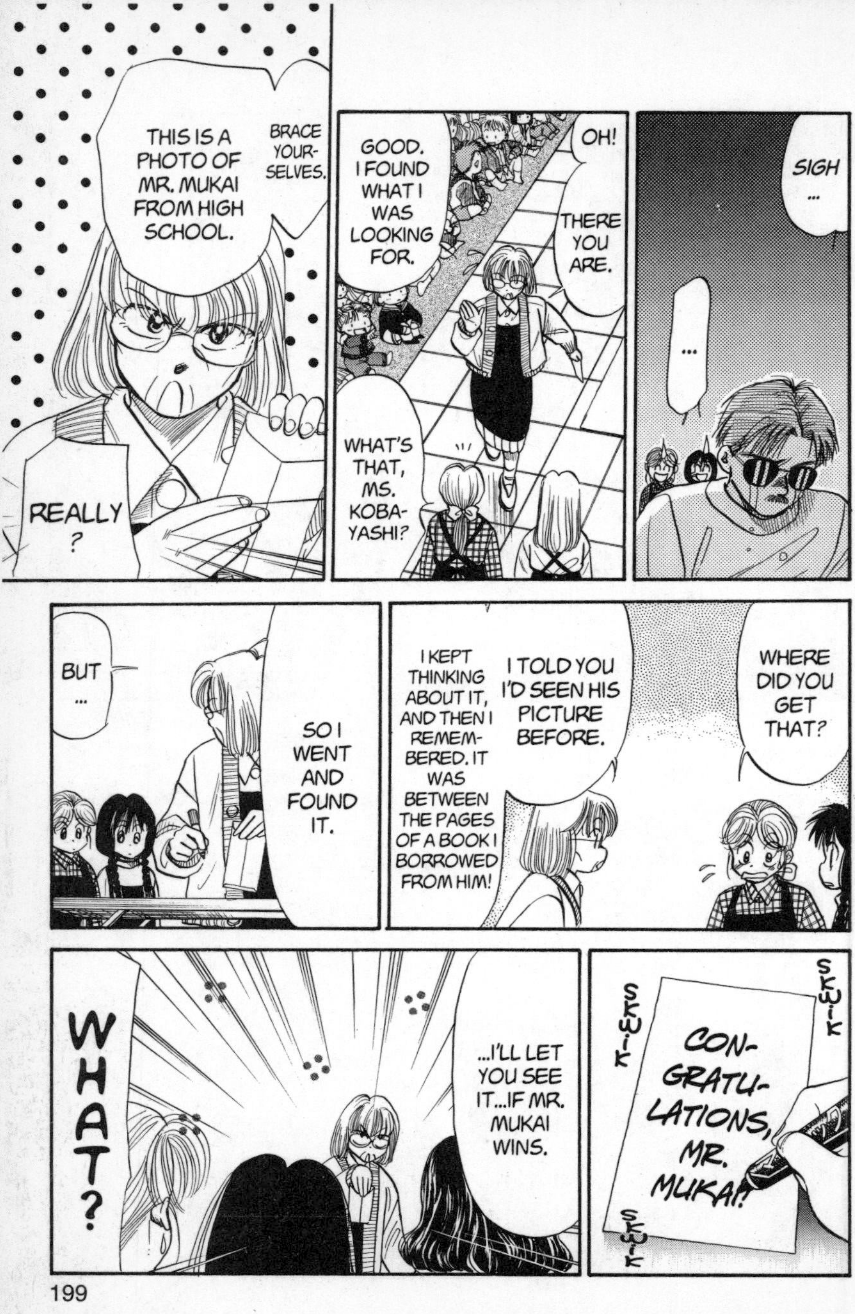
SIGH ...
...
OH!
THERE YOU ARE.
GOOD. I FOUND WHAT I WAS LOOKING FOR.
WHAT'S THAT, MS. KOBAYASHI?
BRACE YOUR-SELVES.
THIS IS A PHOTO OF MR. MUKAI FROM HIGH SCHOOL.
REALLY?
WHERE DID YOU GET THAT?
I TOLD YOU I'D SEEN HIS PICTURE BEFORE.
I KEPT THINKING ABOUT IT, AND THEN I REMEM-BERED. IT WAS BETWEEN THE PAGES OF A BOOK I BORROWED FROM HIM!
SO I WENT AND FOUND IT.
BUT ...
SKWIK
SKWIK
CON-GRATU-LATIONS, MR. MUKAI!
SKWIK
...I'LL LET YOU SEE IT...IF MR. MUKAI WINS.
WHAT?

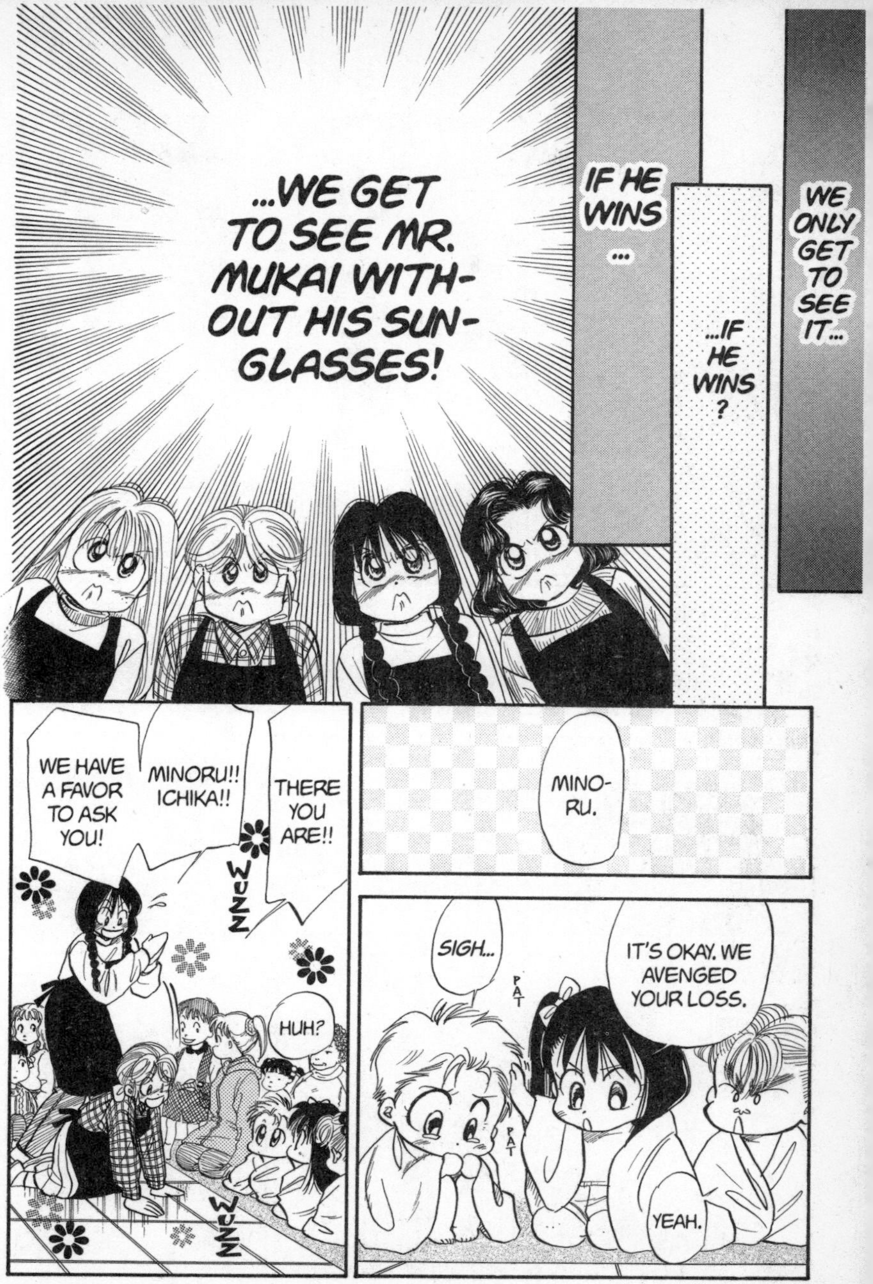
IF HE WINS ...
...WE GET TO SEE MR. MUKAI WITH-OUT HIS SUN-GLASSES!
...IF HE WINS ?
WE ONLY GET TO SEE IT...
MINO-RU.
IT'S OKAY. WE AVENGED YOUR LOSS.
PAT
PAT
SIGH...
YEAH.
THERE YOU ARE!!
MINORU!! ICHIKA!!
WE HAVE A FAVOR TO ASK YOU!
WUZZ
HUH?
WUZZ

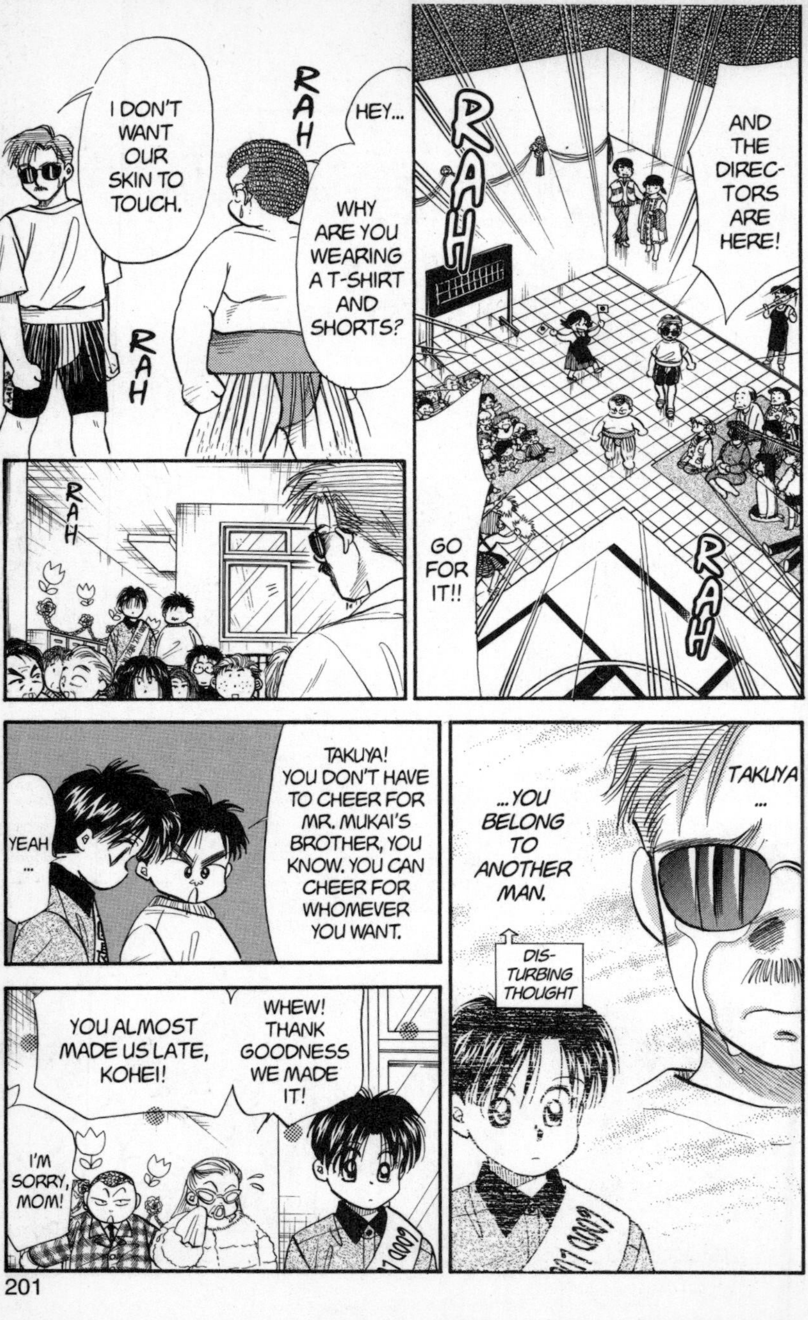
RAH
RAH
AND THE DIRECTORS ARE HERE!
GO FOR IT!!
HEY...
WHY ARE YOU WEARING A T-SHIRT AND SHORTS?
RAH
I DON'T WANT OUR SKIN TO TOUCH.
RAH
RAH
TAKUYA ...
...YOU BELONG TO ANOTHER MAN.
DIS-TURBING THOUGHT
TAKUYA! YOU DON'T HAVE TO CHEER FOR MR. MUKAI'S BROTHER, YOU KNOW. YOU CAN CHEER FOR WHOMEVER YOU WANT.
YEAH ...
WHEW! THANK GOODNESS WE MADE IT!
YOU ALMOST MADE US LATE, KOHEI!
I'M SORRY, MOM!

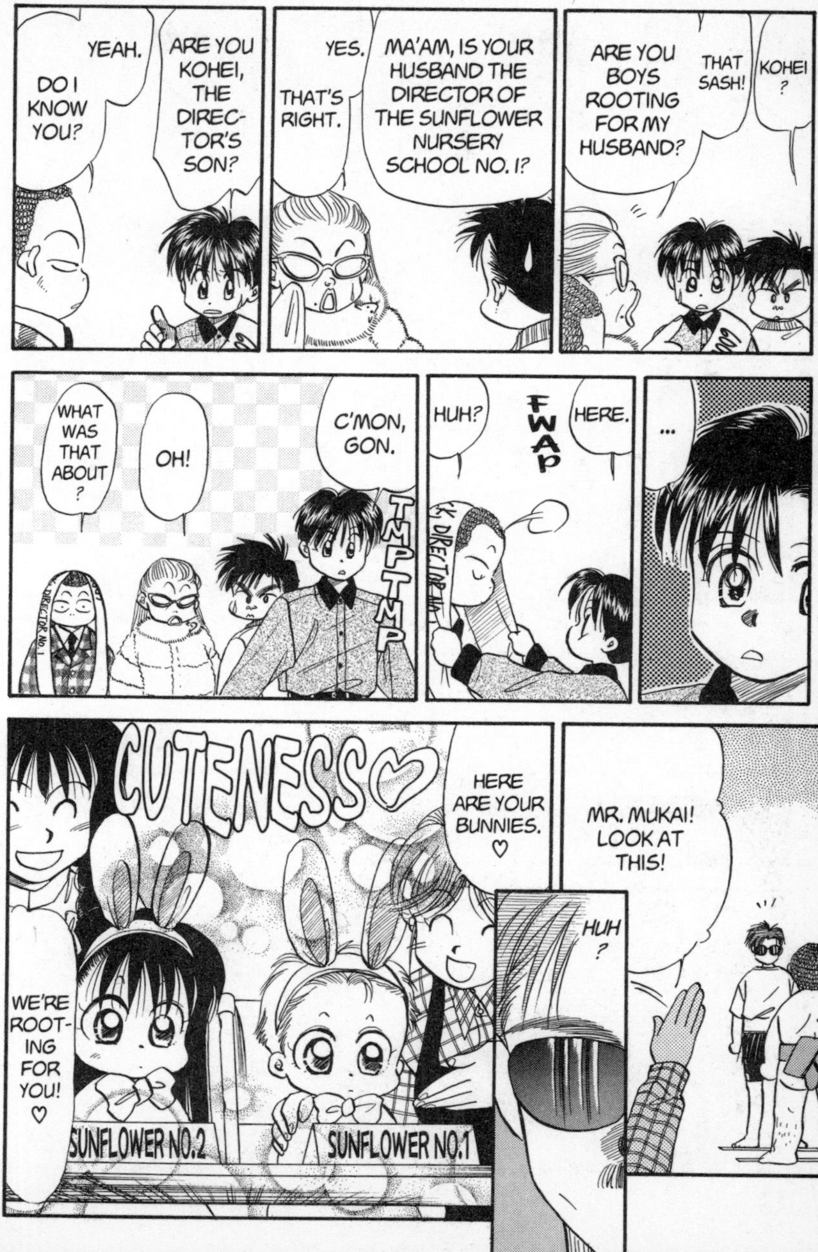
KOHEI ?
THAT SASH!
ARE YOU BOYS ROOTING FOR MY HUSBAND?
MA'AM, IS YOUR HUSBAND THE DIRECTOR OF THE SUNFLOWER NURSERY SCHOOL NO. 1?
YES.
THAT'S RIGHT.
ARE YOU KOHEI, THE DIREC-TOR'S SON?
YEAH.
DO I KNOW YOU?
...
HERE.
FWAP
HUH?
C'MON, GON.
TMP TMP
OH!
WHAT WAS THAT ABOUT ?
DIRECTOR NO.1
MR. MUKAI! LOOK AT THIS!
HUH ?
HERE ARE YOUR BUNNIES. ♡
CUTENESS♡
WE'RE ROOT-ING FOR YOU! ♡
SUNFLOWER NO.1
SUNFLOWER NO.2

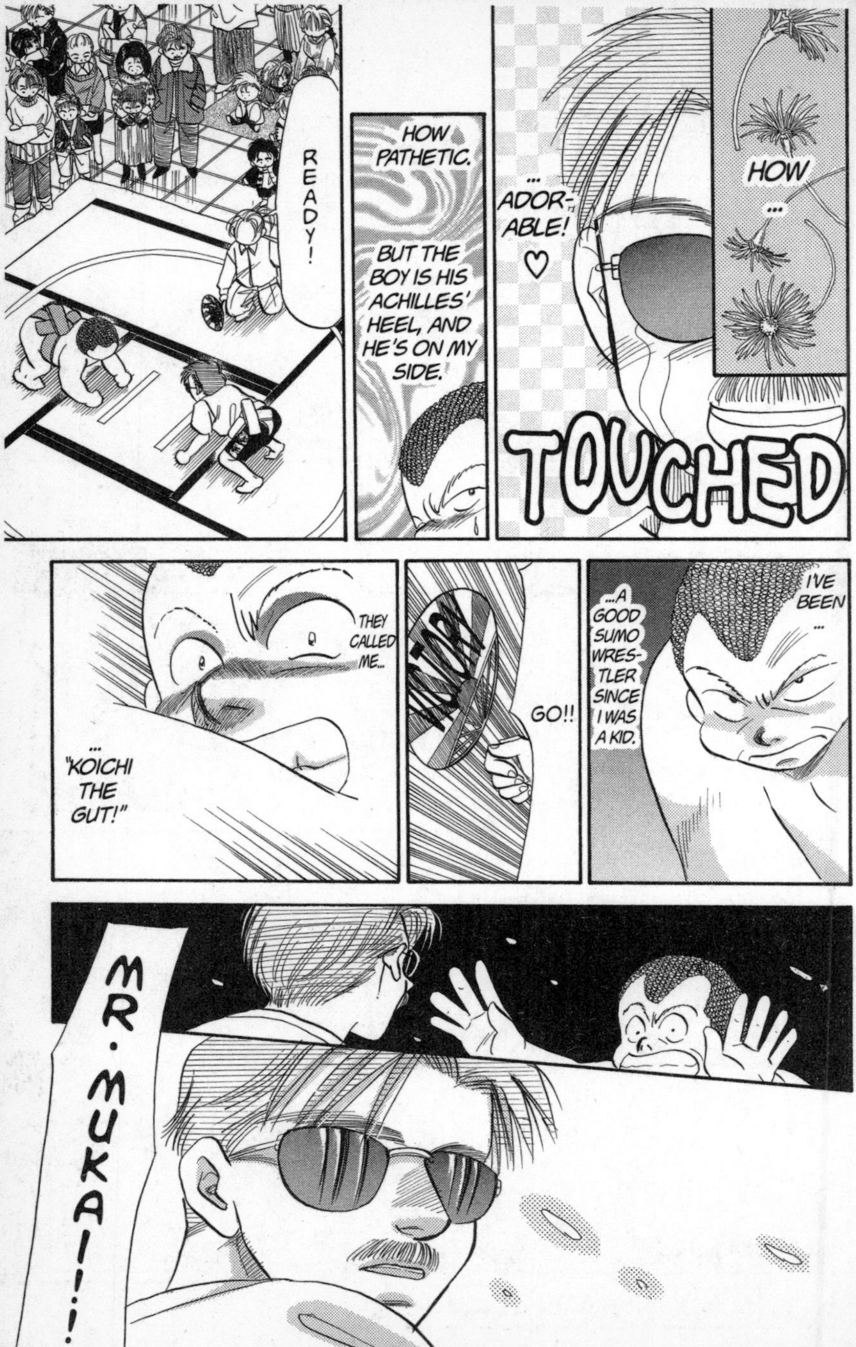
HOW ...
... ADOR-ABLE! ♡
TOUCHED
HOW PATHETIC.
BUT THE BOY IS HIS ACHILLES' HEEL, AND HE'S ON MY SIDE.
READY!
I'VE BEEN ...
...A GOOD SUMO WRES-TLER SINCE I WAS A KID.
GO!!
THEY CALLED ME...
... "KOICHI THE GUT!"
MR. MUKAI!!!!

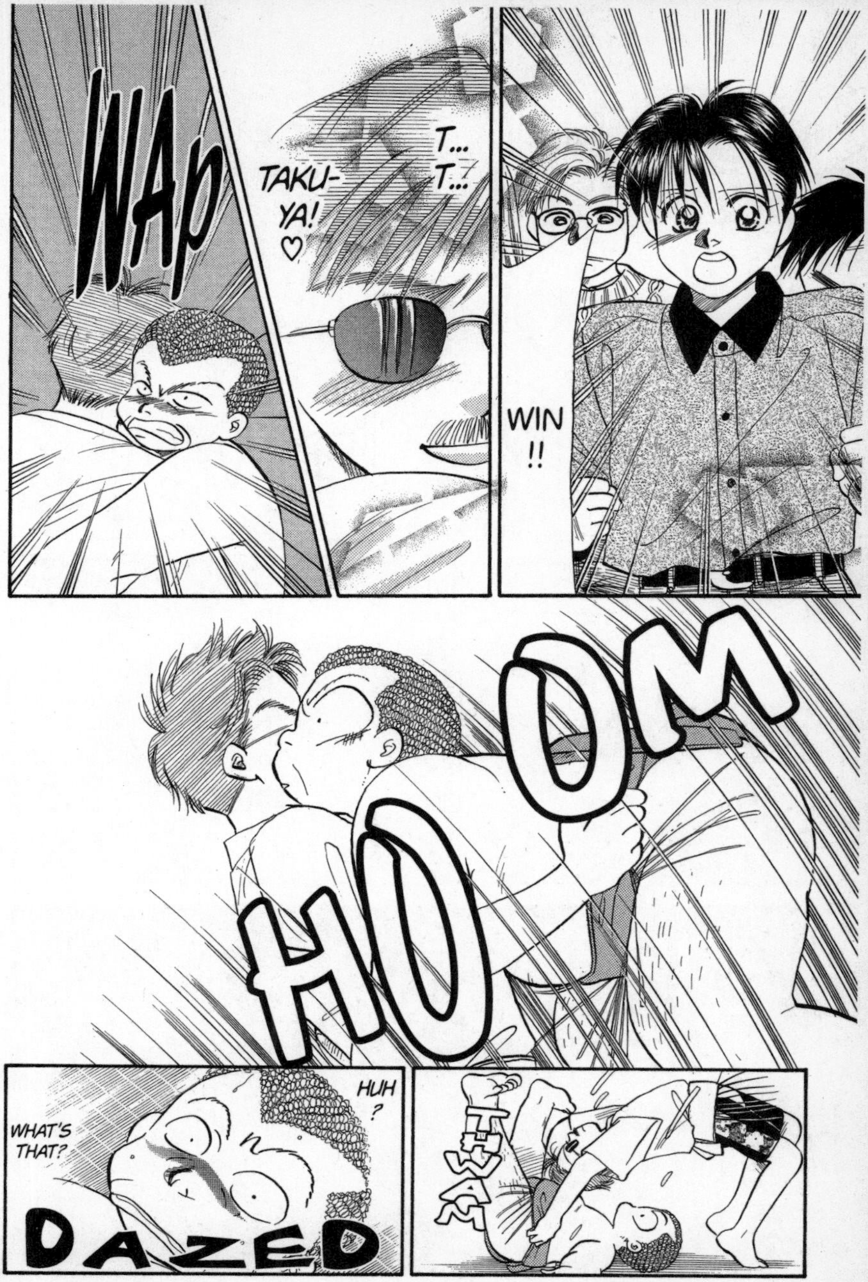

WIN !!
T... T...
TAKU-YA! ♡
WAp
HOOM
THWAM
HUH ?
WHAT'S THAT?
DAZED

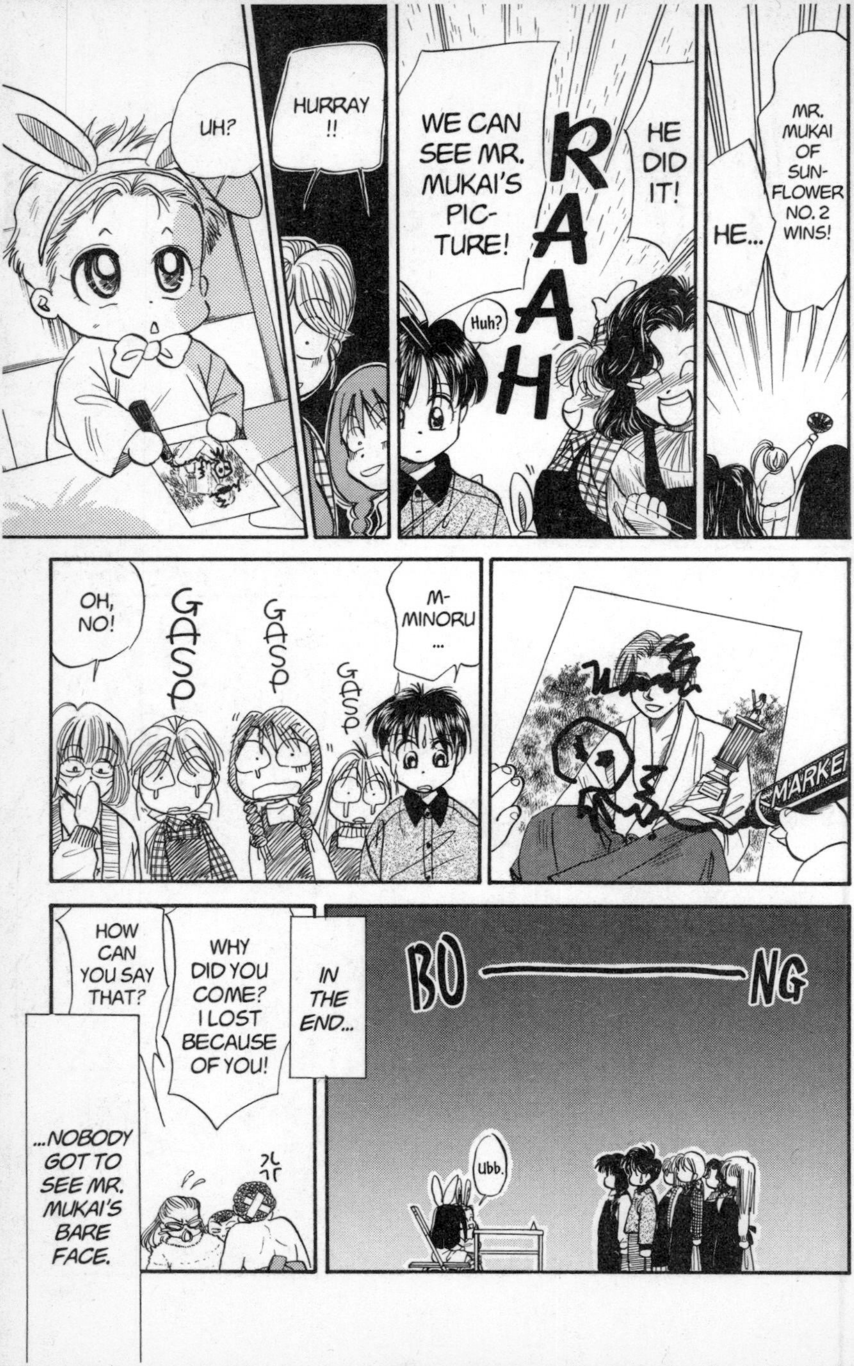
MR. MUKAI OF SUN-FLOWER NO. 2 WINS!
HE...
HE DID IT!
RAAH
WE CAN SEE MR. MUKAI'S PIC-TURE!
Huh?
HURRAY !!
UH?
M-MINORU ...
GASP
GASP
GASP
OH, NO!
BO——NG
Ubb.
IN THE END...
WHY DID YOU COME? I LOST BECAUSE OF YOU!
HOW CAN YOU SAY THAT?
...NOBODY GOT TO SEE MR. MUKAI'S BARE FACE.

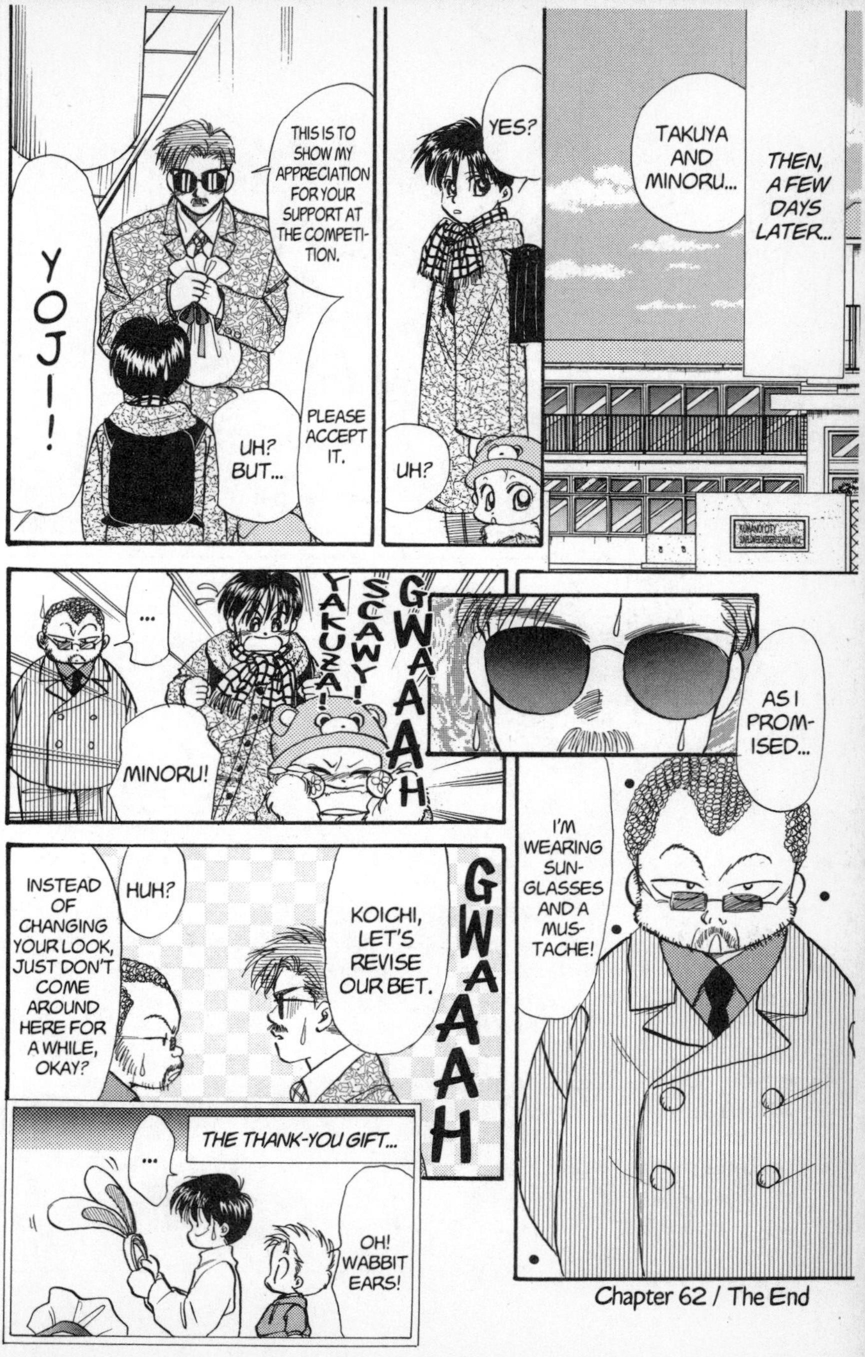
THEN, A FEW DAYS LATER...
TAKUYA AND MINORU...
YES?
UH?
THIS IS TO SHOW MY APPRECIATION FOR YOUR SUPPORT AT THE COMPETITION.
PLEASE ACCEPT IT.
UH? BUT...
YOJI!!
AS I PROMISED...
I'M WEARING SUNGLASSES AND A MUSTACHE!
...
GWAAAH
SCAWY!
YAKUZA!
MINORU!
GWAAAAH
KOICHI, LET'S REVISE OUR BET.
HUH?
INSTEAD OF CHANGING YOUR LOOK, JUST DON'T COME AROUND HERE FOR A WHILE, OKAY?
THE THANK-YOU GIFT...
OH! WABBIT EARS!
...

Chapter 62 / The End